EAST ASIAN SOCIAL SCIENCE MONOGRAPHS

INCOME DISTRIBUTION AND DETERMINATION IN WEST MALAYSIA

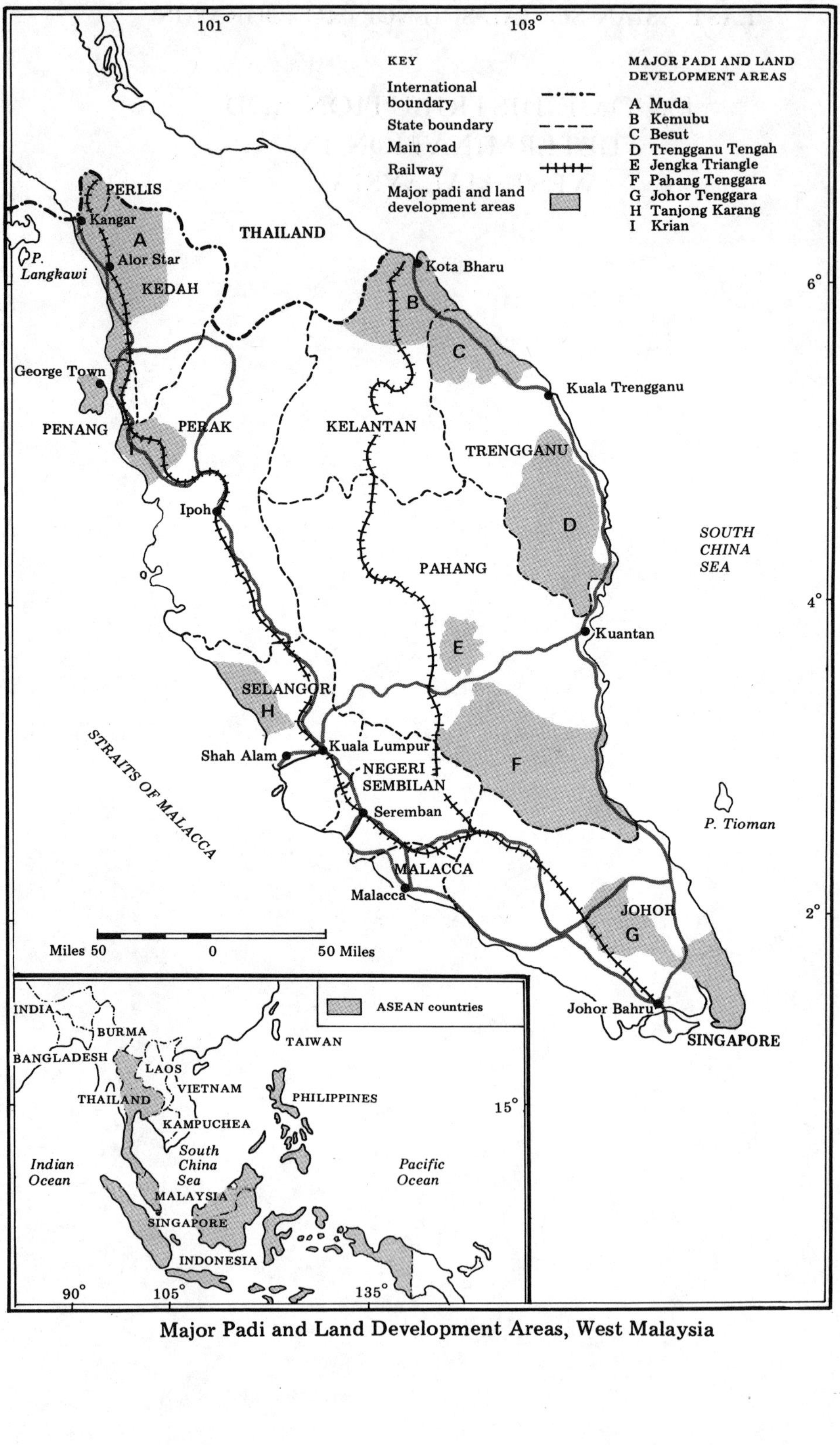

Major Padi and Land Development Areas, West Malaysia

INCOME DISTRIBUTION AND DETERMINATION IN WEST MALAYSIA

TAN TAT WAI

KUALA LUMPUR
OXFORD UNIVERSITY PRESS
OXFORD NEW YORK MELBOURNE
1982

Oxford University Press

Oxford London Glasgow
New York Toronto Melbourne Auckland
Kuala Lumpur Singapore Hong Kong Tokyo
Delhi Bombay Calcutta Madras Karachi
Nairobi Dar es Salaam Cape Town

and associates in
Beirut Berlin Ibadan Mexico City Nicosia

ISBN 0 19 580435 X (boards)
ISBN 0 19 580493 7 (limp)

Printed in Singapore by Dainippon Tien Wah Printing (Pte) Ltd.
Published by Oxford University Press, 3, Jalan 13/3,
Petaling Jaya, Selangor, Malaysia

Preface

THIS book is re-written from my doctoral dissertation with Harvard University. The bulk of the research was concluded by mid-1976. Since then, many changes have occurred, especially in the corporate sector. Many more data have become available.* Although it would have been highly desirable to incorporate all these in the book, the addition and updating of the data have been reduced to a minimum to keep the book to a manageable size and avoid too much delay in sending it to press. However, the minimal editorial work is not a major handicap as the basic conclusions and indications of this book still stand.

The discussion of theoretical concepts and the review of literature have been reduced to the barest minimum in order to facilitate reading by the less specialized general public and to reduce the length of the book. Readers who are interested in more rigorous expositions of the details will have to read the footnotes with greater care and resort to the dissertation, or await a later paper on related subjects. Neither the subject matter in Part I of the book is new, nor are the data; however, they have been organized to provide the necessary backdrop against which the presentation in Part II can be better appreciated. In addition, Part I also provides the conceptual and methodological framework for the study of income distribution and determination. Part II consists of the presentation and analysis of raw and new data. It is in Part II that the attempt is made to establish more clearly the relationships between income distribution and its determinants, such as ownership and control of wealth, structure and size of production, as well as marketing structure.

The late sixties heralded the concern for income distribution when it became increasingly obvious to economists that the past decades of emphasis on economic growth were not able to alleviate the poverty of the masses in the developing nations. In Malaysia, events of 1969 alerted the politicians and social scientists to the potential explosiveness and divisiveness of inequality. The end result has been a proliferation of income distribution studies in general and on Malaysia in particular.

However, surprisingly few, if any, of these many volumes of research have focused on relating the factors of production to the measurement and determination of income distribution. Instead, efforts have been concentrated on the construction of an ideal welfare measure of inequality and various expla-

*Unfortunately, the income data from two recent major surveys—the 1973 Household Expenditure Survey and 1976 Census of Agriculture—have yet to be published.

nations of inequality, such as human capital, culture, monopoly, etc. Such studies frequently can provide no more than a vague picture of inequality with a partial explanation of inequality at best. Hardly any attention has been paid by economists to relating factors of production to the study of income distribution in such a way that the statisticians can have a sound basis with which to design sample surveys that will at once measure income and explain inequality.

It is hoped that the way in which this book seeks to describe income distribution and investigates the origins of income inequality and wealth in Malaysia will serve to advance an alternative methodology in the study of income distribution. The tediousness and difficulties this researcher encountered in the course of research make glaringly obvious the importance of empirical work with raw data. Sadly, orientation of students and teachers of economics at the leading universities has been moving away from this basic foundation of theory—good empirical research—to concentrate on stylizing and modelling in the realm of the more glorifying mathematical economics, frequently without any realization of what is happening in the real world.

In the course of this study, the holdings of many libraries have been consulted, among them Harvard, Yale, World Bank, Bank Negara, Arkib Negara, London School of Oriental and African Studies, and Colonial Office Records. Access to these libraries and the assistance of the librarians are gratefully acknowledged. The proximity of Dr Snodgrass's excellent private collection of materials relating to Malaysia has been extremely helpful.

Acknowledgements are due to the Harvard Yenching Institute which provided me with a fellowship for most of my graduate studies at Harvard and the kind attention of its associate director, Mr Baxter, is particularly appreciated. Over the years, many professors and teachers, my father, fellow students, and friends have, both formally and informally, contributed a great deal to my understanding of economics, history, and other more general topics. Their diverse contributions have been invaluable to the thinking behind this study. The patience and empathy of my two readers, Professor Dwight Perkins and Dr Donald Snodgrass, greatly facilitated the research and writing of the original thesis. Last but not least, I must mention that the editorial work, typing and proof reading help provided by my good friends and family members was especially important in sustaining me through to the completion of the study. To all of them, I owe a great debt and my heartiest thanks.

Kuala Lumpur
1979

TAN TAT WAI

Contents

Tables

Figures

Charts

1 Introduction

1.1 GENERAL BACKGROUND

MALAYSIA[1] is a multi-ethnic country with a total population of 10.385 million in 1975. Of this total, 53.06 per cent was Malay, 35.52 per cent Chinese, 10.64 per cent Indian, while 0.78 per cent came from other ethnic denominations.[2] Historically, developments in the peninsula under British colonial policies have resulted in the segregation of these various ethnic groups by geographical dispersion, economic activity, and political role.[3] The resultant racial tension and conflict is well known and, needless to say, major issues have been coloured by racial overtones.

The largely rural Malay people have been, and remain, among the poorest. As they had a long and well-established history before the influx of the majority of the Chinese and Indians into the peninsula, they consider themselves, and were regarded by the British, to be *Bumiputra* (or indigenous) in contrast to the other ethnic groups.[4] The presence of an established Malay élite (the various Sultanates) enabled them to participate in British indirect colonial rule,[5] albeit as a dominated partner. This has, quite naturally, enabled them to consolidate and continue their more dominant role in government after Independence. It is, therefore, not surprising that post-Independence policies have been most concerned with improving the lot of the Malays.

A casual look at the development budgets of the two Malaya Plans and the First Malaysia Plan would reveal that the emphasis has been on rural development,[6] since that is where the bulk of the Malay populace, and the bulk of the voters in the country, reside. There have also been attempts to advance the position of the Malays in the urban sector through the setting up of Majlis Amanah Rakyat (MARA, Council of Trust for the Indigenous People), Bank Bumiputra, quota guidelines on hiring and allotting shares for the Malays,[7] and encouragement of Malay entrants into an expanding tertiary education system.

Whether these policies have been successful in raising the economic well-being of the Malay people in general and that of the young, capable, and ambitious in particular will be discussed subsequently. Whichever is the case, the younger Malay leaders and political workers have often perceived these policies as being inadequate. Events connected with the 1969 election clearly illustrated that the Chinese were still perceived as the chief beneficiaries of post-Independence economic development.[8] Such perceptions are aggravated by the strong racial identification of two aspects of wealth generation,[9] particular emphasis being placed on what is perceived as:

1. Monopolistic-monopsonistic middlemen control and exploitation of rural Malays;

2. Overseas Chinese control of the South-East Asian economy as a whole, and Malaysia in particular.

Perceptions of the Chinese as economically dominant can and do lead some of the Malays to regard exploitation by the Chinese as the cause of Malay poverty. Resentment and even hatred can be easily involved, especially when the Chinese are still thought of in some quarters as an 'alien' community.

On the other hand, the non-Malays have also been unhappy with recent policies. They feel that they have contributed towards the economic development of the nation. The majority were born in Malaysia and resent continuous references to their 'immigrant' status. They feel that they should have equal rights as citizens and feel threatened by the emphasis on the Bumiputra/non-Bumiputra distinction. Many policies are identified as working to the advantage of the Malays only and thus they feel they have been discriminated against.[10]

After the 13 May riots of 1969, there was a new sense of urgency amongst Malay leaders which led to the formulation of the New Economic Policy (NEP) and the Second Malaysia Plan (SMP). The NEP stresses a two-pronged attack to promote national unity: 'to eradicate poverty for all Malaysians . . . regardless of race [and] to restructure society in order to correct economic imbalances, so as to reduce and eventually eliminate the identification of race with economic functions'.[11]

The first prong has, of course, always been present in the three earlier development plans. However, in the earlier periods, there was heavy emphasis on irrigation projects which would largely benefit the padi farmers. On the other hand, under the SMP, the emphasis shifted to a more active promotion of land development programmes (e.g., Pahang Tenggara and Jengka Triangle).

In terms of urban policies for the poor, there is a shift in emphasis from promoting import-substitution industries to labour-intensive export-oriented industries.[12] There is also more insistence on the hiring of Malay employees at all levels. The first would presumably create more urban employment benefiting the poor generally while the latter would ensure that a significant, though still a minority, proportion of Malays will benefit in the process.

Of the two prongs, the restructuring of society has attracted more attention. Particular emphasis has been placed on the creation of a Malay entrepreneurial class. A necessary step in laying the foundation for creating more Malay entrepreneurs and professionals is to provide more access to education for Malays generally. In the past, efforts have been made to develop the primary and the secondary school system in the rural (and more Malay) areas. As a result, Malay enrolment in secondary schools increased very sharply in the ten-year period from an estimated 16,000 (*v.* 57,000 Chinese) in 1957 to 219,000 (*v.* 178,000 Chinese) in 1967.[13] However, under the NEP, the policy is now to place talented Malay students from all over the country in the more traditional élite schools in the urban areas and to establish a network of Secondary Science Schools in each state to absorb a larger number of rural Malay students. In tertiary education the Government has been, albeit informally, implementing an admission quota for Bumiputras to the local universities. The proportion of Malay students in the total intake of the five local universities rose from 39.7 per cent in 1970 to 75.3 per cent in 1977 while the intake of Chinese and Indian students dropped from 49.2 per cent and 7.3 per cent respectively in 1970 to 20.1 per cent and 4.67 per cent respectively in 1977.[14] In addition, a large number of MARA and Serdang Agricultural College graduates have been sent to the United States both for undergraduate and post-graduate degrees.

There is also the restructuring of wealth objective, aiming at 30 per cent Malay ownership of all corporate wealth by 1990.[15] The implementation of this objective has prompted substantial investment and acquisitions by the Government-controlled corporations and trust funds such as Perbadanan Nasional (Pernas, National Corporation), MARA, the State Economic Development Corporations (SEDCs), and Urban Development Authority (UDA).[16]

1.2 REVIEW OF THE LITERATURE ON MALAYSIA AND PURPOSE OF THE STUDY

There have been more than half a dozen studies on income distribution in Malaysia. One of the earliest was undertaken by Silcock (1963). Lim Lin Lean (1971) wrote a widely quoted monograph using a breakdown of value added figures by industry per employed person to approximate the racial and other distribution of income.[17] Anand (1973) summarized the income distribution data from the post-enumeration survey of the 1970 Population and Housing Census (PES). Snodgrass (1975) presented the trend of income distribution from 1957 to 1970 by pooling the income distribution data from the 1957/8 Household Budget Survey, the Federal Savings Survey of 1959, the 1967/8 Socio-economic Sample Survey of Households (SSSH), the 1967/8 SRM/Ford Survey and the 1970 PES; he (1975a) also evaluated the fiscal policies as a tool of redistribution. Hirschman (1974), Nijhar (1974), and Thillainathan (1975) have also written on related topics: Hirschman focused on the manufacturing sector, Nijhar on the wage structure, and Thillainathan on general policies and income issues.

There are, of course, many other studies that have touched on aspects of the problem of the measurement of income and/or the question of its determination. Snodgrass (1972, 1976) provides very useful and extensive bibliographies on existing materials.

Why is there a need for another study in a field that seems well researched? One motivation stems from a concern with the conceptual apparatus and methodological basis of existing income distribution studies and thus an interest in identifying a more proper approach and scope for future studies. Related to this is the issue of whether existing empirical studies have accurately portrayed income distribution in Malaysia. Who are the rich and poor in Malaysia? What are the dimensions of income inequality? Is disparity in income widening and, if so, what factors cause this to occur? Are the redistributive policies outlined earlier directed at the right groups? What is the likely impact of the NEP on income distribution? A thorough understanding of the main determinants of income in Malaysia, given its economic structure and a knowledge of past and existing patterns of income distribution, will enable us to answer some of these questions with a more objective basis. We can then evaluate the validity of the perceptions of the various ethnic groups as well as identify some trends for the next few years.

Each of the many studies on income distribution in Malaysia has some important drawbacks. Of these, Lim Lin Lean's study calls for the most concern. Value added per worker reflects productivity rather than income. It consists of all factor payments including the return to labour. Value added per unit[18] is a reasonable proxy to income only in the case of the padi farmers, smallholders and small traders, all of whom organize their production around the family's labour and capital resources, provided that rent and interest payments are not significant proportions in the value added. For those working in the corporate sector, value added per worker is a very misleading proxy for the income of the wage workers, who form the overwhelming majority of the employees. This is because depreciation, profit, interest, and other payments, not accruing to the workers, form a significant portion of the value added.[19] Secondly, the professional and managerial employees of any one particular firm who comprise a small minority receive remuneration ten times or more that of the average unskilled worker, and value added is an average figure which does not reflect this.

A second concern with Lim's figures is that she obtained a racial breakdown by *assuming* that the non-Malays receive a higher percentage of the value added and then used the value added figures as the proxy for income since the breakdown for each ethnic group was not available. What follows is the obvious tautological conclusion that the non-Malays earned more than the Malays.

The Anand and Snodgrass studies are much sounder in methodology, and both researchers put in some effort to evaluate the concepts used in defining income. From the point of view of obtaining an overall picture of income distribution for the peninsula, the surveys covered by the two studies are probably adequate, subject to the very careful qualifications Snodgrass attached to the definition of income, the cut-off point of sampling, and the evaluation of the different biases introduced by the various handicaps. However, they are still grossly inadequate if the interest is broader. It is desirable to assess the income characteristics of the different occupation groups, to explain inequality of incomes and examine what determines incomes for a more sound and comprehensive picture of income distribution in Malaysia.[20]

The many studies of income distribution in Malaysia have yet to integrate the study of income distribution with income determination. These studies have indicated the possible increase in income inequality but are unable to explain the reasons for this deterioration. This is hardly surprising as it is the usual practice of economists to separate the measurement of income and the estimation of income inequality from the study of the determination of income inequality.

The study of income distribution is not an end in itself, but a means to an end. Economists and politicians alike should be interested in an income inequality study for three reasons: to ascertain the extent to which it exists, to determine its causes, and to seek possible counter-measures. Any study that, for example, merely reports the current state of inequality without highlighting the causes of it, is useful only in a very narrow sense,[21] and is probably not very effective in the final analysis.

Therefore, the primary focus of this book is to investigate the determinants of income and the consequent pattern of income distribution in Malaysia. The emphasis of each section is to draw attention to the factors determining income and its distribution through which it is hoped will highlight the conceptual problems needing attention in large-scale income surveys and provide a picture of distribution together with an explanation of the causal relations involved.

1.3 THE FRAMEWORK

In the proliferation of literature on income distribution in the late sixties and early seventies, there have been many studies on theories of income distribution and the determination of inequality. Studies of the latter generally centre around the importance of one particular factor in determining income, for example education, or culture, or monopoly. The methodology adopted for studies of income distribution, on the other hand, has been varied but their basic philosophy tends to be of the neo-classical school. Usually income and wealth are not integrated in such studies[22] since most concentrate on labour or employment income without even a foray into income from wealth.

Income is a function of effort, skill, and opportunity. Effort is a function of the individual's subjective will to work which is affected by the opportunities available and perhaps influenced by cultural practices.[23] Skill is determined by the general educational opportunities in the nation, the income of the family, and the chances of receiving on-the-job training. Actual opportunities available to a person are dependent largely on his position within the structure of production and in the market structure. 'Structure of production' refers to the mode of organization and the techniques of production. In the agricultural sector, crucial factors are the size of holdings and condition of land tenancy, how far the production system is labour-intensive and family-oriented and the extent to which agrochemicals are used. In the industrial sector, it is the relative factor intensities. By 'structure of market' is meant the system of distribution in which the extent of market competition and the number of levels of handling involved are important factors.

In the text, whenever possible, the number of man-days worked per person or family will be documented as a reflection of the effort expended. Some attempt will also be made to examine the correlation between effort and the opportunity of making more income within the same occupation or in an alternative career. However, there will be no attempt to investigate how cultural factors affect effort. There will, nevertheless, be a brief comment on the usual tendency to correlate race or culture with propensity to work in the concluding chapter.

The skills of the bulk of the workers are obtained on the job, as the receipt of primary and even lower secondary education is unlikely to change either skill or income significantly. For the smallholding farmers, the skill of planting, cultivation, and harvesting is passed on from generation to generation through on-farm work as unpaid family helpers. Whether they will accept new farming techniques is more dependent on economic factors and the demonstration work of the agricultural extension workers than on the farmers' level of literacy.[24]

It is also true that wage earners, the unskilled and general workers, almost always get trained on the job regardless of educational level. Skilled jobs used to be handed down exclusively through the system of apprenticeship, but vocational training has become an alternative route for the acquisition of skills. However, vocational training is not very widely available in Malaysia and the number of people benefiting from it is limited. The amount of formal schooling a worker has received is probably a secondary consideration compared to how well he can, and is willing to, use his hands. In fact, given the existing emphasis of the present education system, the more formal education a person has, the more likely it is for him to feel superior and despise working with his hands, probably giving rise to a lack of aptitude and dexterity for day-to-day blue-collar work.

Of course getting a primary and lower secondary school education has its benefits in that it qualifies one for admission into vocational school or upper secondary school. The completion of upper secondary school opens up the possibility of clerical work or possible entrance to the university. Obviously, for someone who has the choice of attending a university or not, the difference in his potential income would be very substantial. The starting pay for a university graduate with honours is at least $865 per month in the government sector—a level which is more than six times that of an average farming household. But the number of people who reach this category is rather small. According to the drop-out report, whereas 89 per cent of children aged 11 are enrolled at primary school, only 36 per cent of the 15-year-olds are enrolled in Form Three; the Lower Certificate of Education examination administered at the end of Form Three usually eliminates about 50 per cent of the students from upper secondary school, i.e., less than 18 per cent of the 17-year-olds would be enrolled in Form Five. Children from families with low socio-economic status fare below this average: only 26 per cent of the 15-year-olds are enrolled in Form Three, implying that probably less than 13 per cent would be enrolled in Form Five at best. Only less than 2 per cent of the 19- to 24-year-olds can attend university.[25] For the majority, the point is that termination of one's education at the primary and lower secondary level, and increasingly even at the upper secondary level, does not usually propel one into a higher paying job or make one more skilful.[26]

Moreover, the impact of education on income is quite different from that of a land development scheme or an irrigation project which can raise income in the same generation and in a short time. Education is valued tremendously as a tool for upward mobility because it raises the income prospects of the people of the next generation.[27] But education is very costly, not just to the Government but also to the family. Hence the level of education an individual can receive is dependent on family resources.[28] Only a small minority can receive scholarships and other forms of assistance to undertake higher education.

It is also important to distinguish between the benefits of education in different time periods. When fewer people completed secondary school, the graduates had little difficulty finding relatively 'desirable' jobs after leaving school. But as more and more secondary school graduates enter the market, they increasingly have to be content with becoming blue-collar workers or accepting low-income clerical work and may even face unemployment if the economy cannot respond by creating enough jobs. This situation applies to many underdeveloped countries rapidly expanding their education programme; Malaysia is no exception.[29]

The point here is that there is no single upward sloping labour supply market. Rather, there are several labour markets, each with a labour surplus situation (at least in the case of Malaysia) and hence a horizontal supply schedule. Education becomes a passport for entry into the next higher level of the labour market. But once one gets there, there is no free choice exercised in the usual sense of equating supply and demand. One forms a queue, and the demand can pick and choose. To the individuals lining up in the queue, the 'choice' is to get hired and receive the salary offered, or be unemployed and receive no income at all. There is only a fictitious free choice in how much time, and hence income, one is prepared to put in. For each labour market, the supply situation changes over time. Take the university graduates for instance: in the first twenty years after Independence the number of university graduates was limited, i.e., the queue was short and just about everyone obtained a highly paid job. Once the number of graduates multiplies and the queue becomes longer, the process of hiring (or firing) is no longer one dominated equally by supply and demand. It reverts to a case analogous to that for the unskilled and secondary school graduates.[30] Figure 1.1 illustrates a typical labour market situation for Malaysia.

In short, the argument here is in line with Thurow's concept of the labour queue and the 'defensive' importance of education. Education is a passport for lining up in a queue, but the labour surplus situation lengthens the queue,

FIGURE 1.1
HYPOTHETICAL LABOUR MARKET CONDITION OF MALAYSIA

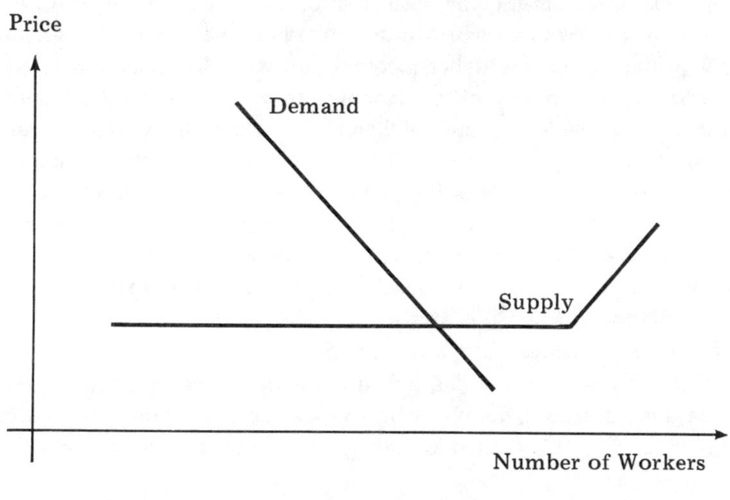

weakens the bargaining power of the individual, and so the available jobs are 'distributed' by the employers to people lining up in the queue, not necessarily according to the order of joining it.[31] Therefore, the employers' decisions to invest or not determine the job opportunities created and hence the job distribution with the consequential effects on income distribution pattern. Clearly effort, skill, and educational level do not constitute important or independent determinants of income.

Therefore, the *main focus* of this book will be on the opportunity available to the people in determining their income. The *core* of the analysis lies in the structure of production and the structure of the market as the main determinants of opportunity available to individuals.

Part I covers the structure of production. This refers primarily to the structure of land tenure and the organization of agricultural production on the one hand, and the capital-intensive bias introduced by the incentive package of the Government in the industrial sector on the other.[32] The labour absorption of the Malaysian economy had yet to create a strong overall upward pressure on the wages and salaries of the different categories of skilled workers up to about 1970. This can be seen by the relative stability of wages over the years.[33] As a result, the choice of technique consideration by the individual entrepreneur, and by the modern sector as a whole, is much less important at this juncture. Therefore the effort here is concentrated at merely identifying the level of income by skill level of the employees. However, since 1970, there has been some pressure on the wage and salary levels due to inflation, union demands, and the introduction of labour-intensive manufacturing industries such as textile and electronics. Unfortunately, there are as yet no detailed studies of the changing wage and salary structure. Nevertheless, we attempt to discuss the impact of this on the overall income distribution pattern in Chapters 4 and 9.

Part II mainly deals with the structure and characteristics of the market and the structure of wealth distribution as a sub-section of it. Conceptually, it is difficult to integrate income, a flow item, with wealth, a stock item.[34] This is particularly so if one is interested in a single index of measurement of inequality.

In order to integrate income with wealth, one must see how fluid conversions between the two can work to an individual's advantage. Let us start by asking why people pursue higher incomes and why they accumulate wealth.

The obvious reason why higher incomes are desired is to satisfy one's ambitions and raise one's standard of living. There are three levels of satisfaction to be fulfilled: necessities, luxuries, and the intangibles. One's society and social exposure establishes the demarcation lines between the necessities and luxuries, and between luxuries and the intangibles. For example, in American society where factories are distant from workers' residential areas, where the public transport system is inadequate, and where overall wealth accumulation (by whatever means)[35] is at a higher level, a car borders on a necessity. In Malaysia, on the other hand, a car is definitely a luxury.

Once the necessities are defined and obtained and a 'suitable' level of luxury has been attained, people begin to look for and accumulate intangibles. Intangibles refer to things such as fame, social status, and influence. One may wish to be elected to the board of a school, or become the president of one's clan association, or the secretary of the local chamber of commerce, or the *penghulu* of a *kampung*, or the branch chairman of the governing party, and so on. All these call for the expenditure of money directly[36] or indirectly. On the other hand, one may want to be recognized for one's riches. Hence, despite a yearly income of such magnitude as to satisfy all of one's luxurious needs and the money to buy influence, it is important to some people to expand their accumulation of wealth so that they can boast of being the largest estate owner, or the biggest sugar tycoon in Malaysia.[37] These are examples of the intangibles.

These three sets of wants motivate the pursuit of high income and wealth. The higher one's income and wealth, the more resources there are at one's disposal to attain the three wants. The expansion of income and wealth can provide for more of these wants, but only by the accumulation of income and conversion of it into the form of wealth can one attain higher income and greater wealth in the future.[38] Hence it becomes necessary to strike a balance between consumed income and wealth, and saved and accumulated income and wealth.

Government imposition of tax on corporate profits, on development, and on income and other taxes introduces still another factor in this spending and accumulation consideration, with its consequences on income and wealth measurement. For an average family of five in Malaysia the personal income tax rate rises above 40 per cent if income is more than $55,000 per year. On the other hand, the corporate profit tax rate remains stationary at 40 per cent regardless of the profit level.[39] Therefore, once a person's income from dividends and salary reaches $55,000 per year, it is advantageous to appropriate only as much dividend as needed for personal use. His access to company funds for entertainment, purchase and maintenance of cars, villas, etc., as well as social and political contributions (all of which should be identified as *de facto* his or his contributions), minimizes his need to receive more in the form of personal income. The unappropriated profit after 40 per cent tax can be used to reduce the need for loan financing in current projects, or accumulated for future expansion. Eventually, these unappropriated profits and their accumulated earnings can be redistributed to the shareholders as bonus or scrip issues not taxable under capital gains. This flexibility not only prevents 'excessive' taxation and raises the amount of funds available for reinvestment, thus enabling the individual to realize eventually greater wealth, it also allows for a lower, in some cases a lower statement of, income in the usual income survey (though perhaps not necessarily in income tax assessment).[40]

Such accumulation of unappropriated profit is, in reality, a voluntary saving-reinvestment on the part of the owner, side-stepping the income loop.[41] These capital reserves, general reserves, and unappropriated profits are future wealth while executive fringe benefits and expenses constitute present hidden consumption and income; both are circulating and accumulating without being registered as accrued present income. It is important to gauge the relative weight of the distributed profits and reported income *vis-à-vis* these unappropriated profits to see how much the usual measurement of income underestimates the income of the rich and hence income inequality. The study of wealth distribution is hence not just important in itself, it is an important and integral part of the study of income distribution.

Furthermore, it is important to realize that complete ownership of the capital, in many cases, is not necessary in order to have effective control over the wealth of a firm. By structuring a firm's shareholding and company integration in some ways (for example, spreading a large portion of the issued capital widely among small investors and utilizing a pyramid control structure), it is possible for one person to exercise control over a number of companies with total capital and assets in the hundreds of millions by merely owning a controlling interest in one single company (the interest may or may not be as much as 50 per cent). The question of what constitutes control will be discussed with examples in Chapter 5. We should just note here that in such cases the controlling shareholder is actually receiving the intangible benefits through the 'generosity' of a large number of small investors. Hence a study of the structure of wealth, and through this economic power, is very important within an income distribution study.

Naturally, the structure of production and market are both related to the structure of wealth. In the agricultural sector, the wealth distribution is closely related to the land tenure structure. The more concentrated the holding of land is in the hands of a minority, the higher the level of land tenure with the result that there is probably a larger number of tenants with lower income after rent payment. It is one of the major objectives of this study to establish that the structure of wealth distribution can also influence the market structure. The income of the farmers is in turn affected by the market structure which will determine the price that they can receive for their produce and the price of consumer goods items they procure.

In this study, some evidence is gathered to illustrate that the wealth of Malaysia is concentrated in the hands of a very few local entrepreneurs and a group of foreign investors with important links to the industrial and financial interests of the leading developed nations. The United Kingdom is perhaps most important, due to her historical links with Malaysia.

In addition to documenting the concentration of wealth, there is also an analysis of the profit level, and hence income and economic power, of the different businesses. This is useful for comparison with the income of the farmers and wage and salaried employees. Such profit data also form an integral part of the investigation of the market structure of Malaysia, the degree of competition at each level of the market distribution, the issue of middlemen monopoly-monopsony, and the question of who makes the pricing decision.

1.4 SCOPE AND LAYOUT

Many of the conceptual problems related to the measurement of income will not be discussed in this book.[42] Data limitations prevented the construction of a detailed income distribution for comparison with that of the PES and other surveys, although some distribution by sector is provided when meaningful data can be compiled.

Part I deals with the great majority of the West Malaysian populace: the urban wage earners, the salaried white-collar employees in the Government and private sector, the rural estate workers, padi farmers, fishermen, smallholders, and the petty traders. These people and their families constitute about 98 per cent of the population.[43] They generally form the lower- and middle-income brackets of this country. Of course, a small percentage of those with higher education really belong to the ranks of the 'lower' high-income bracket, while many of the traders and manufacturers discussed in Part II fall into this lower- and middle-income category.[44]

Part I is organized into three chapters. The first two chapters cover the rural small-farm producers. Chapter 2 primarily covers the 293,000 padi farm households, while Chapter 3 discusses the 417,000 rubber smallholders and about 50,000 coconut smallholders.[45] Chapter 4 summarizes the income of most of the urban dwellers, covering about 215,000 in manufacturing, 200,000 in the distributive trades, 86,000 in transport and communication, 78,000 in construction, 72,000 in mining, 50,000 in hawking, and 300,000 in Government service, including in this case more than 270,000 rural estate workers.[46] The last group has been included with the urban dwellers because the system of production in an estate is organized more like a factory than a small rural farm. Besides, control of these estates and workers is exercised via corporations similar to the practice in the urban wage sector.

The description of income distribution and determination culminates in Chapter 4 with a discussion of the rise of a Malaysian middle and upper class. This group consists largely of the urban well-educated employees of all races, and includes the wealth holders, whose income, wealth, and economic power will be more adequately discussed again in Part II. There will also be a brief evaluation of the status of the lower-income households in association with the factors outlined in the two earlier chapters.

Some factors affecting income in different economic activities will be outlined throughout Chapters 2 to 4 with a view towards a structural explanation of the income determination and distribution for the people of Malaysia in association with the analysis in Part II on wealth.

Part II is organized into four chapters. The first two (Chapters 5 and 6) deal basically with the pattern of wealth distribution, focusing on the extent of concentration of wealth in the hands of a very small minority of large companies. Some attention is also paid to the role of the foreigners, non-Malays, and Malays and Government, over time. Chapter 5 concentrates on the largest companies, i.e., usually the publicly listed companies (with some sprinkling of the private limited ones) which tend to provide relatively more information for analysis, and on some of the most important and dynamic sectors or industries in the country. The analysis is basically micro in nature. By contrast, Chapter 6 attempts to provide a macro picture of the whole corporate sector including large, medium, and small firms by resorting to a retabulation and analysis of the averages and ranges of sales and gross profits of these firms. These will be characterized by legal organization and size as provided by the different censuses and surveys on limited companies and industries conducted by the Department of Statistics. Paucity of data at the medium- and small-sized firm level rules out a detailed study along the lines of Chapter 5 for the large corporations. Nevertheless, an attempt to estimate their performances by defining their level of operating surplus is made on the basis of reasonable assumptions.

Chapter 7 singles out the issue of middlemen for detailed analysis. Middlemen as a group are important not only because they form a core group of the smaller commercial operators dealt with in Chapter 6, but also because of the importance of the question of middlemen monopoly-monopsony in the structure of marketing. The popular impression that poor rural Malays are exploited by Chinese middlemen has been one very important ingredient in racial discontent. Such impressions have been further propagated by officials, social scientists, and journalists of Malaysian and foreign origins alike, and may lead one to have the false impression that all the rich merchants rose from the ranks of coolies and all coolies stood, and stand, a good chance of becoming rich businessmen. It is also often believed that the Chinese middlemen can take advantage of the Government's good intentions and bureaucratic inefficiencies to conspire and depress the prices of rural produce. Some typical quotations from such a perspective will help to illustrate its general sentiments. Alexander (1973) wrote:

> The Chinese were stealthily taking over their economy and their land. The one-time coolies, now flourishing as Chinese merchants, were the real colonizers of Southeast Asia.[47]
>
> The Federal Agricultural Marketing Authority, set up . . . to 'protect padi farmers from Chinese middlemen', had no marketing facilities, was eventually obliged to sell to the middlemen it was designed to by-pass and as a result, caused rice prices to drop to an all-time low.[48]

The distinguished historian Arnold Toynbee was drawn into stating:

> I realised that British Malaya was destined by 'peaceful penetration' to become a new Chinese province and I fancy from what I have heard that the same destiny may be in store for Burma, Siam, French Indochina, Dutch Indonesia and Philippines.[49]

The social scientist Roger Freedman wrote in 1968:

> In Malaysia, as elsewhere, the Chinese play a far more important role in society than their share of the entire population (36 per cent at the present time) would suggest. They dominate the modern sectors of the economy—trade, industry, finance, professionals, mining, plantations (except for a limited number of large units under European control)—and leave to the Malays their traditional occupations: small scale agriculture, fishing, and forestry.[50]

Ungku Aziz's papers are perhaps the works most often cited as the authoritative statement on middlemen exploitation and impoverishment of rural Malays.[51] But Aziz's study, besides not being rigorous, lacks concrete evidence, is outdated and possibly misleading at this juncture, given the very fluid nature of the Malaysian economy.[52] This lack of rigour is not unique to Ungku Aziz. Most studies of middlemen so far do not contain enough careful and substantial data on the degree of monopoly, the profit margin, and the extent of wealth accumulation by the middlemen to validate their conclusion.[53]

In fact, the question of monopolistic-monopsonistic middlemen is of great importance in the determination of income. The degree of competition determines how much control middlemen have in setting the price, i.e., how large a portion of the international price is skimmed by them and how large a portion is passed on to the small producers (which helps to determine their income). Chapter 7 attempts to define the extent of monopolistic-monopsonistic competition in the rural areas, the profit margin and the income received by the middlemen, using data from official and other sources. However, the question of how much control middlemen have over price-setting is closely related to the marketing structure, and so the last section of Chapter 7 outlines the marketing structure of Malaysia.

In investigating the marketing structure, some attempt is made to trace the links of the most important foreign operators in Malaysia to the major financial interests of the developed countries, especially the United Kingdom. The intention is to put the structure of Malaysian business activities into the context of the international economy and point to the possible existence of very strong international oligopolies and cartels in the several major raw materials produced by Malaysia. The possibility of international price-fixing to the detriment of the producers is suggested as well but a more emphatic conclusion awaits the concrete verification of future research. The implications of the price-fixing (if valid) and control over the whole line of distribution (partially documented in the text and notes) on income determination and distribution are obvious.

In the process of research, many interesting examples of the initiation and amalgamation of individuals/families/associates/companies into business interest groups emerged. Such impressions enable a discussion on the hypothetical origin and base as well as the ownership and control structure of the local entrepreneurs at the various levels of the Malaysian economic hierarchy. This treatment of the nature of entrepreneurship in Chapter 8 is made to assess the extent of upward mobility possible from the lower levels of business activities. The difficulties faced by the small businessmen in pushing upwards on the ladder of income and wealth are rooted in the low level of profitability of small businesses in general (Chapter 6) and of the traders in the distribution system in particular (Chapter 7).

The documentation of the upward mobility of the small businessmen serves as a backdrop for an evaluation of the possibility and ease with which the group of Malays who are already in this group can move into the ranks of the big capitalists under the stimulation of the NEP. In light of this, the new tensions and tendencies resulting from the artificial structural changes introduced by the NEP in the economy are also analysed.

Chapter 9 concludes with summaries, inferences as well as some up-dating of data since the bulk of the research was conducted in the early and mid-seventies when only earlier data dating to the late sixties were available.

1.5 LIMITATIONS OF THIS STUDY

As a single well-designed, consistent, and comprehensive income survey is not yet available, the data for this book have been assembled from many different reports, studies, and surveys. These are varied in scope and were conducted at different times with different concepts and rigour. No amount of detailed evaluation of the sample design, the methodology and so on can completely account for, and adjust, the resultant problem of consistency and comparability. The best insurance seems to be extreme care in the overall treatment of the diversified data and this the author has tried to do to the best of his ability. Even then, one should stress that this book hopes only to contribute towards a more basic understanding of the conceptual difficulties and the factors which need to be considered and researched before a satisfactory income survey relating to income determination can be designed. Conclusions are, therefore, tentative and indicative only and not definitive.

In what follows only general difficulties are raised, those arising in each section or chapter will be discussed accordingly.

A. Choice of Year for Analysis

Data for this thesis have been drawn from many different years, but mainly centring around the years 1965 to 1970. In this section, justification for tolerating this choice and possible shortcomings arising therefrom are examined.

For the smallholding agricultural sector, changes in land holding, farming techniques and prices are most likely to affect yearly variance in income. However, the first two factors need not cause undue alarm.

Changes in the distribution of land holding (due to population growth, land development, foreclosure after credit default and other factors) are likely to be small and evolutionary except when drastic changes such as land reform, estate subdivision, or others occur. In fact, the changing tenurial relationship among the padi farmers has taken scores of years to be noticeable. Little is known about land tenancy among the rubber smallholders so that an assessment is not possible.

In terms of farming techniques, important changes have been introduced into the padi, rubber, and coconut industries. For the padi farmers, the most important is the introduction of double cropping. In so far as the Province Wellesley and Krian farmers have been practising double cropping since the Second World War, their production and income pattern should have been stabilized by the late sixties,[54] so that any one year taken would be acceptable. On the other hand, the new major irrigation projects like Muda, Kemubu, and Besut were instituted in the late sixties or early seventies so that by the late sixties, only part of the Muda area had been under double cropping. In short, this important change would not as yet have affected most of the padi areas and hence the estimation and analysis for the relevant years. In fact, drawing on some data of the later years (after double cropping had been extensively practised in Muda) actually allows for an evaluation of the impact of double cropping.

For the rubber smallholders, the question of the choice of year is much more important. This is because the major change involves the replanting of old rubber trees with newer and more productive seedlings. Thus, smallholdings replanted five years later may already have a built-in advantage simply because they may now be using even better seedlings. Moreover, in the years 1969–70, the bulk of the replanted smallholdings was beginning to come into production. By virtue of the six- or seven-year time-lag, it is very likely that most of the smallholders with a reasonable-sized plot would have chosen to replant in stages. Thus, the yearly producing acreage in the smallholdings may change quite appreciably, resulting in fairly important changes in income. This means that one can no longer claim that using 1965 data and 1970 data makes no difference.

Unfortunately, data in the rubber smallholding sector are much more scarce than that in the padi sector. The problem does not lie in having many surveys covering different years, giving rise to the need to reconcile discrepancies introduced by the differences in years. Only two surveys in two areas are available for the sixties, with two more completed even earlier. Consequently, the situation is one of having to draw conclusions and observations based on very sketchy data, constraining the analysis to be non-comprehensive in coverage, and very hypothetical in nature.

With coconut planting, the change in technology is again in the form of replanting with new and better seedlings. Maturing time is again important. But we are similarly confronted with a paucity of data so that the question of choice of year is academic, in the sense that no alternative is available.

The impact of price differences over time varies with the crop. For padi, the guaranteed price has been in operation for many years, including the years when most of the surveys were conducted. Variations introduced by the middlemen or other buyers through deductions for moisture content and transport charges are not likely to swing wild, as they should follow some pattern from year to year and would in general be a modest percentage. Therefore, the farmers' received price should be quite stable, and the difference in years used should not introduce too much distortion.

For cash crops like rubber and coconut, price fluctuations are large, causing wild swings in the income of the smallholders. In these cases, the choice of year is of great importance. However, the question is again not so much distortion when different years' data are employed, but which year, if any, can and should be chosen as representative for comparison with other sectors. This question will be dealt with again in the concluding chapter.

Taking all three factors into consideration, it seems that the only case when data from different years in the late sixties can be used would be the padi sector. For all the others, data constraints dictate that a beggar cannot choose. The concern should really be focused on a more theoretical treatment of how to undertake income measures for such volatile sectors.

With the exception of the rubber estate workers whose wages have been tied to rubber prices beyond the basic minimum wage rate, there are indications that wages and salaries did not change much in the late sixties. This is due partly to the structure of employment in the nation, and partly to the lack of inflation and of strong union organization on a broad front to push for active wage changes from year to year. Part II will show that most of the urban employers, be they commercial or industrial endeavours, are small-scale, family-sized operations with perhaps up to a dozen employees under a patronage system. Wages are usually fixed at a low level and since labour organization is not widely practised and there has been hardly any inflation in the period under consideration, there has been no pressure to increase wages. Any income changes are likely to occur in the form of bonus payments which are very dependent on the business of that year. The profitability of these small enterprises is so small that they cannot sustain any consistent upward trend in wages.[55]

Large-scale employers naturally do not operate under this set of constraints, though again the difference in wages and salaries between 1967 and 1970 is not very large.[56] Those who receive big increases in their pay are generally the very small minority of executives and professionals.

For the estate workers, the variations in rubber price-induced wage changes are likely to be smaller percentages of the price increase, due to the way the wage increase formula was arranged. The distortion should be in the same direction as that introduced by the choice of year for the rubber smallholders.

We turn now to the ownership and control data of Part II. For Chapter 5, the control structure of the firms in 1973 and 1974 has been charted using the published individual company reports and returns to the Registrar of Companies. These have been updated whenever possible and necessary.[57] Chapter 6, on the other hand, depends on census and survey data published by the Department of Statistics which almost always have a three- to four-year time-lag between the end of the calendar year, the initiation of the survey/census, and the publication of the findings. Therefore, it becomes impossible to work on current data. In the end, the year 1968 was chosen for most of the presentation for overall consistency with data used in Part I. Most of the data used for the all-important agricultural sectors in Part I have been based on surveys done around 1967–8. This was also the case with the series of censuses on household expenditure, the manufacturing, mining, and construction industries, distributive trades, and limited companies.[58] Therefore, the choice of the year 1968 would enable one to have a complete coverage of the whole spectrum of activities and on all sizes of operations.

Would this use of different years to construct the picture of ownership and control be inconsistent? Many of the publicly listed companies were already established by 1968 either as private or public, but unlisted, limited companies. When they were subsequently converted into publicly listed companies, there was very little change in their ownership and control pattern.[59] The only important change in that period was the rise of Malay and governmental participation which has been separately highlighted in Chapter 5.

Obviously, some new companies have been established since, and a few of the more aggressive groups have surfaced with an enlarged scale of operation under their conglomeration. Nevertheless with the exception of the most speculative groups (which are few), most of the important groups have been formed or were in the process of finishing their acquisition/expansion, and major changes were, by and large, initiated at least by 1968. In that sense, an examination of 1975 actually permits a clearer picture of the tendencies started in the early or mid-sixties.[60]

In short, for the purpose of tracing the ownership and control pattern, i.e., the wealth structure, the different years do not pose a problem. If the purpose is a comparison of the income of the wealth holders using profit as a proxy of their non-labour income, it is again not a problem for the majority of those in business because their data are for the same approximate year 1967/8. It is only when one wants to contrast the income of those who control the large conglomerates with that of the farmers, employees, and so on that there will be distortions. However, in this case, the size of their wealth and income is so huge that even reducing the figures for 1975 by an arbitrary factor of three to approximate performance for 1967/8 would still leave the wealth holders far ahead. This kind of distortion, especially when it involves only a very small number of families (perhaps no more than several hundred), should not be a major concern.

The picture of the distribution of wealth is up-to-date except for the several groups of Malay capitalists that have risen extremely quickly in recent years and for whom it is not yet possible to document fully. On the other hand, the income data which pertain to the late sixties refer to a period before the advent of the NEP and is somewhat obsolete. Meanwhile, the years 1973 and 1974 ushered in a series of major changes that would have an important impact on the income of Malaysians. First of all, 1973 was the year when there was a worldwide boom; Malaysia was no exception with huge price and profit increases. Wage increases naturally followed suit among the sectors well unionized, with some eventual spillovers to the non-organized sectors. 1973 was also the year of the Fourth Arab-Israeli War followed by the oil price hike which eventually forced up the price of raw material for synthetic rubber and changed the balance in the tussle between natural and synthetic rubber. As a result, the price of natural rubber reversed its cyclical and declining price trend and has hovered around $2.00 per kilo since the mid-seventies. This is bound to raise the income of the rubber smallholders (its impact on estate owners would have been accounted for given the choice of data year for the wealth study). By 1978, the irrigation projects for the major padi areas had already been operational for some time and the various land development schemes had opened up about 1,000,000 acres of land for about 100,000 settler-families, both of which should raise the income of the rural population.

Obviously this study is not able to provide direct data to evaluate the changes to the income distribution pattern introduced by these impulses and policies. Nevertheless, the strength of the approach of this study is precisely the ability to analyse the possible impact of these changes on the income of the different groups of people; and from there, evaluate the change in pattern of income distribution. Accordingly, in the concluding chapter, inferences on the changing picture of income distribution are drawn. There is no necessity to await the conduct of a major income survey to draw conclusions about the changes in pattern. In fact, the next round of agriculture census, or household income and budget surveys, if and when introduced, in the latter part of the seventies should provide cross-checks for the inferences drawn.[61]

B. Choice of Unit for Comparison

In evaluating income, the trend has been moving increasingly from individual income to household income to *per capita* household income (i.e., income per household divided by the number of persons per household). The last is considered the superior unit of measurement because it can smooth out the distortion introduced by a correlation between the size of household income and the size of household if household income is used.

Unfortunately, the nature of the data available does not enable the use of this standardized unit of comparison. In fact, the data are such that household, individual, and corporate income have to be used. This sub-section tries to gauge the amount of distortion resulting from this diversity in unit of measurement.

The family is the unit of organization and measurement in the discussion on rural farm and urban petty traders' income. By contrast, wage earners or salaried persons receive their income as individuals. If there is only one wage earner per household, then the individual income is the household income, hence consistent when compared with the household income reported for the farmers and small businessmen.[62] But this is not always the case and it is necessary to trace the pattern of the number of wage earners per urban family for meaningful comparisons.

For most families, the primary wage earner is most likely to be the husband. People usually marry young, and married women up to the age of 40 generally would not work because of household chores and the need to bring up children. According to the 1970 Census of Population:

> Urban females who enter the labour force before age 15 spend a much smaller proportion of their lives as active members of the labour force, . . . the tendency of the urban women to move into and out of the labour force as their family roles change is manifest. . . .
>
> In the urban sectors, females complete their assession by age twenty. In the next five years of life, in ages 20—24, they retire in large numbers, presumably as they turn to marriage and child care. Retirement frequencies decline rapidly to age 40—44, and increase in the following years of age.[63]

For the women 40 years of age and more, the grown-up children may have started working and moved out, which means lessened pressure to seek employment. Moreover, their physical ability to work would also have been affected.

Those with a hardship condition such as an ailing, unemployed, or deceased husband have no alternative but to work, making them the primary, rather than secondary, wage earners. On the other hand, there are the well-educated women who marry into affluent households and can afford to hire domestic help. They have a choice, but usually work. These would tend to be in such urban occupations as professionals, teachers, and clerks. Another significant group of women workers comprises young unmarried teenagers who work to supplement a low household income. Increasing industrialization is raising the number of such women quite significantly. Thus, apart from the very small number of professional women, the number of teenage workers may be the best indication of the possible upper limit of those households with more than one wage earner, assuming one teenage worker to one household. It is difficult to gauge the number of young male wage earners who are secondary earners from the occupations they engage in. One can only assume that their labour force participation rate at a young age parallels that of their sisters given an almost equal number of males and females in any population. Therefore, the number of young males working as the second earner would be roughly the same as the number of young female second earners.

Data from Table 5 of the same study cited above show that the earlier mentioned pattern of female participation in the labour force is broadly similar for the three major races. However, there is one important divergence from this pattern. For those females aged 10—14, 20.44 per cent of the Malays enter the labour force while 5.62 per cent fewer Indians and 9.8 per cent more Chinese join the labour force. In the age group of 15—19, 11.47 per cent of the Malays join while 4.58 per cent fewer Indians and 2.14 per cent more Chinese enter the labour force. When retirement begins in the next five years, the Chinese withdraw 7.8 per cent more than the Malays while the Indian withdrawal rate of 10.21 per cent is less than half of that of the Malays.[64]

This variation has important implications for income distribution. It implies that almost 10 per cent more of the urban Chinese females participate in the labour force than the Malays for a period of less than ten years. At this age, it is almost certain that the females are the supplementary wage earners. As such, if they all receive salaries or wages, the income of their households would be raised.

At least two qualifications are necessary. The above computation makes no distinction of the unpaid family helpers from the bona fide wage receivers. Since many of the urban Chinese are engaged in the distributive trades using many unpaid family helpers, the difference in the number of second wage earners between the two races may be small after netting out the unpaid helpers.

No comparison has been made of the young employed males by race since there is little difference in their labour force participation characteristics.

The fact that there are only about 214,000 (or less than 9 per cent of total employed) in the 15—24 age bracket working in private limited companies, partnerships, proprietorships, and domestic services[65] indicates the low incidence of two or more family workers with pay, especially at the lower-income band.[66]

The PES data provide more support for this claim. 12.2 per cent of the rural and 20.5 per cent of the urban households have three or more earners per household. In addition, 26.9 per cent of rural and 25.1 per cent of urban households have two wage earners.[67] The difference in percentages of households with two or more earners between rural and urban areas (as a proxy for Malay/non-Malay comparison) is thus not very large. But because of the difference in the number of total rural and urban households, there would be a larger number of rural households with two or more earners. However, the slightly higher wage income received by the urban dwellers in general[68] means that most of these urban dwellers will end up in a higher-income (not high-income) category than those in the rural areas with the same number of earners per household.

In sum, it is probably not inaccurate to claim that perhaps 35 per cent of the households in Peninsular Malaysia have more than one earner per household with some bias towards the urban dwellers. But the bias also operates along income lines in the sense that the richer households tend to have a higher incidence of multiple earners,[69] and these additional earners are probably in the higher-income brackets themselves. The implication is of course that the income bias introduced by not summing the familial income of the multiple earners family will not distort the comparison between low-income Malays and non-Malays, but will underestimate the inequality between low- and higher-income groups, especially the comparison with high-income non-Malay families.

In any case, when a comparison is made of the middle- and higher-income brackets by ethnic group, the data used have been changed from that of the individual to that of household *per capita* income as summarized by Anand; thus this problem of multiple earners per household would no longer pose a problem.

Finally, a word about the use of corporate income to reflect the income of the major shareholder. Under the usual concepts of income, this would have posed a severe problem. However, Chapter 6 argues that corporate revenue and income can be used to the advantage of the major shareholder, and is thus *de facto* his.

1. Throughout the book, 'Malaysia', 'West Malaysia', 'Peninsular Malaysia', and 'Malaya' are used interchangeably to refer to Peninsular Malaysia, as only data from Peninsular Malaysia are available in the study.

2. Malaysia, *Third Malaysia Plan 1976–1980*, Kuala Lumpur, Government Press, 1976, Tables 8—9, p. 150.

3. This is not the place to go into economic history. Neither is it the place to discuss the extent to which British colonial policies were intentionally designed and implemented to segregate and further alienate the various ethnic groups. However, in the introduction to each chapter, there is a brief recapitulation of the socio-economic history relevant to that sector of the economy under discussion. Pertinent references will be given then.

4. The Chinese and Indians have, to some extent, frequently been perceived as 'alien' communities.

5. See for example, R. Emerson, *Malaysia: A Study in Direct and Indirect Rule*, New York, MacMillan, 1937.

6. For more detailed discussion of rural development, see for example: Gayl Ness, *Bureaucracy and Rural Development in Malaysia*, Berkeley, University of California Press, 1967; Martin Rudner, 'The Malayan Quandary: Rural Development Policy under the First and Second Five Year Plans', *Contributions to Asian Studies* (1971), reprinted in David Lim, ed., *Readings on Malaysian Economic Development*, Kuala Lumpur, Oxford University Press, 1975, pp. 80—8; Donald R. Snodgrass, *Inequality and Economic Development in Malaysia*, Kuala Lumpur, Oxford University Press, 1980, Chapter 7.

7. The usual quota for share allotment is 30 per cent and the usual quota for hiring Malays is 30 per cent for all industries and 40 per cent or more for the pioneer industries. Actual practice varies, usually upwards of those mentioned here.

8. See for example, R. S. Milne, 'The Politics of Malaysia's New Economic Policy', *Pacific Affairs*, 49, Summer 1976, p. 237, citing Dr. Mahathir Mohamed, *The Malay Dilemma*, Singapore, Donald Moore, 1970, p. 42. In general, the Milne article provides a good summary and references to pre- and post-New Economic Policy politics.

9. In line with racial stereotypes that tend to distort perceptions, the focus has always been on the wealth generation capacities of a small number

of non-Malays while the low incomes of the large majority of non-Malays is glossed over.

10. This is the general impression gained from a cursory look at newspaper reports and election campaign speeches. In particular, the campaigning and relatively good performance of the opposition Democratic Action Party in 1978 have been built largely on this issue (see newspaper reports during the election). Independently, the discontent has resulted in the convening of a Malaysian Chinese economic convention in early 1978 and the strong support for the setting up of a Merdeka University (see *Quarterly Economic Bulletin*, no. 11, published by the Associated Chinese Chamber of Commerce for the former event and the special report published by the Merdeka University Corporation Limited, for the latter issue; the Merdeka University Corporation was incorporated by Chinese education proponents to promote and fund the proposed University).

11. Malaysia, *Second Malaysia Plan 1971–1975*, Kuala Lumpur, Government Press, 1971, p. 1.

12. See for example, Lutz Hoffmann and S. E. Tan, 'Employment Creation through Export Growth: A Case Study of West Malaysia's Manufacturing Industries', in H. Giersch, ed., *The International Division of Labour: Problems and Perspectives*, Tübingen, Mohr and Siebeck, 1974; Lutz Hoffmann and Tan Tew Nee, 'Pattern of Growth and Structural Change in West Malaysia's Manufacturing Industries, 1959–1968', *Kajian Ekonomi Malaysia*, VIII, December 1971, reprinted in David Lim, ed., *Readings on Economic Development*, Kuala Lumpur, Oxford University Press, 1975; B. L. Johns, 'Import Substitution and Export Potential—The Case of Manufacturing Industries in West Malaysia', *Australian Economic Papers*, 21, December 1973, reprinted in David Lim, op. cit.

13. The estimates were made by Yoshimitsu Takei, John C. Brock, and Bruce Saunders in *Educational Sponsorship by Ethnicity: A Preliminary Analysis of the West Malaysian Experience*, Athens, Ohio, Ohio University, Centre for International Studies, Southeast Asia Series No. 28, 1973. See p. 20 and footnote 16. The article provides good insight into Malaysia.

14. 1970 and 1975 figures are from the *Third Malaysia Plan* while the figures for 1977 have been obtained from reports of the proceedings in Parliament in 1978 in the reply of the Minister of Education to questions. Such a policy had of course generated substantial controversy in 1978 and 1979. On the one hand, the non-Malays have strongly criticized the Government for an admission policy which they see as biased and compromising the future of their sons and daughters. On the other hand, the Government argues that special emphasis on the admissions of Malays to the local universities is necessary to ensure the Malays their fair share in tertiary education and subsequently professional and executive employment and points to the large number of non-Malays studying overseas. However, only the well-to-do can afford to send their children abroad, cutting out the poorer non-Malays. *The Star*'s readers' column carried many statements from anxious readers on this topic in the months of October and November 1978. This is quite apart from the statements by political leaders which were also carried in the press in the same period.

15. Malaysia, *Mid-term Review of the Second Malaysia Plan 1971–1975*, Kuala Lumpur, Government Press, 1973, para. 184, p. 6.

16. The role and importance of these public enterprises will be discussed in Chapter 5.

17. Lim Lin Lean has since written several articles and a doctoral dissertation. The present writer has not seen any of these at the time of drafting this manuscript and hence cannot assess her more recent approach.

18. The unit used was the family for those in the agricultural sector and the self-employed traders and the individual for others.

19. See the tables and discussions of Section 6.1 of this book.

20. This is not the place to discuss this point in detail. Interested readers should refer to Tan Tat-wai, 'Income Distribution and Determination in West Malaysia', Ph.D. dissertation, Harvard University, 1977, pp. 7—8, for a brief discussion and await a forthcoming paper giving fuller details.

21. Of course one cannot say that it is not useful. At least it can tell us whether inequality has increased or decreased. However, the same information can be obtained once the income profile is known. Besides, as will be briefly discussed in the concluding chapter, such single index measurements cannot take into account many value judgements implicit in income measurements. Is the vast amount of effort expended on debating the ideal index that can best reflect welfare justified? For an idea of the issues covered in the debate, see, for example, A. Atkinson, 'On the Measurement of Inequality', *Journal of Economic Theory*, September 1970; D. J. Aigner and A. J. Heins, 'A Social Welfare View of the Measurement of Income Inequality', *Review of Income and Wealth*, March 1967; P. Dasgupta, A. Sen, and D. Starrett, 'Notes on the Measurement of Inequality', *Journal of Economic Theory*, June 1973; D. Rothschild and J. Stiglitz, 'Some Further Results on the Measurement of Inequality', *Journal of Economic Theory*, June 1973; A. Sen, *On Economic Inequality*, Oxford, Clarendon Press, 1974.

22. The article by Joseph Stiglitz, 'The Distribution of Income and Wealth among Individuals', *Econometrica*, 37, July 1969, is one of the few exceptions that tries to integrate wealth distribution into the theory of income distribution in a neo-classical context. However, Thurow (1975) contends that the marginal productivity return to factors cannot adequately explain the divergence in income and wealth. (See note 31.)

23. For example, there has been much discussion on the work-leisure choice the Malays have made in the light of their cultural environment. Chapter 9 briefly discusses this topic, drawing on the exchange between Parkinson and Wilder.

24. See U. Narkswasdi and S. Selvadurai, *Economic Survey of Padi Production in West Malaysia*, Kuala Lumpur, Ministry of Agriculture and Cooperatives, 1967, vol. 1, Table 19, p. 42.

25. The data on education have been obtained from Malaysia, Ministry of Education, Education Planning and Research Division, *Educational Statistics of Malaysia*, various years; Malaysia, Ministry of Education, *Dropout Report*, 1972.

26. Again, it is not the intention here to downplay the role of education. It is just that social scientists should come to grips with the changing role of different levels of education in the process of development. In that sense, the usual human capital approach fails to capture the changing values of the different levels of education at different points in the path of development.

27. Adult education is rather undeveloped in Malaysia (and many other countries), so that the possibilities of self-advancement through adult education once an individual leaves school and enters the labour force are quite limited. Therefore, the usual aspiration for upward mobility through education is usually transferred to the children.

28. Jacob Meerman, *The Distribution of Public Expenditure in Peninsular Malaysia*, Washington, D.C., International Bank for Reconstruction and Development, 1977, summary table. On the average only 2.1 per cent of the population receives post-secondary school education, but only 0.7 per cent of those from the lowest-income quintile can attend post-secondary school

education whereas 5.5 per cent of those from the highest-income quintile do so.

29. This is a casual impression gained by observing the increasing number of secondary and upper-secondary school graduates in blue-collar jobs and the increasing difficulties that some graduates have in seeking employment.

30. This is again the impression gathered from casual observations, from scattered newspaper reports on the number of engineering graduates, as well as graduates in general, still unemployed after months of job hunting.

31. See Lester Thurow, *Generating Inequality: Mechanism of Distribution in the U.S. Economy*, New York, Basic Books, 1975.

32. For an analysis of the possible biases introduced by the incentive package, see C. B. Edwards, 'Protection, Profits and Policy—An Analysis of Industrialisation in Malaysia', Ph.D. dissertation, University of East Anglia, 1975, Conclusion.

33. This can be seen by comparing the representative wages reported by the *Monthly Statistical Bulletin of Malaysia*, Kuala Lumpur, Department of Statistics, various years. However, of late, the wages of some sectors have started to climb. Notable examples are the wages of female operators in Penang due to rapid introduction of the very labour-intensive industries such as electronics and textiles, skilled construction workers because of shortages and the plantation workers primarily because of a long history of organized labour in the industry, and high prices of produce recently.

34. Some people will argue that the inclusion of investment income would have taken care of this problem. We disagree with that view. In later discussion, arguments will be put forward on the intimate flow back and forth between income stream and accumulation of capital which makes a careful treatment of income and wealth integration particularly important. It will be argued that many incomes can be hidden under the capital items and will definitely not be included under income. Such omissions can be very major.

35. From the point of view of the Americans, they may attribute this prosperity to hard work, efficient technology, etc., but from the Third World perspective, the American ability to exercise monopolistic/monopsonistic control over cheap raw material supplies and distribute high-priced manufactured items in the world capitalist system is the more important reason.

36. This can be achieved, for example, by contributing towards a political campaign or a local school expansion fund. It can also be achieved indirectly by entertaining V.I.P.s, giving expensive gifts, or placing villas and cars at the disposal of influential people.

37. This is just a random example; in the context of the Malaysian economy, the more appropriate claim may be a 'rubber king' or a 'tin king', not mentioned here in case of coincidental claim by individuals.

38. There is no intention of implying that this is the only motivation for business expansion, it merely highlights one of them. The usual argument about pressure from competition and relative wage price movement are also important factors.

39. Actually, there is a further 5 per cent of development tax on profit, making the effective profit tax rate 45 per cent. The income tax schedule was revised in the 1980 Budget, hence the estimated $55,000 demarcation line has to be revised upwards.

40. The Inland Revenue Department in their assessment of personal income taxes has taken this into account. Whether they have adequately accounted for it is a separate issue. It is just that in income surveys, this item is generally either not adequately covered or not covered at all.

41. The following figure illustrates the normal route re-cycling income into reinvestment (solid line) and the 'speed-up' route via corporate retained earnings (broken line):

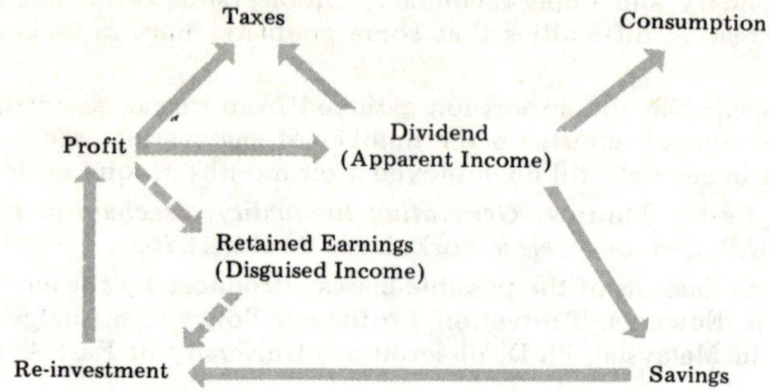

42. Refer to Tan Tat-wai (1977), op. cit., for some discussion.

43. For the estimation on the employment figures, see Tan Tat-wai, 'Employment and Labour Utilisation in West Malaysia' (unpublished World Bank Paper, Income Distribution Division, Economic Research Centre, 1973).

44. See Chapter 6.

45. Tan Tat-wai, op. cit., Table 1. Numerically, the padi farmers are the second largest occupational group, but since they are overwhelmingly Malays, unlike the rubber smallholders almost half of whom are non-Malays, padi farming constitutes the most important Malay occupation.

46. Department of Statistics, *Socio-economic Sample Survey of Households*, Kuala Lumpur, 1971, Table 22.0.0.

47. Garth Alexander, *Silent Invasion: The Chinese in South East Asia*, London, MacDonald & Co., 1973, p. 19. In fact, the intention of Alexander in writing the book is not to promote any anti-Chinese sentiments, but to '. . . show that a racial fear of the Chinese has in fact played a predominant role in starting and keeping alive the cold war in the Pacific' (p. iv, Introduction). Even then, as illustrated here, he is equally susceptible to crude racial stereotypes.

48. ibid., p. 57.

49. Arnold Toynbee, *A Journey to China or Things Which Are Seen*, London, Constable, 1931, cited in Alexander, op. cit.

50. Roger Freedman, *Socialism and Private Enterprise in Equatorial Asia: The Case of Malaysia and Indonesia*, Palo Alto, Stanford University Press, 1968, p. 46.

51. For citations from and discussion of Ungku Aziz, see Chapter 7. It is better to characterize his early works as being provocative first studies to promote more in-depth understanding of Malay rural poverty. As such, it is more a hypothetical theorizing and research proposal than a definitive conclusion. Unfortunately, Ungku Aziz himself and others following him subsequently have not pursued this question in depth in empirical studies and put the problem in perspective. Even more unfortunately, later writers have quoted Aziz liberally as if his propositions had become established facts.

52. In discussing this question of monopoly/monopsony exploitation, it is also important to keep in mind the time perspective. From the account of several referees who are now in the 50—60 age group, middlemen activities were no doubt more 'easy', i.e., more profitable and hence exploitative. For example, the rubber smallholder used to have to deliver the produce to the premise of the first-level dealer at his own expense and leave the buying decision to the dealer. Now, the dealer must send transport to the smallholdings

to collect the rubber. In the past, credit provision was optional, but now, it is mandatory in order to maintain the smallholders' interest in doing business; some part of this loan is in fact non-collectable or 'overhead' cost. While the dealers may be exaggerating their difficulties, as Chapters 6 and 7 will show, the number of dealers in most middlemen activities has grown, since entry is easy and the level of competition has increased.

53. Wharton (1962) did try to conceptualize a sounder theoretical framework and to provide possible tests of the hypothesis. Nevertheless, his study remains non-empirical and unverified.

54. A rough indication of this will be the yield figures of the padi farmers; see *Perangkaan Padi*, Kuala Lumpur, Ministry of Agriculture and Co-operatives, various years.

55. On the size, profit, and income of the small firms, see Chapter 6, especially Section 6.2. A profit level of about $3,000 per year, which is what many of the small firms receive, can hardly sustain wage increases.

56. Data for the years 1968 to 1970 have been computed and compared, but only the result of one year has been presented in this book.

57. This variation in year arises as the bulk of the research was done in 1974 and 1975 and, meanwhile, important changes have occurred in the very fluid ownership and control pattern that this country is undergoing. It is thus not possible to standardize all the data to one single latest year.

58. Subsequent publications have been based on surveys, not census.

59. This is the impression gained by studying the history of several companies and discussing with some referees.

60. However, because their expansion has been completed, their size has also become larger, the total profit of the conglomerates has increased which would introduce an overestimation of their profit and income in comparison with that of others calculated using earlier data. Fortunately, the incomes of these huge conglomerates are already hundreds of times that of the average person; a distortion of several times is minor by comparison.

61. The 1973 Household Budget Survey and the 1976 Census of Agriculture conducted by the Department of Statistics both contain income data. However, their results have not been published and are therefore not available for analysis.

62. For the farm households, the surveys usually report household income including those from outside employment. The profit estimated in Chapter 6 for the small traders is again based on the household as a unit.

63. A. H. Hawley, O. Z. Fernandes, and V. Kandiah, *The Expectation of Working Life in Peninsular Malaysia, 1970*, Kuala Lumpur, Department of Statistics, Research Report No. 83, pp. 6—7.

64. ibid., Table 5, columns 10 and 11.

65. Department of Statistics, *Socio-economic Sample Survey of Households 1967–68*, op. cit., Table 23.0.0.

66. Among the female urban wage earners, relatively few were in manufacturing, mining, and construction, generally no more than one-quarter the number of male workers. Since these are relatively low-paying jobs and the female members of the poorer households are unlikely to get high-paying employment, the low incidence of female workers in these occupations probably indicates a low incidence of poor families with more than one earner.

67. Sudhir Anand, 'The Size Distribution of Income in Malaysia', Washington, D.C., unpublished World Bank Paper, 1973, supplementary tables.

68. Chapters 2, 3 and 4 describe the income of these different groups of occupations.

69. Anand, op. cit., supplementary tables.

PART I

Distribution of Income and Factors of Determination

2 The Padi Farmers and Fishermen

2.1 INTRODUCTION

PADI farmers are numerically the second most important group of Malaysians. In 1970, there were almost 300,000 households involving over one million people engaged in padi cultivation.[1] Padi farming has been the traditional mode of activity among the Malays, the earliest settlers in this land after the Orang Asli[2] (who have by now been pushed into the jungle or jungle fringes).[3] Most of the padi areas and their populations have been in existence for as long as padi cultivation has been prevalent in the Malay community.[4]

Under deliberate British policies, the livelihood of the Malayan padi farmers was least affected by economic changes in this country during the past century until Independence.[5] It is therefore not surprising that they are probably the group who have retained the most traditional values and way of life.[6] This retention of a traditional method of production and way of life in a rapidly changing socio-economic environment has drawn some attention to their plight, from both official and unofficial circles. Most importantly, Malaya's rapidly increasing population necessitated large-scale import of rice from a highly volatile international market. The anguish among colonial officials over this drain of revenue, especially in times of international scarcity and high prices, resulted in some half-hearted steps to bolster padi production.[7] While one could be sceptical about the Colonial Government's true intentions and the import and effectiveness of their limited policies, yet their efforts in this respect stood in marked contrast with their attitude towards smallholding rubber.[8] The next chapter provides some references to the hostile and suppressive policies of the British towards the rubber smallholders. The presence of this dichotomy is striking. The fact that it has persisted after Malayan Independence in 1957 and to some extent even to this day,[9] makes it all the more noticeable.

The lobbying of the plantation interests against the Asian smallholders was one important ingredient of this policy. However, the fact that many of the Malay rubber smallholders were immigrants from Java and Sumatra in the early twentieth century[10] meant that they had less organized political structure with which to influence the Malay royalty and bargain with the British. The Malay royalties in the states of Perak, Selangor, Pahang, and Johor (in which most of the rubber smallholders are found) originated and drew their support from the padi-based landed interests. This meant that they might have been less sensitive to the needs of the newer settlers in their land—the rubber smallholders. Incidentally, a significant proportion of the rubber smallholders were non-Malays who probably commanded even less concern from royalty and the British.

By contrast, the padi farmers are mainly concentrated in the northern former Unfederated States of Kedah, Perlis, Kelantan, and Trengganu. Their concentration in these four predominantly Malay states,[11] their early foothold and strong traditional socio-economic-political pattern probably commanded the attention of the Malay royalty to speak on their behalf in the colonial days. Similarly, these factors probably made it imperative for the post-colonial Malay political leaders to forge a bond with these padi farmers, utilizing them as the political base from which to consolidate their political power. UMNO, the leading political party, was the first and most successful in mobilizing this base.[12] UMNO's concern to maintain the padi farmers' loyalty in the face of challenges from contenders such as PAS is obvious[13] from the emphasis on rural and agricultural development in Government policies since Independence.[14] Of course, the imprint of British legacy and policy may also have something to do with at least some of their policies. The introduction of massive irrigation projects and the promotion of double cropping in the major padi planting areas (Muda and Kemubu in particular) together with a price support programme were the mainstay of Government development efforts in the sixties.[15] By 1975, most of these major areas were well on the way towards double cropping, and presumably higher income.

As a result of this dichotomy in official policies, as well as the changed international economic environment, the relative income of the padi farmers and the rubber smallholders has changed. One of the major aims of this, and part of the next, chapter is to document and explain this change in economic position. Section 2.2 begins with some income characteristics of the padi farmers and continues with an evaluation of the factors determining their income. In the process, the impact of double cropping on farm income generation is also evaluated. Section 2.2.A(c) looks into one of the very important factors in padi farming: the problem of land tenancy—who owns the farms? What percentage of the farmers are dependent on rented land? What are the conditions under which land is rented, and what proportion is rental payment of the total cost of production? Section 2.2.B compares the performance of the Malay padi farmers with the minority Chinese padi farmers, Section 2.3 discusses the livelihood of the fishermen while Section 2.4 sums up the findings of this chapter.

2.2 THE PADI FARMERS

A. Income and Productivity of the Padi Farmers

In this section, the objective is to gain an understanding of the determining factors and distribution of the padi farmers' income, focusing especially on padi farm productivity.

Table 2.1 summarizes the income characteristics and some relevant social features of the padi farmers by state and/or major irrigation areas (mainly for the years 1966–70). Padi farmers in the different states received average incomes ranging from $650 to $2,000; the majority of them earned between

TABLE 2.1

INCOME CHARACTERISTICS OF PADI FARMERS BY STATE (IN $)

Year Surveyed	*State*	*Av. Padi Income*	*Av. Padi Income per Acre*	*Av. Net Padi Income per Acre* (1)	*Av. Other Farm Income*	*Av. Off-Farm Income*	*Av. Total Income*	*Av. Padi Land (ac.)*
1972–3	Kedah and Perlis (MUDA)							
	Acid soil: single crop	$ 531	$186	$134	$210	$ 321	$1,062	2.9
	1st year double crop	1,151	353	205	194	279	1,624	3.3
	2nd year double crop	1,450	384	233	107	128	1,685	3.8
	3rd year double crop	1,341	364	289	254	150	1,745	3.7
	4th year double crop	1,310	313	259	165	125	1,600	4.2
	Non-acid soil: single crop	533	239	186	143	450	1,126	2.2
	1st year double crop	1,465	439	337	176	196	1,837	3.3
	2nd year double crop	1,405	384	307	274	243	1,922	3.4
	3rd year double crop	1,582	386	298	231	204	2,017	4.1
	4th year double crop	1,567	405	319	175	144	1,886	3.9
1966	Kelantan (Kemubu)	271	146	78	90	286	647	2.2
1965–6	Malacca (2)	89	40	–28	495	1,194	1,778	2.2
1968	Penang and Province Wellesley	896	272	200	115	303	1,314	3.3
1970	Perak (Sungei Manik)	594	124		109	446	1,149	4.8
1970	(Changkat Jong)	673	87		497	332	1,501	7.7
1971	(Krian)	691	223		59	302	1,111	3.1
1966	Selangor (Tanjong Karang)	1,004	144	70	170	466	1,640	3.3
1970	Trengganu (Besut)	287	90	–1	226	461	1,030	3.2

Source. Compiled from various tables of all the farm surveys listed in the bibliography.

Notes. (1) Av. Net Padi Income = Av. Padi Income — Imputed Family Labour Cost

(2) Figures for Malacca refer to Central Malacca.

$1,500 and $2,000 per family per year. Their income came from padi farming activity, other farm work (which included supplementary cultivation activities and animal husbandry), and off-farm work (which may be work on other padi farms, on neighbouring estates as well as other petty and semi-skilled activities). These three income sources vary in importance in different areas.

(a) THE ROLE OF OFF-FARM WORK

The state with one of the highest incomes was Malacca with an average annual income of $1,819 per family as opposed to a low income level of $647 for the state of Kelantan, representing two extreme conditions. The Malacca farmers actually had a very low annual average padi income of $89 but obtained the exceptionally high off-farm income of $1,194 which was two to three times that earned by padi farmers in other areas. On the other hand, the Kelantan padi farmers made the lowest family income with both the lowest padi farm and off-farm income.

The variations in the total average income of the other padi cultivation areas, apart from Muda, were smaller. Their off-farm incomes were all comparable, ranging from a low of $302 for the Krian district of Perak to a high of $466 for Tanjong Karang. Therefore, it was the variation in the padi farm income of these regions which accounted for most of the differences in the farmers' income. Trengganu's Besut area had the lowest padi farm income of $513 and Tanjong Karang had the highest figure of $1,174. Their corresponding total average income of $1,030 and $1,640 were also the lowest and highest respectively.

In the most important padi production area of Muda, the off-farm income was more modest than those of the other areas. There seems to be a steady decline in off-farm income as the farmers switch from single cropping to double cropping in areas with acidic soil. The reduction in off-farm income was the most drastic for those who have double cropped for two years as against those who have just started. For those operating on non-acidic soil, off-farm income dropped as soon as double cropping was practised. It probably reflected the increased need to work on one's field with double cropping and hence the decline in available labour for off-farm work. The increased income from double cropping in turn made it less necessary to do supplementary work.

This was also true of the Tanjong Karang area of Selangor. The padi farmers there devoted more effort towards padi cultivation and hence gained a higher padi farm income than those elsewhere.[16]

As such, off-farm work really reflected a need on the part of the poor padi farmers to seek supplementary income rather than the pull of attractive off-farm work, exceptional cases like Malacca notwithstanding. As soon as it was demonstrated that increased effort could bring about higher income, the padi farmers have not hesitated to cut down on their off-farm work to concentrate on padi farm work.[17]

This hypothesis is consistent with other observations. In the major padi producing areas, soil conditions are generally unsuitable for other crops, especially because flooding is needed for wet padi cultivation.[18] This will necessarily constrain the cropping pattern and limit the kind and quantity of off-farm work available to the padi farm families. Only those villages located near the fringes of major padi cultivation areas, and hence possibly close to other cash-crop planting areas or small urban areas, may have more opportunities for, and varieties of, off-farm work. These areas are probably the exception rather than the rule and help to explain the relatively small variations in the size of average off-farm income in most of the areas.

In the case of Malacca, the padi farm income actually brought a negligible return.[19] This, coupled with the unusually high off-farm income, seems to imply that the Malacca farmers may have been lured by the off-farm work opportunity into relegating padi cultivation to a secondary role. The smaller effort would then explain the low productivity there.

Average figures have been used for all farms, and this could disguise much information. In fact, not all farmers and/or their family members worked off-farm. For example, for Province Wellesley and Kemubu, low average off-farm incomes of $303 and $286 respectively were reported. However, 55 per cent of Province Wellesley farmers and 60 per cent of Kelantan farmers who reported off-farm income made an average of $554 and $475 respectively.[20]

Are these the farmers with smaller acreages to farm? Are they the tenants? Or are many of these landless farm workers with only wage income? Are there any differences in the off-farm income earned by the different groups participating in off-farm work? Answers to these questions cannot be deduced from the published results of the surveys themselves, and there is need to resort to sociological studies.

There may be some correlation between the size of farm and tenurial status with the amount of off-farm work. Within the same area, off-farm work may be much more attractive for those with little or no landholding, poor soil condition, and few resources for farm investment. This is because it offers a more steady, higher source of income than that of the more irregular return from a traditional farm. Barnard's (1973) study of a Muda village indicated this sentiment.[21] Kemubu, another traditional area with a prevalence of very small farms, provided further evidence. Seventeen per cent of the farmers there reported earning less than 30 per cent of their income from padi ($130 out of a total income of $1,158 on the average). On the other hand, for those with a higher dependence on padi farm income, average total income is actually lower:[22]

Percentage of Income from Padi	*Average Total Income*
More than 90	$479
70—90	603
50—69	561
30—49	701

One can speculate that the motivation for the 17 per cent with high off-farm income was analogous to that found in the Muda village by Barnard.

Barnard studied in detail four households: one landlord, one tenant, one small landowner-operator, and one landless household. Not surprisingly, the landlord did the least off-farm work and the landless the most.[23]

The Negeri Sembilan padi farmers were reported to rent their small lots from their kin to produce padi for family consumption only, with little intention or orientation towards producing a marketable surplus. Instead, they relied on a variety of non-padi activities to obtain an average off-farm income of $760, which would then push their average total income to around $1,000,[24] a poor and desperate but not impossibly hopeless level portrayed by the cultivation of one or two acres of farmland only.

In this case, the smallness of farm and the dependence on off-farm income probably stemmed from the retention of a traditionally subsistence mode of production. It would be interesting to find out if the persistence of this in Negeri Sembilan (and perhaps in Malacca, Kemubu, and other places) is due to a strict adherence to tradition, or a reflection of the population pressure on land coupled with generations of inheritance practices which have excluded the possibility of farming a larger plot of land. This distinction is crucial in terms of policy measures. If it is the former, farm technique propaganda and education are perhaps more important. If it is the latter, some consideration of land reform may be necessary. A third possibility is the straightforward attraction of the better paid and more stable off-farm work such that the farmers have not been interested in acquiring more land for cultivation. In that case, one must be prepared for a switch back to padi following the success of (say) double cropping in raising the livelihood of other farmers.

Purcal (1964) reported that the average non-farm income of the Province Wellesley farmers declined from $692 for the landless to $420 for those with 2–4 *relong*; however, non-farm income shot up to $785 for those with 4–6 *relong* and then declined again to $454 for those with 6–8 *relong* of padi land.[25] There are no other data that can be used to substantiate the above trend, nor is there any study which tries to explain the rise in off-farm income as the size of holding increases beyond 4–6 *relong*.

Despite the unexplained jump in off-farm income reported above, it does seem that off-farm work helps to equalize the income inequality arising from inequality in landholding. Further research is required before this hypothesis can be confirmed.

(b) INCOME FROM PADI CULTIVATION

Attention is now turned to the main component of the padi farmers' income: the return from padi cultivation and the factors affecting it.

Farmers from two areas have had very high padi income: those from Tanjong Karang and the Muda double croppers have more than $1,000 per farm per year. This higher padi income pushed their total income into the highest bracket among the padi farmers. Those from Province Wellesley, Krian, and Changkat Jong with padi income of $896, $691, and $673 respectively have total income in the next highest bracket (see Table 2.1). Why have these farmers performed better than others?

Three important (and related) factors which determine the income of the padi farmers—size of farm land cultivated, productivity of the farm and cost of production—are discussed in this section. The prices that the farmers receive in marketing their surpluses is the fourth factor, but will be treated as if it is the same as the minimum farm gate price set by the Government.

However, prices still vary with moisture and transport deductions. But such price variation is responsible for only a 10 per cent difference at most and price constancy will be assumed for this discussion. Nevertheless, in view of the charges of monopsonistic buyer markets for farm produce, the larger issue of who really fixes the prices and whether there exists monopolistic-monopsonistic exploitation by the middlemen will be analysed in Chapter 7. Last but not least, the land tenure structure also has an impact on the income characteristics of the padi farmers. The land tenure structure is summarized separately in Section 2.2.A(c) and its impact will only be discussed briefly as rent payment under the cost-of-production item.

There is no presupposition that these five factors are unrelated to one another. For example, there may be some variation in cost and yield with size of the cultivated plot. The land tenure situation may also be related to the size of plot. These possibilities will be addressed in the appropriate sections. Equation (1) on page 43 describes the obvious relation among the three factors considered in this section. The multitude of possible interactions among these factors makes it difficult to attribute portions of income to one factor or another without looking at them in totality. Yet that task would be so huge and tedious as to be almost impossible. Thus, the five factors will be first discussed as if they are independent in order to understand the importance of each separately and, whenever possible, how they interact to determine income. It is hoped that this approach will allow a better appreciation of the need and effectiveness of each policy tool, be it double cropping, price support, land reform, or any other.

(*i*) *Cost of Production.* In looking at the cost of production, only the cost per acre is investigated. Implicitly, the assumption of farm size neutrality in cost determination is made to isolate cost variation due to differences in cultivation practices. Some limited data can be drawn on to show that this assumption is not too unreasonable in our context. The average size of padi farm land for the whole of Malaya is 3.1 acres, and 68 per cent of the farms are less than four acres, with many of the farms fragmented into more than one lot.[26] Both the small scale of farm land and the traditional mode of cultivation are not conducive to much mechanization, nor do farmers use much agrochemicals. Without mechanization, there is not much cost saving as the size of plot increases from zero to four acres.[27] On the contrary, as farm land gets larger than some 'optimum' size for the family (about four acres), the family cannot cope during the busy season and the need for hired labour would greatly raise the cost per acre.[28] The majority of padi-farm households in the late sixties falls into this category of less than four acres of padi land (double cropping was not then prevalent).

Table 2.2 summarizes the cost data for most of the major padi producing areas. The wages paid to the hired labourers (usually during the peak working season), rent for land and fertilizer outlay are the three most important components of production cost, in that order. The wage bill is of particular importance, forming from 25 per cent to over 50 per cent of the total cost. The bulk of the wage bill is incurred during periods of transplanting and harvesting when family labour proves inadequate. The smaller and less

TABLE 2.2
COST OF PADI PRODUCTION PER ACRE PER SEASON

	Region: Muda Area									
	Acidic Soil					*Non-acidic Soil*				
	Single Crop	*1st Year Double Crop*	*2nd Year Double Crop*	*3rd Year Double Crop*	*4th Year Double Crop*	*Single Crop*	*1st Year Double Crop*	*2nd Year Double Crop*	*3rd Year Double Crop*	*4th Year Double Crop*
Hired labour	$ 41.0	$37.6	$33.9	$25.3	$24.3	$ 40.5	$42.1	$ 49.7	$ 39.6	$35.6
Seeds	1.4	0.9	0.9	1.4	1.9	1.8	1.8	1.6	1.5	2.6
Fertilizer and insecticides	8.3	12.7	14.2	16.8	15.5	23.6	13.8	16.0	18.8	15.8
Buffalo and tractor	20.0	6.1	9.7	11.8	10.9	29.5	11.7	18.2	20.4	12.8
Land and irrigation	2.1	0.6	0.8	1.1	1.3	2.7	1.7	2.1	2.2	1.8
Rent	32.8	17.6	10.5	12.8	11.7	33.2	13.6	23.2	17.9	15.4
Sub-total (1)	105.6	75.3	71.2	69.9	65.7	131.8	85.3	114.1	101.5	84.7
Imputed labour cost	49.3	72.0	74.3	36.8	26.7	56.4	53.5	53.2	44.1	41.2
Av. padi area (in acres)	2.9	3.3	3.8	3.7	4.2	2.2	3.3	3.4	4.1	3.9
Yield (in *gantang*)	n.a.	n.a.	n.a.	n.a.	n.a.	n.a.	n.a.	n.a.	n.a.	n.a.

(Continued)

TABLE 2.2 (Continued)

	Region						
	Kemubu	*Central Malacca*	*Province Wellesley*	*Tanjong Karang*	*Besut*	*Sungei Manik*	*Krian*
Hired labour	$12.4	$38.3	$ 82.3	$ 39.6	$15.7	$25.9	$ 84.0
Seeds	5.0	3.0	3.4	2.2	2.3	2.8	2.9
Fertilizer and insecticides	7.2	9.1	19.9	2.5	9.4	7.2	13.8
Buffalo and tractor	4.7	13.7	1.4	1.0	0.3	4.2	—
Land and irrigation	1.8	0.7	2.2	3.3	0.6	1.7	2.5
Rent	34.0	23.4	40.1	12.2	30.9	21.5	39.0
Sub-total (1)	65.1	88.2	149.3	60.8	59.2	63.3	142.2
Imputed labour cost	68.4	54.7	36.0	131.0	91.5	59.9	n.a.
Av. padi area (in acres)	2.2	3.3	3.3	3.3	3.2	n.a.	2.9
Yield (in *gantang*)	215	272	520	398	276	n.a.	403

Source. Compiled from the various relevant tables of all the padi farm surveys listed in the bibliography.

Note. (1) Sub-total is higher than the summation of the major items because of the presence of other items not reported here.

commercialized farms may resort to *gotong-royong* (mutual help) with their neighbours, but the larger and more commercialized ones have to resort to hired labour. The bigger the farm, and the more crops per year, the greater will such need and expenses be. Table 2.3 weighs the importance of family versus hired labour for the major padi areas with some sketchy data for the less important and the mainly single-cropping areas. It classifies several broad groups of farms by the magnitude of labour input.

For the two double-cropping areas of Province Wellesley and Muda with about the same sized plots, the Province Wellesley farmers are more dependent on hired labour while requiring less overall labour input. One possible reason is that it is the most mechanized padi area in the country,[29] the substitution of capital for labour may be responsible for the lower overall labour requirement. On the other hand, its having a smaller number of average working members per family (2.7 for Province Wellesley as opposed to over 3.1 average for Muda)[30] and the attraction of off-farm work opportunity may be two reasons accounting for the greater reliance on hired labour.

For the single croppers, there is a subgroup that has relatively higher dependence on hired labour. Malacca and Muda are both examples of this. It is not clear why the Muda single croppers need more hired labour except perhaps because of their smaller family size. For the Malacca farmers, the need to hire outside labour is particularly surprising in view of the large number of economically active members per household (3.7 per household, among the highest in the country).[31] Their dependence on off-farm work probably draws

TABLE 2.3(a)

LABOUR INPUT CHARACTERISTICS OF PADI FARMS

Type of Farm	*Characteristics*	*Areas*
Single cropping (and partially double cropping)	Low labour input per acre. Very heavy dependence on family labour (15 per cent are hired labour)	Kemubu, Tanjong Karang, probably most of the areas including Besut, Negeri Sembilan, parts of Perak, Pahang
	Lower labour input. Higher dependence on hired labour (about 40 per cent of total)	Malacca, Muda
Double cropping	Low labour input. Very high dependence on hired labour (60 per cent of total)	Province Wellesley
	High labour input. High dependence on hired labour (30—45 per cent of total)	Muda

Source. From Table 2.3(b).

TABLE 2.3(b)
LABOUR INPUT TO PADI FARMS (IN MAN-DAYS PER SEASON)

	Region: Muda Area									
	Acidic Soil					Non-acidic Soil				
	Single Crop	*1st Year Double Crop*	*2nd Year Double Crop*	*3rd Year Double Crop*	*4th Year Double Crop*	*Single Crop*	*1st Year Double Crop*	*2nd Year Double Crop*	*3rd Year Double Crop*	*4th Year Double Crop*
Av. labour input/ac.	45.1	63.2	57.6	73.4	47.9	50.2	69.5	73.4	65.6	73.4
Av. labour input/farm	130.9	208.4	217.9	271.5	201.2	110.4	229.4	249.4	269.1	286.4
Farmer's labour } Family labour }	71.4	136.7	150.2	162.0	105.4	64.5	128.3	129.0	141.7	154.3
Hired labour	59.5	71.7	67.7	109.5	95.8	45.9	101.1	120.4	127.4	132.1
Other farm work Off-farm work	163.6	209.9	69.0	134.9	78.2	205.9	158.1	139.8	47.9	142.1
Av. number of working members per farm	3.31	3.22	2.64	2.89	2.73	2.61	3.00	3.13	3.12	3.05

(Continued)

TABLE 2.3(b) (Continued)

	Region			
	Kemubu	*Central Malacca*	*Province Wellesley*	*Tanjong Karang*
Av. labour input/ac.	39.5	37.2	35.8	41.3
Av. labour input/farm	94.3	122.6	118.0	144.5
Farmer's labour	38.7	76.8	24.5	58.5
Family labour	41.7		22.5	70.5
Hired labour	13.9	45.8	71.0	15.5
Other farm work	33.0	n.a.	n.a.	56.0
Off-farm work	99.0	n.a.	n.a.	92.0
Av. number of working members per farm	2.60	3.70	2.70	3.30

	Av. Labour Input/Ac.	*Av. Number of Working Members per Farm*
Johor	45.0	n.a.
Muda (before double cropping)	36.5	3.0
Negeri Sembilan	45.0	n.a.
Pahang	45.0	n.a.
Penang and Province Wellesley	34.0	2.7
Perak	36.5	n.a.
Selangor	31.5	3.3
Trengganu	39.5	2.8

Source. Compiled from the various relevant tables of all the padi-farm surveys listed in the bibliography.

away the family labour and necessitates the employment of hired labour. The same factor may also account for a lack of time to raise buffalo, hence the reliance on rented buffalo for cultivation, again adding to the cost of production. The hiring of labour and buffalo raises their cost of production by about $30 per acre compared with the other single croppers. Thus, although their yield of about 272 *gantang* per acre and their average labour input of 36.5 man-days per acre[32] are in line with that of the other traditional single-cropping areas, their higher costs of production give them the lowest income generated by padi farming throughout Malaya (only $40 per acre, see Table 2.1).

The rent figures given in Table 2.2 are an average for all farms (i.e., both tenants and landlords) which is quite misleading since only the tenant farmers pay rent whereas the landlords receive rent. However, the possibility of distortion arising from the use of an average rent figure will be dealt with in the next section on land tenancy.

Even though cash outlay for fertilizers and insecticides is the third largest item of cost, it is usually much smaller than wages and rent. The importance of using a suitable quantity of appropriate agrochemicals has been well documented. Its correlation with the generation of income is highlighted in the subsequent discussion of income productivity. Here, the emphasis is on exploring the constraints on the farmers' ability to use more chemicals. The average padi farmer in Malaysia is generally short of cash most of the year. This limits his ability to provide various inputs into his farm. Thus, wage payments, purchase of agrochemicals, and perhaps the hiring of buffalo or tractor compete for his limited resources. In the smaller farms, the tenant may need to put in more labour and fertilizer to raise yield to offset his smaller plot; yet his more modest resources may require a substitution of more family labour for hired labour[33] and a cutback on fertilizer use. The latter may restrict his income receipt and in turn his future ability to expand and raise income. In short, there may be a vicious cycle. Is there really an inverse relationship between fertilizer input and size of cultivation plot? The answer to this question can tell us the dynamics of this aspect of farming.

The most important divergence in cultivation practice relates to the incidence of double cropping. With double cropping, it is necessary to use more agrochemicals and the amount of on-farm work doubles.[34] Given the seasonal aspect of transplanting and harvesting work, hired labour probably at least doubles. Thus, wage payment is likely to be more than doubled. This increase in labour demand is concentrated in several periods during the year and may aggravate labour shortages in those periods and drive up the money wage rate. The rent for padi land may double with two crops especially if the yield per acre per season also increases after the introduction of double cropping and payment is by share-cropping. One or more of the above three factors will raise the cost of production.

The above postulate is reflected in Table 2.2 for the Kemubu, Province Wellesley, and Tanjong Karang areas. At the time of survey, the Kemubu irrigation project was not yet in operation while the latter two areas had double cropping. Wage payments in the two double-cropped areas were much higher than those for Kemubu. The amount spent on fertilizer was much larger in Province Wellesley than in Kemubu, while the amount of fertilizer used in

Tanjong Karang was small.[35] The rent per acre per season had actually gone down with double cropping,[36] contrary to earlier expectation. It may be that the kinship-based land tenure system acted against the raising of rent,[37] or that Government rent control law was effective, or that the market had not caught up with the new economic conditions at the time of survey. The answer cannot be ascertained without further research.

The padi farms can now be classified by the level of production cost. One can identify the following classes of production cost to facilitate discussion in the next section:

Cropping Pattern	*Characteristics*	*Area*	*Cost per Acre per Season*
1. Single crop	(a) Very little reliance on labour hence low labour cost; low level of use of agrochemicals	Besut Kemubu	$60—65
	(b) Moderate employment of labour hence moderate labour cost; fairly high reliance on hired buffalo or tractor; high rent; holding smaller than average plot in Muda; usually pure tenant or owner-operator	Central Malacca Muda	$88—131
2. Double crop	(a) High reliance on hired labour but low wage rate giving moderate to high wage bill; low rent; high level of use of agrochemicals	Muda acid soil area	$65—75
	(b) Low reliance on hired labour but low wage rate giving low wage bill; low rent; low reliance on hired buffalo or tractor; low level of use of agrochemicals	Tanjong Karang	$61
	(c) Very high reliance on hired labour giving high wage bill; low rent; moderate to high reliance on hired buffalo or tractor; high level of use of agrochemicals	Muda non-acid soil area	$85—115

Cropping Pattern	Characteristics	Area	Cost per Acre per Season
	(d) High reliance on hired labour but very high wage bill probably because of high wage rate; high level of use of agrochemicals; high rent; high reliance on hired tractor	Province Wellesley Krian	$139

The complexity of production-cost determination is immediately apparent. There are only six areas under investigation and there are six very different cost categories. Clearly, the different factors can interact to give hundreds of possible cost structures for the different areas.[38]

(*ii*) *Income Productivity*. Normally, productivity refers to labour, land, or capital productivity, i.e., output per labour, yield per acre, or output per dollar respectively. For Malaysian padi farmers, the seasonal variations in labour requirements and the differing proportions of hired labour make the definition and evaluation of labour productivity very problematic. Capital productivity is also difficult to define. The major component of fixed farm capital for those who possess farm land is the value of the land itself, which is dependent on the yield, its location, and other factors.[39] For those without land, there is negligible fixed farm capital though the value of land input is in the form of rent payment, a flow and not a stock item. Since land tenancy is based in part on economic factors and in part on social factors,[40] it is difficult to choose a level of rent that truly reflects the value of land capital input. Therefore, using either capital productivity or rent productivity gives rise to misleading results. Land productivity or yield may not be used instead because of the inaccurate estimation process undertaken by the Department of Statistics.[41] As a result the yield-related concept of income productivity is chosen.

Income productivity is defined as the imputed return from padi output net of the cost of production per acre:

$$\text{income productivity } Y = \frac{pQ-C}{A} \text{ or } Y = p\frac{Q}{A} - \frac{C}{A} \quad \ldots\ldots\ldots \text{ equation (1)}$$

where p = price received, Q = output produced, C = cost of production, A = area of padi land, $\frac{Q}{A}$ = yield per acre, $\frac{C}{A}$ = the cost per acre

Income productivity is directly proportional to the yield if the received price, p, is constant as argued earlier. If the cost per acre is also constant, i.e., similar for all areas, then the two productivity measures should have a one-to-one relationship and can be used interchangeably. This is not the case since there are many different categories of cost per acre possible. However, the interest here is mainly in broad trends, and by using the broad classifications of cost per acre defined in Section (b)(i), it is possible to estimate broad income productivity categories.

Why should data on income productivity be more reliable than yield data? The former is drawn mainly from the various farm surveys which provided income data as given by the farmers themselves cross-checked by the researchers with production data. Thus, its reliability for those interviewed areas should be relatively better than the yield estimates, although there is the problem of how to extrapolate from these more limited samples to a wider picture for the whole country.

It is also important to point out the difference between income productivity and farm efficiency measure. For the former, only the paid-out (in cash and in kind) cost items are deducted from imputed revenue which means that the resultant return is the income due to family labour and whatever little capital investment they put in. For the latter, imputed cost of family labour is also deducted, reflecting the real efficiency of production but not the income of the family.

The income productivity measure is, by virtue of the definition and the family labour-intensive nature of padi cultivation, biased against those areas that have a higher content of hired labour (but not necessarily higher total labour input). As a result, when income productivity is improving with the implementation of a particular policy, the cost-benefit efficiency criteria may begin to show a negative return because an increasingly large element of hired labour has to be used. Thus, from the point of view of raising the livelihood of the poor farmers, the use of an income productivity measure might suggest implementation of a programme while from the overall economic efficiency point of view, one may wish to study the feasibility of other projects to help the farmers. This is fortunately not the kind of trade-off that one faces in the case of evaluating the provision of double cropping to the Malaysian padi farmers.[42]

Table 2.1 presents the income productivity of the different areas. All the padi double-cropping areas (Muda, Province Wellesley, Krian) attained a higher level of income productivity, ranging from over $200 to as high as $439 per acre per year. Muda, which has the highest figures, benefited from the recent huge irrigation project. The Kemubu area income productivity of $146 per acre per year was really quite surprising and impressive. This figure was before double cropping and at a level comparable with the income generated per acre per season in some parts of Muda, and surpassed that of Province Wellesley, Krian, and Tanjong Karang. In fact, the income generated per acre per season in the latter mentioned, more traditional double-cropping areas, was only modestly higher than that in the other single-cropping areas. From this indicator alone, it does not appear as if the Kemubu padi farmers fit one's usual impression of backward and primitive producers in the north-eastern region. Their poverty is caused by other factors.

It is important to understand the divergence in cultivation practices that may result in a divergence in the income generated; this is apart from the different levels of hired labour used in each area. For the highest income-generating area (Muda non-acidic soil), the cultivators put in the most labour per acre, hired more labour and tractors (which can give deeper and more even ploughing), which might indicate greater care in land preparation; they were also among the most conscientious appliers of agrochemicals.[43] On the other hand, in an area like Tanjong Karang, double cropping has not been accompanied by greater input of land preparation and cultivation in the form of increased labour, tractor, and agrochemical input.[44] It is therefore not surprising that yield and income generated were no higher than in an efficient single-cropping area like Kemubu. Province Wellesley has not put in as much labour either but the farmers substituted mechanization which, together with their intensive use of agrochemicals, enabled them to have a very high yield. Unfortunately their higher revenue has been partially offset by their higher reliance on hired labour.

The promotion of double cropping is clearly one policy which can improve the income of the padi farmers though it is most effective when there is enough agricultural extension work to change their farming habits. The Muda area not only attained a high income productivity for the double-cropping area, but the income generated by single-cropping households had also been raised to the highest level in the country. Average padi income has been raised above $1,500 per farm per year for those who double cropped and above $800 for those who single cropped, with corresponding average total income of more than $2,000 and $1,400 respectively.[45] These income levels are superior to those of the rubber smallholders and fishermen and comparable to the wages of the unskilled workers in the urban areas.[46] For Province Wellesley, a traditional double-cropping area, though the income productivity per acre per crop was not higher than that of the Kemubu area before double cropping, the fact that the farmers have two chances to earn some income gave them a padi income of more than $1,000, which contributes towards a total income almost comparable with that of an urban unskilled worker.[47]

(*iii*) *Size of Farm.* It is a self-evident fact that more land means more output and larger income. However, there is some need to understand how this factor is reinforced or balanced by other factors. For example, a small-plot farmer may attain high income with high productivity while one with a large plot may have only a moderate income with low productivity.

For the major padi producing areas, one can further subdivide the padi farms into two groups by area and size (see Table 2.4). Muda and Tanjong Karang are areas with relatively even-size distribution of padi farms. Given that other factors such as soil condition, irrigation, etc., are equal, these areas will tend to have more equal farm income distribution. In the other areas, there is a fairly significant number of very small farms (close to 40 per cent are less than two acres). The common feature of the non-major padi areas is that small farms (i.e. those less than five acres) predominate, forming 74 per cent or more of all padi farmers in these areas (see Table 2.5). However, one should bear in mind that many of them have off-farm income (see the following pages) and a minority of them reported other cropping areas which can also raise their total income.

TABLE 2.4
SIZE DISTRIBUTION OF PADI FARM HOUSEHOLDS BY STATE (IN PER CENT)

Size of Farm (acres)	Region												
	Johor	Kelantan		Malacca	Negeri Sembilan	Pahang	Perak		Penang and Province Wellesley		Trengganu		
		Kemubu	All				Krian	All	Prov. Wellesley	All	Besut	Kuala Trengganu	All
<1	5	9	8	21	38	16	3	14	{ 39	9	1	{ 35	14
1–1.99	60	29	26	32	36	38	22	26		31	14		23
2–2.99	27	30	32	24	19	26	26	19	13	23	27	31	29
3–3.99	3	18	16	7	4	11	20	12	16	13	26	19	11
4–4.99	3	8	10	6	3	5	12	9	12	11	15	10	10
5–7.49	2	5*	7	7	—	3	12*	15	14*	11	9	4	10
7.5–9.99	—	1*	1	2	—	1	5*	4	5*	2	8	1	3
10+	—	—	—	1	—	—	—	1	1	—	—	—	—

(Continued)

TABLE 2.4 (Continued)

Size of Farm (acres)	Region					Size of Farm (relong)	Region: Muda Area					
	Selangor		Perlis	Kedah	West Malaysia		Perlis	Kubang Pasu	Kota Setar		Yan	All
	Tanjong Karang	All							North	South		
<1	—	3	3	8	10	< 2	9.5	7.1	9.7	12.3	15.3	9.5
1—1.99	13.4	14	11	19	23	2—2.99	14.0	11.9	14.4	16.5	13.9	14.2
2—2.99	22.9	5	19	19	21	3—3.99	14.1	11.7	13.8	14.6	13.0	13.4
3—3.99	9.8	40	16	12	14	4—4.99	13.2	12.8	11.9	11.9	11.6	12.3
4—4.99	17.6	13	13	10	10	5—7.49	25.6	27.0	25.1	23.4	20.7	24.6
5—7.49	23.5	18#	25	20	15	7.5—9.99	10.7	11.7	9.2	7.7	8.9	9.7
7.5—9.99	9.8	5	8	6	4	10—14.99	9.6	12.5	11.3	9.0	9.7	10.5
10+	2.5	2	5	6	3	15+	3.3	5.3	4.6	4.6	6.9	4.9

Source. Compiled from various relevant tables of all the padi farm surveys listed in the bibliography.

Notes. * Percentages for 5—6.9 acres and 7—9.99 acres respectively.

Percentage is for 5—5.9 acres; 1 *relong* = 0.711 acre.

TABLE 2.5
SIZE DISTRIBUTION OF PADI FARMS IN SOME AREAS
(IN PER CENT)

Size of Holding	*Muda*	*Tanjong Karang*	*Trengganu*	*Province Wellesley*	*Kelantan*	*Perak*
Less than 2 acres	23.7	13.4	37 (15)*	39	34	40
2—3.5 acres	25.7	27.8	35 (40)	21	40	25
3.5—5.0 acres	24.6	22.5	15 (28)	20	18	15

Source. Compiled from Table 2.4 assuming that half of the farmers in the 3—4 acres category belong to the 3—3.5 acres group.

Note. * The figures in parenthesis refer to those of the Besut area of Trengganu.

With the prevalence of small farms, income generated in these areas would most likely be differentiated by the presence or absence of adequate irrigation facilities for double cropping. Thus, as discussed earlier, in Province Wellesley and Tanjong Karang, income level was at a low but bearable level of $1,500 when padi and non-padi incomes were summed. However, in Kemubu and Trengganu before double cropping, the income level was less than $1,000 on average and less acceptable.

In the less important padi areas scattered in the states of Johor, Negeri Sembilan, Pahang, and Malacca,[48] 65 per cent, 74 per cent, 54 per cent and 53 per cent respectively are farms smaller than two acres. Part of Perak also falls into this category. These are generally areas where modern irrigation facilities are not prevalent which means that yield is likely to be low. Drawing on data from other areas, it is highly unlikely that they can obtain a padi farm income of more than $200,[49] probably not even $150. This is hardly a level adequate for the most frugal survival.

In these areas, there are hardly any padi farms of economic size. Only 2 per cent, 0 per cent, 8 per cent and 10 per cent of the farms are larger than five acres of padi land in the states of Johor, Negeri Sembilan, Pahang, and Malacca respectively (and for the last state, they are almost all present in the central section).[50] With low yield and hence low income productivity, five acres is not adequate to generate an income of more than $500, unless there are other farm and off-farm sources of income.

However, Johor, Negeri Sembilan, and Malacca are all states with large tracts of rubber and oil palm land, both estate and smallholdings; they are also more urbanized. The presence of other cash crop areas and urban activities presumably provides the opportunity for off-farm work, with which the padi farmers can supplement their income. In Section 2.2.A(a) we have already shown that off-farm income was very important for the landless and very small farm operators. In some parts of Kemubu, Malacca, Muda, Negeri Sembilan, and Province Wellesley, off-farm income even formed the backbone of the farmers' income, bringing their otherwise very low income to a total of $1,000 or more. While it is not clear whether these examples can be extended to cover all the very small farms, they do caution against a simplistic use of size of farm to approximate income distribution without very careful and systematic modifications. This also serves to substantiate further the FAO–World Bank call for caution on using farm-size distribution to explain income inequality, because size neutrality and constant management levels are not conditions universally true.[51]

Nevertheless, for those who depend on padi as their main source of income and are present in the same area and facing the same natural conditions, larger farms do provide a higher income. The higher receipt of income implies that there is a larger cash outlay with which to pay for the increased hired labour, fertilizer, and eventually tractor use necessary for double cropping. Therefore in the Muda area, it is not surprising that those who have double cropped for four years have a larger total plot than those with fewer years of double cropping. In fact, the size of padi farm is directly proportional to the number of years double cropping has been practised.[52] The single-cropping households have the smallest plots of padi land, not surprisingly.

(c) LAND TENANCY

Cultivation of padi is the economic activity which Malay villagers know best and one which they can be fairly confident will provide them with a living. This is reflected by a pilot survey of six Muda villages in 1968 which showed that 34.5 per cent of the farmers preferred to have padi farming only and another 35.6 per cent preferred to have padi farming as their main source of income with other sideline activities. Only 1.6 per cent expressed a wish to quit padi farming.[53] The corollary is that the possession of land is highly valued and the loss of land is met with grief and despair. After all, land secures more than just potential income. It is in this light that land tenancy is discussed separately here.

While the possession of a very small plot of padi field in itself need not be the cause of the prevalence of poverty, yet it is true that not all the small padi-land holders and landless can have off-farm jobs or possess other farm land to raise their income. For example, Barnard reported that the landless household had a yearly income of less than $500, lived in poverty and was in general looked down upon by other villagers for its poverty, dependence, and lack of effort. But how many households fall into this category? Do they not put in enough effort or is it that opportunities for adequate off-farm work are inadequate to sustain them? Their poverty-stricken condition would prevent adequate accumulation for the purchase of cultivation land. Their poverty would give rise to low credit standing which may block the ability to rent farm land and purchase supplies for the improvement of the lot which may in turn perpetuate their poverty.

As for the owner and tenant farmers, the differences in cost of production may affect their respective long-run income trend. Table 2.6 shows that the difference in the owners' average cost of production and that of the tenant farmers' in the major padi areas of Kelantan and Province Wellesley were $54.5 and $68.8 per acre respectively (the approximate amount of rent payment). In Sungei Manik it was smaller, at $36.3 per acre. For an average farmer in those areas, the difference in cost of production between owner and tenant farmers translates into a potential income difference of $206, $135, and $200 per

TABLE 2.6
COST OF PRODUCTION OF KEMUBU AND PROVINCE WELLESLEY PADI FARMS BY TENURIAL STATUS (IN $/AC.)

	Region/Status							
	Kemubu			*Province Wellesley*			*Sungei Manik*	
	Owner	*Tenant*	*Owner-cum-Tenant*	*Owner*	*Tenant*	*Owner-cum-Tenant*	*Owner*	*Tenant*
Hired labour	$20.1	$10.5	$10.1	$ 77.6	$ 89.6	$ 78.9	$26.2	$25.5
Seeds	4.7	5.0	5.1	3.6	3.3	3.4	3.0	2.6
Fertilizer and insecticide	8.2	6.4	7.2	21.2	19.6	20.6	8.4	5.9
Buffalo and tractor	0.5	7.9	5.1	0.7	2.5	0.9	0.2	0.7
Land and irrigation	3.3	—	1.8	4.7	—	2.7	3.6	—
Rent	—	61.5	36.1	—	61.6	44.6	—	43.0
Sub-total	36.8	91.3	65.4	107.8	176.6	151.1	41.4	77.7
Imputed labour	68.9	67.4	68.6	37.5	38.3	27.9	61.6	38.2
Percentage of farmers under category	58	20	22	44	39	17	n.a.	n.a.
Av. owned area in acres	1.9	—	1.3	2.9	—	4.6	n.a.	n.a.
Av. rented area in acres	—	2.4	1.6	—	3.2		n.a.	n.a.

Source. Compiled from the relevant tables of the padi farm surveys on Kemubu, Province Wellesley, and Sungei Manik.

farm for the three areas of Sungei Manik, Kelantan, and Province Wellesley respectively, i.e., between 15 and 20 per cent of the tenant farmers' total average income.[54] The owner-cum-tenant farmers in Kelantan and Province Wellesley paid on the average $36 to $45 more in cost per acre for rent, which translates into an income difference of $100 and $207 per farm per year.

As adequate resources are necessary to hire more labour, purchase agro-chemicals, and hire tractors to benefit fully from double cropping,[55] the owner-operators, especially those with a larger plot, will be in a better position than the tenant farmers to take advantage of the newly improved irrigation condition with their 15 to 20 per cent margin in income. The FAO–World Bank Muda survey confirms this general trend; the average fourth-year double cropper cultivated a larger plot of land owned than those who have double cropped for a shorter period of time with the first-year double croppers averaging the smallest owned plot and the largest rented plot.[56] This pattern, if generally true, will mean that land tenure conditions can accentuate income inequality in the long run.

A fair amount of information exists on land tenancy and related problems. The range in time and space and the differing rigour with which many very small-scale micro-studies at the village or district level were conducted make it extremely difficult and hazardous to pool them together into a national land tenure picture. Three, however, provide sufficiently detailed information for a relatively large area: T. B. Wilson on Krian (1956), Purcal on Province Wellesley (1965), and Lim *et al.* on Muda (1973). It is possible to combine the data from these studies (especially the above three) with some recapitulation of historical development to trace the evolution and general characteristics of land tenancy relationships.

Table 2.7 illustrates that the major padi areas such as Muda, Perak, Province Wellesley, and Trengganu all tended to have the highest incidence of tenants (about 40 per cent of all farmers). In the less important padi areas such as Negeri Sembilan, Pahang, and Johor, farms were occupied almost exclusively by small owner-operators with a very small proportion of tenants. Kelantan was the only major padi area that had a small proportion of pure tenants (only 20 per cent of all farmers), though it had the largest percentage of owner-cum-tenant farmers (55 per cent). The owner-cum-tenant farmers formed only a small proportion of the total number of farmers in all the other areas (15—20 per cent).

The average holding of the tenants and owners varied from state to state; but in each area it was the tenant-owner who generally possessed the largest operational plots of land in that area.

Lim *et al.* advanced a life-cycle hypothesis of land tenancy among the Muda District II farmers which can explain the larger land operation by owner-tenant and other tenurial characteristics. Briefly stated, '. . . young farmers begin as tenants, later acquire land through inheritance or purchase and may well dispose of rented land in later years to complete their farming life as owner-operators'.[57] As the farmer gets older with more grown-up children, his need for a larger income and his pool of family labour increases, necessitating and enabling the expansion to the point when his children disperse and then both decline thereafter.[58]

TABLE 2.7

LAND TENURE CHARACTERISTICS OF THE PADI FARMERS BY STATE (AREA IN ACRES)

	Region												
	Johor	*Kelantan*		*Malacca*	*Negeri Sembilan*	*Pahang*	*Perak*		*Penang and Province Wellesley*		*Trengganu*		
		Kemubu	*All*				*Krian*	*All*	*Province Wellesley*	*All*	*Besut*	*Kuala Trengganu*	*All*
Av. padi area	1.5	2.2	2.3	2.2	1.1	1.7	3.1	2.6	3.3	2.5	3.2	n.a.	2.3
Av. farm area	n.a.	3.0	n.a.	4.8	n.a.	n.a.	n.a.	n.a.	n.a.	n.a.	6.8	n.a.	n.a.
Owner farmer (%)	70	58	25	52	87	70	37	50	44		45	18	55
Av. area		1.9		1.5			3.3		2.87		3.2		
Tenant farmer (%)	10	20	20	30	6	16	41	37	39		34	70	22
Av. area		2.38		2.66			2.7		3.21		3.0		
Mixed farmer (%)	20	22	55	18	7	14	22	13	17		21	10	23
Av. area		2.87		3.4			3.6		4.6		4.6		
Av. rented area		1.58					2.1				2.6		
Av. owned area		1.29					1.5				2.0		
No. of padi farmers (in thousands)	4		56	12	19	20	16	44	11	16	3.5		19

(Continued)

TABLE 2.7 (Continued)

	Region					*Muda Area (Area in* relong*)*					
	Selangor		*Perlis*	*Kedah*	*West Malaysia*	*Perlis*	*Kubang Pasu*	*Kota Setar*		*Yan*	*All*
	Tanjong Karang	*All*						*North*	*South*		
Av. padi area	4.5	3.6	4.1	4.0	3.1	5.5	6.0	5.7	5.4	5.9	5.7
Av. farm area	5.8	n.a.				6.2	6.9	6.6	6.3	6.7	6.5
Owner farmer (%)	62.3	60	45	45	48	48.3	41.6	48.3	48.4	30.5	44.1
Av. area	4.2					5.1	5.2	5.4	4.8	4.6	5.1
Tenant farmer (%)	14.5	15	31	35	27	33.8	38.3	40.4	40.5	56.3	40.9
Av. area	23.2					4.9	5.6	5.2	5.4	5.5	5.3
Mixed farmer (%)	6.1	25	24	20	25	16.1	17.7	10.7	9.4	13.2	13.5
Av. area	6.1					7.5	9.2	9.0	8.9	10.6	9.0
Av. rented area						3.9	4.8	4.7	4.6	6.2	4.8
Av. owned area						3.6	4.2	4.3	4.3	4.4	4.2
No. of padi farmers (in thousands)		13	12	81	296						49.7

Source. Compiled from the various relevant tables of all the farm surveys listed in the bibliography.

The existence of kinship land tenancy, rather than an outright exploitative system, may actually be a built-in mechanism within the padi farming system of Malaysia for the equalization of income. The authors concluded as much.[59] This is another factor to be considered in the evaluation of farm size distribution as a reflection of income distribution.

In line with this hypothesis, the young landlords (below 40 years of age) with inherited land are themselves farmers. The old landlords (those over 60 years of age) do not farm their land (mainly inherited rather than purchased) but live on rent income. Thirty-six per cent of the landlords are dependent on rent as their sole source of income while another 21 per cent depend on it as their main source of income. Those heavily dependent on rent income are probably old landlords.[60] Both old and young landlords are very resistant to selling their land, supposedly confirming the life-cycle hypothesis: '. . . many young landlords are reluctant to sell inherited land because of the expectation that they will need a bigger farm later in life, and that some old farmers become landlords when they retire from active farming because of age or ill-health but still retain their land to support them in their old age'.[61] In fact, 55 per cent of landlords rent to their kin, while 52 per cent of the tenants rent from their kin.[62]

This brings to light a very important feature of Malaysian land tenure relationship: the kinship ties between the landowners and tenants. Other surveys have confirmed the same picture. For example, Kenzo Horii reported that 78 per cent of all tenancy in Kampong Sungei Bujor in Muda was arranged between kin; Affifudin reported that 74 per cent of the owners-cum-tenants and 83 per cent of the tenants rented from kin in Muda; Kuchiba and Tsubouchi reported that 65 per cent of the tenants rented from kin, again in Muda; the same was true for other padi farm areas.[63] The most important kinship tie in land tenancy appears to be that between parents and children, suggesting that the level of rent cannot be taken simply as a reflection of exploitation. There is a high probability that high rent supports retired parents, or perhaps ageing siblings.[64] This led Horii to argue that the land tenancy structure reflected a 'reciprocity resulting in shared poverty'.

On the other hand, parents may rent land to their newly-wed children for a token rent to help them establish themselves. While there are no data to support this directly, it is not an unreasonable proposition since the small-scale tenant cultivators are frequently rentiers of their parents' land.[65] Because farmers with (say) two acres of land do not get a very high return anyway, it is not reasonable to expect the parents (who would be middle-aged at this point and not dependent on rent income) to impose stiff rents.

At the same time that one stresses the importance of kinship ties, it is imperative to recognize other tendencies in the land tenure arrangement. Lim *et al.* classified the land tenure arrangements into three categories: those between kin where social factors dominate economic considerations, those which have some interplay between the two factors and those where economic considerations reign supreme.[66]

The first category has already been dealt with. The second category presumably refers to the group where the landlord-tenant relationship is one which does not involve the immediate family.

The second category may form more than half of the kinship land tenure arrangements.[67] From Horii's study, we know that thirty of the ninety-four kinship-related (out of a total of 147) rental arrangements were in this category.[68] No other study provides data on this.

The third category of land tenure arrangement where economic conditions dictate refers to the cases when landlords and tenants are not related. In Muda District II, 48 per cent of the tenants rented from non-relatives; in Horii's survey, fifty-one of the rental cases (35 per cent) did not involve relatives.[69] It is necessary to consider a sub-category of land tenure arrangement, that exercised by absentee landlords. For example, Horii showed that 186 acres of the total 230 acres rented in Kampong Sungei Bujor (or 80 per cent) were owned by people living outside the village.[70] Lim *et al.* reported two absentee landlords with large plots, one with 151.7 *relong* and the other with 146.5 *relong*.[71]

Perhaps it is more useful to discuss these three categories of tenurial arrangement in a historical perspective.

Long ago, when peasants did not produce for trading purposes and faced relatively few constraints on land clearance/acquisition, there was less need for land rental. Whenever rental was necessary, it was arranged among relatives. As commercialization increased, land clearance was obstructed by new laws and regulations, and with population growth one would expect more land tenure. Besides more incidences of renting from non-kin and even from absentee landlords, rental contract would change from share-cropping or rental in kind to prepaid rental in cash.

As early as 1955, T. B. Wilson (1956) claimed that there had been shifts away from fixed rent in kind to fixed rent in cash, which by now has become the dominant form of rental payment in Muda, Province Wellesley, and Krian.[72] Most of the other less commercialized areas such as Kemubu and Trengganu still had payment in kind as the dominant mode in the late sixties.[73] Lim *et al.* followed up on Wilson's investigation and found that the level of cash rent has been increasing; by 1973, 40 per cent of the tenants were required to pay their cash rents in advance of the harvest, and 67 per cent could expect no reimbursement in the event of a poor harvest. The level of cash rent was $72 per *relong*, while the rent in kind of about 83 *gantang* per *relong* (or about $100 per *relong*) has not changed much over the years.[74] As for the other areas, there have not been enough in-depth studies for one to compare with what Lim *et al.* did for Muda. One could perhaps speculate from sketchy data that their development may parallel that of Muda to some extent. Krian has a level of cash rent as high as $93 per acre, while Province Wellesley and Kemubu tenant farmers have to pay about $61 per acre.[75]

To sum up, it is clear that the land tenure system in the Malayan peninsula has been changing slowly, the change coming particularly in the major areas with a relatively large marketable surplus like Muda. The change has been away from the traditional kinship arrangements still prevalent in the less important padi areas towards one where economic considerations have begun to outweigh social factors. This trend is likely to be aggravated by the increase in double cropping because the latter tends to increase commercialization and the importance of economic considerations with increased production and income, not to mention the favourable bias to the landowners and large cultivators (discussed earlier). This trend together with experiences of the green revolution in places like Pakistan and the Philippines may point to increasing land concentration and income inequality.[76] Of course, extensive double cropping has only begun in Malaysia and it may take some time for such effects to materialize, though as Lim *et al.* tried to argue in 1973, the initial stages of double cropping have yet to result in a rise in land rent in the Muda region. This, in itself, is not conclusive, since the slowly-changing land tenure structure is still heavily influenced by the kinship structure. As economic factors gradually override the social factors, one may see increasing concentration of land in the hands of the rich Malays. Some authors, notably Mokhzani (1973), have already expressed concern that Malay Reservations may have provided an opportunity for the rich Malays to build up land holdings at a relatively cheap price with their role as money-lenders in the absence of competing non-Malay money-lenders.[77] In the various surveys, there has already been scattered evidence of some fair amount of absentee landlordism existing side by side with the traditional kinship landlords who hold not more than ten acres of land and only rent a part of their holdings to kin. The most significant claim of land concentration has been by Wilson in 1956: '. . . not more than 2,000 families own not less than $\frac{2}{3}$ of the padi lands of North Malaya'.[78] His data came from a 10 per cent sampling of 102 deceased landlords in Krian which showed that the three largest held 180 lots covering 50 per cent of the total area.[79]

This question of landownership is a very difficult topic in which to conduct research, both technically and politically. There has been no substantive work to verify or disprove Wilson's assertion. Even the very substantive study by Lim *et al.* of land tenure in Muda has failed to cover the big absentee landlords. Nevertheless, it is important to keep this question in mind to project future income distribution patterns among Malaysian padi farmers following extensive farm technique improvement.

B. Racial Comparison of the Padi Farmers

In numerical terms, the number of non-Malay padi farmers is small. They consist of several thousand Thais in the northern states and several thousand Chinese, mainly in Sekinchan in Tanjong Karang, Selangor, and Changkat Jong in Perak. The only rationale for devoting a section to a racial comparison is that the Chinese have been singled out for comparison with the Malay cultivators on many occasions, frequently in a misleading fashion.

The great complexity in determining padi farm income, even without taking into account the variations of soil condition within each locality, means that the conclusions drawn can be quite misleading if one were to choose any two random villages for comparison. It is important to choose the villages from broadly similar general geographical locations so as to eliminate differences due to soil and other natural conditions. Simply to highlight income differences, as has been separately stressed before, is uninstructive. In this case, data from Tanjong Karang are chosen as it is one area where there is a major concentration of Chinese padi farmers among the Malay padi cultivators. The sharing of many common socio-economic characteristics by the two neighbouring Malayan farmers makes much more meaningful comparison than if Tanjong Karang Chinese farmers are compared with Sungei Manik or Muda Malay farmers.

The Sekinchan Chinese farmers have the average income per acre, average cost of production per acre, and average net income per acre of the farmers in the different districts of the Tanjong Karang area.[80] However, they have the highest yield due to their greater use of agrochemicals and tractors, as well as their concentrated and extensive effort on their own farm (having the second highest number of work days per family and spending 70 per cent of it on their own farm).[81] Narkswasdi and Selvadurai, the surveyors, concluded, 'Obviously, since they focus their attention on their own farm work only, the standard of cultivation will be higher, and the income earned from farm operations will be greater and should help in maintaining their farm family.'[82]

However, it is important to point out that while they were among the most hard-working, they did not work the hardest. The Malay farmers in the Sungei Panjang subdistrict, with about the same number of members in the household (7.2 compared to 7.3 for Sekinchan), worked more man-days.[83] This demonstrates that effort alone was not the explanation of their higher yields, but that concentrated effort with better farming techniques were. Secondly, they were more receptive to better farming techniques not because they were more literate or received more Ministry of Agriculture help. In fact, they were no more literate on the average than farmers in neighbouring areas. (Sungei Burong has a higher literacy level and comparable yield.)[84]

If they had the highest yield per acre per season, why did they make only average income per acre? This was because the percentage of double cropping in Sekinchan was the second lowest in the region (only 60 per cent),[85] resulting in an average per year no higher than other areas with a higher percentage of double cropping. This, however, is misleading because another 13.3 per cent chose to plant a second crop of vegetables.[86] Whether this was in response to the more attractive return from vegetable planting or the result of unsuitable land for double cropping padi is not clear. In fact, it was precisely the growing of vegetables which gave them a higher income than their Malay neighbours with no tradition of planting vegetables. Unfortunately, since 1965, vegetable planting, an off-season crop, has no longer been possible on most farms because of flooding of padi land.[87] This no doubt causes a reduction in their income and serves as an example of how a development effort which should benefit the people generally in one area acted to the disadvantage of a small minority within the community.

They have to pay the highest level of cash rent ($144) in this area.[88] This, together with the higher input of agrochemicals as well as hired tractors, should have given rise to a higher cost of production, save for their greater reliance on family labour reducing wage payment to a very low level. Their average farm area was among the smaller within the area, though larger than the average in Peninsular Malaysia.[89] Further, with smaller farms, they have to operate on the largest number of land parcels in the area, which suggests that most of these might have been acquired piecemeal as their earnings improved;[90] another indication that this might be true is their highest percentage of marketable surplus[91] reflecting a higher propensity to save.

In short, the Chinese padi farmers in Sekinchan have a higher income than their Malay neighbours, not because they have larger plots, better irrigation, or other natural conditions, nor because they were more literate or made greater efforts, but because they were among those farmers (of both races) who have made the most use of the more modern farming techniques in their padi farms. Some benefited from their acquaintance with vegetable gardening. They were able to put in greater efforts because married children stayed with the family and provided more family labour. This meant that the higher income would also be divided among a larger family and the resultant welfare *vis-à-vis* the Malay padi farm households might not be so very different after all. (The Malay families were generally smaller as the married children would move out and rent, if necessary, two or three acres of padi land to start another household.) This example also shows the complex nature of income measure and its welfare considerations.

2.3 THE FISHERMEN: TO TRAWL OR NOT TO TRAWL? THE PARADOX OF THE FISHERMEN

The poverty of the fishermen is not new. Much has been written on the subject. What is new is the introduction of trawler fishing in the coastal waters, especially along the West Coast of Malaya, on a fairly large scale in the early sixties. The larger catch landed by the trawling fishermen depressed the price of fish in the market and affected the income of the inshore fishermen whose catch continued to be modest. The problem became worse when some of the trawlers fished very close to the coastline, making off with the catches which the inshore fishermen depended upon, and upsetting the cycle of fish breeding. Many fights, the cutting of trawler nets, and the burning of boats took place,[92] highlighting a new dimension in the problems of the fishermen.

A. Conversion to Fishing by Motor-boats

The common view is that the inshore fishermen are primitive, with very outdated gear and using sails or outboard motor-boats. On the other hand, the offshore fishermen are conceived of as modern and advanced. While both images have some element of truth, both are incorrect. In fact, the fishing sector of the economy has not been a static sector, as evidenced by the introduction and fairly extensive use of trawlers. Even the inshore fishermen, who are considered to be primitive, have experienced a fair amount of change, involving mechanization and use of newer gear. Munro and Chee (1976) have done a very effective job of refuting the assertions of the primitiveness of the inshore sector, at least for the West Coast fishermen. They documented the increase in the number of motorized boats in Penang and Kedah, as well as the change in fishing gear by describing the different types of gear used.[93] Mechanization can be approximated by the change in proportion of boats equipped with outboard and inboard motors. It is easier, cheaper, and more logical for a small fisherman to try first to install an outboard motor on his small boat,[94] and perhaps at a later stage combine with a few friends to acquire a larger boat with an inboard motor. However, one can expect some fishermen to be too poor to change from a non-powered to an outboard motor-

TABLE 2.8
PROPORTION OF MECHANIZED FISHING BOATS IN MALAYA

Year	*Non-powered Boats (%)*	*Outboard Motor-boats (%)*	*Inboard Motor-boats (%)*	*Total Number*
1955	80.6	16.8	2.6	23,429
1957	73.6	19.9	6.5	23,824
1958	68.1	20.0	11.9	25,045
1959	64.6	21.4	14.0	22,263
1960	62.1	21.2	16.7	23,549
1961	57.9	21.1	21.0	22,958
1962	55.6	19.7	24.7	22,183
1963	54.0	17.8	28.2	22,754
1964	50.4	17.3	32.3	21,630
1965	45.4	17.3	37.3	22,520
1966	40.0	15.5	44.5	20,906
1967	35.6	14.3	50.1	20,236
1968	32.4	13.0	54.6	19,453
1969	29.2	11.3	59.4	19,184
1970	26.0	10.7	67.1	20,306
1971	22.8	9.6	67.6	21,141
1972	21.6	9.3	69.1	21,619
1973	20.6	9.0	70.4	22,167
1974	18.2	9.4	72.4	22,377

Source. Malaysia, Ministry of Agriculture, Fisheries Division, *Annual Fisheries Statistics*, various years.

boat. Thus, as time goes on, the decrease in the proportion of non-powered boats will level off. Similarly, a group of outboard motor-boat owners would not be able to afford the conversion from outboard to inboard motor-boats, and the proportion of boats with outboard motors should decrease and then level off at some point after an initial increase (Table 2.8).

From Table 2.8, the extent of the conversion of fishing boats into motor-boats over a seventeen-year period is quite impressive. The proportion that has become inboard motor-powered is even more impressive (72.4 per cent). That is to say, the fishing industry has gone from one largely unpowered to one largely motor-powered. However, the extent of mechanization is probably not the same for all states. Table 2.9 shows the mechanization trend for some of the states. In 1955, mechanization was insignificant in all states except Perak, Selangor, and Pahang. Even in these cases, the power was provided mainly by outboard motors. Inboard motor-powered boats were the exception rather than the rule, and Kedah surprisingly had the largest proportion of these with 4.3 per cent. By 1971, mechanization, especially the use of inboard motor-boats, had made much headway, certainly in all the West Coast states including the more backward Kedah. As for the East Coast states, principally Trengganu, mechanization does occur, but to a lesser extent, and the

TABLE 2.9
DEGREE OF MECHANIZATION OF THE MALAYAN INSHORE VESSELS

Class of Power	*1952*	*1955*						*1965*		*1971*	
		Kedah	*Penang*	*Johor*	*Trengganu*	*Perak*	*Malaya*	*Kedah*	*Penang*	*Kedah*	*Penang*
Non-powered		91.1%	66.4%	86.3%	93.0%	—	80.6%	70.7%	26.7%	55.0%	19.0%
Outboard motors	Few	4.5	30.0	15.8	4.5	38.7%	16.8	15.9	44.0	15.0	38.3
Inboard motors		4.3	3.6	—	2.5	2.9	2.6	13.4	29.3	30.0	42.7
Total		2,016	2,197	4,327	5,049	3,787	23,439				

Sources. Report of the Commission to Investigate the Fishing Industry 1956, Appendix 'B'; Munro and Chee, 'Fishermen and Fishing Development in Penang and Kedah', mimeographed, Penang, Universiti Sains Malaysia, 1972, Table A, p. 18.

emphasis is on the outboard motor-boats. With such changes on both the West and East Coasts, it is very difficult to argue that the fishing industry in Malaya is primitive and static. What has prompted this change? Munro and Chee argued that the sharp increase in mechanization in a state like Kedah can be linked to the rise of trawling.[95] While they did not think that the rise in Penang can be attributed to the challenge of trawling, it is felt here that the earlier introduction of trawlers into the state of Penang in the early sixties could have been an important stimulus in the conversion to inboard motors. The proportion of boats using outboard motors has not changed much, simply because it started with a higher degree of mechanization. This explanation also fits the East Coast. Trengganu still lags behind in terms of mechanization because of its generally less developed economy, the disadvantage of geographical location, and also the lack of challenge from trawlers.

While trawler fishing is more profitable than the traditional inshore fishing, their wasteful mode of production,[96] and the quick entry of large numbers of trawlers since the sixties, may have brought them close to 'saturation' point. This can be seen from the estimates of return to capital and owner's share made by Munro and Chee. For the trawlers of Penang, the return to capital with management costs excluded dropped from the highly profitable 55 per cent per annum in 1966 to 10 per cent in 1971.[97] The owner's share of the net income per trip dropped from $58.6 in 1966 to $25.1 in 1971. This occurred because the gross value of the catch dropped from $201.8 per trip in 1966 to $115.5 in 1971.[98]

Given the continued rapid increase in the number of trawlers from 2,486 in 1971 to 3,973 in 1972 for the whole of Malaya,[99] it seems likely that the trend in Penang would spread to Kedah and perhaps even the East Coast in a fairly short time.

It is also interesting to note that the smaller trawlers (a 30-ton boat with about ten crew) performed better than the large trawlers in terms of profitability.[100]

B. Income of the Fishermen

The inequality of income between the ordinary crew member and the boat and/or net owner has been a standard feature of the fishing sector for years, both for inshore fishing as well as offshore and trawler fishing. Traditionally, when a group of fishermen team up to fish with larger nets needing more than one boat and a dozen men to operate, the boat owner and the net owner usually take 50 per cent of the catch with the crew members dividing the remaining 50 per cent. Furthermore, the owner-operators can take their share of wages in the pool for the crew members. The *Taikong* [skipper] and/or the most experienced member usually get an extra share. The details, of course, vary with the gear.[101] The trawlers have retained an analogous catch-sharing structure.[102]

The earnings of the crew members on the trawlers have decreased from 1966 to 1971, as have that of the owners. However, since the crew's share has to be divided among ten or more people, their lower income means that they would feel the pinch of the decrease in income more than the owners.

Table 2.10 summarizes the income distribution among the surveyed Penang

TABLE 2.10
SIZE DISTRIBUTION OF THE INCOME OF PENANG AND KEDAH FISHERMEN (IN PER CENT)

Income Bracket	*Penang*	*Kedah*	*Total*	
			Ordinary Crewmen	*All*
< $600	—	3.7%	2.2%	1.5%
600—1,199	21.5%	20.9	32.3	21.3
1,200—2,399	39.7	27.2	39.6	35.2
2,400—3,599	17.9	14.7	10.9	16.8
3,600—4,799	10.6	11.0	8.6	10.7
4,800+	7.4	17.3	5.1	10.9
No information	2.7	5.2	1.3	3.6
Total number of fishermen	340	191	313	531

Source. Munro and Chee, 'Fishermen and Fishing Development in Penang and Kedah'.

and Kedah fishermen, including the trawler and other fishermen. 22.8 per cent received less than $1,200 per year, another 35.2 per cent received $1,200 to $2,400 per year. Among those who received more than $4,800, forty-two of the fifty-six were not ordinary crew members. Among the crew members, 34.5 per cent received less than $1,200, and 39.6 per cent between $1,200 and $2,400.[103] That is to say, the level of income of the majority of fishermen was about on par with that of the average padi farmer with a small plot of land in the more productive padi areas.

There has been no new published study of the East Coast fishermen for an assessment of their income level. However, the general impression is that they receive less than the West Coast fishermen. This can be seen from the relatively lower mechanization ratio (Table 2.9), and the effect of the two monsoon seasons (the East Coast is open to the South China Sea with no natural protection). On the other hand, the East Coast Malay fishing village is quite unlike its West Coast Chinese counterpart. The West Coast fisherman concentrates on fishing whereas the East Coast fisherman frequently engages in a multiplicity of economic activities with the help of his family. Padi cultivation is not uncommon.[104] In this way, his income becomes larger than it otherwise would be from just fishing, though it is probably true that the income level still cannot be compared with that of the West Coast.

2.4 CONCLUSION

The first point to emerge in this chapter is the great complexity in padi farmers' income measurement. Small farms normally yield lower income, but in the Malaysian case, many of the farmers with small plots have resorted to other work, raising their income to a level comparable with that of the medium-sized farms. Moreover, the size of the farm cannot be considered in isolation from the other socio-economic characteristics such as land tenure, age of farmer, size of household, and so on. The most interesting aspect is the possibility of a life-cycle hypothesis of the traditional kinship-determined land tenure and farm cultivation system. In this hypothesis, farm size and tenancy are directly related to the age of the farmer and the size of his household. Thus, the farmers with small plots frequently are the youngest and also have the smallest families. On the other hand, the in-village landlords are usually old people, retired with a few acres of padi land the rent from which is their main source of income and means of survival. As such, even if the younger farmers with smaller farms are to make more modest incomes and are without the help of off-farm income, their livelihood may be no worse than that of the middle-aged owners-cum-tenants with larger plots and larger families, or the older landlords with small families. This highlights the problem of the inability of income-per-family to reflect the true state of the padi farm households that have a built-in equalization structure.

However, as padi farming becomes more commercialized, and especially with the introduction of double cropping which can speed up this process, economic factors would increasingly replace social considerations as the main determinant of land tenancy and distribution of farm size. One may thus see the raising of rent, concentration of land holdings, increase in the number of absentee landlords, and increasing income inequality. As the traditional system becomes less important, the built-in equalization process via the life-cycle process will increasingly play second fiddle. In that case, the smaller farms may no longer be operated by the younger farmers with smaller families, and the distribution of farm size will become a better approximation of income distribution by family (and *per capita* too).

Therefore, it is of some importance to have a good estimate of the farm size distribution, and preferably one that is cross-classified with other socio-economic characteristics such as the farmer's age, the size of his family, tenurial status, source of rental (from kin or non-kin), and extent of off-farm work. This would enable one to verify the life-cycle hypothesis and to form a basis for future comparison as the trend shifts. Unfortunately, there are no good estimates of these socio-economic characteristics related to farm size distribution at present and it has not been possible to build up a set of income distribution statistics from this distribution using production data.

Nevertheless, the reasons for the poverty of the padi farmers can be summarized. The level of their income is dependent on three major factors: land tenure (including the size of their cultivated plots), productivity, and price. In this chapter, the price factor has not been discussed at all, partly because the Government has set the farm gate price at a relatively constant level above international prices and partly because there will be a more detailed discussion in Part II. The productivity for most parts of Malaysia has been low because of the lack of mechanization and application of agrochemicals as well as the original lack of double cropping and new seedlings. Clearly, the land tenancy factor is also important. It is usually the smaller farm operators and tenants who make the lower income and it is also this lower income which generally pushes them into more off-farm work.

Two important policies have been pursued by the Government to improve the income of the padi farmers; the earlier mentioned price support is one and encouragement of double cropping is the other (mainly through the provision of irrigation facilities). Double cropping, by virtue of its more intensive cultivation nature, requires the farmers to have more resources for the undertaking. Therefore, there is a difference in time when the farmers can take advantage of it. It would generally be the landowner-operators and the larger farm cultivators who would have the resources to be among the pioneers of double cropping. This would serve to accentuate further the income inequality and, potentially, the landholding inequality among padi farmers in the same area. There is, of course, no doubt that the income of everyone within the area would have improved relative to those outside.

Furthermore, it is important to bear in mind that, so far, the thrust of the double-cropping policy has been in the major padi production areas. These are already areas with a larger average plot and higher productivity. The advent of double cropping will further widen the difference between their income and those of the less important padi areas. It is a cause for concern since hardly any survey has been conducted in these less important areas and very little is known about their livelihood. It is not clear, *a priori*, whether the structure of their land distribution and location would have made it advantageous to introduce irrigation projects and push for double cropping there. At least one researcher has concluded from his study of the other double-cropping areas that it may be preferable to promote the cultivation of other crops in these areas in lieu of double cropping. His contention is that the farmers who are not used to commercialized cultivation are not likely to be able to profit from double cropping.[105] However, the most important need is for more in-depth research in these areas.

In the fishing sector, as with the padi farmers, the possession of non-labour factors of production is an important determinant of income. To the padi farmers (or the rubber smallholders to be discussed in the next chapter), it is land. To the fishermen, it is the possession of a boat and/or a net. Unfortunately, most of them are too poor to possess either, and they have to work as crew members for those who own the boat and gear. At best, some of them are able to own small boats with or without an outboard motor. This inequality in the ownership of the means of production is the major constraint on the alleviation of poverty and the equalization of income.

The introduction of trawlers resulted in initial affluence to the trawler fishermen, but this has since declined. Even then, their level of income is still higher than that of the traditional fishermen. This illustrates the potential of trawler fishing in raising the income of fishermen in the areas where they are not yet saturated. But it also illustrates the limitation of trawling. If trawler fishing is continued in trawler-intensive areas like Penang, the income of all the fishermen would be further depressed due to the depression of fish prices with increased output. The intensive trawling might even threaten the future supply of fish because of the destruction of marine life along the coast.

It is therefore important to have a well-conceived overall fishing policy: perhaps limiting the number and range of trawler fishing, setting up co-operatives with subsidies to encourage the cultivation of marine products and farming, and relocating the surplus manpower to alternative sectors. However, it is necessary to bear in mind that marine products are important sources of protein (especially for lower-income groups) and future policies should ensure a growing supply at reasonable prices for the populace at large, in addition to raising the income of the fishermen.

1. See Tan Tat-wai, 'Income Distribution and Determination in West Malaysia', Appendix Table 1.

2. 'Orang Asli' refers to the aborigines.

3. For some idea about the livelihood of the Orang Asli, please refer to N. Maeda, *Economic Activity among the Orang Hulu*, Research Paper No. 23, Center for South East Asian Studies, Kyoto University, May 1971.

4. For a summary of the history of padi cultivation in Malaysia, see Cheng Siok Hwa, 'The Rice Industry of Malaya—A Historical Survey', *Journal of the Malaysian Branch of the Royal Asiatic Society*, XLII, Part 2, December 1969.

5. See for example: Lim Teck Ghee, 'Peasant Agriculture in Colonial Malaya: Its Development in Perak, Selangor, Negeri Sembilan and Pahang 1874–1941', Ph.D. dissertation, Australian National University, 1971; Zahara Haji Mahmud, 'The Period and Nature of Traditional Settlement in the Malayan Peninsula', *Journal of the Malaysian Branch of the Royal Asiatic Society*, XLIII, Part 2, December 1970; R. Bonney, *Kedah 1771–1821*, Kuala Lumpur, Oxford University Press, 1971; Syed Husin Ali, *Malay Peasant Society and Leadership*, Kuala Lumpur, Oxford University Press, 1975.

6. This can be ascertained by comparing the description of padi cultivation techniques of the earlier periods contained in Cheng (op. cit.) with that of the present day.

7. Lim, op. cit., pp. 96—100, 128—37, and 213—20.

8. See introduction to Chapter 3 and especially the notes to that section.

9. Compare with the rubber smallholders as summarized in Chapter 3. The most important difference in policy that the two groups face is the tax payment. The padi farmers receive in effect a subsidy in the form of a Government-supported minimum farm gate price while the rubber smallholders have to pay an export duty, a surcharge, the replanting cess, and the research cess. See R. Goldman, 'Staple Food Self-Sufficiency and the Distributive Impact of Malaysian Rice Policy', *Food Research Institute Studies*, XIV, September 1975, for an analysis of the impact of the padi price support programme on the welfare of other Malaysians, especially that of the rubber smallholders.

10. See Lim, op. cit.; R. N. Jackson, *Immigrant Labour and the Development of Malaya 1786–1920, passim*, for evidence. These immigrant Malays were primarily located in the Federated Malay States of Negeri Sembilan, Selangor, Perak, and Pahang, and the state of Johor.

11. Table 2.1. By contrast, in states like Penang, Perak, and Selangor, the non-Malays form the majority of the population.

12. This is not the place to try to establish the socio-economic bases of UMNO leadership and cadres. For interested readers, the following suggestions can provide basic information for the validity of this point by taking into consideration the major thrusts of the policies advocated by UMNO as well. This author does not necessarily concur with the interpretation of some of these authors. See J. M. Gullick, *Indigenous Political Systems of Western*

Malaya, London, Athlone Press, 1958; Chandrasekaran Pillay, 'Protection of the Malay Community: A Study of UMNO's Position and Opposition Attitudes', M.Sc. thesis, Universiti Sains Malaysia, 1974; William Roff, *Kelantan: Religion, Society and Politics in a Malay State*, New York, Oxford University Press, 1974; Gordon Means, *Malaysian Politics*, London, University of London Press, 1970. Interested readers can also read the several studies on the background of UMNO leaders and form their own impressions.

13. It is in these states that the major Malay opposition party, the Pan Malayan Islamic Party (renamed Partai Islam, and had a short-lived alliance with UMNO in the ruling coalition, the National Front, from 1973 to 1977), has the greatest strength. It has had enough following to capture control of the state of Kelantan for more than ten years and to rule Trengganu briefly. While it does not have enough following in the states of Kedah and Perlis to become the ruling party, it is sufficiently strong to pose as a major opposition group.

14. This is not to imply that there was no concern for the poor Malay rubber smallholders. But at that point in time, the cyclical and secular fall in the price of rubber had not yet reached the more alarming state it did later on. Besides, as implied in the above argument, the rubber smallholders mainly consist of immigrants; even when they are Malay in origin, they may not be as well organized and entrenched in the political process of the nation.

15. See, for example, Martin Rudner, 'The Malayan Quandary: Rural Development Policy under the First and Second Five Year Plans'; Snodgrass, *Inequality and Economic Development in Malaysia*; and Goldman, op. cit., for a summary of the first decade of rural development policy.

16. Udhis Narkswasdi and S. Selvadurai, *Economic Survey of Padi Production in West Malaysia (Selangor, Collective Padi Production at Bachang, Malacca)*, 3 volumes, Kuala Lumpur, Ministry of Agriculture and Co-operatives, 1967, Vol. 1, p. 51.

17. In a pilot survey of the Muda region in 1968, the Department of Agriculture found that 70.1 per cent of those farmers interviewed want padi farming as the only or main occupation. Malaysia, Ministry of Agriculture and Co-operatives, Department of Agriculture, 'Socio-Economic Survey of 6 Pilot Project Areas in Kedah 1968', Kuala Lumpur, mimeographed, 1968, Table 9.

18. M. J. Purvis, 'Evaluation and Use of Underdeveloped Agricultural Statistics: The Food Economy of Malaysia', Ph.D. dissertation, Cornell University, 1966, p. 41; Section 2.2B, citing data from Tanjong Karang.

19. Table 2.1.

20. S. Selvadurai and Ani bin Arope, *Socio-Economic Study of Padi Farms in Province Wellesley 1968*, Kuala Lumpur, Ministry of Agriculture and Fisheries, 1969, Tables on the income of the padi farmers. S. Selvadurai, Ani bin Arope, and Nik Hassan, *Socio-Economic Study of Padi Farms in the Kemubu Area of Kelantan 1968*, Kuala Lumpur, Ministry of Agriculture and Fisheries, 1969, Tables on income of the padi farmers.

21. Rosemary Barnard, 'Organisation of Production in a Kedah Rice Farming Village', Ph.D. dissertation, Australian National University, 1971, p. 24.

22. Selvadurai, Ani bin Arope, and Nik Hassan, op. cit., Table 59, p. 119.

23. Barnard, op. cit., Tables 6.12 and 7.4.

24. Loh Meng Kei, Thomas Weaver, and Tan Bock Thiam, 'A Study of Rice Double Cropping', Faculty of Agriculture, University of Malaya, 1969, mimeographed, p. 1, cited in footnote 15 of Huang Yu-kon, 'Some Reflections on Padi Double Cropping in West Malaysia', *Malayan Economic Review*, 17, April 1972.

25. John T. Purcal, *Rice Economy, Employment and Income in Malaysia*, Honolulu, University of Hawaii Press, 1972, Tables VII and VIII.

26. S. Selvadurai, *Padi Farming in West Malaysia*, Kuala Lumpur, Ministry of Agriculture and Fisheries, 1972, relevant Tables. The basis of Selvadurai's data seems to be from the *Census of Agriculture 1960* which may not be the most accurate. However, one can get some ideas from the individual padi farm surveys. For example, Province Wellesley has 20 per cent of the farms with two parcels, 19 per cent with more than two parcels (Selvadurai and Ani Arope, op. cit., Table XV); Kemubu has 31 per cent with two parcels and 25 per cent with more than two parcels (Selvadurai, Ani Arope, and Nik Hassan, op. cit., Table 24, p. 57); the Besut area of Trengganu averaged 1.4 parcels per farm (Yap Kim Lian and John Dixon, *Socio-Economic Study of Padi Farms in the Besut Project Area of Trengganu*, Trengganu, Pejabat Daerah Besut, 1972, p. 25); Malacca has 33 per cent with 2 parcels, 17 per cent with more than 2 parcels and averaged 1.8 parcels per farm (Narkswasdi and Selvadurai, op. cit., Table 17, p. 279); and Tanjong Karang, Selangor, averaged 2.2 parcels per farm (ibid., Table 23, p. 53).

27. Of course there are still some economies of scale. For example, for those farmers who cultivate a very small plot, say less than two acres, the overhead and variable cost of raising a buffalo is too high for them, and the cost of renting buffalo is high compared with the average cost to a farmer with a large enough plot to sustain the rearing of buffalo.

28. Barnard claimed that a couple can work only 1.5 to 2 acres; unmarried daughters cannot work on the field because of Islamic custom. If the son and mother of the farmer can work, then the family can handle 3 to 4 acres, Barnard, op. cit., p. 12. Lim *et al.* reported that the yield of a farm with more than 7 *relong* (about 5 acres) declines because of labour shortage, Lim *et al.*, *Preliminary Report of a Pilot Survey on Land Register in Locality II, Kubang Pasu, Muda*, Muda Agricultural Development Authority–Universiti Sains Malaysia, 1974, paras. 166–8. See also Purcal, op. cit., and Tan Tat-wai, op. cit., Chapter 2, footnote 37.

29. From Table 2.2, one can see that the Province Wellesley farmers spent more on buffalo/tractor on the average than did the farmers of other regions. Seventy per cent of the padi farms in this area reported using tractors, Selvadurai and Ani Arope, op. cit., Table XXV, p. 29.

30. Selvadurai and Ani Arope, op. cit., relevant Table. Food and Agriculture Organisation, *The Muda Study: A First Report*, Rome, FAO/World Bank Cooperative Programme, 1975, Tables 13 and 14.

31. The figure here refers to central Malacca only, as the northern and southern regions farm padi only as a supplementary occupation. See Narkswasdi and Selvadurai, op. cit.

32. Their yield was 356 *gantang* for 1970 which was comparable with that of other single-cropping areas but not with the double-cropping areas. See *Perangkaan Padi* (Rice Statistics), various years.

33. One implication of this is that a high proportion of hired labour is a 'luxury'. This seems to be the implication of Barnard's discussion too (p. 13 and pp. 155–62 on the third surveyed household).

34. ibid., p. 252. Besides, for Province Wellesley, because of the higher incidence of mechanization, the requirement of labour cannot be compared in a straightforward manner with that of other areas that have less mechanization.

35. It is difficult to use simply the size of wage payment to imply that the amount of hired labour has increased or decreased. There are several factors that can offset one another. In the last note, it was mentioned that the increased labour need may be offset by the use of mechanization. On the other hand, in an area like Province Wellesley, which is closer to a major urban area, the wage rates in off-farm work may be high. This will have the

effect of drawing away the family labour to the better paid off-farm work and substituting with hired labour on the farm. In that case, the higher wage payment may simply reflect this substitution as well as the generally higher wage level of that area. While insufficient data have been provided in the various surveys to make a clear distinction among these different factors, an examination of the labour input data of Table 2.3 shows that the double-cropped areas do utilize more labour per season per acre than the single-cropped areas, and wage payment can be taken as an approximate indicator of greater hired labour input arising from the needs of double cropping (but the amount of increase in payment in itself is not necessarily indicative of the increase in labour input).

Another indication of the increased labour need (and hence increased hired labour and wage payment) comes from reports that East Coast labourers crossed over to the Muda area during the peak labour demand season. See Barnard, op. cit., p. 73, and Malaysia, Muda Agricultural Development Authority, *The Economic Implications of Machinery Use in Padi Production: A Study of the Muda Irrigation Scheme*, Table 1, pp. 5—6.

On the use of fertilizers, see Table 2.2, and Selvadurai and Ani Arope, op. cit., p. 33, for the greater use of fertilizers in Province Wellesley.

36. This refers to rent per season. From the data given, it is not possible to tell if rent per year has changed since before double cropping. Barnard claimed that the level of rent in the village she studied has risen following double cropping (p. 49).

37. Kindred land tenancy is frequently arranged to assist landless close relatives; it is thus not necessary to charge a level of rent comparable to the economic conditions. For more details, see Section 2.2.A(c) on land tenancy

38. For example, if each of the five factors has two possible outcomes, there are 120 possible combinations of outcomes.

39. Eighty per cent of the capital is accounted for by the value of land; the exact value varies with the size of holding, location in or out of Malay Reservation land, etc. See the relevant tables of the various padi farm surveys.

40. Section 2.2.A(c).

41. Purvis, op. cit., and FAO and International Bank for Reconstruction and Development Co-operation Programme, *The Muda Survey—A First Report*, have both criticized this inaccuracy.

42. If double cropping were to provide an income productivity per crop that is higher than that for one single crop, then one can conclude that the income benefit of double cropping is greater than 100 per cent and is obviously desirable. This will happen as long as the increased income generated by double cropping is large enough to offset the rising cost due to double cropping. In Malaysia, the Muda and Province Wellesley double croppers were the most efficient with over $100 per crop per acre using the cost-benefit criteria. Using the income productivity criteria, the Muda farmers were still the most efficient (see Table 2.1).

43. Table 2.2, and Selvadurai and Ani Arope, op. cit., p. 33.

44. Narkswasdi and Selvadurai, op. cit., Part I on Tanjong Karang, p. 84.

45. Table 2.1.

46. Compare these income figures with those in Chapters 3 and 4.

47. Chapter 4, Tables 4.1 to 4.3 and 4.5.

48. The percentage pertains to north and south Malacca, Narkswasdi and Selvadurai, op. cit.

49. Using the income productivity of Besut as a basis for calculating that in the other non-major padi areas, two acres of padi land producing $90 of income per acre will generate a total padi income of $180.

50. Table 2.4.

51. FAO–IBRD Programme, op. cit., p. 38, para. 6.32.

52. Tables 2.1 and 2.2.

53. 'Socio-Economic Survey of 6 Pilot Areas . . .', Table 9.

54. The percentage is calculated by dividing the area times the difference in income between an owner and a tenant farmer per acre by total income per acre. For some areas of Muda, the percentage is as high as 25 per cent, Malaysia, Ministry of Agriculture and Co-operatives, 'Farm Economic Survey of the Muda River Project 1966', Kuala Lumpur, 1967, Table 28.

55. The capital and labour available are constraints, Lim *et al.*, op. cit., para. 176.

56. Lim *et al.*, however, claimed that there is no link between the tenurial status and the extent of double cropping; if there is any pattern at all, the tenants actually double cropped a little more than the owners. They claimed that 90 per cent of the mixed farms double cropped, 73 per cent of the tenants double cropped and 67 per cent of the owners double cropped. Lim *et al.*, Summary, p. xviii. For the FAO–IBRD Programme data, see summary in Tables 2.1 and 2.2. These data with seemingly conflicting conclusions need further close scrutiny before any conclusive result can be reached. One possible explanation of the difference is that one set of data (the FAO–IBRD Programme study) is reported by average area while the other (Lim *et al.*) uses percentage of farms. There seems, however, no doubt that the larger farmers do double crop first.

57. Lim *et al.*, Summary, p. xx, also para. 223.

58. ibid., pp. xx—xxi, also paras. 228 and 229.

59. ibid., p. xxv, if rent is for close kin.

60. ibid., p. xxii, paras. 258, 266—9, p. 119, and Table 60, p. 127. However, there is a group of twelve landlords in the 20—39 age-group that is a departure from the model described.

61. ibid., p. xxiii.

62. ibid.

63. Kenzo Horii, 'The Land Tenure System of Malay Padi Farmers—A Case Study of Kampong Sungei Bujor in the State of Kedah', *The Developing Economies*, 10, March 1972, Tables IV and V; Affifudin bin Haji Omar, 'Some Aspects of the Socio-Economic Value System of the Muda Rice Farmers in Development Perspective', Alor Star, Muda Agriculture Development Authority, 1973; M. Kuchiba and Y. Tsubouchi, 'A Padi Farming Community in Kedah, Malaysia', *The Developing Economies*, 5, 1967.

64. Twelve out of 40 rented from parents according to Barnard, op. cit., p. 47; high rents are paid to needy parents (ibid., p. 51). Horii, op. cit., reported that 40 of the 94 kin related land tenancy were from parents to children, 5 from children to parents, and 19 between siblings; 54 were non-kin related tenancy arrangements (Table V). See also Horii, pp. 19—20.

65. ibid., p. 19.

66. Lim *et al.*, para. 160.

67. Lim *et al.* defined four characteristics of close kin land tenure arrangements and found that only 34 per cent of the tenancy arrangements exhibit these four characteristics. ibid., Table 20.

68. Horii, op. cit., Table V.

69. ibid., also Lim *et al.*, p. xxv.

70. Horii, op. cit., Tables IV and V.

71. Lim *et al.*, op. cit., p. 125. The two figures are equivalent to 106.2 acres and 102.5 acres respectively.

72. ibid., Table 17, p. 55: 71 per cent of the tenants paid in kind in 1955, but 73 per cent paid in cash in 1973; Horii, op. cit., 51 per cent paid in cash in 1966 in that Muda village; 'Farm Economic Survey', op. cit., 51 per cent paid in cash in 1966 in the six pilot areas of Muda; Affifudin, op. cit., 52 per cent paid in cash in 1972 in Muda; Selvadurai and Ani Arope, op. cit., 74 per cent paid in cash in Province Wellesley.

73. See Yap and Dixon, op. cit.

74. Lim *et al.*, op. cit., pp. 56—8, using their own data as well as those reported by other researchers.

75. Robert Ho, 'Rice Production in Malaya: A Review of Problems and Prospects', *Journal of Tropical Geography*, 29, December 1969.

76. This is not to deny that a first round of increase in income does occur.

77. The Reservation Act prohibited the owning of a class of land by non-Malays which naturally made those lands under the Reservations more restrictive in marketability and unattractive as a surety for the relatively big loans the Chettiar money-lenders used to give. Yet, there continued to be a need and a market of profitable credit lending to the Malay farmers with land as a mortgage. As soon as the few rich Malays (chiefly the landholders) realized the potential of this market, they would step into the role of money-lender. This led Mokhzani to remark:

'. . . The profitable nature of Malay moneylending continually attracts new lenders. Extensive lending and foreclosure by lenders, who are generally the village rich and other high income and high-status Malays, lends to the concentration of landed property which amplifies the wealth and social differences between Malays. . . .'

'. . . With increasing demand for loans among rural Malays there is a real danger that more high income Malays in urban employment will enter into the money lending scene . . . and acquire an increasing proportion of rural Malay land over and above the accumulation of Malay land in the hands of the Malay rich who are residents in the villages.' Mokhzani bin Abdul Rahim, 'Credit in a Malay Peasant Economy', Ph.D. dissertation, University of London, 1973, pp. 2 and 437 respectively.

78. T. B. Wilson, *The Economics of Padi Production in North Malaya*, Part I, Kuala Lumpur, Ministry of Agriculture and Fisheries, 1958, pp. 63—7.

79. ibid.

80. Narkswasdi and Selvadurai, Volume 1 on Tanjong Karang, op. cit., Table 62, p. 100.

81. ibid., p. 48 on the use of agrochemicals; Table 21, p. 51 on the proportion of time on own farm; Table 42, p. 78 on the total number of work days per household per year.

82. ibid., p. 51.

83. ibid., Table 19, p. 42.

84. ibid., Table on literacy rate.

85. ibid., Table 27.

86. ibid., Table 30, p. 60.

87. ibid., p. 61.

88. ibid., Table 36, p. 67.

89. ibid., Table 24.

90. ibid., Table 23 reported that 73 per cent of the farmers in Sekinchan purchased their farm land, the highest percentage of purchased land in the region of Tanjong Karang.

91. ibid., 75.8 per cent are marketable surpluses, Table 51, p. 87.

92. This has not been formally documented, but can be seen from the local dailies; see, for example, *Nanyang Siang Pau*.

93. Munro and Chee. The initial report was entitled 'Fishermen and Fishing Development in Penang and Kedah', Penang, 1972. This was published in 1978 by Universiti Sains Malaysia Press under the title of *The Economics of Fishing and the Developing World, a Malaysian case study*. See pp. 19—24, especially Tables I and II, of the initial report.

94. It costs several thousand dollars to convert an old lorry engine and $10,000 for a new motor, ibid., pp. 22—3.

95. ibid., p. 19.

96. The trawlers are wasteful in the sense that they scoop up any sea life that is in their path, including the smaller fishes and prawns which should be left to breed.

97. Munro and Chee, op. cit., Table 4.

98. ibid., Table 4.

99. This figure of 2,486 trawlers in 1971 is in itself an increase over the 1,389 in 1970. Table in *Annual Fisheries Statistics*, 1973. For another discussion of the trawler question, see Yap Chan Ling, 'Over-expansion in the Trawler Industry with Special Reference to the Dindings District of West Malaysia', *Kajian Ekonomi Malaysia*, X, December 1973, pp. 79—90.

100. The crew members of the small trawlers made $286 per month on average *v.* $155 for the crewmen of all trawlers in Penang. Munro and Chee, op. cit., Table VIII. In Kedah, the average monthly income for crewmen was $309 for those on small trawlers and $262 for those on the large trawlers. ibid., Table XI.

101. R. Firth, 'Economics of the Malayan Fishing Industry', *A Record of Anthropological Society*, August 1941.

102. Munro and Chee, op. cit., Table N.

103. Summarized from the Income Tables in Munro and Chee, op. cit.

104. Y. L. Lee, 'Kukup: A Chinese Fishing Village in South West Malaysia', *Journal of Tropical Geography*, 16, September 1962, p. 135. See also Firth, op. cit.

105. Huang Yu-kon, op. cit., last section on profitability of padi farming.

3 The Rubber and Coconut Smallholders

3.1 INTRODUCTION

In this chapter, the production and distribution characteristics of two groups of rural producers will be discussed: the rubber and coconut smallholders. The rubber smallholders are, in fact, the most numerous small-scale rural producers in this country, numbering in excess of 400,000 households.[1] However, compared with the padi farmers, there is a relative lack of written material on the rubber smallholders, and especially a lack of detailed surveys on a wide range of rubber smallholding villages. Works by Bevan (1962), Voon (1967), Barlow and Chan (1968), Lim (1968 and 1972), Selvadurai (1972), and, to a lesser extent, works by Ho (1967), Fisk (1961), Mohamad Ismail Ahmad (1968), and even earlier works by Arshad Ayub (1959) and Sallehudin (1960) are informative. However, they cover Selangor mainly and not other parts of the peninsula. As for the coconut smallholders, the extent and depth of data are even more limited. This limits discussion and it is not possible to give as much detail as in the chapter on padi farmers. And as will be obvious in the course of discussion, none of these groups has received much attention on how each group can improve its livelihood. Yet they have to shoulder the burden of the padi price-support policy as Goldman (1975) has shown.[2]

The method of investigation is analogous to that in the last chapter. The impact of the size of plots, differences in seedlings, application of agrochemicals, the extent and date of replanting as well as the necessity and availability of other on- and off-farm work for the generation of income for the planters will be traced.

Section 3.2 contains the discussion on the rubber smallholders, Section 3.3 deals with the coconut smallholders, while Section 3.4 concludes with a brief statement about the landless agricultural labourers; only the fruit and vegetable growers numbering 49,812 householders among the agriculture-related activities will not have been covered by this book.

3.2 IN CYCLE OF POVERTY AND AGONY— THE RUBBER SMALLHOLDERS

A. Historical Background

The rubber smallholders have always been in difficulties. Ever since the commercial cultivation of rubber was successful, the ordinary Malaysian has been interested in this obviously profitable cash crop. However, the British Colonial Government tried two measures to block the first attempts by ordinary farmers to plant rubber:

(1) alienate the most suitable land for European estate-planting only;

(2) legislate to prohibit the Malay peasants from switching to rubber, ostensibly to preserve their way of life![3]

However, the profit from the early estate rubber planting proved to be too attractive, and large numbers of Malay peasants either replanted their padi land with rubber or opened up jungle land for rubber planting. Many non-Malay immigrants were also attracted into opening up land for planting. Law or no law, boom or depression, the British colonial administration was not able to stamp out this wave of planting.[4] From this very early date, the rubber smallholders have operated under handicaps. Not only were they denied access to financial assistance (who would lend to a small peasant in an uncertain venture?) and hence forced to rely on their own resources, but they also had to wrestle with official disapproval, obstruction, and even sabotage.[5] Naturally, they were at a competitive disadvantage under such circumstances, apart from their possible lack of economy of scale and non-commercial organization.[6]

Are there, however, any remaining disadvantages as a result of these early handicaps? This is an area into which researchers have yet to venture. Heuristically, one can ask: when the British delineated land for estate rubber planting, would they not have reserved the most suitable land?[7] Would it not be true then that the remaining land subsequently opened by smallholders for rubber planting was less suitable? The British reserved land closest to or with access to roads, railways, and transport in general,[8] implying that the smallholding land may be less accessible. As for the land converted from padi fields, this would again be inferior, as the land and soil suitable for padi cultivation is more often than not unsuitable for rubber. In sum, it is possible that the land now occupied by rubber smallholdings cannot expect to match the estates in productivity even if it is converted to an estate mode of production via amalgamation and reorganization. And the reason for that may be due to these historically determined handicaps.

Just as quickly as rubber planting became successful, and European as well as small Asian planters crowded into this new endeavour, rubber prices came crashing down with the business downturn in the industrialized countries, and a glut on the natural rubber market occurred in the 1918–21 period.[9] Profits turned into losses, many estates ran into difficulties, and small planters were forced into bankruptcy. The producers in the then Federated and Unfederated Malay States were quick to get organized.[10] The white-dominated Rubber Growers' Association and, to a lesser extent, the non-Malay dominated Rubber Estate Owners' Association, persuaded the colonial administration to introduce production quotas among the local producers and to negotiate with the Netherlands East Indies (Indonesia) to limit production in consonance. In between the war years, there were to be several such attempts; some were successful, others failed. Yet, in every instance, since the small producers were not organized, their interests were not represented before the larger producers and the colonial administration. It was also not in the interest of the estate owners to protect the smallholders. Thus no fair allocation of quota was given to the smallholders.[11] It was probably the wish of the estate owners that the low prices together with the restrictive production would totally squeeze out the smallholders and revive the profitability and health of the industry.[12] Regardless of the effectiveness of the schemes of control, the point is that the rubber smallholders were once again the target of discrimination by the wealthy, powerful and organized estates, if not actually the Colonial Government as well.

It was not until the fifties, after Malaya's dependence on rubber had become overwhelming, and when it was clear that the smallholders were here to stay, that some measures were devised to assist the smallholders. The rubber research and replanting cesses were introduced in that period and a replanting fund was set up to encourage rubber replanting. In view of the historical record of the colonial administration, one cannot help but wonder if such steps had really been undertaken to lift the smallholders out of difficulties and poverty. One cannot help but think that, by then, the economic health of Malaya as a whole has been linked to the ability of both the estates and smallholders to compete effectively with synthetics, and that the political realities of that time were the real reasons motivating the initiation of smallholding replanting schemes. Even in these circumstances it was not until after the Independence of Malaya in 1957 that smallholding replanting was pushed forward with full steam.[13] Besides, it was the estates with superior organization and access to information which were able to quickly take advantage of the Government replanting incentives and to implement the fruits of research.[14] In fact, to this day, the whole structure of research and replanting cesses collection is still biased against the smallholders. In so far as the smallholders, who produce the lower grades of rubber, have to pay the same export duty and research cess per lb. as the estates producing the higher grades with substantial price differential, the smallholders are paying proportionately higher tax rates.[15] The regressive nature of this would be even more apparent if one evaluated the benefits of research accruing to each of the two groups in detail. Besides, the estates receive a full refund of their paid-out replanting cess while the replanting smallholders receive a flat sum in yearly instalments as a replanting subsidy. Are the replanting smallholders getting more or less than their payment of replanting cess? Further, the smallholders who do not replant obviously would be perpetually subsidizing those who have replanted and who are presumably on the way to a relatively better life.

It is not the intention of this book to document and interpret the historical development of the Malayan rubber industry.[16] The brief historical recapitulation is intended to highlight some aspects of the development of the rubber industry in Malaya in which it is necessary to put the discussion of rubber smallholders in poverty into perspective. In this section, the income range of the rubber smallholders will be presented first, followed by a discussion of the factors affecting income receipt. The next part of this section deals with the possible picture of income distribution among races in the rubber smallholding sector. Finally, there is a brief foray into the question of the general livelihood of the rubber smallholders *vis-à-vis* the padi farmers. As in the last chapter, concern centres on factors affecting income receipt.

B. Income Determinants

(a) GENERAL

Table 3.1 is a summary of the estimated income of rubber smallholders in some parts of Malaya. The bulk of the rubber smallholders falls into the income category of $500–$1,499 per family per year (51 per cent and 74.4 per cent of those from west Johor and Selangor respectively) which is roughly in the same range as in the case of the average padi farmer.[17] Actually, neither the series for Selangor nor that for west Johor is representative of Malaya and their spectra should not be taken to be applicable for Malaya. The average holding for Malaya is about 6.55 acres whereas that for the surveyed Selangor smallholders is only 5.21 acres and that for the west Johor farmers is 9.9 acres.[18] However, since the average for each of the two spectra falls slightly off to each side of the mean for Malaya, together they do furnish a sense of the range of some possible distributions. More importantly, they can be used to reflect the major factors influencing the income of the smallholders. In fact, due to the many steps undertaken and assumptions made in arriving at the figures in Table 3.1 from the Selangor survey data, its distribution should be interpreted with great care.

The most striking feature for Johor is that despite having an average farm acreage almost twice that of the national average, a full 33 per cent earned less than $1,000 in 1971, and another 23 per cent earned $1,000–$1,499. For the other areas, with smaller acreage, it is most likely that at least half of

TABLE 3.1

INCOME DISTRIBUTION OF RUBBER SMALLHOLDERS

Income Group	Johor			Selangor		
	% of Holdings	*Average Rubber Income*	*Average Total Income*	*% of Holdings*	*Average Rubber Income*	*Average Total Income*
< $500	5	$ 201	$ 338	—	—	—
500– 999	28	428	779	51.3	$ 219	$ 856
1,000–1,499	23	674	1,215	23.0	993	1,276
1,500–1,999	18	986	1,726	5.9	1,626	1,626
2,000–2,999	14	951	2,428	12.7	2,240	2,440
3,000–3,999	5	1,024	3,412	—	—	—
4,000–4,999	3	379	4,518	7.2	4,841	4,841
5,000+	4	2,046	8,029	—	—	—

Sources. Tables 3.2 and 3.6, Chapter 3, Tan Tat-wai, 'Income Distribution and Determination in West Malaysia'; Table 19, Selvadurai, *Socio-Economic Survey of Rubber Smallholdings in West Johore*, Ministry of Agriculture, 1972.

Note. The figures for Johor have been taken straight from the survey. The figures for Selangor are less reliable as they have been estimated from the surveyed data by combining the two Tables mentioned in the sources using some assumptions.

TABLE 3.2
ESTIMATED INCOME OF RUBBER SMALLHOLDERS IN 1968

	Size of Holding (in acres)				*Total Surveyed*
	< 3	*3–5*	*5–10*	*> 10*	
Percentage of total smallholding area (1)	13	16	30	41	100
Percentage of total smallholder (1)	41	23	23	13	100
Av. size of holding (1)	2.08 ac.	4.5 ac.	8.55 ac.	20.67 ac.	5.21 ac.
Percentage with high-yielding clones (2)	22.7	30.3	33.2	30.0	29.9
Av. household members per farm (3)	4.6	3.0	5.4	6.4	5.1
Av. number of workers per farm (4)	2.0	2.2	2.4	2.8	2.2
High-yielding material (5)					
Revenue ($) (6)	$819.9	$1,797.6	$3,370.4	$8,148.1	$2,053.8
Labour cost	116.3	312.8	738.7	2,573.6	383.9
Other expenses	178.5	391.3	391.3	733.6	447.0
Net family return	525.1	1,093.5	2,240.4	4,840.9	1,222.9
Low-yielding material					
Revenue ($) (7)	$383.8	$841.3	$1,577.5	$3,813.6	$961.3
Labour cost	64.2	189.9	448.3	1,561.8	233.0
Other expenses	63.0	138.2	259.1	626.3	157.9
Net family return	256.6	513.2	870.1	1,625.5	570.4

Sources. (1) Tables 2, 4, 8, Barlow and Chan, *Toward an Optimum Size of Rubber Holding*. Average size of holding calculated on the basis of the first two rows of this Table and the following:

	Surveyed	*In Sector*
Total area (acres)	912,865	2,521,500
Number of smallholders	175,284	384,700

(2) Table 3, ibid. This refers to percentage of smallholdings with high-yielding clones.

(3) Table 10, ibid.

(4) Calculated from row (4) on the basis of one worker to 1.3 dependants, see ibid, page 8.

(5) Table 19, ibid. The imputed cost of labour given in Table 19 has been adjusted using percentage of family labour given in Table 11. For example, for three acres or less, 78 per cent are family labour and the inputed labour cost given in Table 19 is $254. Thus after deducting the 78 per cent family labour cost, the paid labour cost is $58/acre. The cost and yield estimated are based on a survey of 495 high-yielding smallholders and 576 low-yielding smallholders done in 1963/4. The concept here is similar to that used for padi. Revenue per farm = price per lb. x yield per acre x average acreage. Cost = cost per acre given in Table 19, ibid., x average acreage. Family return = revenue – labour cost – other expenses.

(6) The revenue is estimated using a yield of 1,086 lb./ac. valued at 50¢/lb. FOB RSS 1 or 36.3¢/lb. to smallholders.

(7) The revenue is estimated using a yield of 514 lb./ac. valued at 50¢/lb. FOB RSS 1 or 35.9¢/lb. to smallholders.

TABLE 3.3

INCOME CHARACTERISTICS AND DISTRIBUTION OF JOHOR RUBBER SMALLHOLDERS, 1971

Size of Farm (ac.)	*Size Distribution of (in %)*				*Average Rubber Area (ac.)*	*Income Characteristics (in $, averaged)*				
	Total Area	*All Farmers*	*Malay Farmers*	*Chinese Farmers*		*Net from Rubber*	*Net Farm*	*Off-Farm*	*Gifts*	*Total*
< 3	3	11	14	—	2.2	$ 257	$ 262	$912	$ 63	$1,237
3.0—4.99	8	18	18	18	4.1	449	632	732	43	1,407
5.0—6.99	29	16	18	3	7.4	748	912	539	64	1,515
7.0—9.99	21	23	24	20						
10.0—14.99	22	17	16	23	12.1	1,010	1,179	596	48	1,823
15.0—29.99	—	12	9	25	18.6	1,038	1,858	963	44	2,865
30.0+	17	3	1	11	54.7	2,884	4,036	240	240	4,516
All	100	100	100	100	9.9	814	1,044	666	61	1,771

	All Farmers	*Malay Farmers*	*Chinese Farmers*
% Reporting farm income only	59	58	60
Average farm income	$1,044	$ 905	$1,689
% Reporting off-farm income	38	38	36
Average off-farm income	$ 666	$ 593	$1,008

	All Farmers	*Malay Farmers*	*Chinese Farmers*
(Av. for those reporting)	($1,753)	($1,561)	($2,800)
% Reporting gifts	3	4	4
Average gifts	$ 61	$ 52	$ 99
(Av. for those reporting)	($2,033)	($1,300)	($2,475)

Source. Selvadurai, *Socio-Economic Survey of Rubber Smallholdings in Western Johore*, Tables 17, 20, 23, and 24.

them would fall into the category of less than $1,000, probably more. However, one word of caution is also necessary: the holders of smaller plots of rubber land tend to hold them as supplementary plots to their other holdings.[19] This means that their low rubber income is also a supplementary income. Therefore, it would also be unwise to jump to the conclusion that many smallholders are so poverty-stricken as to earn much less than $500 per year. It is crucial to estimate the number of farmers with truly small plots of land for rubber cultivation as the only or major source of living.

(b) SIZE OF HOLDING

From Tables 3.1—3.3, rubber income forms only part of the smallholders' total income, and this proportion tends to vary with the acreage they own. Not surprisingly, their income from rubber increases absolutely, and relatively up to a point, as their acreage increases. Referring to Table 3.3, for west Johor, the rubber income increases from $257 for holdings of less than 3 acres to just over $1,000 for holdings of 10—30 acres and then jumps to $2,884 for holdings in excess of 30 acres, but less than 100 acres. As a proportion of total income, income from rubber increases from 20.78 per cent for holdings of less than three acres to 63.8 per cent for holdings of more than 30 acres, with a dip to 36.23 per cent for holdings with acreage between 15 and 29 acres. This is illustrated in Figure 3.1.

This trend is hardly surprising. When one's holding is small, rubber income is low. An income level of $257 per year from rubber necessitates a search for off-farm income. This need and the availability of excess family labour (due to substantial under-employment of the family on-farm) cause a higher incidence of, and increased income from, working off-farm. As the family hold-

FIGURE 3.1
INCOME FROM DIFFERENT SOURCES BY SIZE OF RUBBER SMALLHOLDING IN JOHOR

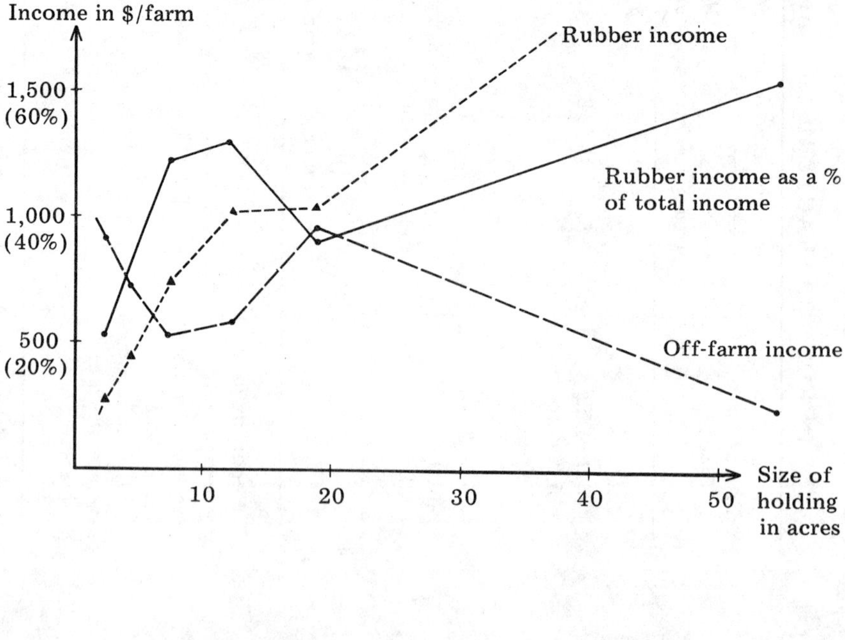

ing increases, the amount of on-farm work increases and absorbs most of the family labour. Off-farm income would taper off since the availability of family labour and the necessity for supplementary income both decrease.

A family of six or seven, with at least two full-time working adults and perhaps two or three part-time family helpers, is able to handle most of the maintenance, tapping, and coagulation work of a plot up to about ten acres without seeking outside labour help.[20] For a holding in excess of ten acres, an increasing amount of hired help becomes necessary. However, while hired help could be profitable and may add to the family income, the use of it for holdings below a certain size may not bring about a higher return for the lack of economy of scale. This is because the holding of less than 30 acres may put the cost structure in the rising marginal cost-curve portion and increasing return to scale portion of the production curve is not reached until the holdings become larger. If so, this would explain the levelling off of income from rubber in holdings ranging from ten to twenty-nine acres (Fig. 3.1). This hypothetical cost-curve is illustrated in Figure 3.2.

One irregularity occurs in the holding range between fifteen and twenty-nine acres: just as income from rubber levels off, off-farm income increases sharply before decreasing again to the lowest level. Unfortunately, there is no evidence to indicate if this is a 'freak' occurrence for this particular area due perhaps to the presence of particularly attractive off-farm work.

Another related observation is the increase in other farm income as the size of holding increases (see Table 3.3). The low point is $5 for holdings smaller than three acres, increasing to $1,052 for those with more than thirty acres. The explanation for this is simple. When one's holding increases, it becomes more possible (i.e., relatively less costly) to delineate or to acquire some acreage for the planting of other crops (usually coconut or vegetable, rather than padi, except for some of those neighbouring major padi areas where the soil

FIGURE 3.2
COST OF PRODUCTION OF RUBBER SMALLHOLDING BY SIZE OF HOLDING

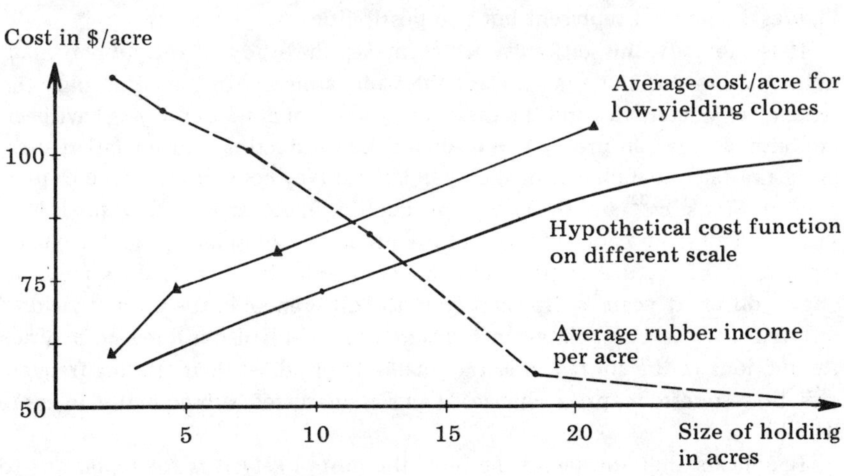

conditions may be more suitable for the growing of padi).[21] Presumably these serve to supplement the rubber income and also to prevent a total dependence on rubber. However, that also means that the income distribution pattern is quite unequal: the smallholders with the larger rubber plots also possess larger other-crop plots, reinforcing their higher rubber income with larger other-farm income.

In making these remarks, the analogy with the padi farmers is clear. In each case, the size of the main crop holding is an important determinant of their income. However, that is not the only determinant and a simplistic use of distribution of size of main crop holding to approximate distribution of income is misleading. In the case of rubber, the year and extent of replanting are also important.

(c) REPLANTING

During the sixties most of the smallholders undertook some replanting. Since rubber trees take six to eight years to mature, i.e., before tapping for production, it becomes necessary to replant one's holding in stages to ensure a minimal flow of income in the waiting period. After the first production date, an average tree can produce for about twenty years before production begins to taper off to an extent requiring another round of replanting several years later. Thus the matured acreage of rubber in possession is the more important reflection of current income of the smallholders.

In Figures 3.3 and 3.4, curves A, B, C, and so on represent the production curve of different portions of the holdings in different replanting cycles. In the absence of a phased replanting cycle, presumably some smallholdings would have just one production cycle and hence a yield and income cycle depending on the type of seedlings available when the replanting began. That would mean absolute poverty during the replanting years and perhaps decent living during the peak production years, if the smallholder has a big enough plot. However, with a phased replanting programme, there are numerous combinations possible depending on the size of the plot, the number of phases, and the timing of the initiation of each phase. The curves representing the numerous production and income streams cannot and need not be graphed here. Figures 3.3 and 3.4 represent but two possibilities.

It is precisely this difficulty which makes the study of the rubber smallholders more difficult than that of the padi farmers. For the latter, once the tenancy characteristics and the presence/absence of double cropping have been established, one can proceed to estimate the production and income figures, using the fairly detailed annual crop-cutting survey conducted by the Department of Statistics[22] and the cost of production figures from various small farm surveys. The same cannot be said of the rubber smallholders, given the changing acreage of mature crops and the differences in the yield of the same seedling in different years, quite apart from the differences in the average yield of different species of seedlings. In addition, the yield is also influenced by price fluctuations in the short run as the smallholders adjust their tapping frequencies in response to price changes. (This is discussed subsequently in more detail.)

It appears that the larger the plot, the more likely it is for replanting to

FIGURE 3.3
OUTPUT OF A HYPOTHETICAL FARM REPLANTING IN TWO STAGES

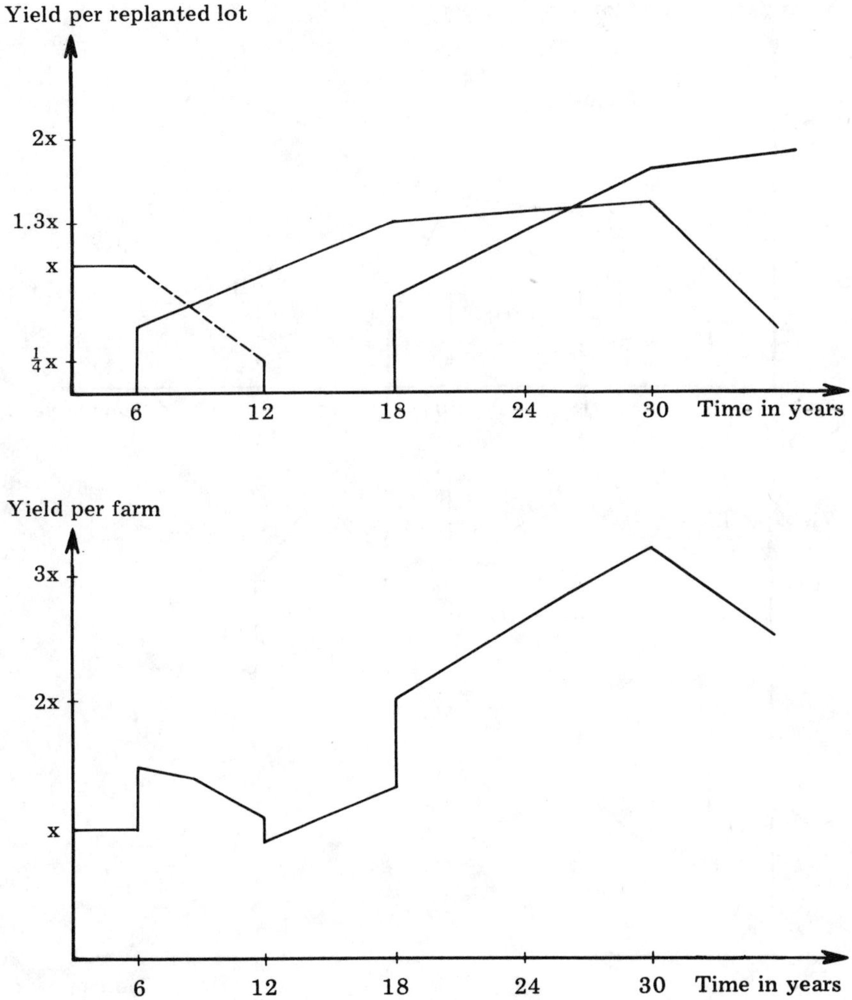

have occurred.[23] However, the average replanted area tends to be less than 50 per cent of the total rubber area, except for those with holdings of less than five acres, in which case the bulk of the land would have been replanted. In terms of mature area, the average mature acreage as a percentage of the total acreage is about 75.8 per cent with a downward trend as the size of holding increases. These observations provide some preliminary indication of the validity of the hypothetical replanting behaviour among the smallholders in west Johor. However, it is not conclusive verification.

More importantly, both our hypothetical construction and these observations suggest the existence of another built-in potential for income inequality

FIGURE 3.4
OUTPUT OF A HYPOTHETICAL FARM REPLANTING IN THREE STAGES

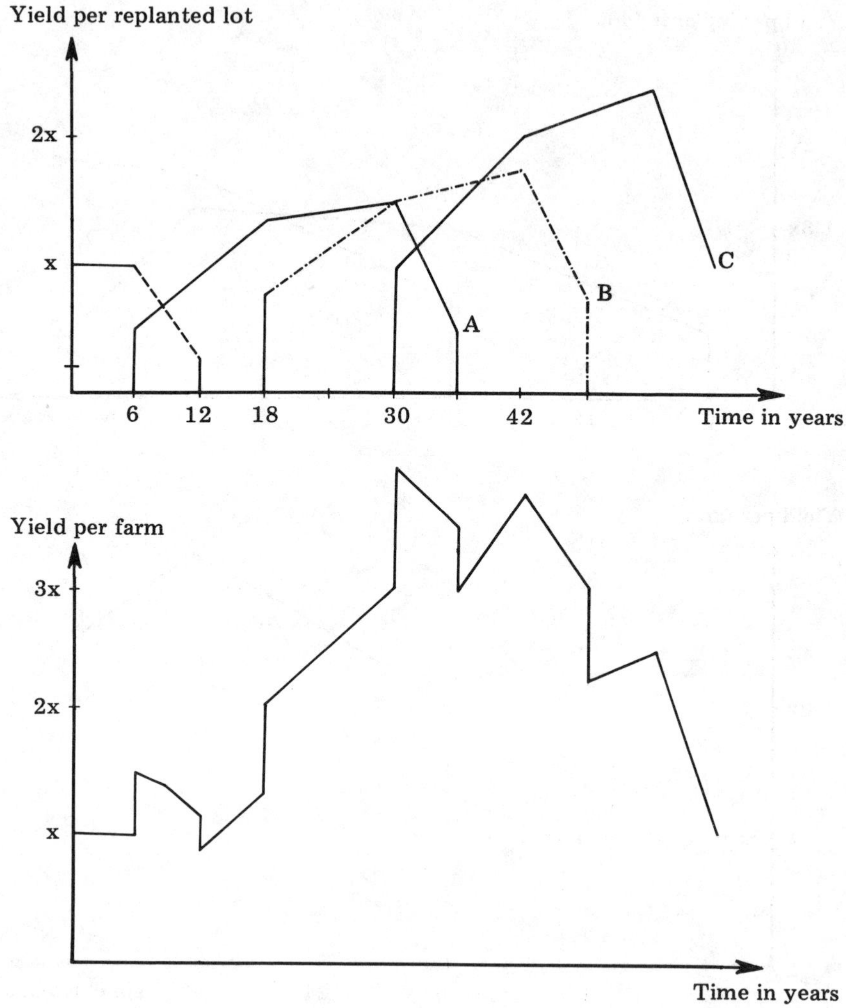

to increase as time goes on. This is of course not surprising. With larger acreage, the large smallholders have already more income than those with smaller plots. The higher income would have enabled more savings, more capital improvement, application of fertilizer and weed control, etc., under normal operation, all of which would have yielded higher income subsequently. Now with replanting, the bigger ones tend to replant in more phases than the smaller, which means that they can continually have trees with increasingly higher yield coming into production (presumably those replanted at a later date can take advantage of newer seedlings with higher yield) resulting in higher yield and income per acre.

In 1971, the large smallholder made $4,036 in farm income compared to $912 by the smaller ones (442 per cent as large—see Table 3.3). However, the large smallholder has a potential of making $5,282 in farm income as opposed to the $1,081 for the smaller ones (489 per cent as large), primarily because of the very substantial difference in the potential increase of rubber income.

To the policy planner, the choices of action are varied. Encourage frequent and well-spaced replanting which can provide a more constant production and income stream, all other things being equal; it is possibly less costly to the Government since the loss of income by the replanting smallholder would be a smaller portion of his total income, giving rise to less pressure for bigger subsidies. Encourage one massive shot, or a few phases of replanting effort, and it may give rise to an impressive gain in production and income (if the increase does not glut the market and depress the price more than the percentage increase in production) in the medium run but perhaps at a much higher cost of public finance and maybe difficulties in the long run if similar massive replanting cannot then be organized for various reasons.

(d) PRICE

There is one other factor which affects the income of rubber smallholders much more than it does the padi farmers: price. The price of natural rubber fluctuates wildly from year to year, and from month to month (even from week to week). Since there is no Government set farm-gate price as in the case of padi, international price fluctuations are mainly passed back to the producers.[24]

The impact of price changes comes in many ways. First there is the obvious, direct effect on the income received for a similar level of production. Additionally, when the price is really high, there is an incentive to tap more frequently out of the usual tapping cycle, in order to capitalize on the short-run gain. When the prices are low, the smallholder may also be forced to harvest more latex in order to compensate through the sale of an increased volume for income loss due to low prices.[25] Such increased tapping has a direct and an indirect impact on income. The income is now artificially higher than it would otherwise be in the short run. In the long run, such tapping practices are suicidal for the trees are injured, which would affect long-run latex outflow, and might even be killed if practised in excess. Such fluctuations in prices, and subsequently production, would make the income of the smallholders quite different from year to year even in the absence of any changes in seedling, replanting phases, proportion under matured trees, and so on. It makes extrapolation or estimation, based on one well-surveyed year's data, hazardous and misleading. It also poses the very difficult question of which year to choose as a common-base year comparison between the rubber producing sector and most of the other sectors. It is fair to suggest that the choice of any one single year for such an overwhelmingly important sector[26] will inevitably be unsatisfactory; the better way would be to take at least two years close to one another, one with high prices and the other in depressed conditions, in order to gauge better the true income differential between this and other sectors.

C. Differences by Race

Turning now to the racial composition of rubber smallholders and their respective income distribution, the absence of any good and comprehensive agricultural survey that can provide a distribution of either income or holding acreage by race[27] necessitates making estimations and drawing inferences from several area surveys.

Table 3.4 summarizes the estimated number of rubber smallholdings and the corresponding acreages established under different schemes. The different schemes fall into three categories:

(1) The individual schemes refer to those holdings established historically by individual settlers through land clearance or crop conversion. While no information exists on the racial breakdown for this category, one can speculate on the number of Malay and non-Malay smallholders. These individual plots are located in the West Coast states of Selangor, Johor, Perak, and southern and eastern Kedah as well as in the East Coast states. As the first three West Coast states, i.e., excluding Kedah, are predominantly non-Malay, it can be deduced that the plots there tend to be non-Malay.[28] On the other hand, the population structure of Kedah and the East Coast states is chiefly Malay, implying that the overwhelming number of rubber smallholders in these areas are Malay. The summation of these two distributions may give rise to slightly more Malay than non-Malay rubber smallholders.

(2) 'Subdivided' refers to smallholdings established as a result of the subdivision of estates. There is no detailed racial breakdown for this category. However, one knows from Aziz's study of subdivision that a very small proportion of the estate subdivided land went to Malay smallholders.[29] It is therefore reasonable to surmise that the great majority of these are still non-Malay, assuming that very few transactions have occurred to change the ownership from non-Malay to Malay.

(3) The remaining schemes were set up by the Government in the fifties and sixties; some of these schemes continue to provide new land to new and existing holdings (for example, Felda, Felcra, and Fringe schemes). In 1968, smallholdings that had been established through land clearance after the Second World War accounted for only 18.61 per cent of the estimated 379,884 holdings. The bulk of these (74.25 per cent) were Malay.

If one were to look at all three categories, it would appear that there are slightly more Malay smallholders than non-Malay. It is probable that the non-Malays would have larger plots on the average than the Malay smallholders since some non-Malay smallholders obtained their plots in the post-war period from estate subdivision with delineation in blocks of ten acres.[30] However, since 1968, the plots delineated under FLDA and Felda schemes have been raised to ten acres and in some cases even 12.5 acres; again, the bulk of these go to the Malay farmers and the difference in average Malay and non-Malay acreages should have narrowed.[31] By 1973, 526,900 acres of land had been developed by Felda, benefiting at least 52,690 households; 96.2 per cent of the land was owned by Malays.[32]

The older, individual holdings form the bulk of the rubber smallholdings, and have a broader distribution pattern due to differences in the original land clearance effort and the process of selling, foreclosure, inheritance, and expan-

TABLE 3.4

COMPOSITION OF RUBBER SMALLHOLDINGS BY SCHEMES AND RACE, 1968

Type of Holding	*Total Planted Area (in thousand acres)*	*Total Partici-pants*	*Av. Planted Area per Holding (acres)*	*High Yielding Material (%)*	*Malay Partici-pants (%)*	*Chinese Partici-pants (%)*	*Other Partici-pants (%)*
Individual	1,758.0	274,600	6.4	45.1	n.a.	n.a.	n.a.
Subdivided	345.6	34,600	10.0	62.3	n.a.	n.a.	n.a.
In Fringe schemes	123.0	27,991	4.4	92.0	87	11	2
In FLDA schemes	116.3	10,720	7.5	100.0	92	5	3
In unsubsidized schemes	113.0	18,858	6.0	90.5	36	63	1
In state schemes	46.9	7,791	6.0	72.8	92	7	1
In other schemes	18.6	5,324	3.5	54.2	75	19	6
Total	2,521.5	379,884	6.6	54.9			

Source. Tables 2 and 6, Lim Sow Ching, 'A Study of the Marketing of Smallholders' Rubber at the First Trade Level in Selangor', University of Malaya, unpublished M.Sc. Thesis, 1968.

sion through the years. By contrast, the shorter history of the other smallholdings (hence fewer changes likely), the rather uniform plots that have been alienated, and the more stringent conditions imposed on land transfer[33] all serve to reduce income variations. Besides, the Fringe schemes instituted have added small supplementary acreages to the holdings of the smallholders. This serves further to balance inequality in holding and income between the really small plot owners and the large plot owners, as well as between Malay and non-Malay smallholders, as the bulk of these went to the Malays.[34]

Bearing in mind the above qualification to the landholding distribution structure, we proceed to summarize the pattern in the late sixties.

For Selangor (Table 3.5) the Chinese smallholders with an average of 4.43 acres have a larger average acreage than the Malays with 3.17 acres. There is a higher percentage of Malays in the smallest holding group of less than 3 acres while there are more Chinese in the larger plot categories above 3 acres. However, families operating less than 6 acres are very poor; they earn about $500 per year with low-yielding material and a little over $1,000 with high-yielding seedlings, and this includes off-farm income![35] In fact, more Chinese smallholders than Malay smallholders in Selangor have holdings of less than 6 acres: 45.9 per cent of all smallholdings are Chinese with an average holding of 4.06 acres and 37.6 per cent are Malay with an average of 3.02 acres, though the Chinese poor are one-third better off on the average than the Malay poor. It is in the medium-farm category that the Chinese and the other non-Malays dominate with an average holding of 7.35 acres, with only a very small number of Malays in this category. These Malay and non-Malay medium-sized smallholders with 7.35 acres earn above $2,500 a year, but are a far cry from the wealthy and affluent estate owners.

The above can be confirmed by another independent study on Selangor. Voon (1965) collected data pertaining to Selangor from 1910 to 1965. He reported that in 1952, the average holding for the Malay, Chinese, and Indian smallholders was 4.9, 10.1, and 9.9 acres, respectively. This statistic hides the fact that the majority of the non-Malay smallholders were poor: 35.68 per cent, 41.84 per cent and 8.06 per cent were Malay, Chinese, and Indian smallholders with holdings of less than 25 acres respectively.[36] The relatively higher averages of the non-Malays were due to the larger numbers (14.78 per cent) among them who had holdings of more than 25 acres.[37] The averages had been inflated by having 20 per cent and 32 per cent in the ranks of the Chinese and Indian smallholders who owned more than 25 acres each. The bulk of those owning less than 25 acres had less than 10 acres: 30 per cent of the Chinese had less than 5 acres with an average of 3.8 acres and 46 per cent had between 5 and 15 acres, averaging 8.6 acres.[38] One has to remember that these figures apply to the year 1952. By the late sixties, many changes could have occurred to alter this pattern. But the most important event was likely to be the estate subdivision, boosting the number of Chinese smallholders with about 10 acres each. Some land foreclosure to the Chettiar money-lenders and some consolidation among the Malay landholders may also have occurred, giving a more unequal landholding distribution between and within the races.

In terms of either Selangor or the Malayan population distribution, the non-Malays were clearly over-represented in the category of large-scale small-

TABLE 3.5
SIZE DISTRIBUTION OF SELANGOR'S RUBBER SMALLHOLDINGS BY RACE AND TENURIAL STATUS

Size of Holding (acres)		Malay			Chinese			All		
		Owner Tapper	*Hired Tapper*	*Both*	*Owner Tapper*	*Hired Tapper*	*Both*	*Owner Tapper*	*Hired Tapper*	*Both*
< 3	% of Farmers	4.5	8.9	13.4	—	7.0	7.0	5.1	15.9	21.0
	Av. Area Operated (ac.)	2.37	2.37	2.37	—	2.36	2.36	2.29	2.36	2.35
3—5.9	% of Farmers	10.2	14.0	24.2	2.5	38.9	41.4	12.7	54.1	66.9
	Av. Area Operated (ac.)	3.33	3.42	3.38	4.00	4.11	4.10	3.46	3.91	3.82
6+	% of Farmers	0.6	1.3	1.9	0.6	8.9	9.5	1.3	10.8	12.1
	Av. Area Operated (ac.)	6.00	6.00	6.00	6.00	7.45	7.35	6.00	7.19	7.07
Total	% of Farmers	15.3	24.2	39.5	3.1	54.8	57.9	19.1	80.8	100.0
	Av. Area Operated (ac.)	3.16	3.17	3.17	4.40	4.43	4.43	3.32	4.04	3.90

Source. Table 2, Bevan, *A Study of Yields, Labour Inputs and Incomes on Rubber Smallholdings in the Coastal Area of Selangor*, Kuala Lumpur, University of Malaya, 1962.

holders, especially the Indians. The latter occurrence can probably be partly attributed to the dominant position of the Indian Chettiar money-lenders among the medium and small (especially small) producers and their land being foreclosed as compensation for not servicing their debts.[39]

From Table 3.6, one gathers that this picture was roughly true for Negeri Sembilan in 1968, with the qualification that the Malays were even more concentrated in the less than three acres category as compared with Selangor.

The case of west Johor presented in Table 3.3 is again consistent with the analysis above. The major difference here is that the average holding for the Malay and non-Malay smallholders was almost twice as large as that in the other two states.[40]

How does this distribution of size of holding by race translate into income distribution by race? As argued in the earlier pages, this is something that one cannot predict without accurate information on the extent of replanting, the dates of replanting, types of seedlings, and the size of other farm plots in addition to the size of holding information. Therefore, it is inadvisable to attempt to construct an income distribution picture here beyond drawing attention to the west Johor case. There, with an average holding size of 17.4 acres for the Chinese smallholders, which was about 112 per cent larger than the 8.2 acres average owned by the Malay smallholders, the farm income made by the Chinese smallholders was $1,689 per year, or 86.6 per cent higher than that made

TABLE 3.6
SIZE DISTRIBUTION OF NEGERI SEMBILAN RUBBER SMALLHOLDINGS BY RACE

Size of Holding (acres)		*Race*		
		Malay	*Chinese*	*All*
< 3	% of Farmers	28.6	1.1	29.7
	Av. Area Operated (in acres)	1.9	2.1	1.9
3—5.9	% of Farmers	11.7	12.2	23.9
	Av. Area Operated (in acres)	3.8	4.5	4.2
6—8.9	% of Farmers	3.9	19.7	23.6
	Av. Area Operated (in acres)	6.4	6.4	6.4
9+	% of Farmers	0.9	21.9	22.8
	Av. Area Operated (in acres)	10.8	16.3	16.1
Total	% of Farmers	45.1	54.9	100.0
	Av. Area Operated (in acres)	2.9	9.8	6.7

Source. Tables 1—5, pp. 13—18, Robert Ho, 'Rubber Production by Peasants of the Terachi Valley, Malaya'.

by the Malay smallholders.[41] This excluded the off-farm earnings made by both. Even this level of income was not high compared to the double-cropping Muda farmers. Moreover, this is hardly representative of the pan-Malayan differences since the holdings in this sample were larger than the average. In general, one expects the differences, both absolutely and relatively, to be smaller for the smaller holdings. One salient feature which needs to be re-emphasized is the almost equal number of Malay and non-Malay rubber smallholders in the small farm category (less than 10 acres) in the West Coast states, all of whom are quite poor.

As for the East Coast smallholders, their holdings are probably even smaller on average than the West Coast ones.[42] As such, if their acreages are included, since they would mainly be Malays, the number and hence percentage of poor smallholders who are Malay would be raised significantly. The Felda schemes, by virtue of their providing a larger plot of land (an average of 7.8 acres for those surveyed) and better seedlings, enable the settlers to achieve an income range of $718 for those with trees in the first years of production to $4,926 for those producing under the best conditions and peak production. This is a level superior to the average of less than $1,100 before they joined Felda.[43] Even those settled under the State schemes and those supplemented by the Fringe schemes have achieved superior incomes, though not as much as the Felda settlers. The State schemes' settlers made between $1,076 and $3,141 per family per year, while the Fringe settlers made between $547 and $1,623 per family per year.[44]

The peak income years are between the sixteenth and twentieth years of production when it is possible for the Felda rubber settlers to receive between $3,198 and $4,926 per household per year. By contrast, during the planting years until the early production years, the incomes of the settlers have not been projected to exceed $3,000 even under the most optimistic estimates, and they can make less than $1,300 per year up to the fifteenth year under pessimistic estimates, or a level no better than the income level of the bulk of the settlers before joining the schemes.[45] This level is even worse than what settlers on State schemes could obtain, primarily because of the extremely severe loan repayment schedule exceeding $140 per month or between 46 and 52 per cent of income in the first ten years and 41 per cent from the eleventh to fifteenth years.[46]

The results of the 1976 Felda Settlers Census (1978) provide supporting evidence for the above as well as some additional insights. Unlike the Lim survey, which has small and very partial coverage, the Census surveyed 37,158 settlers with 34,433 providing income data. A total of 38.4 per cent of the settlers received income of between $1,200 and $2,400 per household per year, 27.0 per cent between $2,400 and $3,600, 12.1 per cent between $3,600 and $4,800. Perhaps one can assume that the 10.6 per cent with less than $1,200 yearly income were new settlers whose trees were not yet in commercial production at the date of survey. This is in fact one major weakness of the reported data: one cannot surmise the correlation of income with the length of settlement. Only 9.2 per cent of the settlers earned above $4,800 per year and could be considered to be in the ranks of the middle-income bracket.[47] At the time of the survey, the rubber settlers had a better income distribution than the oil palm settlers with the latter category's income concentrated in the less than $3,600 group (80.6 per cent).[48] Perhaps this is a reflection of the later settlement of the oil palm farmers in general, meaning that few of them have farms in their prime production years.

Of the settlers, 62.2 per cent reported increased income compared to their income level prior to joining the Felda schemes. Not surprisingly, about two-thirds of these came from those who earned less than $1,200 previously. Most of the increases in income have been modest, moving the settlers' income level up one rung. Two- or three-fold increases are the exception rather than the rule.[49] The surprising thing is that 1976 was a good year for rubber prices which hovered around $1.90 per kilo—way above those when the surveys quoted earlier were done.[50] Prices for oil palm were also at a fair level. In view of the good prices and the generally larger plots under Felda, one would have expected greater increases in income. Unfortunately, the published report of the Census does not provide information on income correlated with years of settlement and cost structure (especially loan repayment schedules) to enable a more in-depth analysis.

Two features from the Census report call for some concern. Firstly, while 56.2 per cent of the settlers earned less than $1,200 per year before joining the schemes, only 439 settlers had no income (less than $1\frac{1}{2}$ per cent), and a surprising 44.9 per cent earned between $1,200 and $2,400 per year. Over 1,000 of the settlers actually earned in excess of $3,600 per year prior to joining Felda![51] Heads of households numbering 1,432 were unemployed and 3,802 were odd-job labourers (i.e., 4.1 per cent and 10.9 per cent of the settlers respectively) prior to joining the scheme.[52] One would have expected greater numbers to come from the ranks of the unemployed, odd-job labourers, landless, and those with less than $1,200 yearly income in general. Those earning between $1,200 and $2,400 per year, while poor, are not amongst those in grave poverty and the first years of Felda settling can hardly raise their income. One should look into alternative ways of assisting them, while reserving the Felda development schemes for the really poor.

The second disturbing feature was the high incidence of settler children who had completed schooling but were unemployed: 17,087 or 44.4 per cent of the 38,584 settler children![53]

D. Land Tenure

As hard data are non-existent, it is necessary to resort to some educated speculation. It might be recalled that the average padi farm area is generally smaller than the rubber smallholding area and is fragmented.[54] One important determinant is the Muslim law of inheritance whereby a deceased parent would have his holding divided among his offspring. After several generations, several subdivisions might have occurred, reducing substantially the size of land owned, or cultivated, or both. However, important qualifications apply to the Malay rubber smallholders. First of all, a sizeable number of the rubber smallholdings are fairly new (though the smallholders are not necessarily new) under schemes set up by the Government in the post-war period. With greater Government effort in this direction since the NEP, this number and proportion must be increasing.[55] Since these holdings have such a recent past, most of them are likely to be still occupied by the original owners. This is assuming that the smallholders in these schemes, with slightly larger plots and newer seedlings, would be less poor and indebted and would be under less pressure to mortgage their land over the years.[56] Given the recent history, the proportion of grown and married sons from these holdings is probably small. Hence, presumably there has as yet been little subdivision or fragmentation of these plots.

Even for the Malay smallholdings not in the Government schemes, their history is still short relative to the padi land: two or three score years versus more than a couple of hundred years of settlement. Some subdivision or fragmentation could have taken place, but it does not appear as if more than three cycles (three generations) of division could have occurred. With less division and fragmentation, each household would have a relatively larger plot of land to cultivate; it would also mean fewer landless adults, both tending to reduce the need for land tenancy. Since rubber cultivation and production is a year-round endeavour, rather than one with seasonal peaks and troughs as in padi cultivation, it is attractive for the landowning farmers to hire long-term farm-hands (tappers, weeders) rather than lease out land like the padi landowners. The supply of land for tenancy may thus be reduced. There are some countervailing forces, however. The location of rubber smallholdings away from the traditional farming concentrations may reduce the political and social pressures of transferring land (sale, mortgage, or foreclosure) to someone outside the community, especially of another race. If this is true, it would naturally increase the marketability of the smallholding land.[57] This possibility, when realized, would increase landlessness, and the concentration of plots of land in the hands of landlords, many of whom may be absentee. However, the presence of Malay reserve areas would operate against this trend. In particular, if land were to change hands as a result of foreclosure or forced sale, the new owner might not be able to consolidate the land into one single homogeneous plot. It would then discourage the employment of hired labour and would increase the desirability of renting out the land. The relative importance of each factor and the consequential land tenancy situation is not known.

As for the non-Malay rubber smallholders, many of the factors affecting the Malay farmers would probably have applied to them.[58] Their recent origin since the turn of the century would not have allowed for the inheritance factor to rise to its full importance. In so far as they are also small, poor farmers, they should be equally in need of credit, tend to be in debt and thus face the problem of foreclosure and forced selling.[59] There are also few political and social obstacles to the sale or foreclosure of land of a non-Malay. The first factor would work against fragmentation and land tenancy while the latter factor would increase landlessness among the unfortunate and land concentration by the more fortunate. The latter tendency may be alleviated somewhat if the non-Malay smallholders have higher incomes and are thus better able to pay off at least part of the debt to avoid foreclosure. On the other hand, it is also more difficult for a non-Malay to obtain land under Malayan land law that has been in operation since colonial days. Therefore, apart from the luckier ones who were able to open up land which was subsequently converted to permanent titles or became *de facto* long-term 'temporary operating licences' or had sufficient savings to purchase a plot of subdivided land, there would be increasing pressure to subdivide as the family grew. Again, it is not possible to ascertain which factor prevailed.

We can now summarize the sparse and scattered evidence on the tenancy situation. For some Malay Reservations in the late fifties, Fisk (1961) reported very high incidence of landlessness (42 per cent of households owned no land), high incidence of absentee landlords with land aggregation (20–25 per cent of land belonged to absentee landlords), and consequently, very high percentage of share-cropper tenants (79.9 per cent of the farms were operated by tenant farmers).[60] A surprisingly high proportion of the land not operated by the owners was operated by the Chinese smallholders (63 per cent of the land!). Rent was rather steep with 64.3 per cent of the tenants reporting a fixed rent in kind of 7 *kati* of rubber per acre per month (equivalent to 118 lb. per acre per year, or more than 20 per cent of the yield of old seedlings plots), 14.3 per cent paid $85.20 per acre per year, and the rest were share-croppers paying 40–50 per cent of their crops as rent (equivalent to 12.5 *kati* per acre per month).[61] The high rent tenancy with absentee landlordism is undoubtedly an important reason for low income, and has been identified as such.[62] However, the presence of outside operators (in this case the Chinese tenants, one presumes) had also been identified as a reason for poverty. This is surprising, since the Chinese tenants would have to face the same adverse conditions themselves; perhaps they have been viewed as the culprits who auctioned away the land.

The above situation may not be, and probably is not, typical of the tenancy situation in Malaya, especially since it refers to a Malay Reservation. However, the presence of tenancy in Selangor cannot be denied. In his 1965 study, Voon reported the presence of tenancy arrangements in the Chinese rubber smallholder-dominated area of Semenyih.[63] In west Johor, especially around the district of Muar, about 23 per cent of the farmers reportedly leased out some of their land. The Muar farmers, with an average holding of 14.5 acres, leased out an average of 8.4 acres.[64] Details of rent and other tenancy arrangements were not known.

3.3 COCONUT SMALLHOLDERS

There are no accurate statistics on the number of coconut smallholders. Existing data on cropping area and size distribution conflict.[65] Only three published socio-economic surveys exist on the coconut smallholders in Malaysia. The first one by T. B. Wilson (1959) in west Johor seemed to have covered mainly the smaller holdings averaging 3.73 acres per household with little other farm land such as rubber holdings.[66] On the other hand, the second one by Selvadurai (1968) in 1964 seemed to have covered the larger farms while probably missing some of the smaller ones. From Table 3.7 the average holding for west Johor surveyed by Selvadurai was thirteen acres, almost four times that reported by Wilson, and about 16 per cent of these were mixed farms with fairly large holdings of rubber plots. This naturally makes one sceptical about the reliability of Selvadurai's estimate of 50,000 coconut farmers.[67] Considering the large number of small farms present in west Johor and the possible

TABLE 3.7

FARM AND INCOME CHARACTERISTICS OF COCONUT SMALLHOLDERS IN 1964–1965

Total Area (ac.)	*Area*	*Av. Farm Area (ac.)*	*Av. Coconut Area/ Farm (ac.)*	*% of Pure Coconut Farm*	*% of Mixed Farm*	*% of Farmers Having Coconut Income as*			*Av. Size of House-hold*	*Av. No. of Earners*	*% with Own Land*
						Sole Income	*Major Income*	*Subsid-iary Income*			
86,000	Johor	13	9.5	60	16	25	20	55	7.2	1.6	86
67,500	Batu Pahat	12	8.6	68	12	30	24	46	7.3	1.6	83
18,900	Pontian	16	11.1	50	22	15	12	73	6.8	1.7	91
38,200	Kelantan	5	2.7	24	27	2	6	92	4.9	2.3	84
96,100	Selangor/Perak	13	11.6	87	5	47	36	17	7.4	1.6	87
20,400	Kuala Selangor	9	8.7	90	6	51	36	13	6.2	1.5	91
31,700	Sabak Bernam	8	5.8	69	4	31	41	28	8.1	1.6	85
44,000	Lower Perak	21	20.6	93	5	61	29	10	7.5	1.6	87

(Continued)

TABLE 3.7 (Continued)

Total Area (ac.)	*Area*	*Income from Coconut*	*Income from Rubber*	*Income from Padi*	*Total Farm Income*	*Income from Outside Farm*		*Total Income*	*% Reporting*	
						Agri-culture	*Non-agri-culture*		*Outside Agri-cultural Income*	*Outside Non-agri-cultural Income*
86,400	Johor	$ 389	$ 147	$ 1	$ 561	$ 303	$ 490	$ 1,354	55	39
67,500	Batu Pahat	444	102	2	598	322	687	1,607	56	—
18,900	Pontian	270	223	—	505	276	171	952	54	—
38,200	Kelantan	165	21	168	359	293	163	815	70	45
96,100	Selangor/Perak	1,034	8	167	1,210	488	253	1,951	73	33
20,400	Kuala Selangor	720	—	62	782	724	400	1,906	70	—
31,700	Sabak Bernam	783	—	357	1,140	352	185	1,677	91	—
44,000	Lower Perak	1,594	19	40	1,656	437	207	2,300	56	—

Source. Selvadurai, 'A Preliminary Report on the Survey of Coconut Smallholdings in West Malaysia', Tables 22, 23, 26, 28, 50, 52, and 54.

under-sampling of the small farms throughout Malaya,[68] perhaps it is not unreasonable to estimate that there may be more than 70,000 coconut smallholders throughout the peninsula.

In Selangor/Perak, the great majority of the coconut farmers (about 87 per cent) are purely coconut farmers and only 5 per cent are mixed farmers with padi as the other crop planted. This is also reflected in the composition of their total income: only 17 per cent reported coconut farm income as their subsidiary source of income. This is in marked contrast with the coconut smallholders of Kelantan and of Pontian in Johor. The Kelantanese have the smallest average total holding and coconut holding (5.0 and 2.7 acres respectively). Not surprisingly, 92 per cent reported coconut income as their subsidiary source of income, with 27 per cent reporting mixed farms mainly consisting of padi land. (See Table 3.7.)

Therefore, there was an interesting range of income amongst the coconut smallholders in the three different regions. Not surprisingly, the Selangor/Perak smallholders with the largest average farm and coconut holdings also made the highest average coconut and farm incomes of $1,034 and $1,210 respectively. However, this did not result in less participation in off-farm work, perhaps due to the presence of off-farm work opportunities on the one hand, and the larger than average household on the other.[69] They ended up having $741 in off-farm income which is only slightly less than the $900+ made by the Johor smallholders.

By contrast, the size of household of the Kelantanese was only 4.9. This, coupled with the lack of other work opportunities in that general area, meant that their off-farm income was only $456. As their farm incomes were already the lowest by comparison with the rest (since they farm small lots), it is not surprising that the average total income of Kelantan coconut smallholders was only $815, in contrast to the $1,951 for those in Selangor/Perak, or the $1,354 for those in west Johor.

However, as pointed out earlier, Selvadurai may have under-sampled the smaller farms and therefore the average figures given above probably do not accurately reflect the income of the smaller cultivators. In fact, a closer look at the figures would show that even for the Selangor/Perak and Johor smallholders, 49 and 51 per cent respectively have between 3 and 9.9 acres of farm land, giving them a holding smaller than the area average, and, by implication, an income also lower than the area average. Therefore, the average earnings of the Kelantanese coconut smallholders may be more representative of the true earnings of the coconut smallholders in the country.

3.4 CONCLUSION

The paucity of data and the greater complexity of inter-relationships amongst socio-economic factors in determining the income and its distribution among rubber smallholders prevented a fuller exploration of these factors and actual income distribution. Nevertheless, some of the determinants of poverty in rubber smallholdings were discussed. In cases where data were inadequate, the problems involved in attempting an analysis have been outlined.

The income of the smallholders is dependent on the size of the holding, the density, age, and seedling of the trees, the number of replanting phases and the price of rubber at the time of tapping, as well as the cost of production. At first glance, a small holding, old trees, oil seedlings, and low prices all work against a reasonable income to the smallholders in a direct and straightforward manner. In reality, these feed into one another to form a vicious cycle. Low prices and small holdings both mean that replanting with higher-yielding clones is all the more imperative; and yet, the low income arising means that the smallholder would be handicapped by the lack of accumulated capital to replant.[70] The long waiting time following replanting dictates that replanting should best be done in stages to avoid excessive loss in income. Each phase of replanting allows for the introduction of newer, higher-yielding clones. However, once planting is done, the yield pattern of the plot for the next twenty to thirty years is largely determined. Therefore, the average yield per smallholding varies from year to year, all things being equal, which means that the yield, and hence income, of all the smallholders in the country also vary from year to year in a non-trivial manner. Such variations critically affect the choice of year and sample to arrive at a proper income survey. The variations in yield pattern naturally also influence the unit cost from year to year. The price of rubber acts as a short-run yield stimulant as well. In times of low prices, intensive tapping can be practised to raise artificially short-run yield and income at the expense of longer-run yield and income.

This summary brings out another important factor not dealt with in the text: the role of replanting, research cess, and export duty. Collecting replanting cess and then providing replanting grants when there is actual replanting is tantamount to imposing a savings, if the replanting grant received equates the life-time pay-out in replanting cess per acre of land.[71] If the smallholders do not replant, or replant only part of their holdings, or if the grant received is less than the life-time pay-out, the cess becomes in effect a regressive tax whereby those least able to save or to be taxed are made to subsidize those who are in a relatively better position to do so. Once the burden of the research cess, export duty and the export surcharge (which was at one time levied) are added, the tax burden on the smallholders becomes very severe, amounting to at least 13 per cent of their output value or 30 per cent of their current income on the average and in excess of 55 per cent on the margin at current prices.[72] The research cess has an added element of inequality in that the smallholders pay the same amount of absolute rate as the estates (but a proportionately higher percentage of received price), only to receive smaller benefits, partly due to the emphasis of RRI research, and partly due to the difficulties of disseminating research results to the smallholders.

These are not the only tax burdens facing the rubber smallholders. In so far as they have to purchase their food and consumer goods, whenever there is any protective tariff for domestic production of consumer goods or padi farm-gate price support, they have to provide the effective subsidies to these other sectors. The case of the burden on the rubber smallholders and other non-padi producing poor, in both the urban and rural areas, has been well documented by Goldman (1975).[73] It is just that the burden on the rubber smallholders may be doubly severe because of the twin squeeze by this subsidy and the other taxes described earlier. They have been subjected to these squeezes for a long time, and will probably continue to be subject for a long time to come.

Of course, with the higher level of rubber prices that have been sustained since 1976, the income of all the rubber smallholders should have been raised, but the increase would amount to no more than 30 per cent of the price increase.[74] The provision of larger plots of land under Felda schemes should also help to raise the income of those fortunate enough to be included in the scheme. This does happen; generally the income of the settlers on rubber plots is pushed to a range between $2,400 and $4,800. Unfortunately, as has been pointed out earlier, the bulk of the settlers do not come from the poorest households, and loan repayments hold down their income in the first decade and a half of settlement. Moreover, relatively few of the really poor rubber smallholders appear to have benefited under this programme: only 9,505 or 27.2 per cent of the settlers were former rubber tappers which presumably includes some rubber smallholders.[75] This of course is another element in the contrast that has been drawn between the treatment received by the padi planters *vis-à-vis* that received by the rubber smallholders.

Over the years, RRI researchers have discussed the advantages of, and experimented with, the setting up of Group Processing Centres to promote the production of Ribbed Smoked Sheet rubber to the advantage of the smallholders.[76] This has gone on for a few years now, and its impact needs more investigation. The profitability of intercropping has also been promoted by RRI researchers.[77] What has been the progress out in the field? There are other important questions relating to the production of smallholder rubber: the extent and the factors influencing the use of fertilizers, insecticides, weeders, stimulants, the availability of off-farm work versus the adequacy of on-farm work, the land tenancy pattern and so on, which this book is unable to cover.

As for the coconut smallholders, they appear to be in even greater difficulties than the rubber smallholders. However, probably because of their smaller numbers and lack of political influence, few studies are available on them and little effort seems to have been devoted to alleviating their difficulties.

In neither this nor the last chapter has any mention been made of the livelihood of a very large group of Malaysians: the landless agricultural labourers. There is no precise estimate of their numbers, but 175,000 is probably a good estimate.[78] It is also probable that there are as many non-Malays as there are Malays in this category. Most of the non-Malays living in the New Villages or estate quarters are generally working in the estates or larger rubber smallholdings or in vegetable and fruit gardens, while the Malays in this category may be divided between the padi-farming villagers and the rubber smallholding villagers. From the discussions in Chapters 2 and 3, it seems unlikely that these labourers would have a level of income exceeding $1,500 per year.

In addition, there are a fair number of pineapple, tapioca, and vegetable cultivators scattered in various parts of the Malayan peninsula and of which the non-Malays form an important proportion. Scattered information on them is also available to show that their income levels are also modest. However, in-depth study of them must await a more energetic researcher.

1. For a discussion on the accuracy of the various estimates of the number of smallholders, see Tan Tat-wai, 'Employment and Labour Utilisation in West Malaysia'.

2. Richard H. Goldman, 'Staple Food Self-Sufficiency and the Distributive Impact of Malaysian Rice Policy'.

3. The following quotations can provide some insight into the Colonial Government's intention and policies in encouraging plantation rubber on the one hand, and discouraging smallholding rubber on the other:

'. . . The rapid expansion of rubber planting after 1900 is related closely to an intensification of Government encouragement. Special land regulations were introduced in the Federated Malay States to encourage rubber planting as early as 1897. . . . Moreover, under the existing land regulations, virgin land could be acquired at attractive terms, indeed, one of their basic purposes was to promote the opening of estates.' See James Jackson, *Planters and Speculators: Chinese and European Agricultural Enterprise in Malaya 1786–1921*, Kuala Lumpur, University of Malaya Press, 1968, p. 235.

By contrast, '. . . the Resident did not regard rubber as a "suitable undertaking for desultory workers", and considered that the Malays were attracted primarily by the windfall profits to be made from selling land to rubber companies'. See J. H. Drabble, *Rubber in Malaya 1876–1922: The Genesis of the Industry*, Kuala Lumpur, Oxford University Press, 1973, p. 73.

The land rates imposed by the Colonial Government were also unfair: '. . . The rates for areas not exceeding 10 acres remained unchanged so that in the years immediately following alienation, First class land of this type, rental of $1.20 to $3.20 per acre in the west-coast Malay States was more heavily taxed than the same class in the category over 10 acres.' Drabble, op. cit., p. 37. The effective land rent over a fifteen-year period that a planter and a peasant had to pay was $21.5 and $37.5 respectively in Kuala Selangor in 1915. ibid., footnote 13 of Chapter III, p. 123.

So was the granting of loans:

'. . . This [the granting of loans] became a feature of Government agricultural policy in the Federated Malay States when the High Commissioner gave his approval to a special "loans to Planters" scheme in July 1904. . . . Sizeable loans were taken up by both individual Planters and companies in each of the three western Malay States. The vast majority of these went to Europeans; amongst the few exceptions are loans made to Japanese planters in Negeri Sembilan and to Chinese in Perak.' James Jackson, op. cit., p. 237.

Drabble also reported that estates got at least £30 per acre with a total loan allotment of £1.5 million while the smallholders (mainly the Malay ones) got a total of $100,000 with a $500 ceiling on single loans, forcing them to turn to high-cost Chettiar money-lender loans. Drabble, op. cit., p. 64.

4. It is important to point out that even during the depression of 1913–14, the interest of the smaller planters in taking up rubber planting remained unabated, at least among the Chinese if not the Malays as well:

'. . . In contrast, in many parts of Western Malaya, the Chinese continued to acquire and to plant new land, and in Kedah in 1913 the Chinese Towkays had in no way "lost their confidence in the future of plantation rubber, and Chinese planters, of the market-gardener class, who own and cultivate their separate smallholdings of 10 or 15 acres, [were] clearing and planting with undiminished vigour".' Jackson, op. cit., p. 254; see also Drabble, op. cit., p. 69.

The equal enthusiasm of the Malay smallholders can be seen from the continued and rapid increase in their acreages. See Lim Teck Ghee, 'Peasant Agriculture in Colonial Malaya: Its Development in Perak, Selangor, Negeri Sembilan and Pahang 1874–1941', pp. 186—7.

5. Lim, op. cit., organized the various facts into a forceful argument about the discriminatory policies by the Colonial Government against the smallholders. See ibid., pp. 89—94, 110—17, 259; see also Jackson, op. cit., Chapters 10 and 11, and Drabble, op. cit., *passim*. While some readers may be uncomfortable with the argument that the British merchants, planters, and Colonial administration conspired to prevent the small farmers from participating in rubber planting and to preserve the field for themselves, there can be no doubt that the end result of their various actions, co-ordinated or otherwise, achieved the result of placing smallholder rubber planting at a great disadvantage. In fact, this point has gained acceptance even among latter-day Western writers such as Bauer, Benham, and Silcock. See Lim, op. cit., p. 231, footnote 50.

6. At that time, the economy of scale and commercial organization of the estates may not have been overwhelmingly superior. Lim showed that the yield of at least some of the smallholders was at a very high level, one comparable with that of the estates, though their yield figures were under-reported by the officials (see ibid., pp. 173—80). This need not be the case after years of innovative changes mainly benefiting the estates.

7. It is not possible to document fully this point. It can only be argued that if biases can be introduced in some aspects (for example the differential land tax and loan provision documented in note 5), it is not very far-fetched to make this postulation, especially in view of official pronouncements such as the one by the then Resident of Selangor, Belfield: 'Meanwhile . . . I am attempting to concentrate native gardeners in specified areas, and to discourage the occupation by them of land which may be usefully reserved for scientific planting.' Jackson, op. cit., pp. 236—7; see also Lim, op. cit., pp. 147 and 157; Drabble, op. cit., pp. 26—7. Of course, this quotation is meant only to provide a glimpse into another discriminatory aspect of Colonial policies.

8. For example: 'One of the complaints made by the Association [United Planters' Association] was that the alienation to Asian smallholders of land with a road frontage seriously retarded European enterprise, as such grants "locked up" considerable areas behind them. The request was made that Asian holdings should be confined to distinct blocks, two to three miles apart. The High Commissioner's reply was that whilst existing alienations could not be disturbed, the wishes of the planters would in future be acceded to as far as possible.' Drabble, op. cit., quoting from the Annual Report of the Federated Malay States, 1904. See Drabble, op. cit., pp. 72—6 for the application of this policy.

In many cases, at the time of the first rubber boom, European planters bought up existing Malay smallholdings in order to acquire road frontage for their estates, '. . . At the same time, the growing bias in favour of European planters is revealed by the action taken by the Selangor Government to "abate this nuisance"' [i.e., the need to buy up the smallholdings for road frontage]. Wherever possible, roadside smallholdings that could be classified as 'abandoned' were resumed by the Government. Moreover, in 1905, Belfield issued an order to all District Officers to the effect that no land abutting on a Government road was 'to be alienated to a native without the previous sanction of the Resident'. Jackson, op. cit., p. 236; see also Drabble, op. cit., pp. 26—7, and Lim, op. cit., pp. 147 and 157.

9. The first depression occurred in 1907–8, a bigger one was in 1913–14, but that of 1918–21 was the most severe. See Figure 36, Jackson, op. cit.

10. The first organization was started in 1907. See Drabble, op. cit., pp. 52—7.

11. See Jackson, op. cit., pp. 260—3, Drabble, op. cit., pp. 142, 145, and 148—9. However, the best account of the total disregard for the interest of

the smallholders has been presented by Lim, op. cit., pp. 167—71. He has documented the total lack of consideration for the smallholders' interests by the Rubber Growers' Association as well as by Colonial officials to the extent of distorting smallholders' aspirations and positions. He also reported the strong spontaneous opposition by the smallholders to the strangulation of their interests (p. 172), and the various subtle ways in which the smallholders had been further squeezed under the Stevenson restriction scheme (pp. 173—80). These methods included under-assessment of smallholding yield, area under smallholdings (which were used to assess quota allocation), and further reduction of the smallholders' share in the quota by using the presence of fruit crops all over the smallholdings as an excuse.

12. Indeed, Lim argued that the heavy capitalization structure of the plantations, the greedy and short-sighted dividend policy, and the lack of supplementary income alternatives caused the plantations to be non-competitive in a very low price context (pp. 167—8). Smallholders did not indulge in any of these practices.

13. See for example: P. T. Bauer, 'Malayan Rubber Policy', *Pacific Studies Quarterly*, March 1957; J. M. F. Greenwood, 'Rubber Smallholdings in the Federation of Malaya', *Journal of Tropical Geography*, 18, 1964, pp. 81—100; Lim Chong Yah, 'The Malayan Rubber Replanting Taxes', *Malayan Economic Review*, 6, October 1961, pp. 43—52; Malayan Rubber Fund Board, *Annual Report*, various years.

14. Lim claimed that earlier research was not geared towards the need of the smallholders (p. 89), and the Department of Agriculture in the earlier periods was not concerned about the smallholders (p. 141). No doubt these contributed towards the inability of the smallholders to benefit from innovations in the earlier period. However, the research direction of the Rubber Research Institute in the sixties and seventies has to be carefully researched to assess its bias. A cursory look at a list of their research papers would seem to indicate that the emphasis on smallholders may still be inadequate, though it began to pick up towards the late sixties.

15. Section 7.2.B(b). See also Lim Chong Yah, op. cit., and also 'Export Taxes on Rubber in Malaya. A Survey of Post-war Development', *Malayan Economic Review*, 5, October 1960, pp. 46—58. In fact, Edwards constructed a hypothetical example to show the burden of taxes on smallholders of different income characteristics and found that the poorer ones pay a higher proportion of their income in taxes (C. T. Edwards, *Public Finance in Malaysia and Singapore*, Canberra, Australian National University Press, 1970, Table 50, p. 369).

16. Unfortunately such a study is lacking. The studies by Lim Teck Ghee, Jackson, and Drabble cited earlier have all covered important aspects of the development of the rubber industry, but there is still the need for one integrating the development of smallholdings, estates, remilling, and distribution system.

17. See Section 2.2.

18. See Table 3.3.

19. Unfortunately, it is not possible to assess the real income of the mixed-farm operators, not to mention constructing an income distribution profile. This is because inadequate information exists on the crop cultivating pattern of the mixed farms. However, we know that the number of mixed farms is quite high, judging from the data provided by the *Census of Agriculture 1960*, Kuala Lumpur, Department of Statistics.

20. Voon Phin Keong, 'Chinese Rubber Smallholding Industry in Selangor', M.A. dissertation, University of Malaya, 1967, p. 66; P. T. Bauer, *Report on a Visit to Rubber Growing Smallholdings of Malaya*, London, H.M.S.O.,

1948, p. 9; Robert Ho, 'Labour Inputs of Rubber Producing Smallholders in Malaya', *Malayan Economic Review*, 12, April 1967.

21. S. Selvadurai, *Socio-Economic Survey of Rubber Smallholdings in West Johore*, Kuala Lumpur, Ministry of Agriculture, 1972, Tables on pp. 14 and 29 seem to imply that it is the larger farmers (those with over 30 acres) who tend to have other crop land.

22. Although as pointed out in Chapter 2, the method of estimation is shaky, the overall pattern can be used because the distortions probably occur in the same direction.

23. S. Selvadurai, op. cit., pp. 14 and 23.

24. Lim Sow Ching, *A Study of the Marketing of Smallholders' Rubber at the First Trade Level in Selangor*, Kuala Lumpur, Rubber Research Institute, Economics Research Division, Report No. 4, 1968, Tables D and E. Only 20—30 per cent of the price increase goes to the dealers. As for the remaining 70—80 per cent, the smallholders have to share with the Government. At the lower ranges of prices, the smallholders retain the bulk of it as the export duties are charged on a lower marginal rate of about 20 per cent. However, once the prices go beyond $2.00 per kilo, the marginal tax rate rises to about 60 per cent which means that the Government takes the lion's share. This is the case at current (1978) prices. However, at the time of the research, the price level was lower and hence the Government's share was at the lower end.

25. See for example, C. R. Wharton, 'Malayan Rubber Supply Condition: Some Policy Implications', in T. H. Silcock and E. K. Fisk, eds., *Political Economy of Independent Malaya*, Canberra, Australian National University, 1963, pp. 131—62; Francis Chan Kwong Wah, 'A Preliminary Study of the Supply Response of Malayan Estates between 1948 and 1959', *Malayan Economic Review*, 7, October 1962, pp. 77—94.

26. If one were to plot the price of rubber against the GDP of Malaysia, there is an almost straight line relationship between the two. While the importance of rubber to Malaysia has fallen relative to other major exports, it is still the most important sector, not counting its indirect impact on the economy.

27. The *Census of Agriculture* is not adequate in providing accurate and comprehensive farm data. In particular, it has substantially understated the number of small farms. For an excellent discussion of the Census, see Lee Kok Huat, 'The 1960 Agriculture Census', *Kajian Ekonomi Malaysia*, December 1967.

28. Tables 3.3, 3.5, and 3.6; Voon, op. cit., Table 5, p. 54, reported that there were 35.8 per cent Malay, 52.3 per cent Chinese and 11.9 per cent other races out of 105,347 smallholders with less than 25 acres each in 1952.

29. Ungku Aziz, *Subdivision of Estates in Malaya 1951–1960*, 3 volumes, Kuala Lumpur, 1963.

30. Table 3.5, column 3; Voon reported that the number of Chinese smallholders increased from 1910 to 1965 because of subdivision (Voon, op. cit.).

31. Of course the old small Malay holdings remain very small.

32. *Third Malaysia Plan 1976–1980*, Table 9-8, footnote 13. See also Felda, *Felda Settler Census 1976: Survey on Household and Socio-economic Conditions of Felda Settlers*, Kuala Lumpur, Institute Pembangunan Tanah dan Jabatan Memperoses Data, 1978.

33. This refers to the land laws governing most of the newly alienated areas prohibiting the transfer of Malay land to non-Malays, and in some cases to other Malays. For a description of the operation of land laws historically, see D. Wong, *Tenure and Land Dealings in the Malay States*, Singapore, University of Singapore Press, 1975.

34. See Lim Sow Ching, *Land Development Schemes in Peninsular Malaysia*, Kuala Lumpur, Rubber Research Institute, 1976, Chapter 9, for a discussion of the composition, income, and farm characteristics of some new land settlers in the late sixties to early seventies period. Some of these will be discussed in later pages.

35. Tables 3.2 and 3.5.

36. Voon, op. cit., Table 5, p. 54.

37. ibid., Table 9, p. 62.

38. ibid., p. 63.

39. Twenty-nine per cent of the Selangor smallholders Voon studied were foreclosed in 1965. ibid., Table 6, p. 56, and footnote on p. 55. See also Paul Kratoska, *The Chettiar and the Yeoman: British Cultural Categories and Rural Indebtedness in Malaya*, Singapore, University of Singapore, Institute of Southeast Asian Studies, Occasional Paper No. 32, 1975.

40. Again, there is a bias here because of the presence of a number of farms with greater than 25 acres holding. See earlier pages and Lim Teck Ghee, op. cit., p. 229, footnote 45.

41. Table 3.3.

42. See figures from the *Census of Agriculture 1960* also.

43. Lim Sow Ching, *Land Development* . . . , Table 9.15, reported that the Felda settlers received an average income of $88.9 per month or $1,070 per year before joining the scheme. See Table 9.2(a), p. 212 for the figures on income after joining Felda.

44. Lim Sow Ching, *Land Development* . . . , Table 2(b) and (c), pp. 213—14.

45. ibid., Table 2(a).

46. ibid.

47. *Felda Settler Census*, Table 6.5, p. 400.

48. ibid., Table 6.5.9 and Table 6.5.10, pp. 416—17.

49. ibid., Table 6.6, p. 418.

50. Bank Negara Malaysia, *Quarterly Economic Bulletin*, September 1978, Appendix Tables.

51. *Felda Settler Census*, Table 5.1, p. 269.

52. ibid.

53. ibid., Table 8.4, p. 513.

54. It is necessary to distinguish between the effects of subdivision and that of fragmentation. There has been a lot of confusion over these. See Lim *et al.*, op. cit., for a very good discussion of the difference, although their discussion relates specifically to padi farmers.

55. See figures cited earlier for the significant increase in the number and areas of the Felda settlers. With their numbers increasing while that of other rubber smallholders stagnated, the proportion in Felda schemes has to increase.

56. However, as we have documented in note 45, the loan repayment to the Government can be quite steep. This has been the focus of many criticisms directed at the Government's running of Felda schemes.

57. See for example, E. K. Fisk, 'Productivity and Income from Rubber in an Established Malay Reservation', *Malayan Economic Review*, 6, April 1961; and Kratoska, op. cit.

58. The Chinese are also in the habit of subdividing their land and giving it to their offspring. This can be seen from fragmentation of land among peasants in China pre-1949 which enabled the concentration of land.

59. See Voon, op. cit., and Kratoska, op. cit.

60. This occurred in Kampong Genting Malik, Selangor (Fisk, op. cit., p. 16, p. 17 and Tables 1 and 2).

61. ibid., pp. 18—19.

62. ibid., conclusion.

63. Voon, op. cit., pp. 66 and 68.

64. S. Selvadurai, *Socio-Economic Survey of Rubber Smallholdings in West Johore*, Kuala Lumpur, Ministry of Agriculture and Fisheries, 1972.

65. S. Selvadurai, *A Preliminary Report on the Survey of Coconut Smallholdings in West Malaysia*, Kuala Lumpur, Ministry of Agriculture and Fisheries, 1968, p. 15. Compare his findings with those of T. B. Wilson, 'The West Johore Coconut Production Survey', Kuala Lumpur, Department of Agriculture, Ministry of Agriculture and Fisheries, 1958.

66. ibid., Tables 11, 14, and 15. In fact, 79 per cent of the 39,961 farms consisted of less than 5 acres.

67. ibid., Table 4.

68. Compare the figures with those reported by *The Census of Agriculture 1960*, Kuala Lumpur, 1962, Table 562. On the possible underestimation of small farms by this census, see Lee Kok Huat, 'The 1960 Agriculture Census', *Kajian Ekonomi Malaysia*, December 1967.

69. It is hardly surprising that areas like Kelantan and Pontian in Johor should have less off-farm opportunity when compared with an area like Kuala Selangor. Kelantan is a state that is generally less developed than Selangor, with few industries and mines as well as fewer plantations. In the case of Pontian, it has been mainly a pineapple and coconut growing area, again giving rise to few other economic opportunities.

70. Voon, op. cit., pp. 83—90.

71. Life-time taxation works out at $562.5 per acre using 4.5¢ per lb. of replanting cess, a yield of 500 lb. per acre, and a production life of 25 years. This is of course a very conservative estimate. For a yield of 1,000 lb., cess collected becomes $1,125 over the production life. The replanting 'grant' was originally $500, which was raised to $750, then to $900 and finally to $1,200 for those holding less than 10 acres in 1978. The calculation here is not a cost-benefit analysis, otherwise the stream of increasing income following replanting has to be imputed to the benefits accruing to the smallholders.

72. The calculation is based on a combined replanting cess and a research cess of 5.5¢ per lb., a yield of 1,000 lb. per acre, an average of 6.5 acres per farm, and an export duty based on the current price level of about $2.00 per kilo.

73. See Goldman, op. cit.

74. This is discussed in note 24 of this chapter, as well as in Chapter 7.

75. *Felda Settler Census*, Table 5.1, p. 269.

76. Yeoh Choon Hoe, Ghazali Noor, and G. Iyer, *A Report on the Survey of Group Processing Centres*, Kuala Lumpur, Rubber Research Institute, 1974.

77. Lim Sow Ching, *An Agro-Economic Study of Intercrops on Rubber Smallholdings*, Kuala Lumpur, Rubber Research Institute, 1969.

78. Department of Statistics, *Socio-Economic Sample Survey of Households 1967–68*.

4 Income of the Salaried and Urban Workers and the Rise of the Malaysian Middle Class

4.1 INTRODUCTION

THE factors affecting the income of farmers can be easily quantified and analysed. But the same is not true for wage and salaried employees. *A priori*, there would be no difference in income among people with the same level of schooling and training. However, in reality, how well a person learns in school and on the job would ultimately differentiate his income from that of his peers. Unfortunately, these are not factors that can be easily quantified and analysed.

The income of the worker depends on his skills which embody learning, both in school and on the job, apart from market supply and demand conditions. With the exception of the professionals, managers, and technicians, most occupations require very little formal training or educational attainment but the latter is usually necessary as a passport to the job (see Chapter 1). As such, it is fairly easy for another person to be trained into a position recently vacated. Moreover, population growth and rural-urban migration give rise to a high rate of unemployment which means a ready pool of labourers for such jobs. Consequently, it is possible to characterize the supply of labour for most of the job categories as generally fairly elastic (i.e., an almost horizontal labour supply curve). Labour demand, on the other hand, is less elastic due to the structure of the economy.[1] Therefore, one can expect little change in the general wage rate, a few pockets of critical skilled jobs notwithstanding. If any change is to occur, it is more likely to be affected by a change in the demand condition in the present-day Malaysian economy.[2]

The demand conditions are determined by the structure of the economy, the market, and the production function of each industry. How these structures influence the income of the wage workers and farmers is discussed elsewhere in this book (Chapter 1 and Part II), suffice it to mention here that the structure of the economy is likely to change very slowly over time, even with active Government policies to influence the choice of technology and alter the structure of the market. As a result, short-run wages and salaries are less likely to be affected by such minor structural changes, the market force of demand and supply will determine the approximate wage and salaries level, the range of which will change gradually over the years.

Once a person leaves school and enters the labour force, his formal education ends and his chances of re-entering school and moving up to a higher level of education (and hence earnings) are quite small, given the present market economy and its education system. Therefore, his income level is largely determined by his point of entry into the labour force, in particular the category of job. After this, his income level is raised by small increments over the years (both Government and private sectors have some built-in formal and informal wage increment, with or without union negotiations), presumably reflecting changing market conditions.

Although we have pointed to general wage stability in the context of the development of a generally labour surplus economy, it is also important to recognize that at a later stage of development, there can be general upward pressure on wages as a result of rising wages in specific sectors. Such pressures can be the result of bottlenecks in dynamic sectors which require skills not easily forthcoming. They can also be the result of unionization and wage demands. As the number of wage earners in the manufacturing sector increases, the degree of unionization with wage demands is likely to increase.[3] The net result is that wages amongst these workers would rise initially followed by a more general wage increase. In times of inflation, such pressures are likely to mount as well. On the other hand, for surplus labour not fortunate enough to be employed, employment opportunities are likely to be as elusive as ever. In short, we can have rising wages in spite of a labour surplus. However, rising wages can seldom improve the livelihood of the employed workers *vis-à-vis* those in the upper-income brackets whose incomes are likely to rise at least proportionately. The experience of Malaysia seems to fit this general characterization with overall wage-price stability in the fifties and sixties but rising prices and wages with more unionization in the seventies.

With this brief expose on the determination of wages and salaries as a background, the rest of this chapter will paint the income ranges and trends of the wage and salaried workers. Section 4.2 covers the description and analysis of the broad range of income of wage earners by skill categories and sectors. Apart from urban wage and salaried employees, the estate workers who are located in the rural areas have also been included because the determination of their wage level and organization of their employment is rather similar to that of the urban wage workers. In Section 4.3, the income of the petty traders is documented. This category includes the hawkers, caterers, and small retailers who are not wage earners, but have been included because they are located principally in the urban areas with a low level of income comparable with that of urban wage workers. Section 4.4 discusses the rise of the middle-, upper middle-, and upper-income groups. These are mainly the professionals and executives but include some technicians and clerks who have attained a level of income exceeded only by the wealth holders. This group also has more upward mobility than most of the other categories of workers. Each change in job can command a significant increment in salary for those who are capable. More importantly, they are the main beneficiaries of post-Independence economic development. By contrast, the lower-income brackets have not fared so well despite the rural development programmes and the push of industrialization.

4.2 INCOME OF THE WAGE AND SALARIED EMPLOYEES

A. Manufacturing

Table 4.1 classifies the manufacturing workers under different income brackets by seven categories of skill. In the late sixties and early seventies the income distribution of the 137,925 employees in this sector had the following characteristics:

(1) 14.5 per cent of these workers received less than $1,000 per year, 48.9 per cent received between $1,000 and $1,999, and a further 24.7 per cent received between $2,000 and $2,999,

(2) Almost all unskilled workers (96.5 per cent), 65.2 per cent of skilled workers and 64.4 per cent of general workers received less than $2,000 per year,

(3) Only the managers, professionals, and 36.4 per cent of the technician-supervisors received more than $5,000 per year.

Two qualifications are, however, necessary.

Firstly, at the upper end of the skill level, it is not clear if the reported income adequately covered dividends from stock holdings, the size of which would be very substantial for the owner-managers of large firms. Here we assume that the managers received only salaried income, bearing in mind that this would be a gross underestimation of the income of some of them.

Secondly, the distribution tabulated in Table 4.1 is biased upward because employees in many small enterprises with less than five employees and the craftsmen and artisans servicing small urban areas have not been included. It is not possible to estimate the distribution of income among these manufacturing employees but it is possible to assess the size of their probable earnings. The earnings of the employees in the smaller enterprises included in the pan-sector distribution of Table 4.1 (such as manufacturers of pickles and sauces, coffee and spices, ice, iron products, vegetable and animal oils) were much lower than the sectoral average: managers and professionals earned between $2,350 and $5,000 per year; technicians and supervisors between $2,000 and $3,000; clerks between $1,500 and $2,500; skilled workers between $1,000 and $2,000; unskilled workers from less than $1,000 to $1,500.[4] Therefore, it is not likely that the earnings of the employees of the very small manufacturing establishments and craftsmen excluded in the survey would greatly exceed the above ranges. There are no accurate data on the numbers of such manufacturing workers. However, estimates based on the data of the number of manufacturing workers given by the 1967/8 Socio-Economic Sample Survey of Households in Malaysia (67/8 SSSH) and that of 1968 Census of Manufacturing Industries indicate that there may be about 90,000 of them.[5]

B. Mining and Construction

As for the mining and construction sectors, Tables 4.2 and 4.3 summarize their employees' income distribution data. Again, the picture that emerged is that a near majority or majority (45.0 per cent and 50.45 per cent for the mining and construction sectors respectively) of these workers earned less than

TABLE 4.1

WEST MALAYSIAN MANUFACTURING EMPLOYMENT BY INCOME CLASS, 1970

Annual Income Range in M$	Total Employed		Managerial and Professional		Technical and Supervisory		Clerical	
	No.	%	No.	%	No.	%	No.	%
500— 999	19,993	14.50	—	—	—	—	—	—
1,000—1,499	38,761	28.10	—	—	—	—	34	0.35
1,500—1,999	28,682	20.80	—	—	—	—	556	5.65
2,000—2,499	22,510	16.32	42	1.27	31	0.59	2,442	24.82
2,500—2,999	11,606	8.41	—	—	12	0.23	763	7.76
3,000—3,999	7,528	5.46	23	0.70	1,467	27.68	4,683	47.60
4,000—4,999	3,674	2.67	41	1.24	1,860	35.10	1,361	13.83
5,000—5,999	1,877	1.36	444	13.45	1,433	27.04	—	—
6,000—6,999	641	0.47	190	5.75	451	8.51	—	—
7,000—7,999	343	0.25	343	10.39	—	—	—	—
8,000—8,999	162	0.12	117	3.54	45	0.85	—	—
9,000—9,999	554	0.40	554	16.78	—	—	—	—
10,000—14,999	544	0.39	544	16.48	—	—	—	—
15,000+	1,003	0.71	1,003	32.38	—	—	—	—
Not available	47	0.03	—	—	—	—	—	—
Total	137,925	100.00	3,301	2.39	5,299	3.84	9,839	7.13
Total manufacturing employment 1970	143,838		3,791		6,026		10,689	

(Continued)

TABLE 4.1 (Continued)

Annual Income Range in M$	*General*		*Skilled*		*Unskilled*		*Employed through Contractors*	
	No.	*%*	*No.*	*%*	*No.*	*%*	*No.*	*%*
500— 999	—	—	2,359	5.02	17,022	37.42	612	3.53
1,000—1,499	744	7.66	13,585	28.93	21,905	48.15	2,493	14.39
1,500—1,999	5,509	56.75	14,687	31.28	4,992	10.97	2,938	16.95
2,000—2,499	2,517	25.93	13,899	29.60	1,383	3.04	2,196	12.67
2,500—2,999	891	9.18	1,179	2.51	191	0.42	8,570	49.45
3,000—3,999	—	—	1,147	2.44	—	—	208	1.18
4,000—4,999	—	—	99	0.21	—	—	313	1.81
5,000—5,999	—	—	—	—	—	—	—	—
6,000—6,999	—	—	—	—	—	—	—	—
7,000—7,999	—	—	—	—	—	—	—	—
8,000—8,999	—	—	—	—	—	—	—	—
9,000—9,999	—	—	—	—	—	—	—	—
10,000—14,999	—	—	—	—	—	—	—	—
15,000+	—	—	—	—	—	—	—	—
Not available	47	0.48	—	—	—	—	—	—
Total	9,708	7.04	46,955	34.04	45,493	32.98	17,330	12.57
Total manufacturing employment 1970	10,454		49,262		50,153		17,930	

Source. *Survey of Manufacturing Industries 1970*.

Notes. (1) If the percentages add up to a little less than or more than 100.00, it is due to rounding off the figures.

(2) The last row, total manufacturing employment 1970, is larger than second last row, total, because the detailed skill level breakdown is not provided for several industries: preparation and preserving of meat, canning, preparation and preserving of fish and other seafood, other food manufacturing, distilling, rectifying and blending of spirits, breweries, manufacture of miscellaneous wearing apparel and made-up textile goods, wood preservation, pre-fabricated wooden buildings, compressed and liquefied gases, industrial chemicals, products of petroleum and coal, cutstone and stone products, other non-metallic mineral products and miscellaneous metal products, manufacture and assembly of bicycles, tricycles, trishaws and their parts and accessories, manufacture and assembly of motor cycles and scooters, musical instruments, pens, pencils and office supplies, surgical, dental supplies, measuring, controlling, laboratory and scientific instruments and miscellaneous.

TABLE 4.2

1969–1970 MINING EMPLOYMENT AND AVERAGE EARNINGS IN WEST MALAYSIA

	1969		1970			
	Number	*Average Earnings (in $)*	*Male*	*Female*	*Total*	*Average Earnings (in $)*
Working proprietor and partners	1,001		1,165	42	1,207	—
Managerial and professional	3,386	8,624	1,287	15	1,302	8,681
Technical and supervisory			2,821	20	2,841	4,302
Clerical	2,681	3,671	2,086	186	2,272	3,679
General	39,787	2,152	3,985	436	4,421	1,927
Skilled			15,098	930	16,028	2,222
Unskilled			21,230	2,843	24,073	1,662
Employment through contractors	9,433	2,632	10,365	798	11,163	2,401
Total	56,288	2,558	58,037	5,270	63,307	2,305
Net value added	$495,376,000		$542,443,000			
Number of mines	1,446		1,506			
Unpaid family helper			61	7	68	
Part-time white collar employees			187	6	193	1,081
Part-time skilled and unskilled			876	242	1,118	845

Sources. (1) Tables 1.1, 3.6 and 4.3, *Census of Mining Industries 1969*.
(2) Tables 1.1 and 3.1, *Census of Mining Industries 1970*.

TABLE 4.3

EMPLOYMENT AND EARNINGS IN WEST MALAYSIAN CONSTRUCTION INDUSTRIES, 1969–1970

	1969		1970			
	Number	*Average Earnings (in $)*	*Male*	*Female*	*Total*	*Average Earnings (in $)*
Working proprietors	896	—	971	9	980	—
Managerial and professional	1,296	2,576	409	14	423	11,057
Technical and supervisory			859	4	863	4,216
Clerical	1,550	2,795	960	459	1,419	2,616
General	9,461	2,151	1,234	53	1,287	1,867
Skilled			4,421	108	4,529	2,303
Unskilled			5,323	475	5,798	1,366
Employed through contractors						
Skilled	30,887	2,373	16,722	608	17,330	2,566
Unskilled			16,554	2,367	18,921	1,747
Total	44,090	2,495			51,550	2,140
Unpaid family workers	141	—	110	42	152	—
Value added	$175,898,000			$207,775,000		

Sources. (1) Tables 1.1, 3.1 and 4.1, *Survey of Construction Industry*, 1969. (2) Tables 1.1, 7.1 and 8.1, *Survey of Construction Industry*, 1970.

$2,000 (and as expected these were the general and unskilled workers); a great majority (87.95 per cent and 59.24 per cent for the two sectors respectively) received less than $2,500 (these included the skilled workers). Only a few technicians and supervisors received about $4,000 and even fewer belonged to the high-income bracket.

C. Estate Workers

Table 4.4(a) furnishes the average earnings of rubber estate workers. It can be seen that 22.9 per cent received about $1,000 or less per year; 72.8 per cent received between $1,000 to $1,500; and only 4.2 per cent received as much as $3,600. The 11,848 oil palm estate workers were reported to receive $128 monthly or about $2,536 a year. The earnings of the tea estate workers was an average of only $93 per month or $1,116 a year (Table 4.4(b)). This income did not include payments in kind such as free housing with electricity and water, some medical attention, and perhaps primary schooling for some of the dependants. It is hard to compute these benefits but perhaps $400 for imputed rent and another $100 a year for miscellaneous services are not unreasonable figures. These would put estate workers' incomes in line with the higher ranges of the income of the unskilled manufacturing labourers and the larger farmers.

An important feature is that the income of the rubber estate workers changes automatically on a sliding scale pegged to the price of rubber as a result of collective bargaining. While the margin of increase is not very large, it is significant because it is a scheme unique to the rubber estate workers. Unlike other workers, therefore, the welfare of these estate workers varies from year to year.

TABLE 4.4(a)
RUBBER ESTATE EMPLOYMENT, 1970

	Number	*Average Earnings per Month*	*Earnings per Year*
Tappers	160,100	$116	$1,392
Weeders	35,800	68	816
Factory workers	18,400	87	1,044
Others	12,100	117	1,404
Foremen (included in 'Others')		151	1,802
Administrative staff	10,000	300	3,600
Total	236,400		

Source. Tables 12.1, 12.2, 12.3 and 12.4, *Rubber Statistics Handbook*, 1970.

D. Distributive Trades

Table 4.5 provides information on employment and earnings for the distributive trades. In this industry, there are only three categories of workers of interest to this study: the owner-operators, the unpaid family helpers, and

TABLE 4.4(b)

EMPLOYMENT AND INCOME IN PINEAPPLE, TEA, COCONUT, AND OIL PALM ESTATES IN 1970

	Tea				Coconut	Pineapple	Oil Palm			
	Directly Employed	*Employed through Contractors*	*Average Earnings*	*Total*	*Number Employed*	*Number Employed*	*Directly Employed*	*Employed through Contractors*	*Average Earnings*	*Total*
Administrative and technical staff	200	—	$317		n.a.	n.a.		11,848	$128	
Agricultural workers	3,210	170	93		n.a.	n.a.	22,172			
Factory workers		n.a.			n.a.	n.a.				
Total	3,410	170		3,580	4,200	2,200				36,409

Sources. Tables 3.1 and 5.1, *Monthly Statistical Bulletin of West Malaysia*; Tables 35 and 36, *Oil Palm, Coconut and Tea Statistics West Malaysia 1970*, Department of Statistics.

Note. The figures for oil palm do not add up because of the presence of 2,389 'other' workers.

TABLE 4.5
EMPLOYMENT IN THE DISTRIBUTIVE TRADES IN WEST MALAYSIA, 1966

	Owner-Operators					*Family Helpers*				
	Full Time		*Part Time*		*Total*	*Full Time*		*Part Time*		*Total*
	Number	%*	*Number*	%		*Number*	%	*Number*	%	
Retailing										
Provisions	24,392	38.5	326		24,718	20,588	32.5	8,693	13.7	29,281
Clothing and textiles	3,074	34.8	54		3,128	1,983	16.8	255	8.5	2,238
Fruit and vegetables	5,076	54.1	68		5,144	2,924	31.2	960	10.2	3,884
Total	55,922	40.1	842		56,764	38,521	27.7	16,036	11.5	54,557
Wholesaling										
Household and personal goods	4,251	19.7	48		4,299	1,373	6.4	591	2.7	1,964
Business, industrial, and agricultural goods	4,815	25.9	46		4,861	1,740	9.3	1,086	5.8	2,826
Large general whole-sales	72	1.0			72	4	0.1	1	—	5
Total	9,138	19.2	94		9,232	3,117	6.6	1,678	3.5	4,795
Catering										
Coffee shops, drink stalls, bars	11,496		103		11,599	10,627		4,332		14,959
Food stalls, restaurants	5,725		81		5,806	4,638		1,212		5,850
Total	17,221	34.3	184		17,405	15,265	30.4	5,544	11.1	20,809
Total	82,281	34.7	1,120	0.5	83,401	56,903	24.0	23,258	9.8	80,161

Source. Malaysia, Department of Statistics, *Census of Distributive Trades, 1966*, Tables 7, 21, and 35.

Notes. *All the figures in percentage refer to per cent of total participants in that trade.

(Continued)

TABLE 4.5 (Continued)

	Paid Employees					Total			Av. Income of Paid Full-time Employee**
	Full Time		Part Time		Total	Full Time	Part Time	Total	
	Number	%	Number	%		Number	Number		
Retailing									
Provisions	8,855	14.0	556		9,411	53,835	9,575	63,410	n.a.
Clothing and textiles	3,403	38.5	77		3,480	7,960	886	8,846	n.a.
Fruit and vegetables	306	3.3	41		347	8,306	1,069	9,375	n.a.
Total	26,518	19.0	1,497		28,015	120,961	18,375	139,336	$1,733
Wholesaling									
Household and personal goods	14,640	67.9	672		15,312	20,264	1,311	21,575	n.a.
Business, industrial, and agricultural goods	10,252	55.1	684		10,936	16,807	1,816	18,623	n.a.
Large general wholesales	7,100	96.9	147		7,247	7,176	148	7,324	n.a.
Total	31,992	67.3	1,503		33,495	44,247	3,275	47,522	$3,097
Catering									
Coffee shops, drink stalls, bars	4,616		275		4,891	26,739	4,710	31,449	n.a.
Food stalls, restaurants	6,670		404		7,074	17,033	1,697	18,730	n.a.
Total	11,286	22.5	679		11,965	43,772	6,407	50,179	$1,307
Total	69,726	29.4	3,679	1.6	73,405	208,910	28,057	236,967	$2,292

Note. **This figure is computed by assuming that all the full-time paid employees are employed by those firms with accounts. This is clearly untrue and would underestimate their income. However, bearing in mind that wages are probably lower for the smaller establishments and hence wages for firms with accounts would be higher, our underestimation is to some degree counterbalanced. In reality, the amount of underestimation is likely to be small. By checking the number of workers (including operators and family helpers) for establishments with gross turnover less than those with accounts, it can be concluded that these smaller establishments generally cannot afford (and it is unnecessary) to hire workers. Therefore, a very high percentage of full-time employees would be hired by those firms with accounts only.

the employees, who are best classified under salesmen and related occupations. The owner-operators also serve as managers and the unpaid family helpers and sales employees frequently serve as clerks concurrently. Here, the income of 11,286 catering employees (or 4.77 per cent of the total number of economically active persons in this sector) averaged $1,307 annually; 26,518 retailing employees (11.19 per cent) averaged $1,733; and 31,992 wholesaling employees (13.47 per cent) averaged $3,097. The remaining persons (roughly 164,000) were the owner-operators and unpaid family helpers who shared in the profits of running the businesses. Their income will be estimated in Part II.

E. The Services

Most of the urban sectors have now been covered, the only exceptions being the civil service, teachers, and clerical workers in banking and other commercial activities. Government employees totalled 309,042 including the civil servants, labourers, and teachers. They formed more than 13 per cent of the labour force.[6] The labourers employed by the Government received a wage that was not likely to exceed greatly that in the private sector described above. As for the other Government employees, while it may be argued that the pay at each of the higher levels of the Government services was not competitive with that given to the executives in the private sector, it is a fact that university graduates in teaching and the civil service received over $750 per month.[7] White-collar workers who finished secondary school, a pre-university course, or a teachers' training course received income of more than $250 per month. For the clerks, it was a level over $200 per month which was a rate of pay comparable with the clerks in the private sector.

For the professionals, i.e., the engineers, accountants, lawyers, doctors, etc., their level of income varies quite substantially depending on whether they work as salaried employees for the Government or the private sector, or establish their own professional firms. Their income is fixed but at a very lucrative level—usually in excess of $1,000 per month and frequently several thousand per month. If they established their own firms, their income would be even higher, ranging from a low of $18,000 per year in profit for the average Malaysian surveyor in 1971 to over $100,000 for an average non-Malaysian accountant.[8]

Rather than singling out each profession in Government and the private sector for separate discussion, they will be discussed in Section 4.4 on the rise of the middle- and upper-income groups.

4.3 THE SELF-EMPLOYED PETTY TRADERS

Petty traders refer to the large number of hawkers, small retailers, and caterers. There were at least 50,000 hawkers scattered throughout Peninsular Malaysia in the seventies, the majority of whom were concentrated in the major cities and towns. There were 71,853 establishments engaged in catering and retailing in 1966; the number probably has increased since.[9] Each of these two categories of traders probably represented one family with little duplication, i.e., one family operating only one hawking stall or retail shop. Together there were a very significant 120,000 plus families engaged in such petty hawking and trading activities. The petty craftsmen, artisans, and very small manufacturers should have been covered here, but the lack of reliable data on their numbers and income precluded their inclusion.

Due to the complex nature in the evaluation of the returns to business organizations, the estimation of the profit and income of the caterers and retailers is left to Chapter 6 in Part II. Here, only the relevant income data will be cited. In 1966, 8,711 of the caterers (mainly the coffee shops and drink stalls) were estimated to have an average net turnover of $1,993 or a possible income per family of about $1,500 while 36,405 of the retailers had an average net turnover of $1,212 and income of about $1,000 per year.[10] In short, a total of 45,116 caterers and retailers belonged to the very small traders' category with very modest incomes no higher than that of the farmers and blue-collar workers.

The rest of this section focuses on the hawkers.[11] There are very few studies on hawkers; the notable exceptions are those by Fujio Hara (1975) on Penang hawkers, and Lam (1976) on Kuala Lumpur and Malacca hawkers, from which the bulk of the data in this section are drawn.

The Penang Hawkers' Association estimated that there were between 7,000 and 7,500 hawkers in Penang out of a population of about 777,000. The Chief Minister of Penang, Dr Lim Chong Eu, reported on 7 June 1973 that there were more than 10,000 hawkers.[12] The latter figure is likely to be more accurate as the number could have been estimated from the large number of hawkers with Georgetown City Council's licence and a further 4,000 or so who hawked without permits.

The number of hawkers in any one place depends on two major factors: (i) the size and income of its population and hence the number of hawkers it can support; (ii) the rate of unemployment. Hara hypothesized a strong correlation between high unemployment rate and the increase in the number of hawkers. Following a period of unsuccessful job-hunting in a period of high unemployment, the unemployed may turn to hawking, raising the number of hawkers. He found supporting evidence from direct interviews as well as a breakdown of sociological data. A large number of the young hawkers had never held any job and had been idle for some time prior to becoming hawkers.[13] With these two factors in mind, one can try to make a very rough estimate of the total number of hawkers in the major cities and in West Malaysia.

Table 4.6 summarizes estimates made for the ten major metropolitan areas in 1970. The approximately 50,000 hawkers formed a very sizeable group supporting about 300,000 people or 3.5 per cent of the population of West Malaysia. As will be obvious in subsequent presentation, the hawkers were among the poorest in Malaysia. Moreover, with persistent high unemployment since the sixties, the ranks of the hawkers must have swollen in recent years. With this intensified competition and the recent high inflation, their real income would have been reduced substantially.[14] For these reasons, it is necessary to gain a clear picture of their livelihood and difficulties.

Hara was not very precise about his sampling method which is a biased and narrow one.[15] Nevertheless, it represented an indicative data base. The information available pertained only to those hawkers with a moving stall in Penang, a hardly representative sample base. We can expect the fixed-stall

TABLE 4.6
ESTIMATED NUMBER OF HAWKERS IN
WEST MALAYSIA, 1970

Area	*Population in the Greater Area*	*Estimated Number of Hawkers*
Kuala Lumpur Municipality	706,997	15,000
City of Georgetown	332,128	10,000
Ipoh Municipality	257,309	7,000
Johor Bahru Town Council	144,921	3,500
Melaka Municipality	99,782	3,000
Seremban Town Council	90,062	2,500
Alor Star Town Council	85,748	2,000
Kota Bharu Town Council	69,756	1,500
Kuala Trengganu Town Council	59,494	1,000
Kuantan Town Council	43,391	1,000
Sub-total		46,500
Estimated total of other areas		3,500
Total		50,000

Source. Population figures from 1970 Population and Housing Census. Number of hawkers is estimated heuristically, based on the percentage of hawkers population in Georgetown adjusted by casual observation of the purchasing power of that community.

Note. Comparing the figures in this table with those given by T. F. Lam, op. cit., p. 75, we get reasonably good concurrence. In 1972, the Melaka and Kuala Lumpur municipalities issued 1,329 and 7,734 hawking licences respectively, to which must be added an unknown number of licensed hawkers in the Petaling Jaya municipality. In addition, once we allow a percentage of unlicensed hawkers, the number of hawkers within the vicinity of Kuala Lumpur (including Petaling Jaya) would come close to our estimate here. The number of unlicensed hawkers can be indicated by the data from p. 77 of Lam: 41.7 per cent of the prepared-food hawkers had no licence!

hawkers to receive higher incomes, some of the very popular ones even making upwards of $500 per month, though they are the exception, not the rule. On the other hand, Lam's technique is based on a stratified sampling and can be more representative, though his information was not as detailed.[16]

The following is a summary of Hara's major findings, supplemented by results from Lam when possible:

1. The hawkers worked very long hours, 10.6 hours per day on the average; 29.0 per cent worked between 9 and 11 hours, 28.2 per cent between 11 and 13 hours and 16.8 per cent more than 13 hours a day. They worked an average of 28.2 days per month; 55 per cent worked 30 days and a further 16.0 per cent worked 27 days a month. The length of the working day and the number of days worked a year far surpass that of any other occupation, except some of the shopkeepers.[17]

2. Of the Penang hawkers, 24.8 per cent received an average net income of

$5 per day or about $1,692 per year; 22.1 per cent received $4 per day or about $1,373 per year; 19.5 per cent received $7 per day or $2,369 per year. This is generally in line with the income levels of the hawkers located outside markets presumably not with fixed stalls in Kuala Lumpur, Petaling Jaya, and Malacca: 27.3 per cent, 13.6 per cent and 29.1 per cent respectively made $5 per day and 37.2 per cent, 35.6 per cent and 31.4 per cent respectively made between $5 and $10 per day. However, in these three places, there is a higher proportion making in excess of $10 per day than in Penang. Furthermore, for those located inside markets, i.e., with fixed stalls, the percentage making between $10 and $20 increased to over 35 per cent. There was, however, a difference between the net income of those who owned their stalls and those who rented their stalls. For the owner-operators, their net daily income ranged from $4.5 to $5.9 while that of the tenants was between $3.7 and $5.2. The lower income of the tenant-operators was attributed to an average daily rent of about $0.73 or about 14 to 20 per cent of their net income.[18] The above average net income figures were income of the individual hawkers, not counting the income of their family members whose average daily net income ranged from $4.4 per day to $5.7 per day, i.e., $1,489—$1,929 per year.

3. The average monthly income of the eighty-four families who were willing to supply information on family income was $219.9 or the equivalent of $2,639 per year. This income level compares unfavourably with the West Malaysian average family income of $268.7 per month or $3,224 per year and the West Malaysian urban average family income of $328.1 per month or $3,552 per year. A further breakdown of the size distribution of income of hawkers revealed that poverty among this group was prevalent: 29.8 per cent belonged to the $100—$150 per month or $1,200—$1,800 per year bracket while 15.5 per cent received between $50 and $100 per month and 6.0 per cent less than $50 per month. Overall, 51.3 per cent received a family income of less than $150 per month. This would certainly put the earnings of the last category among the lowest in West Malaysia, especially in view of the extraordinarily large families. Twelve families (14.3 per cent) had incomes larger than $500 per month but three of these have eleven to fifteen members in the same household and another three have between eight and ten household members; i.e., the higher income was probably a reflection of more working household members. On the other hand, of the eighteen families with an income of less than $100 per month, eight have less than three members, while thirty of the thirty-seven earning between $100 and $200 per month have between four and seven members.[19]

4. The ratio of net income to gross income varied from a low of 2 per cent to a high of over 60 per cent. However, the great majority fell within the range of 20 to 25 per cent for gross income of up to $30 per day. It was generally true that in the lowest-income bracket of less than $7 gross income per day, the ratio was much higher; while at the other extreme, when the gross daily income reached $100 per day, the net income was as low as 5 per cent, i.e., no more than that earned by many with very low gross incomes.[20] This variation in gross income and net income was probably closely associated with the type of food or merchandise sold. Unfortunately, Hara did not present any such correlation.

5. The average household size for these hawkers was 5.58 with an average of 2.62 (1.93 male and 0.69 female) per household in the labour force. The very high number of persons in the labour force per family reflected the pressure of poverty and the necessity to have more family members working to earn a decent living. Unemployment was very high, twenty-four were unemployed giving an unemployment rate of 11.76 per cent.[21]

6. The educational level of the hawkers and their family members was below that of the average West Malaysian. Moreover, there was a drop in the percentage of those in the 15—19 age-group who attended lower secondary school as opposed to that for the 20—24 age-group. This may indicate that the 20—24 year olds might have been able to attend lower secondary school in their teens whereas their siblings in their teens at the time of survey could not afford to. Of the 104 male teenagers and 27 female teenagers lucky enough to be admitted to secondary school, 55.77 per cent and 66.67 per cent respectively were forced to drop out because of poverty.[22] This deterioration in educational background in a nation with generally broadening educational opportunities probably indicates the poor conditions faced by the hawkers.

Hawking is, in fact, not a priority occupation. People resort to it only if they fail to find satisfactory alternative employment; they would not leave it because the prospects of finding other adequate means of living are not very bright.[23]

The striking feature of hawking is its extremely long hours. Since hawking is an occupation of last resort, the only avenue for raising income level at relatively little material cost is to lengthen the vending time. However, there are limits to what can be done.[24]

To what extent would the above summary be applicable to other parts of Malaysia? Bearing in mind that Kuala Lumpur, Penang, and Malacca were respectively the largest, second, and seventh largest urban centres in Malaysia, one can speculate that their income data are representative of that of the larger towns. Given that Kuala Lumpur is in general wealthier and larger, one can expect the hawkers there to attain a generally higher income as evidenced by a comparison of hawkers' income among those in Kuala Lumpur and Penang/ Malacca. For the smaller towns, with their smaller population and lower purchasing power, the numbers and income of hawkers would be correspondingly lower.

4.4 THE RISE OF THE MIDDLE- AND UPPER-INCOME GROUPS

A. Introduction

In the last two chapters as well as the two preceding sections of this chapter, we have dealt with each group of Malaysians by occupation to assess their respective levels of income and the factors affecting income. There is a need to provide an *overview* of the changing pattern of income distribution within the country to tie up these various sections, providing a *microscopic* view and to lay the background for the second part of the book dealing with the distribution of wealth and economic power. This is the main purpose of this section.

Table 4.7 provides a breakdown of the share of the total income for each of

TABLE 4.7

INCOME SHARE OF THE THREE RACES BY INCOME BRACKETS (IN PER CENT)

Income Bracket	*Malay*			*Chinese*			*Indian*		
	1957/8	*1970*	*Change*	*1957/8*	*1970*	*Change*	*1957/8*	*1970*	*Change*
Top 5%	18.1	24.6	6.5	19.6	25.3	5.7	19.5	28.2	8.7
Next 5%	9.5	11.6	2.1	11.9	11.8	—0.1	10.0	11.4	1.4
Next 10%	14.9	16.3	1.4	15.3	15.5	0.2	14.2	14.6	0.4
Next 40%	38.0	34.8	—3.2	36.2	33.5	—2.7	36.6	31.5	—5.1
Bottom 40%	19.5	12.7	—6.8	18.1	13.9	—4.2	19.7	14.3	—5.4
Gini Coefficient	0.342	0.466	0.124	0.374	0.455	0.081	0.347	0.463	0.116
Gini Coefficient for those with monthly income of less than $1,000	0.332	0.386	0.054	0.331	0.351	0.020	0.303	0.355	0.052

Source. Adapted from Snodgrass, Table XIII, p. 264 in David Lim, ed., *Readings on Malaysian Economic Development*.

the three races by income brackets from 1957/8 to 1970. The most striking, and alarming, feature is that the share of income of the top 20 per cent has increased for each of the three races, all at the expense of the bottom 80 per cent. In fact, it is the top 5 per cent who have benefited most: 5.7 per cent, 6.5 per cent and 8.5 per cent gain by the Chinese, Malay and Indian top 5 per cent respectively. The share of each top 5 per cent group of the total income of the respective racial group in 1970 was: Malay 24.6 per cent, Chinese 25.3 per cent and Indian 28.2 per cent. The next 5 per cent and the following 10 per cent of the Indians and Malays registered modest gains, whereas the Chinese second top 5 per cent lost 0.1 per cent and the following 10 per cent gained 0.2 per cent. At the other end of the scale, the bottom 40 per cent lost the most, especially the Malay poor who lost 6.8 per cent of income share to the Malay rich; the Indian and the Chinese bottom 40 per cent lost too, albeit by slightly less than that lost by the Malay bottom 40 per cent.

The mean income of every group has increased absolutely, except that of the bottom 40 per cent. The latter suffered a decrease in income of $11 per month per household (or $132 per year), a decline of 13 per cent. For the other groups, the absolute and relative increase in income was the largest for the top 5 per cent who, by 1970, made an average of $18,240 per year per household. This level of income was more than twice that of the next 5 per cent. As a result of the increased share by the top 20 per cent and the decrease by the rest, especially the bottom 40 per cent, inequality in Malaysia has increased up to 1970, especially intra-race.[25] And income inequality within race has widened the most for the Malays, followed by the Indians (Table 4.8).

In this section, we attempt to identify the different income brackets with economic activities upon which correlations with policies can be traced. This will enable us to identify the main beneficiaries and understand the overall changes in income inequality outlined above. We begin by first defining and relating the composition of the several major income brackets in subsection 4.4.B, followed by an overview of how these income brackets have expanded or contracted and how their income shares have changed over time, including a discussion of the relative benefits of the three major races (Section 4.4.C).

TABLE 4.8
AVERAGE INCOME PER MONTH OF THE MALAYSIANS BY INCOME BRACKETS

Income Bracket	*1957/8*	*1970*	*Increase*	*Increase in %*
Top 5%	$953	$1,520	$567	59
Next 5%	477	680	203	43
Next 10%	334	414	80	24
Next 40%	191	218	27	14
Bottom 40%	86	75	−11	−13

Source. Snodgrass, Table X, p. 262 in David Lim, ed., *Readings on Malaysian Economic Development.*

B. Definition and Composition of Income Classes

From Table 4.8, the Malaysian populace has a very large lower-income group consisting of the bottom 80 per cent of the population. The bottom 40 per cent generally earned less than $1,000 per household per year. They consisted of the landless, the very small farmers (padi farms of less than three acres with no double cropping, rubber smallholdings of less than five acres), most of the fishermen, and some of the hawkers and the unskilled and general workers. The next 40 per cent were the less poor households earning usually no more than $3,000 per year, though a minority might earn up to $4,000 per year. These were the farmers with medium-sized plots and those with double cropping or matured new seedlings areas, some of the unskilled workers, hawkers, the skilled workers, the new land settlers, most of the clerical workers, some teachers, the sales and related workers, and some of the different categories of service workers, as well as most of the small traders-cum-middlemen who are discussed in Part II.

It is possible to define a 'middle' class of about 10 per cent of households (i.e., the top eleventh to twentieth percentile) that made an average yearly income of about $5,000. Those who earned between $3,000 and $4,000 per year in the next 40 per cent group mentioned in the last paragraph should be included in this category as well. These were mainly the larger farmers with more efficient cultivation conditions chiefly in the better padi areas, clerical workers and teachers, many of the medium-sized distributive trade owners, and some technicians and managers.

The next category is the 'upper middle'-income group consisting of 5 per cent of the households (i.e., the second 5 per cent from the top) averaging an income of about $9,000 per year. Many of these were the more experienced and the college-trained teachers, the more qualified technicians, some administrators and managers, many of the junior civil servants, some professionals, etc.

By elimination, the remaining 5 per cent was the upper-income group consisting of the professionals, executives, and wealth holders.[26]

Clearly, this distinction between middle and lower income, or between middle- and upper middle-income groups, is quite arbitrary. The choice of $3,000 to about $6,000 in annual household income for the range of the middle-income group has been influenced by a general impression of how they are able to live and the nature of the jobs required to reach this level of income. Analogously, the choice of perhaps about $9,000 average annual household income (implying a range of $6,000 to $12,000 per year) has been influenced by such casual observation as well.

C. The Rise of the Middle- and Upper-income Groups

Following the lines of division suggested above, we can identify the changing proportion and composition of the people of different income groups from 1957/8 to 1967/8 and probably 1970 by analysing the changing numbers in each occupation presented in Table 4.9. Since the rate of inflation and rate of wage/salary increase in the country in this period had been very modest, we can safely assume that the change in occupational distribution reflects the change in income distribution and relative welfare.[27]

TABLE 4.9

EMPLOYMENT OF THE THREE RACES BY OCCUPATION (IN THOUSANDS)

Occupation	*Malay*			*Chinese*			*Indian*		
	1957/8	*1967*	*Change*	*1957/8*	*1967*	*Change*	*1957/8*	*1967*	*Change*
1. Professional and technical	27	61	34	27	53	26	7	18	11
2. Administrative and executive	4	10	6	15	30	15	3	4	1
3. Sub-total (1 and 2)	31	71	40	42	83	41	10	22	12
4. As % of total employment	3.1	5.3	12.2	5.6	8.1	14.9	3.3	6.8	63.2
5. Clerical	16	33	17	28	60	32	12	17	5
6. As % of total employment	1.6	2.5	5.2	3.7	5.8	11.6	3.9	5.2	26.3
7. Sales and related workers	29	63	34	121	175	54	30	23	—7
8. Craftsmen and labourers*	106	221	114	210	320	109	76	87	11
9. Sub-total (7 and 8)	135	284	148	331	495	163	106	110	4
10. As % of total employment	13.5	21.3	45.0	43.8	48.0	59.1	34.5	33.7	21.1
11. Total employment	1,001	1,332	329	755	1,031	276	307	326	19

Source. Adapted from Table 2-19, Snodgrass, 'Inequality and Economic Development in Malaysia', mimeo., 1977.

Note. *Including workers in mining, transport, and communication sectors. Numbers may not add up because of rounding of figures.

For the bottom 40 per cent, the bulk were Malays, perhaps as many as 75 per cent.[28] For those in the next 40 per cent, the proportion of work force under clerical workers increased from 2.8 per cent to 4.0 per cent, that of sales-workers, craftsmen and semi-skilled workers increased from 27.6 per cent to 33.1 per cent which would imply that the proportion of the next 40 per cent occupied by these categories of workers should have increased. The remainder of these clerks, sales-workers, and craftsmen probably belonged to the lower middle-income group earning in excess of $3,000. Concurrent with the expansion of this group of workers generally in the urban areas, the proportion of Malays within it had also been rising rapidly with a net gain of 148,000 from 1957/8 to 1967/8. They formed 21.3 per cent of the total Malays employed in 1967/8 in contrast to the 13.5 per cent in 1957/8. On the other hand, the number of Indians in this category rose by only 4,000 in the ten-year period. The largely urban-based Chinese increased their employment in this category by the larger absolute number of 163,000, but only increased their proportion in this category by a smaller 4.2 per cent. The implication of the above changes is that the proportion of Malays within this second 40 per cent had risen as a result of their increasing employment in the urban non-professional/executive employment as well as rural development.[29] Nevertheless, the non-Malays still formed the majority within this 40 per cent, but perhaps by only a very slim margin.[30]

For the rest of the 20 per cent of the work force, we have to analyse their development from both the changes in clerical and sales employment as well as the changes in professional/executive/technical/administrative employment. In the last paragraph, we have documented the increases in the clerical and sales employment and remarked that those with higher incomes would fit into the lower middle-income group. The same is true for those in the professional/executive/technical/administrative employment. Their proportion of total work force had increased from 4.0 per cent in 1957/8 to 6.5 per cent in 1967/8.

Within the middle- and upper-income groups and the subgroup of professionals/executives/technicians/administrators, the proportion of Malays had been on the rise, as was the case of those Malays within the second bottom 40 per cent and the clerks/craftsmen/sales-workers/semi-skilled workers discussed earlier. This can be seen from the absolute and relative increase in the number of Malay professionals and executives in Table 4.9 and the proportion of Malays among the rich in 1970 (21.5 per cent).[31] Their numbers more than doubled from 31,000 in 1957/8 to 71,000 in 1967/8, accounting for the bulk of the top 5 per cent and some of the next 5 per cent of the Malays. On the other hand, the number of Chinese and Indians in these occupations had increased absolutely by a slightly larger, but proportionately slightly smaller, number of 53,000 to 105,000, giving rise to the increase in the share of income by the top 5 per cent in their respective races.

Or looking at it another way, from 1957/8 to 1967/8, the proportion of workers in the middle- and upper-income occupations within each race changed as follows: the Malays increased from 8.8 per cent to 14.4 per cent, a gain of 5.6 per cent; the Chinese from 19.4 per cent to 23.7 per cent, a gain of 4.3 per cent; but the Indians declined from 6.2 per cent to 5.5 per cent. In so far as the Malays formed the bulk of the work force and had the larger rate of increase in these occupations by race, their relative proportion within these occupations had to increase relative to the other races. Clearly, the Malays had been able to benefit as much in sharing in the significant increase in the middle- and upper-income groups of this country in the decade of development since Independence. Of course the share of the rich, at 21.5 per cent, was still less than the proportion of Malays in the population, and also smaller than the share by the Chinese and Indians (55.8 per cent and 16.9 per cent respectively with 5.8 per cent others).[32] Nevertheless, it was not as unequal or unrepresentative as the impression conveyed by looking at the distribution of shares of limited companies.[33] This discrepancy can be explained by the more balanced number of professionals and executives as well as the earnings of the bigger landlords and/or cultivators.

Significantly, it was those in the 20—29 age-group who had the highest incidence of high income,[34] about 10.7 per cent, while those in the 30—39 age-group among the professionals and managers formed 24.4 per cent of the rich. These two statistics reflect the process of economic expansion and Malaysianization as well as the manpower supplied by an expanded tertiary education. In so far as the Malay share of the tertiary student population rose to about 50 per cent from a much smaller proportion before Independence, young Malay university graduates can be highlighted as the main Malay beneficiaries in post-Independence economic development.

Thus, the changing occupational distribution summarized implies that less than 5 per cent of the households in 1957/8 belonged to the upper middle-income bracket, no more than 10 per cent belonged to the middle-income bracket and less than 5 per cent to the upper-income bracket; however, by 1970, perhaps slightly more than 5 per cent of the households were in the upper- and upper middle-income brackets respectively and more than 10 per cent formed the middle-income bracket.

Excluding the very small number of wealth holders (of any race), the non-Malays were still better off than the Malays in general, occupying the upper strata in each income bracket, whether the lower 80 per cent, middle 15 per cent, or the upper 5 per cent. However, the differential between the two groups at each level could not be considered outrageously large. In terms of the size of income, the differences between Malays and non-Malays working in the same occupation, especially the wage earners and salaried ones, were small. This difference ranges from an approximately similar level for the services workers to no more than 50 per cent for the professionals and technical workers.[35] Among the poor, the non-Malay farmers and wage workers generally earned between $1,500 and $3,000 which was ahead of the $1,000 to $2,000 range made by the Malay farmers.[36]

From this exercise, we can perceive the following pattern of income distribution for the Malays and non-Malays:

Important events have occurred in the seventies since the bulk of the surveys drawn upon by this book were concluded. The most important is the steep price inflation of 1973 and 1974 which has pinched the purchasing power of income. Partly as a result of this, three major Governmental wage and salary revisions have been administered, though they tended to favour the higher-income brackets.[37] Another is the introduction of labour-intensive manufacturing activities such as electronics and textiles and footwear which have brought in many young female workers formerly not in the work force. The expansion of labour employment in the labour-intensive industries of course was not confined to female workers; this development together with the drain of some skilled workers to Singapore and the general organization of labour movements exerted an upward pressure on the wages of both the unskilled and skilled workers. The incomes of the farmers of padi, rubber, and oil palm have also generally improved, due to the concurrent improvement in commodity prices in the wake of petroleum price increases and world inflation, as well as the coming on-stream of Government rural development projects. Meanwhile, the few more years of economic expansion together with the NEP have meant a further expansion of the middle- and upper-income brackets and a further acceleration in the Malay share in these two groups.

While the detailed impact of these movements cannot be assessed until a good comprehensive income census is conducted, we can nevertheless draw some general conclusions. This will be done in some detail in the concluding chapter. However, it is clear that the improvement in income of the farmers would at least be matched in part by wage and salary increases. The likely outcome is that income inequality by income brackets would not improve on a relative scale, although that between the Malays and non-Malays may improve a little as a result of the increased farm income, the faster pace of Malay absorption into the more urban and 'modern' economic activity and the higher non-Malay unemployment rate.

4.5 CONCLUSION

The income of the lowest 40 per cent declined in relative terms by 13 per cent in the thirteen-year period, and from the discussions in Chapters 2 and 3, by 1970 the poorest Malay farmers had yet to benefit significantly from the rural development policies. One reason is because the major irrigation projects were being completed only in 1969 or later, and had not generally reached the smaller farmers. Analogously, the land development programme was accelerated only in the seventies. The impact on farmers' incomes would not have been reflected in the 1970 survey. Secondly, even for those areas blessed with development projects, the poorer, less efficient farms are either not able to take advantage of farm improvement because of capital and other constraints, or have not been given enough priority to be the most important, much less sole, beneficiary in land allocation. Thirdly, the benefits of the rubber replanting programme have not been as great for the smaller and poorer smallholders. Besides, the increases in yield have been offset by the decline in prices up to the early seventies.

One can expect that as the Muda, Kemubu, and Besut irrigation projects became fully operational in the seventies, the income of many padi farmers would have improved and this would probably move some of the padi farmers from the bottom 40 per cent income bracket in 1970 to the level of the next 40 per cent. Some of the larger owner-tenants could even earn more than \$3,000 and join the ranks of the lower middle-income bracket. Analogously, the participants of the more successful land development projects will also join this group of more fortunate padi farmers. This trend has been confirmed by the scattered evidence summarized in the two earlier chapters. Concurrently, the rural to urban migrants can obtain jobs in the modern sector and earn an income of $1,500 to $2,500 like their non-Malay counterparts, and more if they become skilled workers. The number of these, which has been rising in the sixties, will rise at an even faster rate with the intensified suasion and legislation introduced under the NEP to promote Malay employment in these sectors. Nevertheless, it is probably unlikely that the industrial expansion can offset the sum of population growth and net rural-urban migration. This will likely aggravate the squatter problem which is already quite serious.[38]

The expansion of the Malay middle- and upper-income brackets, at a faster rate than the other races, would have picked up momentum with the advent of the NEP.[39] However, the proportion of this group within the Malay households is unlikely to be as high as that of the non-Malays by the second half of the seventies; nor would the Malay share of the middle- and upper-income brackets catch up with their share of the population. In rough order of magnitude one can speculate that the Malay share within these income brackets would come close to 30 per cent by then. At any rate, Figure 4.1 presents the possible shape of within-Malay income distribution.

The non-Malays also benefited from the post-Independence rise of the middle- and upper-income groups. Since more of them have lived in urban areas and been exposed to better education opportunities and facilities, more non-Malays than Malays joined the ranks of the professionals and managers in the post-Independence period. Such a scenario might not have occurred in a

FIGURE 4.1
INCOME DISTRIBUTION PATTERN BY RACE

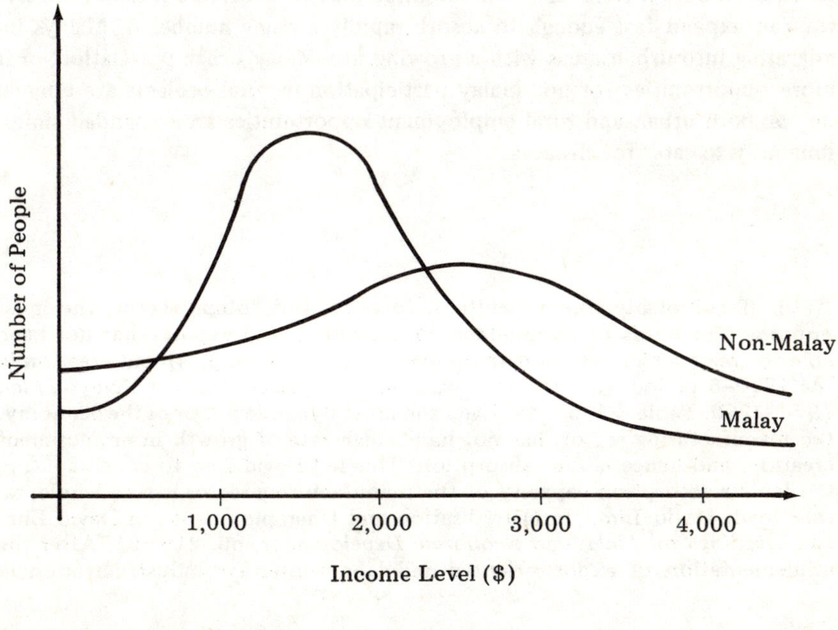

colonial context. Of course, the number of those who could move into this rank would still be a minority.

Some benefits also accrued to the non-Malay poor in the post-Independence developments through the expansion of industrial activities which provided additional employment opportunities for the young in the urban areas. The number of new jobs created in the manufacturing, mining, transport, and communication sectors for the Malays and non-Malays in the post-Independence decade were roughly equal. However, as the industrialization and urbanization processes have been concentrated in the Klang Valley where the capital, Kuala Lumpur, is located, non-Malays in other parts of the country probably could share little in the fruits of this progress.[40] Unemployment in the other major urban areas therefore stayed high; Georgetown, for example, carried a higher than 13 per cent rate of unemployment towards the end of the sixties.[41] At the same time, the existing land policy, the political sensitivity of the land allocation problem and the reversal of the ruralization spread of the non-Malays caused by the creation of New Villages under the Emergency[42] meant that the non-Malays could hardly benefit from the rural development policy and increased employment opportunities in the rural areas.[43]

In this context, the creation of urban employment becomes the only major means whereby their poverty can be eased and prospects of some upward mobility safeguarded. Therefore, while active promotion of Malay employment in the urban and modern sector is an extremely desirable step in promoting some possibility of integration and the eradication of the identification of economic activity with race, it can result in a rising non-Malay unemployment rate and its attendant socio-political implications, in particular, antagonism towards such policies. This is already happening to some extent, especially to the Indian poor, as evidenced by the paltry increase of 4,000 in Indian urban, non-professional/managerial employment highlighted earlier. The implication is that unemployment among the Indian poor, already the highest of the three races, must have increased.[44] This situation may be alleviated if the urban sector can expand fast enough to absorb rapidly a rising number of Malays inmigrating into urban areas with a growing non-Malay urban population, or if more opportunities for non-Malay participation in rural projects are opened up, or both urban and rural employment opportunities are expanded simultaneously to cater for all races.

1. Traditionally, the agriculture, forestry, and fishing sector, the most important in terms of value added, employment, and exports, has not been able to create a high rate of employment. The rate of employment creation in the 1970–5 period by this sector was only 1.6 per cent, *Third Malaysia Plan 1976–1980*, Table 8-1, p. 140. Even the most dynamic sector of the economy, the manufacturing sector, has not had a high rate of growth in employment creation, and hence labour absorption. This led David Lim to conclude: '. . . the labour absorption capacity of the manufacturing sector is, as a whole, rather low'. David Lim, 'Industrialisation and Unemployment', in David Lim, ed., *Readings on Malaysian Economic Development*, pp. 219—21. After the implementation of export-oriented and labour-intensive industrialization in

the seventies, manufacturing employment grew at the rate of 6.6 per cent from 1970 to 1975, *Third Malaysia Plan*, op. cit., Table 8-1.

2. The following diagram illustrates the impact of a change in demand schedule for labour in the general labour surplus Malaysian economy:

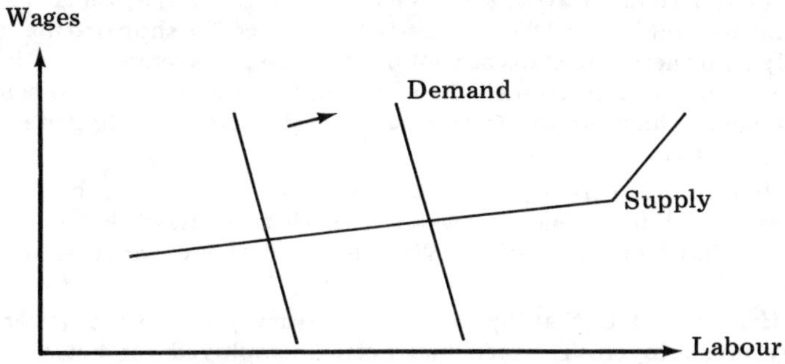

3. Even the white-collar workers have unions. Two are particularly strong and are leaders in setting salary demands for the white-collar segment of the labour market. They are the National Union of Bank Employees (NUBE) and the Congress of Unions of Employees in the Public and Civil Services (CUEPACS).

4. Tan Tat-wai, 'Some Aspects of Income Distribution in Malaysia', unpublished World Bank paper, 1973, Table 1.

5. The *1967/8 SSSH* reported about 220,000 manufacturing employees while the *Census of Manufacturing Industries 1968*, Kuala Lumpur, Department of Statistics, reported 130,000; the balance of 90,000 left out in the 1968 Census are presumably the artisans and small enterprises' employees.

6. *1967/8 SSSH*, Table 22.0.0.

7. The starting pay of a college or university graduate varies with his field and degree. The $750 per month figure was the pay for a new graduate with a B.A.(Honours) degree working in the civil service. In fact, since 1970, several pay revisions have been given whereby by 1980, the pay at each level of Government service, from the labourers right up to the professionals, has become more than competitive with the private sector. This, however, is outside the scope of this book.

8. Department of Statistics, *Census of Professional and Institutional Establishments 1971 and 1972*, Kuala Lumpur, Tables 1, 26 and 33.

9. For the number of catering and retailing establishments, see Table 6.5. The perception that the number of these establishments has increased is based on the report of the FAO–IBRD Programme *Muda Survey*, Table 72. There, the number of provision stores alone increased by 100 per cent from 1968 to 1973. Of course, there was an exceptional pace of development because of the introduction of double cropping.

10. These figures have been obtained from the preliminary tables with which Table 6.5 is constructed. They have been obtained by deducting the expenses of the establishments with accounts from that of all establishments, and then subtracting these figures from the total sales value of the establishments without accounts for the total net turnover for those establishments without accounts. The average net turnover figures are thus obtained by dividing them by the number of establishments without accounts.

11. Who are the hawkers? They include people with mobile carts or hand carriages either moving from street to street, or stationing themselves in par-

ticular streets or at street corners, as well as those vendors renting a spot at a coffee shop or a market-place. Their merchandise ranges from drinks, food and snacks, to toys, utensils, and apparel. This section of writing draws very heavily on the survey by Hara. 81.6 per cent of those hawking with a movable stall or carriage own their own stall, though sometimes they are borrowed, rented, or shared. (Fujio Hara, 'Hawkers in Penang', アジア经济 (Ajia Keijai Kenkyujo), XVI, January and March 1975.) Those selling in a coffee shop or a market-place probably own their own stalls as well but have to pay a rental fee to the coffee-shop owner or the city council. In addition, there are some who sell only at '*Pasar Malam*' which are in effect rotating night-markets selling in each place for a few days at a time.

12. ibid., p. 81. Perhaps one explanation for the discrepancies in the two estimates is that the Penang Hawkers' Association's figure has excluded the number of hawkers in Province Wellesley and the more rural sections of Penang.

13. Hara reported that 38 of the 131 surveyed (29.1 per cent) were formerly unemployed. Thirteen had been unemployed for between 10—15 years and another 10 had been unemployed for 5—10 years before turning to hawking (ibid., Table 20, p. 81). While 81 of these did not want to switch occupations, 8 who were willing to did not want to switch for lack of capital, 8 due to old age, and 5 for lack of skill. Forty-five of the 58 who offered an assessment of their chances of changing occupation felt that it was difficult, 7 felt that it was very difficult, and 2 felt that there was no chance at all; only 2 felt that they had a 50 : 50 chance and 2 more felt more optimistic (ibid., Table 23, p. 90). These figures speak very clearly.

14. Inflation means that the cost of raw materials has risen. Since the hawking activity seems to be an occupation for the unemployed, entry should be easy, and competition can be assumed to be keen. It is therefore not unreasonable to expect that the elasticity is such that any increase in price that the hawkers can introduce may not be as much as the rise in cost. Moreover, rising prices may also deter some customers. ibid., p. 87 (Part I) and p. 85 (Part II).

15. He mentioned that interviews were conducted between 12 noon and 5 or 6 p.m. from the end of July to the beginning of September in 1973. As a result, he has missed out completely those vendors who cater for the early morning market selling meat, vegetables, fish, fruit, and other perishables, as well as those catering for the marketers' breakfast with processed food. Also missed were those who catered for the night market. Hara probably obtained from the hawkers' associations a list of streets where there were hawkers' concentrations and then proceeded to interview them based on their merchandise and street locations. Thus, the sampling frame may be problematic. Nevertheless, his study can provide some ideas about the livelihood of hawkers. ibid., Introduction.

16. See Lam Thim-Fook, 'Urban Poverty: The Case of Hawkers and Vendors', in Mokhzani bin Abdul Rahim and Khoo Siew Mun, eds., *Some Case Studies on Poverty in Malaysia, Essays Presented to Professor Ungku Aziz*, Kuala Lumpur, University of Malaya Press, 1977.

17. Hara, op. cit., Table 5, p. 78, on the working hours; he compared his findings with those reported in Department of Statistics, *Cycle of Occupational Wage Survey*, Hara, Tables 6 and 13, pp. 78 and 83. It is not clear from his report whether the time taken to prepare the food for vending has been included. In so far as the family has to assist in these preparations, it is unlikely that all the preparation time would have been included. The supporting evidence for this claim can be found in the long hours that the hawkers' assistants reported. The male helpers reported working 13 hours a day, 7 days a week, while the female helpers averaged 7.9 hours a day and also 7 days a week (obviously, the time these females spent on housework has not been included).

It is important to stress this point because there seems little doubt that they probably put in more effort than any other occupational group.

18. Income per year has been calculated on the basis of income per day times 338.4 days per year (the average number of working days among those interviewed). Hara, op. cit., Tables 6 and 8, pp. 77—8.

Of the 204 (126 males and 78 females) family members who were working, 19.12 per cent (20 males and 19 females) were hawkers' helpers, which probably implies that they did not bring in additional income. 15.69 per cent (28 males and 4 females) were also hawkers, 27.94 per cent were casual labour, 8.82 per cent were trishaw pedlars and the rest were shopkeepers, maids, laundrymen, and apprentices. The notable feature is that they all have extremely long hours, most in excess of nine hours a day, some even in excess of twelve hours! As for the distribution of family income, see Table 3 of the text.

19. ibid., Table 10, p. 80, and Malaysia, *Mid-term Review of the Second Malaysia Plan*, Kuala Lumpur, Government Press, 1973, p. 3.

20. Hara, op. cit., Table 7, p. 78.

21. ibid., Table 12, p. 81, part II.

22. ibid., Tables 14 and 15.

23. ibid., Table 20, p. 81.

24. Their efforts at lengthening vending time to generate higher income are limited by physical endurance on the one hand and the pattern of buying behaviour on the other. The following two figures illustrate the probable buying pattern pertaining to two types of hawkers. From them, it will be obvious

LIKELY PATTERN OF INCOME STREAM OF A
(a) PROCESSED-FOOD HAWKER

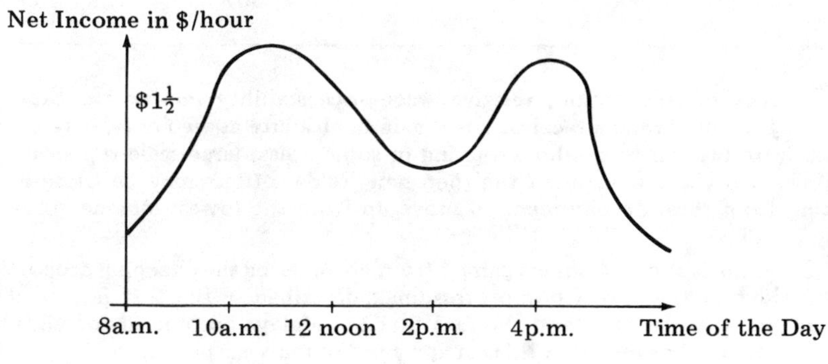

(b) COLD-DRINK HAWKER

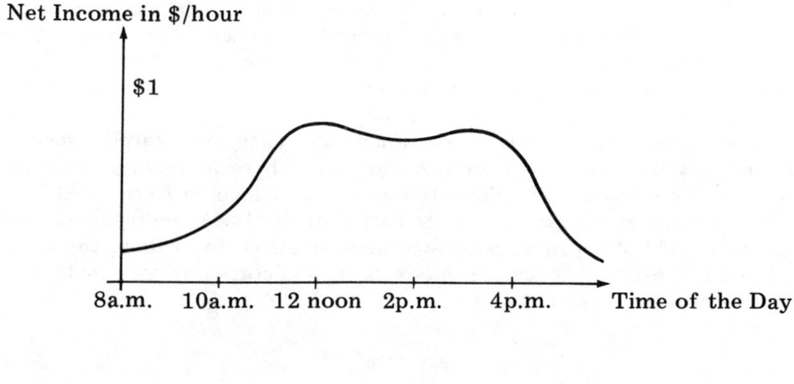

that effort other than those around the peak hours will bring in a very marginal return.

25. See also Snodgrass, 'Trends in Income Inequality', in David Lim, ed., *Readings*, conclusion.

26. See Anand, 'The Size Distribution of Income in Malaysia', p. 29, and supplementary tables on the rich: 32.4 per cent of the rich (i.e., those households with a *per capita* income of more than $185 per month or about $14,000 per household per year) were professionals and managers; 30.1 per cent of the professionals and technicians, 31.0 per cent of the managers and administrators and 16.3 per cent of the clerks belong to the rich.

27. However, as pointed out in Chapter 1, since 1973, this relative wage-price stability is no longer true. In the concluding part of this chapter and the concluding chapter, we will draw some inferences on the impact of this change on the income of this group of people and the relative change to the whole population.

28. Using Anand's poverty criterion of $25 *per capita* household per month, 78.1 per cent of the poor were Malays, 12.9 per cent Chinese, 8.0 per cent Indians, Anand, op. cit., Table 6, p. 3.

29. One way to look at this changing pattern is to postulate the following probable scenario:

	1957/8	*1967/8*
Proportion of the households earning less than $1,500 per year	50%	40%
Proportion of the households earning between $1,500 and $3,000 per year	30%	40%

Note that in this period, relative wage-price stability implies that anyone moving up in earnings receives a real gain in absolute as well as relative terms. The introduction of double cropping in some areas, large-scale replanting of rubber and the few cases of the then new Felda settlers may be those benefiting from rural development to move up from the lowest-income group to the next level.

30. This is the assessment gained from considering the changing proportion of Malays in the urban non-professionals described in the text immediately preceding this sentence and the fact that the Malays accounted for 45.0 per cent of new jobs created in this category in the ten-year period.

31. See Anand, op. cit., p. 29.

32. ibid.

33. The most commonly quoted figures for wealth distribution came from the *Second Malaysia Plan*: the Malays owned 2 per cent, the Chinese 21 per cent of corporate shares in 1970. The difference between the upper-income bracket defined here and the distribution of corporate share ownership can be accounted for by the inclusion of income from wealth of the rich Malay landowners, as well as those professionals and executives earning very high salaried or self-employed income in our case. There is, however, a need to note that there has been inadequate treatment of income from wealth in all the surveys and studies cited here. In Part II of this book, we try to assess the importance of holding wealth on income generation. Even then, there is still inadequate treatment since the interests in non-corporate land held by individuals have not been covered.

34. It is interesting to note that the proportion of non-labour income was high for this subgroup, probably indicating that some of them must have come from families of substantial wealth, quite apart from their holding degrees and serving in well-paid jobs.

35. See Anand, op. cit., Table 8. The following summary of income per month by occupation group and race provides some evidences:

Occupation	*Malays*	*Non-Malays*	*Difference in %*
Professional, technical	$319	$488	53
Managers, administrators	574	632	10
Clerks	238	291	22
Sales	118	259	119
Services	172	162	6
Farmers	84	210	150
Farm labour	74	104	41
Production workers	132	172	30

36. See Chapters 2 and 3.

37. Interested readers can consult the Harun Report, Ibrahim Ali Report, and the Cabinet Committee Report, all on wage and salary revisions of public sector employees. Even in some cases when workers at the lower level receive a slightly higher percentage of wage increase, the absolute difference between their income and those of the high level administrator is so great that little relative improvement would have occurred. This has not taken into account the greater ability of more senior staff to take advantage of better fringe benefits such as acquiring a good house at a concession price (through the Syarikat Perumahan Pegawai Kerajaan or Government Officers' Housing Co.) and having access to loans at lower than market interest rates.

38. The squatters include the traditional non-Malay squatters in the urban centres, the new Malay rural-urban migrants, and the non-Malays in the New Villages. There are many studies from which one can assess the livelihood and income of the squatters, for example, P. Pirie and others, 'Squatter Settlements in Kuala Lumpur', paper presented at the 3rd Conference of the Malaysian Economic Society in Penang, 21—24 August 1976; Ishak Shari, 'Urban Poverty and Urban Life in Kuala Lumpur: A Case Study', paper presented at the 3rd Conference of the Malaysian Economic Society, Penang, 21—24 August 1976; Azizah binti Osman, 'The Squatter Problem in Kuala Lumpur with Special Reference to Datuk Keramat', unpublished graduation exercise, University of Malaya, 1970; Kuala Lumpur Municipality, *Report on Surveys of Squatters on State Land and Private Land 1966/68*, Kuala Lumpur, 1970. There are many more governmental studies and graduation exercises which deal with this topic. The income of this group has not been reported separately here because most of it has been included in the summary of other occupations, such as casual and unskilled labour and so on.

39. This is clear from the trend in tertiary education admissions since 1970 cited in Chapter 1, the increasing number of tertiary education students as well as post-graduate students of the Malay ethnic group that the Government has been sending to the United States. The pressure to hire Malay executives exerted on the private sector will of course help to secure high-paying jobs for at least some of these graduates.

40. This is reflected by the very rapid urbanization of the greater Kuala Lumpur area, the concentration of factories in the Klang Valley, and the fact

that the residents of Selangor earned the highest average income in the country.

41. This is the figure quoted by Dr Lim Chong Eu, the Chief Minister of Penang, in a speech.

42. Interested readers can refer to a paper drawn up by Paul Leong on the problems in the New Villages for the MCA Task Force in 1971.

43. Most of the rural development programmes have rightly been aimed at Malay areas since these have been the poor areas. Even in the Felda schemes, the non-Malays participated in less than 4 per cent. While there is no doubt that the poor Malays should get priority treatment, the fact remains that current emphasis leaves the poor non-Malays with little opportunity to take part in rural development programmes.

44. See *Third Malaysia Plan*, Table 8-2, for a verification of this. Indian unemployment has been reported to have risen from 11 per cent in 1970 to over 12 per cent in 1975. The lack of opportunity is one factor; so is the switch from the more labour-intensive rubber planting to oil palm planting by the estates. In fact, in the estimation of Indian unemployment, no account has been taken of the sizeable Indian net migration out of Malaysia from 1957 to 1970 amounting to 174,000, mainly in the young age-groups. Had they not left, this would have raised the unemployment rate effectively. See Charles Hirschman, 'Net External Migration from Peninsular Malaysia 1957 to 1970', *Malayan Economic Review*, XX, October 1975, pp. 38—54. What has happened since 1970 has not yet been researched.

PART II

Distribution of Wealth and its Impact on Income

5 Ownership and Control of the Largest Corporations

5.1 INTRODUCTION

IN Chapter 1, the importance of incorporating a study of wealth distribution into a study of income distribution was stressed. Part II of this book (consisting of Chapters 5 to 8) researches into two major aspects of wealth distribution in relation to income distribution. (1) Chapters 5 and 6 outline the ownership and control pattern in West Malaysia. Control of the corporate sector is important in itself as it reflects the *concentration of wealth and economic power* in the hands of the few. (2) The demonstration of the extent of control will enable an appreciation of the *impact of the wealth and income from wealth of the highest-income bracket on income distribution.* Chapter 7 deals with the marketing structure and the extent of competition at the different levels of distribution, culminating in a discussion of the concentration of decision-making on the prices and sales pattern in the marketing structure. Since prices are an important factor in the determination of the income of the small rural producers, the study of ownership and control can also form a basis for estimating the control of flow of income to the rural sector by the leaders of the corporate sector. Chapter 8 traces the origins and bases of the Malaysian businessmen and executives of the three races which together with the data on the concentration of wealth ownership and pyramid marketing structure enable us to establish the extent of upward mobility within the group of people engaged in business. The last section of Chapter 8 also attempts to summarize the salient characteristics and perspectives of the businessmen of various races in terms of their origins, bases, and the pressure and promises of the NEP.

The pioneering work on ownership and control in the Malayan economy was written by J. J. Puthucheary in the fifties. He observed the very extensive and clustered control of Malayan rubber, tin, and wholesale trade by the British investors primarily through the vehicle of the agency houses.[1] Since Puthucheary, there have been at least six other studies: that of Mamajiwala (1965), Yip (1968), Hirschman (1973), Lindenberg (1973), Lim (1978), and Sieh (1977). Hirschman's, Lindenberg's, and Sieh's works dealt with the manufacturing sector while Lindenberg's work was limited to the pioneer industries only. All three provided interesting insights, but were too limited both in scope and depth.[2] The Mamajiwala study was very thorough for the section of the estate sector it covered—the publicly listed rubber companies incorporated in Malaya—which unfortunately held only 1.4 per cent of all estate land.[3] Yip gave a general view of the ownership structure of the publicly listed tin mining companies in a very aggregative manner like the latter-day study of the manufacturing sector by Sieh; thus it is similarly flawed with a lack of depth and scope, especially the inability to account for the interlocking structure by the controlling interests. Lim's work was the most comprehensive, with a wealth of information on shareholdings and social backgrounds of the businessmen and executives. Unfortunately, however, his rigid imposition of graph theory in classifying and analysing business linkages is too mechanistic and frequently misleading as to the true linkages among important business groups.[4]

In the next section, some general observations on the 'typical' ownership and control pattern of large Malaysian companies will be made to provide the basic methodology for this chapter. Subsequently, the ownership and control pattern of the Malaysian economy will be discussed in three sub-categories:

(1) the traditional activities which cover the rubber and oil palm estates and tin mines[5] (Section 5.3);
(2) the financial sector which includes the banks, finance, and insurance companies (Section 5.4); and
(3) the manufacturing, real estate, housing and other sectors. All these have been lumped together as their development has become important and dynamic only after Independence and the concentration of control in these sectors is not generally so severe as that in the other sectors (Section 5.5).

Under the NEP, the Government has taken various steps to achieve 30 per cent Malay ownership of share capital and the creation of a Malay entrepreneurial group. Such steps are bound to create very important changes in the structure of ownership and control in this economy. Section 5.6 summarizes the Government's effort in this direction, discusses some of the welfare and procedural questions involved in the restructuring policies, summarizes the changes in Malay ownership and control of the economy, discusses in a desultory manner the three earlier sections and provides a few examples of important Malay businessmen with significant concentration of wealth.

Most of the data in this chapter have been based on publicly listed companies, although where possible private companies are included. Generally, the public companies tend to be large, while the private ones cover a wide range from the very small to the really large. As such, the analysis will cover most of the large enterprises and it can be construed as representative of the wealthiest companies. This point will be further substantiated in Chapter 6 which provides a more aggregative view of the pattern of ownership and profitability.

5.2 GENERAL OWNERSHIP AND CONTROL CHARACTERISTICS OF MALAYSIAN COMPANIES

A. What Constitutes Control?

In sole proprietorships and partnerships, ownership is almost synonymous with control. In private limited companies, the number of shareholders is usually limited, with the shares tightly held by members of several partnership families.[6] In the larger and/or more modern of these firms, some executive employees may be allotted a few shares. Hence, the distinction between ownership and control is not important.

The picture is very different with the publicly listed companies. Within these companies, a whole range of concurrence between ownership and control is possible. The stock exchange in Malaysia has a very short history dating only from post-war days, with really active local floating of companies coming as late as the sixties.[7] Prior to 1960, perhaps fifty companies were listed, most of which were rubber and tin companies originally floated by the British, with a sprinkling of financial and industrial companies. Most of the companies floated since then are relatively smaller in scale, freshly emerging from the realm of private limited companies with tightly held shares. For this reason, it is necessary to distinguish the many different combinations in the pattern of ownership and control.

In statistics provided by the Government (e.g., the *Financial Survey of Limited Companies*), a minimum ownership of 50 per cent of the outstanding shares of a company is regarded as control of a company; this is too stringent a definition of control.[8] Theoretically, the shareholders vote on how profits should be allocated. But, by and large, it is the executives who can propose and allocate the profits either for dividend or more investments, thus having effective control of this pool of funds accruing to the shareholders. Research for this chapter has shown that the dispersal of shares other than those belonging to the major directors coupled with general shareholders' apathy have enabled effective control with less than 50 per cent ownership. Therefore, a broader definition of control, in this case the ownership of a large block of shares adequate to dominate decision-making by the company, may be a better gauge of the real wealth of the major executive shareholders.

As a result, many of the companies classified as being under local control in the terminology of Government surveys would actually be classified as foreign controlled by the above criterion. While this distinction is insignificant in the case of the private limited companies, a higher degree of foreign control of the publicly listed companies will necessarily be reported in this book compared with those reported by the financial surveys.[9]

B. Control of Malaysian Companies at Different Levels of Operation

The shares of the smaller companies with paid-up capital of less than $10 million tend to be held very tightly. Half of these publicly listed companies were recently floated by the several families that owned them in the preceding private limited companies. Some may be partially owned by a foreign corporation with one or more local partners, again with a fairly recent history of quotation on the Stock Exchange. Their small capital makes them easy targets for take-over bids, prompting the original owners or controlling interest to hold substantial amounts of stocks directly or through associates. In these cases, it is not unusual to see more than 50 per cent of the shares tightly held, though the owning of 30 per cent of the shares by one family may begin to constitute control provided that the other large shareholders are either passive or sympathetic. The distribution of directorships usually reflects the distribution of the original ownership of capital.[10]

At this level of operation, more often than not, the local directors are themselves the major shareholders.[11] The other directors nominated by the same block of shareholders are frequently either close relatives or long-time business associates. Rarely does it happen that the block of shareholders nominate an executive employee as the director. As for the foreign partners, it is unusual for their original controlling shareholders or even major director(s) to be representatives on the local board since the local operation is only a small part of their global operation. It is probably the managing director and/or executives of their Far Eastern subsidiary who represent their interests in Malaysia.

Those firms with paid-up capital of more than $10 million but less than $30 million[12] could have ownership structures and directorship set-ups broadly similar to the smaller firms. However, the percentage of capital floated may be slightly higher; and one may begin to observe the appointment of senior executives to sit on the board by, and together with, the local major shareholders. Naturally the senior executives themselves would hold significant but minority numbers of shares. Nevertheless, it is important to distinguish the original entrepreneur from their hired executives-turned-partners.[13]

Once the firms have paid-up capital in excess of $30 million, especially when they reach $50 million or more, they are among the largest firms in Malaysia. This is when the volume of shares in circulation can be quite large and may be much more than 50 per cent of the total issued share capital. In such cases, it is not easy for anyone to bid for the company and a 10—20 per cent shareholding may constitute working control if the remaining shares are well dispersed.

The above pattern has been drawn to serve as a guideline. In analysing the pattern of ownership and control in Malaysia, it is more important to realize that most of these companies are newly listed, or even newly established. They are in a great state of flux; take-over, merger, and bidding abound, all of which tend to make generalization too rigid and hazardous.

The discussion in this chapter is conducted with the above broad identification of the control of business organizations in mind. While it would have been ideal and much more accurate to trace and document the actual number of shares owned and controlled by a particular director, group of directors, or shareholders, the process is too involved. It requires not just the compilation and classification of all stock registers, but also a great familiarity with the nominee and trustee arrangements. This is done whenever possible. But full and complete documentation is unnecessary and almost impossible. Rather, the limited information has been combined with interviews with a score of knowledgeable persons in various commercial and industrial activities to establish the control by particular director(s) in the various conglomerations. The identification of key directors is frequently taken as an indication of key ownership and control as it is not always possible to verify the precise proportion of their share ownership.

5.3 THE TRADITIONAL SECTOR

A. A Review

In his pioneering work, Puthucheary detailed the system of interlocking directorship, management and secretarial arrangements by which the major agency houses controlled the Malayan rubber and tin industries with only some equity participation.[14] In the few years preceding Independence, many British investors, fearing the uncertainties, sold their shares and sometimes even whole estates. Many of the estates were subdivided and sold to local groups; some of these were later further subdivided and sold to the smallholders.[15] The selling of shares and estates opened up the opportunity for local investors to buy into hitherto European companies at what was perhaps a fairly good price. Apart from this, the years of economic development had by then established a small core of businessmen affluent and sophisticated enough to plan for expansion and acquisition.[16] We would expect that the pattern of ownership and control in these two industries would have fundamentally altered. Has it?

Preliminary evidence has shown that it was mainly the relatively smaller British investors who sold out and the Malaysian and Singaporean investors who bought the shares of these companies prior to the seventies were, with few exceptions, small Chinese investors or those with dispersed holdings. Only a few local groups were able to take over ownership as well as control of the smaller companies.[17] Control continued to rest in the hands of the agency houses. The changes in the control of the major planting and mining companies did not occur till the seventies.

B. The Estates

(a) GENERAL

In 1974, West Malaysia had approximately 2.184 million acres of rubber and oil palm estate land, of which 1.430 million acres had been planted with rubber and 0.754 million acres with oil palm.[18] As Table 5.1 indicates, the five largest planting groups together with Highlands & Lowlands Bhd. (H & L), which three of them jointly controlled, owned more than 493,975 acres (or 34.64 per cent of the total) of rubber estates and 340,025 acres (or 45.10 per cent of the total) of oil palm estates. In addition, they controlled at least another 42,196 acres of estates through management and secretarial duties for other plantations. The two next largest groups, Plantation Agencies Sdn. Bhd. (P.A.) and Socfin Co. Bhd., controlled/owned 136,504 and 68,563 acres respectively. Following these, the next twelve large independent planting companies/groups owned and controlled 356,739 acres, with the following twenty big planting companies/groups owning and controlling another 183,117 acres of estates. Table 5.1 lists each of the top twenty groups/companies. However, at the level of the next twenty, some have been omitted because of the lack of published or confirmed acreage. Their number, however, is not likely to exceed ten. In all, after eliminating double counting (see Table 5.1), this group of forty companies/groups accounted for more than 75.8 per cent (1,655,640 acres) of the total estate rubber and oil palm acreage; and there are indications that this amount may be growing,[19] i.e., greater concentration.

There is, thus, a striking concentration of ownership by two or three score companies. But the extent of foreign domination or control at this level up to the mid-seventies is even more striking. Of the five largest groups, only that headed by Tan Sri Dato Lee Loy Seng and the Sime Darby Bhd. group are locally owned and controlled; and control of both passed to local hands only

TABLE 5.1
THE MAJOR PLANTATION GROUPS AND THEIR HOLDINGS, 1974+++

Name of Group***	Owned Acreage (1)			Controlled Acreage (2)			Total	
	Rubber	Oil Palm	Total	Rubber	Oil Palm	Total	Acreage	%
1. Harrisons & Crosfield Ltd., Group*	120,698	73,635	222,387	14,447	4,579	19,026	241,413	11.05
2. Sime Darby Bhd. Group*	112,418	83,859	197,196	10,549	—	11,262	208,458	9.54
3. The Guthrie Corporation, Ltd. Group++	107,609	76,290	185,255	—	—	—	185,255	8.48
4. Lee Loy Seng Group (3)	62,116	53,743	123,786	—	—	—	123,786	5.67
5. Boustead Holdings Bhd. and Barlow Group*	57,574	18,269	82,578	9,004	1,804	11,908	94,486	4.33
6. Highlands & Lowlands Bhd. (4)	33,560	34,229	77,016	—	—	—	77,016	3.53
Sub-total	493,975	340,025	888,218	34,000	6,383	42,196	930,414	42.60
7. Plantation Agencies Sdn. Bhd.*	—	—	—	109,184	20,754	136,504	136,504	6.25
(a) Plantation Holdings Ltd.	17,601	9,180	28,830					
(b) National Land Finance Co-operative Society Ltd.	15,099	462	20,360					
(c) Amalgamated Rubber Estate Ltd., Rubber Trust Ltd., and Shanghai Kelantan Ltd.	30,711	144	33,656					
(d) Kuala Reman Rubber Estate	9,524	515	11,705					
(e) Others (5)	36,249	10,453	54,551					
8. Socfin Co. Bhd.*	34,568	29,161	68,563				68,563	
(a) Plantations des Terres Rouges	—	28,565	30,439					

(Continued)

TABLE 5.1 (Continued)

Name of Group	Owned Acreage (1)			Controlled Acreage (2)			Total	
	Rubber	Oil Palm	Total	Rubber	Oil Palm	Total	Acreage	%
(b) New Selangor Plantations Co. Bhd.	16,969	225	18,340					
(c) Compagnie du Cambodge	10,151	371	12,176					
(d) Compagnie du Caoutchouc de Padang	7,448	—	7,608					
9. Dunlop Estates Bhd.	36,363	18,164	54,527				54,527	
10. Goh Tjooi Kok Group (6) @	—	15,177	42,260				42,260	
11. Trengganu Development Malaysia Bhd. @	—	8,500	8,500	—	24,904	24,904	33,404	
12. Ko Rubber Plantations	25,393	—	31,783				31,783	
13. Uniroyal Malaysian Plantations Sdn. Bhd.	27,819	—	29,728				29,728	
14. Johor State Government			29,000				29,000	
15. Unipamol Malaysia Sdn. Bhd.	—	26,411	26,411				26,411	
16. Malacca Group (7)*	18,235	4,085	23,122	2,659	—	2,659	25,781	
17. United Plantations Bhd.	395	23,371	23,766				23,766 (+9,142 ac. Other Crops)	
18. Kulim (M) Bhd.	4,653	14,595	19,248				19,248	
19. Yule Catto Ltd. (8)	10,339	4,924	16,873				16,873	
20. Associated Estate Agencies Bhd. (9)*	—	—	16,011	—	—	—	16,011	
21. M. P. Evans & Co. Ltd.*	—	—	—	13,501	1,733	15,846	15,846	
22. Tsang @	—	15,348	15,348	—	—	—	15,348	
23. The East-Asiatic Co. (Malaysia) Bhd.	5,560	—	5,604	—	—	7,966	13,570	

(Continued)

TABLE 5.1 (Continued)

Name of Group	*Owned Acreage (1)*			*Controlled Acreage (2)*			*Total*	
	Rubber	*Oil Palm*	*Total*	*Rubber*	*Oil Palm*	*Total*	*Acreage*	*%*
24. Loh Boon Siew			12,076				12,076	
25. Keck Seng (Malaysia) Bhd.	7,156	4,700	11,856				11,856	
26. Lee Plantation (10)	—	—	10,972				10,972	
27. Kemayan Oil Palm Bhd. @	—	7,983	10,080				10,080	
28. Kew Man Co. Sdn. Bhd.	8,481	—	8,481				8,481	
29. West Country Sdn. Bhd.	5,087	1,305	7,343				7,343	
30. Perbadanan Kemajuan Negeri Kedah	5,500	—	7,200	acreage included in 'Others' of Plantation Agencies			7,200	
Sub-total 7 to 30	293,233**	194,478**	620,654				659,431	30.19**
31. Austral Enterprises Bhd.	1,053	4,638	7,144				7,144	
32. Chee Tat Realty Pte. Ltd.– Kheng Hup Co. Pte. Ltd.	—	—	6,662				6,662	
33. Riverview Rubber Estate Bhd.	5,848	—	6,634				6,634	
34. Neoh Choo Ee	5,805	150	6,177	acreage included in 'Others' of Plantation Agencies			6,177	
35. Pelam Estate Sdn. Bhd.	5,559	—	6,319				6,319	
36. Lee Thor Seng (11)	5,915	—	5,915				5,915	
37. Gopeng Consolidated Ltd.			5,003				5,003	
38. Arumugam Pillai++	4,381	—	4,545				4,545	
39. Gan Teng Siew Realty Sdn. Bhd.	4,372	—	4,486				4,486	
40. See Hoy Chan	2,957	1,223	4,287				4,287	
Total 40 companies/groups	823,098	534,503	1,559,867				1,640,840	75.13
Total West Malaysia	1,430,000	754,000	2,184,000					

Sources. *Straits Times Directory*, 1967, 1974. Zorn & Leigh-Hunt, *Manual of Rubber and Tin Companies*, 1974. Fraser & Co., Fraser's *Facts and Figures of South East Asian Plantations*, 1970. Various Company Reports. Barlow and Chan, *Towards an Optimum Size of Rubber Holding*.

Notes. (1) Owned Acreage includes all acreages owned by companies in which the group has a controlling interest (may be less than 50 per cent).

(2) Controlled acreage includes only managed acreage.

(3) Lee Loy Seng's group includes all the companies in Chart 5.2.

(4) Highlands & Lowlands Bhd. is currently under the joint holdings of Sime Darby Bhd., Lee Loy Seng's group and Pernas.

(5) Others include the acreage of all the companies managed by Plantation Agencies Sdn. Bhd., some of which are listed separately.

(6) Goh Tjooi Kok's group includes all companies in Chart 5.5, Tan Tat-wai, 'Income Distribution and Determination in West Malaysia'.

(7) Malacca group is that managed by Unitac presented in Chart 5.6.

(8) While Yule Catto had come under the joint control of the original British investors, Lee Loy Seng's K.L. Kepong Bhd. and the Johor State Government by 1980, it was independent in 1974.

(9) Associated Estate Agencies Bhd.'s managed acreages are all owned by the directors.

(10) Lee Thor Seng's group includes Jeram Kuantan (M) Bhd., Kluang Rubber Co. (M) Bhd. and Sungei Bagan Rubber Co. (M) Bhd.

* Estate agencies.

** Incomplete figures.

*** Names of some companies have been changed from their 1974 ones to those currently in use.

@ Companies which have large new oil palm acreage.

\+ The figures here do not include the 10,300 acres of rubber and oil palm estate purchased from the Heah Joo Seang Rubber Estates Sdn. Bhd. in the mid-seventies, but which have been included in the sub-total of nos. 7 to 30.

++ Since 1974, Arumugam Pillai has lost a court case to the Income Tax Department and has had some of his estates auctioned by the Government. The Kedah State Government (no. 30) purchased the biggest Arumugam Pillai estate to raise its total area to more than 11,000 acres.

+++ Since 1974, some new development has occurred in the estate sector. The Lee Loy Seng group has acquired 26 per cent of Yule Catto with the Johor State Government a 35 per cent share of Yule Catto's plantation subsidiary. In addition, the Johore State Government has acquired 43 per cent of Kulim by injecting some of its estates into Kulim. The Trengganu State Government, through Kompleks Ladang Getah Bukit Besi and Kompleks Ladang Sungai Tong, has become operator of more than 30,000 acres of estates. Amalgamated Rubber Estates Ltd., Rubber Trust Ltd., and Shanghai Kelantan Rubber Estates Ltd. were taken over by Genting Bhd. Several business groups have also commenced the opening-up of new estates of 10,000 acres size each.

recently. Harrisons & Crosfield Ltd. (H & C), The Guthrie Corporation, Ltd., and Boustead Holdings Bhd. and Barlow group are all British agency houses with majority ownership and control resting in the hands of the British. At the next level, P.A. is a Hong Kong–British company and Socfin Co. Bhd. is a French company. Six of the next twelve planting groups are European- and American-owned and controlled, and each has at least 15,000 acres; of the remaining six, the Goh group, Trengganu Development Malaysia Bhd., and Ko Plantations are all controlled by Singaporeans, though Trengganu Development has important Malaysian partners. Only three, the Johor State Government, Malacca group and the Associated Estate Agency Bhd., are truly Malaysian in ownership and control. Down the list, the Keck Seng (Malaysia) Bhd., Lee Plantation, Chee Tat, Lee Thor Seng group and Gopeng Consolidated Ltd. are all Singaporean; M. P. Evans and Co. Ltd. is a foreign planting agency; East Asiatic Co. (Malaysia) Bhd. and Riverview Rubber Estate Bhd. are European; Pelam Estate Sdn. Bhd. is a company on which the author has no information, while the remaining eleven are Malaysian in ownership and control.[20] In short, only two of the five largest (in 1974 it was actually only one, since Sime Darby was not then controlled by Malaysians), three of the next twelve planting groups and three agencies, and eleven of the next twenty were Malaysian in ownership and control. If Sime Darby is included under Malaysian control, the Malaysians controlled about 462,000 acres or 19.3 per cent of the total estate land. By contrast, the dozen largest foreign-controlled groups owned and/or controlled 45.6 per cent. If Sime Darby is treated as foreign controlled, as was the case in 1974, the Malaysians controlled and/or owned only 9.8 per cent.

The control by the agency houses remained as strong as ever in the plantation sector.

(b) THE AGENCY HOUSES: THEIR DEVELOPMENT

Although the agency houses as a group have maintained their predominant position in the plantation sector up to this day, the development of each agency house has been different.

Of all the agency houses, Sime Darby (SD) has had the most striking development. Though it has been a major agency for some time, it was never among the largest five. As recently as 1968, it managed only nine planting companies with a total area of 110,692 acres. However, through a series of reorganizations, estate sellings and acquisitions, and share swapping,[21] its owned and/or controlled acreage had swollen to 197,199 by 1974, making it the second largest estate owner-manager in Peninsular Malaysia. In addition, having initiated or acquired extensive industrial and commercial enterprises in Europe and South-East Asia, it has become the major conglomerate in this part of the world and is no longer simply an agency house. Over the years, an increasing proportion of its shares has been acquired by Malaysians with no change in the structure of management and control until 1976.

Harrisons & Crosfield has been the largest plantation agency house. The acreage under its control has remained above 220,000 acres since 1953,[22] unlike the other major agency houses. Its control over the associated estates has become even tighter with its successful offer in 1978 for the bulk of the shares of Malayalam Plantations, Ltd., Harcros Investment Trust Ltd., and

Harrisons Malaysian Estates Ltd., itself a merger of the three sister companies of London Asiatic Rubber and Produce Co. Ltd., Petaling Rubber Estates Ltd., and Golden Hope Plantations Ltd. only in 1976.

In the same period, The Guthrie Corporation, Ltd. slightly increased its ownership of estates from 175,044 acres to 185,255 acres in 1974, continuing the trend from the fifties[23] and moving into the number three position in view of the faster pace of expansion of SD. Control remained in the hands of the British though part of its estate holdings was grouped into a new publicly listed company, Guthrie Ropel Bhd., through which some Malaysian participation was facilitated.[24]

Plantation Agencies also expanded to manage eight large independent planting companies and a number of smaller ones giving it an expanded management acreage of 136,504, compared with 108,634 acres in 1968, and 51,526 acres in 1953.[25] Unlike other major agency houses, this associate of Jardine Matheson & Co., Ltd., one of the largest British financial interests in the Far East, has concentrated its activity in estate management for the planting companies belonging to British financial interests based in Hong Kong. In the sixties there seemed to be a coincidence in the building up of P.A.'s management activities and Jardine's expansion of its estate holding. However, with Jardine Matheson selling off its substantial estate holding in 1978,[26] it is not clear whether there will be any change in P.A.'s activity.

By contrast, two former major agency houses have curtailed their estate management activity substantially. Meagl Sdn. Bhd., 36 per cent owned by Syarikat Harper Gilfillan Bhd., and which used to own and manage the third largest acreage, has since ceased its management activity and gone into voluntary liquidation.[27] More recently, Barlow–Boustead appear to be similarly reducing their activities in Malaysia. The recent relinquishment of controlling ownership of H & L reduced their owned acreage to 82,854 acres and is of particular significance. This reduced their owned and controlled acreage from 219,973 in 1968 to 102,991 in 1974.[28] The other big planting agencies have been able to maintain their level of activities, though there has also been some reorganization.[29]

It is interesting to ask why some of the major agency houses seem to have been forced into a curtailment of activity. Was this due to the aggressive acquisition policy of the Lee Loy Seng and Sime Darby groups? Or was there a conscious decision to withdraw from this region which then opened up the opportunity for the other two groups to go on the acquisition trail? In particular, the timing of the Barlow group's withdrawal following its merger with the Boustead group and the latter's expansion in planting activities in the fifties is quite intriguing. Incidentally, Harper Gilfillan also expanded its plantation activities in the same period, only to withdraw soon after. By contrast, a group like REA–Cumberbatch & Co. chose to phase out their plantation operation quite early.[30] It would be interesting to know what prompted the policy reversals of Barlow–Boustead and Harper Gilfillan, though it appears as if the Barlow–Boustead group decided very early to comply with the NEP and started to restructure. Chart 5.1 appears to support this contention.

Why has there been realignment and amalgamation of estates? For the biggest agency houses and planters who were well informed and therefore more

CHART 5.1
THE BARLOW–BOUSTEAD GROUP

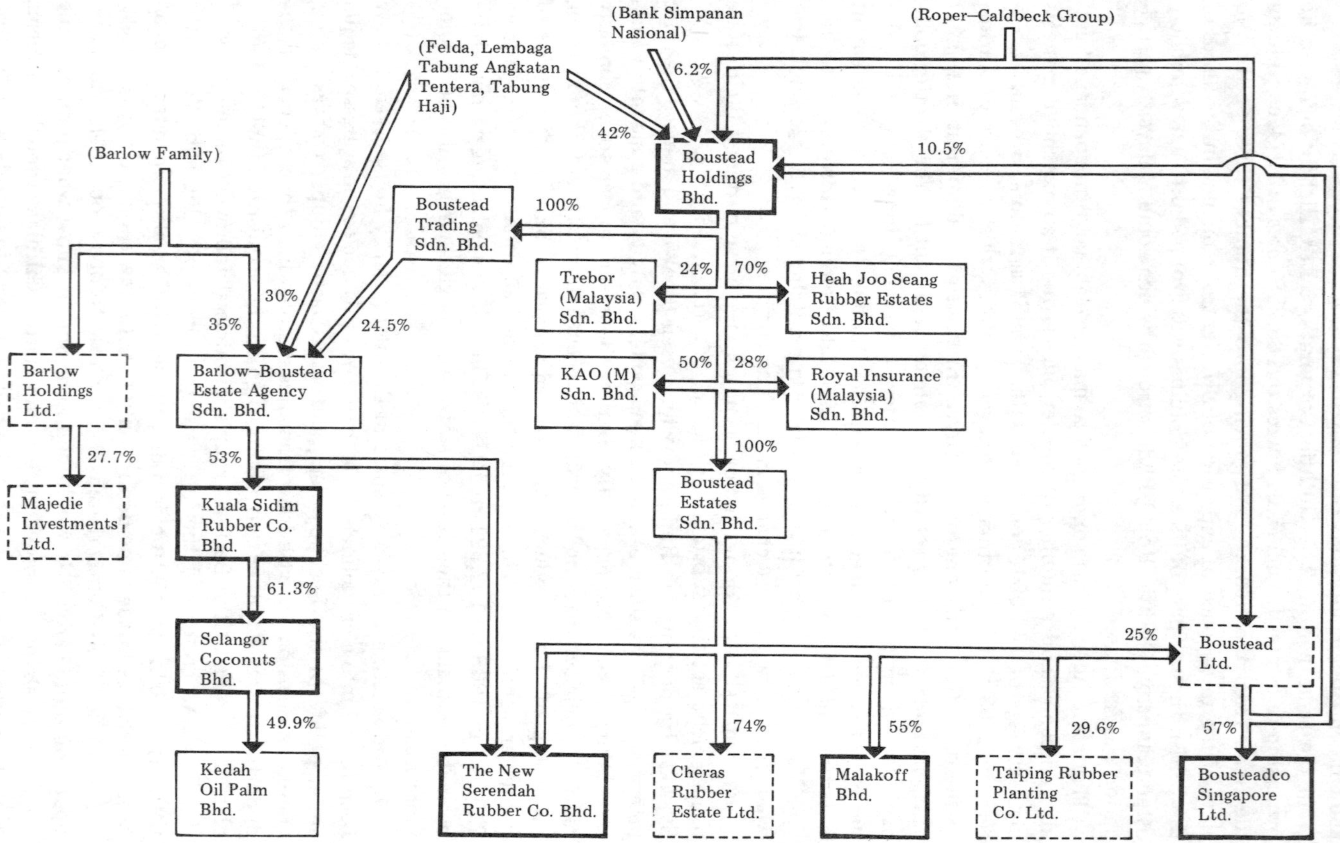

Introductory Notes and Sources to Charts 5.1 to 5.19.

These charts have been constructed based on a vast number of articles, documents, records, and interviews. Rather than listing all the sources separately for each Chart, all the relevant major sources are listed here:
Stock Exchange Handbook, Singapore, various years.
Stock Exchange Handbook, Kuala Lumpur, various years.
Gazette, Kuala Lumpur Stock Exchange, various months.
Journal of Singapore Stock Exchange, various months.
Fraser & Co., *Facts & Figures*, various volumes, especially 1964, 1967, and 1970.
Zorn and Leigh-Hunt, *Manual of Planting Companies*, various years.
New Straits Times, Business Times section, 1971 onwards.
Nanyang Siang Pau 南洋商報 column written by 冷眼.
Malaysian Business, various months, especially the monthly feature write-up by Solomon on different companies.
Far Eastern Economic Review, 1971 onwards.
Annual company reports of the various companies.
Company files with the Registrar of companies.
Company files with the Kuala Lumpur Stock Exchange library.
Jane's Major Companies of Europe, 1973, 1974.
Stock Exchange Official Year Book, London, 1975–6.

(heavy-bordered box)	Publicly listed limited company incorporated in Malaysia/Singapore
(plain box)	Private limited company incorporated in Malaysia/Singapore
(dashed box)	Publicly listed company quoted in a foreign stock exchange
A —*x%*→ B	Company A holds x per cent of shares of Company B
( ), [ ]	Controlling interests
d or director	Appointed a director of that company, but shareholding not known

confident of the economic prospects of this country after Independence, it was a unique opportunity for them to improve their economic position. In the years preceding the war, they were not in a position to expand as they had to consolidate their holdings in the estates and planting companies which they had helped to set up and manage. At that time, it was also more difficult to expand as there were more agency houses all competing to consolidate their foothold in the industry. After the war, many of the estates lay in ruins, and time, energy, and money were needed for the rehabilitation.[31] The high prices resulting from the Korean War enabled them to recover substantial funds and resume more aggressive activities. With the withdrawal of some investors when Independence seemed imminent, the opportunity to acquire good estates at bargain prices pushed the agency houses into acquiring and amalgamating estates and planting companies. Their management and secretarial duties had probably given the agency houses better insight into choice acquisitions. As their holdings became larger, it became sensible to look into ways to take advantage of economies of scale. One natural way was to 'exchange' estates such that the companies could now manage a large tract of adjoining estates rather than many widely scattered ones. The exchange of estates also offered an opportunity to realize additional profits as capital gains. This served the dual function of evading tax payments and raising the book value for a better bargaining position in case of a nationalization policy. These are, however, postulations which need further substantiation.

(c) LOCAL PENETRATION OF THE ESTATE SECTOR

(*i*) *The Big Estates.* In the post-war period, when some of the European planting companies began to withdraw, very few of the local businessmen would have been able to buy controlling interests in the large plantation companies. First of all, few of them owned the kind of capital needed for gaining control of a large company.[32] Secondly, few of them had enough access and expertise to trade on the London Stock Exchange where the bulk of the major planting companies (for that matter, the tin companies also) were traded. Thirdly, the tight control exercised by the agency houses through share ownership, management, and secretarial duties made it unlikely that the best and most profitable would be allowed to change hands.[33]

Indeed, despite the increasing interest of Malaysians, especially the non-Malays, to buy into the foreign-owned and controlled companies,[34] only the Lee Loy Seng group (Chart 5.2) managed to wrest control from major planting companies and expanded its ownership to 123,786 acres by 1974. This group also has several important minority stakes in other big planting companies which may lead to eventual control.[35] The take-over of SD in 1976 occurred under rather different circumstances: it was probably initiated by the Government-owned corporation, Pernas, or at the very least, had its tacit support.[36] As late as 1976, when another major locally-controlled company, Genting Highlands Bhd., tried to bid for Golden Hope Plantations Ltd. under the H & C wing, it failed.[37] In fact, over the same period, several major local estates passed into the control of the expanding foreign-owned and controlled companies.[38]

Other take-over bids occurred on a much smaller scale, generally conducted by businessmen-planters with a long history of involvement in this sector. The setting up of United Malacca Rubber Estates Bhd., Associated Estate Agencies Bhd., Heah Joo Seang Rubber Estates Sdn. Bhd. and Kew Man Co. Sdn. Bhd. are examples of this. Their size at the peak of their operations ranged between 15,000 and 30,000 acres only.[39] Therefore, it appears that the withdrawal of European capital in the estate sector has opened up few opportunities for the average Malaysian businessman. This assertion can be further supported by examining the statistics provided in Tables 5.2 and 5.3. There were only 414 rubber estates and 127 oil palm estates larger than 1,000 acres in 1973, the great majority of which would have been included in the tabulation in Table 5.1. Among these, the Malaysian-owned estates accounted for 35.8 per cent of rubber acreage and 45.9 per cent of oil palm acreage, including those owned by Malaysians but managed by the agencies. The position occu-

CHART 5.2
THE LEE LOY SENG GROUP

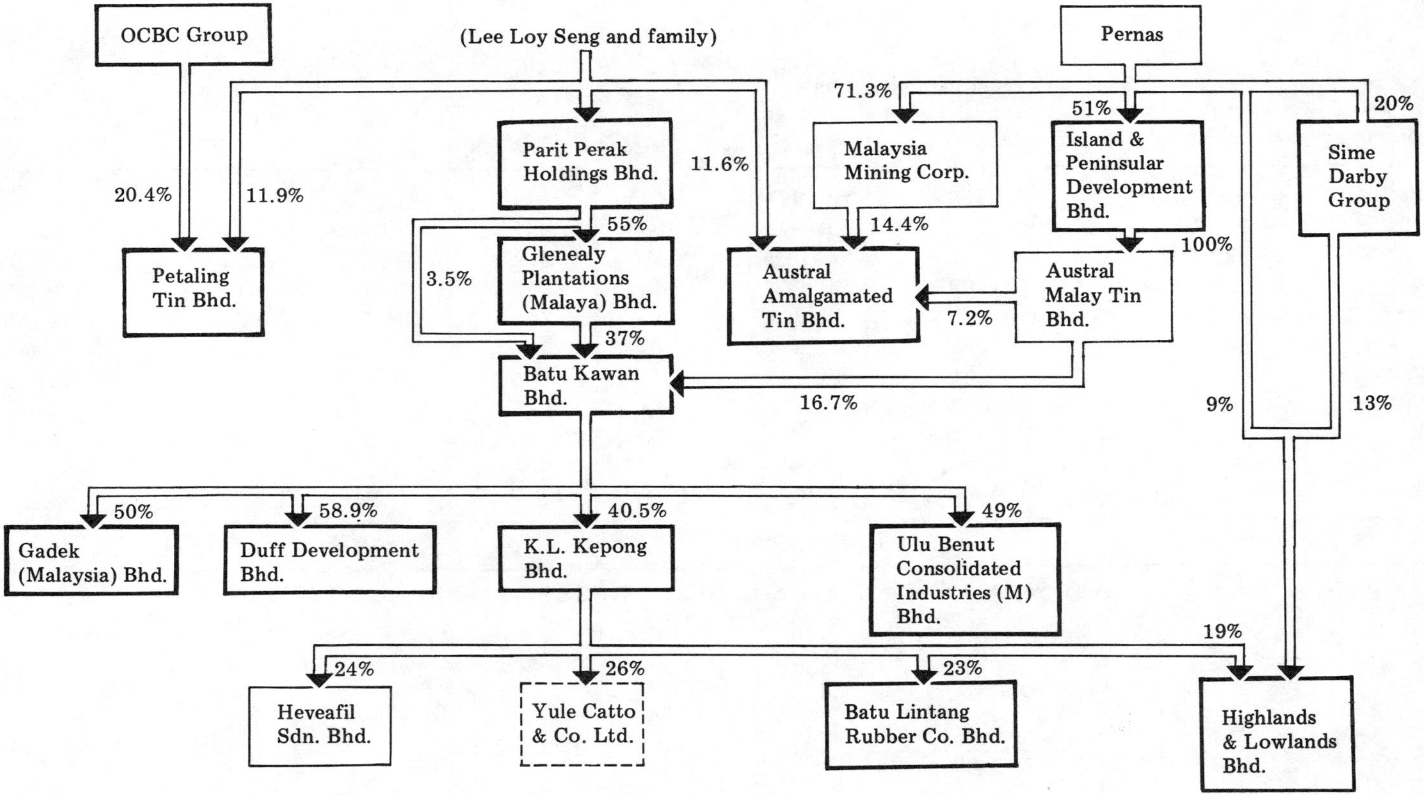

TABLE 5.2
RUBBER ESTATES STATISTICS, 1973 (IN ACRES)

Size Group (ac.)	*Malaysian*			*Non-Malaysian*			*All*		
	Number	*Total Area*	*Average Area*	*Number*	*Total Area*	*Average Area*	*Number*	*Total Area*	*Average Area*
0—499	1,103	205,719	187	158	32,305	204	1,261	237,924	189
500—999	158	115,508	731	75	55,333	738	233	170,841	733
1,000—1,999	112	153,772	1,373	101	145,975	1,445	213	299,747	1,407
2,000—2,999	29	71,099	2,452	57	136,247	2,390	86	207,346	2,411
3,000—4,999	19	71,126	3,743	59	229,822	3,895	78	300,948	3,858
5,000+	12	79,386	6,616	25	160,276	6,411	37	239,662	6,477
Total*	1,433	696,610	486	475	759,858	1,600	1,908	1,456,468	763
All*		913,126	637		1,135,604	2,391		2,048,730	1,074

Source. *Rubber Statistics Handbook 1973*, Table 2.6, p. 14, Table 3.5, p. 29.

Note. *The area under 'Total' is for the estates with rubber as the sole or major crop, whereas the area under 'All' refers to all estates with planted rubber area.

TABLE 5.3

OIL PALM ESTATES STATISTICS, 1973 (IN ACRES)

Size Group (ac.)	Malaysian			British			Other			Total		
	Number	*Total Area*	*Average Area*	*Number*	*Total Area*	*Average Area*	*Number*	*Total Area*	*Average Area*	*Number*	*Total Area*	*Average Area*
0—99	20	1,429	71	1	20	20	3	166	55	24	1,615	67
100—499	82	17,849	218	2	532	266	8	1,900	238	92	20,281	220
500—999	26	17,903	689	5	3,668	734	7	4,664	666	38	26,235	690
1,000—1,999	24	35,069	1,461	8	11,746	1,468	4	4,522	1,131	36	51,337	1,426
2,000—2,999	14	35,191	2,514	12	28,748	2,396	2	4,523	2,262	28	68,462	2,445
3,000—4,999	17	60,491	3,558	12	46,608	3,884	2	9,253	4,627	31	116,352	3,753
5,000+	12	93,570	7,798	11	79,712	7,247	9	78,386	8,710	32	251,668	7,865
Total*	195	261,502	1,341	51	171,034	3,354	35	103,414	2,955	281	535,950	1,907
All*	341	315,568		112	250,278		53	113,159		506	679,005	

Source. *Oil Palm, Coconut and Tea Statistics, West Malaysia*, 1973, Table 7, p. 14, Table 16, p. 26.

Note. *The area under 'Total' is for the estates with oil palm as the sole or major crop, whereas the area under 'All' refers to all estates with planted oil palm area.

pied by the Malaysians was clearly inferior to that of the foreigners. That Malaysians had a larger precentage of oil palm acreage than rubber is a testament that the foreigners have by and large held on to their rubber estates with the exceptions noted in the preceding paragraphs. The Malaysians could expand their holdings of oil palm by planting it on newly cleared land. As this was a newer crop promoted only in the late sixties, the holdings of the State Governments and groups like the Tsang Estates are notable examples.

(*ii*) *The Small Estates.* There were not many small estates. Only 1,494 rubber estates and 154 oil palm estates in 1973 were less than 1,000 acres but more than 100 acres each (Tables 5.2 and 5.3). The most likely owners of these small estates are the planters who began in a small way, but then through the cycle of land clearance, planting, and possibly the selling and buying of estates built up small estates of a couple of hundred acres. It is of course possible for the small- to medium-sized traders, the civil servants or professionals to accumulate enough wealth to buy a small estate for investment purposes. But nevertheless their number cannot be large, as they usually lack the expertise and aptitude to run the estates themselves and small estates probably would not interest the agency houses for a management agreement. In particular, for the traders who have sufficient wealth, interest in investing in the estate sector would usually come in a big way rather than piecemeal purchases of small estates.[40] Moreover, there are indications that the subdivision of estates which occurred in the fifties most probably passed through the hands of land speculators for further subdivision into smallholdings.[41] The number of small estate owners which might have been created by European withdrawal and the subsequent subdivision is, therefore, likely to be very small. In these circumstances, it seems most likely that local participation in the small estate sector was the result of parallel planting interest on the part of the Malaysians to the development of the big foreign-owned estates. As such, their number and importance were unlikely to have been affected by trends in the larger estate sector. A family-run small estate probably would not be able to manage more than 200 acres; the fact that 1,261 of the 1,494 small rubber estates averaged only 188.7 acres may lend added weight to this postulation.

(d) CONCLUSION

First of all, it should now be apparent that the agency houses taken as a whole have not only maintained their dominance in the rubber industry, but have also moved in a big way into a new and growing industry: oil palm. With control over 674,864 acres of rubber (44.52 per cent of the total estate rubber land or 13.18 per cent of the total rubber acreage) but 396,162 acres of oil palm (58.34 per cent of the total estate oil palm land, 28.52 per cent of the total oil palm land), the hold by the big five and the two leading agency houses in oil palm is even stronger than in rubber. The difference in dominance is affected by the presence of several thousand medium-sized local rubber planters and the lack of corresponding medium-sized local oil palm planters. At the level of large planting companies, foreigners predominate. There are less than a handful of local businessmen who can penetrate the ranks of the top twenty groups.

The second observation is that there seems to be a flow from business activities into ownership of large (but not the largest) rubber estates by local businessmen, whereas the reverse is not true. From the informants interviewed, there seem to be very few planters moving into commerce and industry following the accumulation of wealth. A highly possible explanation from casual observation may be that planting activity is relatively simple compared to trading and industrial activities in terms of organization and know-how.

Thirdly, it is the Chinese businessmen among the local groups who possessed the bulk of *estate* land not owned by the foreigners. They (and to a much lesser extent, Indian traders) have moved into the larger rubber estates. Apart from two or three exceptions, all the Malaysian-owned estates listed in Table 5.1 were owned by Chinese companies. While some of them have Malay or Indian partners, there is no doubt that the Chinese partners predominate. The biggest Indian estate owner appeared to be Arumugam Pillai with over 4,000 acres.[42] It is at the medium-sized level that there are more Malay and Indian owners; these increase towards the end of the scale. There is no ready figure at hand for such breakdown by race in the seventies.

Finally, there are now some very large Government estate holdings on behalf of the Malays.[43] This is a recent development and is the result of substantial effort at both Federal and State level. Pernas' control of the 197,000 acres of SD, the 7,200 acres owned by Perbadanan Kemajuan Negeri Kedah in Ladang Ra'ayat Laka-Temin, the 28,000 acres owned by the Johor State Development Corporation, and those by other State Government agencies, not documented here, are some examples. Furthermore, under the NEP, efforts have been made to bring about the transfer of residence of British-registered rubber and tin companies to Malaysia.

In the process of transfer, restructuring is necessary and there are pressures to allot 30 per cent of the shares to the Malays.[44] As such, Malay ownership and control of the modern agriculture sector (including the estates and Felda schemes) is no longer negligible; it has been on the rise and will continue to rise. By 1973, the Malays already owned 21.0 per cent of the modern agriculture sector compared with 26.3 per cent for the Chinese and 42.3 per cent for the foreigners. The Indians owned a paltry 2.6 per cent.[45] If control is taken as an indicator, Pernas' control of SD has to be included in the Malay-controlled figure which would significantly raise the percentage.

C. Tin

In tin, tight foreign control and domination has been even more pronounced than in the estates. Overall, the publicly listed tin mining companies produced 58.6 per cent of the 1973 Malaysian output using mainly dredges, but 85.5 per cent of this (or 50.2 per cent of the total Malaysian output) was produced by companies owned and controlled by foreigners, mainly British and South African, and to a much lesser extent, Singaporean (Table 5.4). Furthermore, the only two smelters in this country are owned and controlled by foreigners.

Prior to 1972, the two largest tin mining groups in Malaysia, London Tin Ltd. (LT) and Charter Consolidated Ltd. (CC), were independent in structure. LT had control over eleven listed tin mining companies and a number of private ones. CC controlled four listed tin mining companies and some private ones. LT appeared to have made the first moves for a withdrawal from total

TABLE 5.4
TIN OUTPUT BY PUBLICLY LISTED MALAYSIAN COMPANIES IN 1973 BY GROUP

	Output (tons)	*% of Total*
London Tin Group	18,269	25.03
Charter Consolidated Ltd.	8,786	12.04
Aokam Tin Bhd.*	2,146	2.94
The Straits Trading Co. Ltd.–Osborne & Chappel International Sdn. Bhd.	6,480	8.88
The Pahang Consolidated Co. Ltd.	2,577	3.53
Austral Group	1,190	1.63
Kuchai Development Bhd.	919	1.26
Selangor Dredging Bhd.	898	1.23
Rahman Hydraulic Tin Bhd.	865	1.19
Larut Tin Fields Bhd.	658	0.90
Total produced by publicly listed corporations	42,795	58.63

Sources. Stock Exchange of Singapore, *Company Handbook*, 1975; the relevant companies' Annual Reports; Table 8.1A, pp. 174–5, Treasury, *Economic Report*, 1973–4.

Notes. *Jointly owned by London Tin and Charter Consolidated.
Under the London Tin Group, all the companies shown on Chart 5.3 in which London Tin has a controlling interest have been included. Similarly, all the Tronoh Mines Group of Companies are under Charter Consolidated.

participation beginning from the sixties. There were capital repayments in at least three of its companies: Kamunting Tin Dredging (M) Bhd., Kuala Kampar Tin Fields Bhd., and Lower Perak Tin Dredging Bhd.[46] In 1973, following CC's purchase of the largest single block of Haw Par Brothers International Ltd. (HPBI) shares and the appointment of one of its directors, Mr Gammell, as the chairman of HPBI, the latter bought about 30 per cent of LT shares.[47] Probably acting in unison, Pernas Securities Sdn. Bhd. bought another 20 per cent stake of LT. This set in motion a complicated series of events which ultimately established Pernas–CC joint control of all the tin mining companies previously held by LT and CC (Chart 5.3), but without HPBI participation.[48]

With this marriage, the new company, Malaysia Mining Corporation Bhd. (MMC), now controls about 42 per cent of Malaysia's tin output and is the single largest tin mining entity in the world. This deal has of course resulted in cutting down drastically the former predominating role of the foreigners in tin company ownership. However, until Pernas has the technical and managerial expertise, CC can exercise effective management and control while paying some respect and deference to Pernas priorities.

This benefit to CC, a subsidiary of the leading South African mining and financial conglomerate, cannot be underestimated. Its participation in the control of 42 per cent of Malaysian tin output together with its tin mining

CHART 5.3

PERNAS GROUP OF COMPANIES

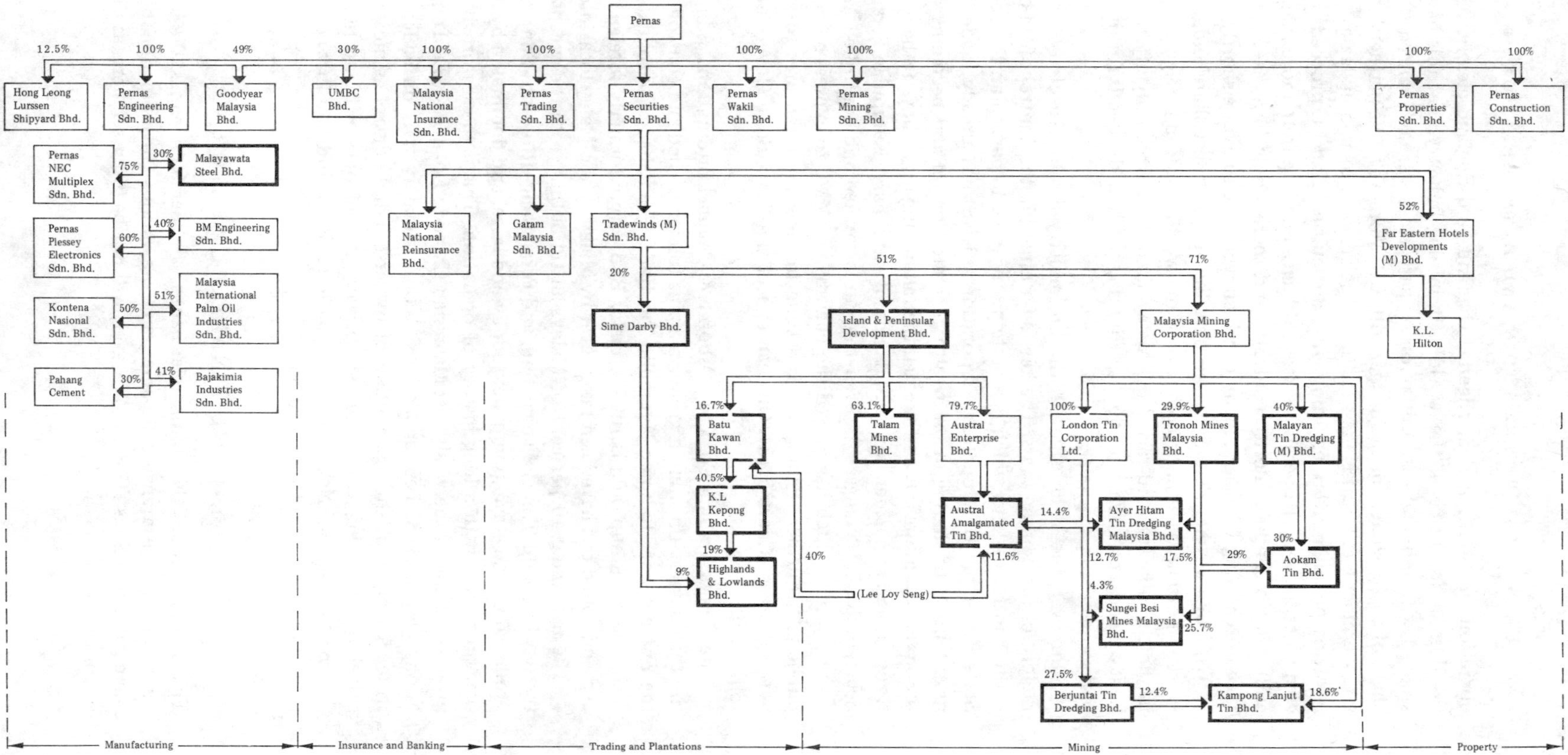

operations in South Africa, Nigeria, Thailand, and England clearly makes it the dominating force in the world's tin mining industry. Yet this had been secured with minimal cash outlay on its part, since Pernas financed the purchase of all LT shares for the merger with CC. Moreover, this partnership with a Government enterprise may facilitate the renewal of mining leases[49] or in resolving possible future environmental difficulties. Had CC proceeded on its own to take over LT operations, it would have had to put up more than $100 million for a simple majority control[50] and there would have been no assurance of renewing LT leases, many of which were due to expire shortly.

With one stroke, Pernas has become the single largest shareholder of the most important tin mining company in the world, reduced foreign ownership in the tin industry, and raised the Malay share in it from insignificance to at least 30 per cent.[51] This, no doubt, will bring political dividends for the ruling party engineering this deal.

Moreover, the Malay share in the tin industry can be expected to increase rapidly in the coming years. The key determinant in the control of tin output is the control of land which is a State prerogative. In particular, the Selangor State Economic Development Corporation (PKNS) has already made known its intention of sharing in the wealth generated by tin and becoming one of the major tin miners. It has directed that all mining leases have to be renewed through, and in partnership with, its mining subsidiary, Kumpulan Perangsang Selangor Bhd. (Perangsang). Even the Pernas-owned and controlled MMC is no exception, which has caused the chairman of MMC to express his concern publicly.[52] Further, Perangsang is setting up new joint ventures to exploit new tin areas (Chart 5.13). One can expect the Perak State Government to follow suit.

The Straits Trading Co. Ltd.–Osborne & Chappel International Sdn. Bhd., the third largest tin mining group, remains foreign-owned and controlled. All the rest but one—Rahman Hydraulic Tin Bhd., The Pahang Consolidated Co. Ltd., Austral group, and Larut Tin Fields Bhd.—were formerly foreign owned and controlled but have been taken over by Malay or non-Malay local interests.

The remaining 40 per cent of Malaysian tin output, with the exception of the newly set up Timah Langat Bhd. and Perangsang–Rio Tinto Sdn. Bhd., is produced by the gravel-pump method, by and large, and dominated by Malaysian tin miners with a long history of operation. This is the sector which has produced some of the wealthiest Malaysian Chinese: Loke Yew, Eu Tong Sen, Foong Seong, H. S. Lee, and others.[53] Unfortunately it is difficult to construct a picture of the distribution of ownership and control as most of the gravel-pump mining companies are private limited ones with no published records to draw on. Nevertheless, casual impressions indicate that concentration of ownership is also substantial.

5.4 THE FINANCIAL SECTOR

This sector includes the commercial banks, the merchant banks, the borrowing companies, insurance companies, and the various Government-controlled financial institutions. The last, however, will not be discussed here, as the seat of control is obvious.

A. Commercial Banks

(a) THE RISE OF DOMESTIC BANKS

To quote Bank Negara Malaysia's *Annual Report* for 1975:

> Before Independence, the banking system was dominated by a few foreign banks, engaged primarily in the mobilisation of savings to finance plantation agriculture, mining and international trade. . . . A total of 20 commercial banks, with 88 offices centred mainly in the major towns, were operating in Malaysia at the end of 1957. Twelve of them, with 77 offices, were foreign banks.[54]

The foreign banks which played a leading role, then, were The Chartered Bank Ltd., The Hongkong & Shanghai Banking Corporation Ltd. (HSBC), and Oversea-Chinese Banking Corporation Ltd. (OCBC).[55] The Chartered Bank and HSBC represented British interests in the Far East. The OCBC was established after the turn of the century by Singaporean and Malayan businessmen with wide-ranging interests in both Singapore and Malaya.[56] The only major Malaysian shareholder group in this bank is the Malacca rubber planting group mentioned earlier.[57]

Before Independence, the only local banks in existence were very small. Ban Hin Lee Bank Bhd., Kwong Yik Bank Bhd., Kwong Lee Bank Bhd., and Oriental Bank Bhd. have all been established for some time, while Hock Hua Bank Bhd., Wah Tat Bank Bhd., and Bian Chiang Bank Bhd. were established in the fifties in East Malaysia. They represented a very outdated and conservative way of banking, having been set up to cater for the banking needs of the owners, who were among the wealthiest local business families or groups.[58]

Since Independence, the sympathetic supervision of the Central Bank fostered a more favourable banking climate for the locals which led to the flourishing of domestic banking activities. To quote Bank Negara again:

> . . . At the end of 1975, there were 36 commercial banks, of which one-half were domestic banks and they operate nearly two-thirds of a total 403 banking offices in this country. . . . Since Independence, the total assets of the banking system have increased from $852 million at the end of 1957 to $10,811 million at the close of business on December 31, 1975. Domestic banks accounted for nearly one-half of these assets, compared with only about 20% in 1957.[59]

Clearly, the domestic banks have grown in the last eighteen years to such an extent that they need no longer play second fiddle to the large foreign banks.

Most of the twelve new local banks established since 1957 were incorporated in the sixties by businessmen who made their money in the rubber and tin sectors and were then diversifying into the financial sector for security, fame (as a banker), and to facilitate future industrial and property development activities.[60] In performance, Malayan Banking Bhd., Bank Bumiputra Bhd., and United Malayan Banking Corporation Bhd. (UMBC) tower over the rest. By 1975, Malayan Banking and Bank Bumiputra had overtaken The Chartered Bank to be the largest and second largest banks, while UMBC had moved into the fourth spot ahead of HSBC and OCBC. Their combined total assets, deposits, and loans formed 37.7 per cent, 40.6 per cent and 26.8 per cent of the whole banking industry respectively.[61]

CHART 5.4
THE GOVERNMENT-CONTROLLED BANKS AND FINANCE COMPANIES

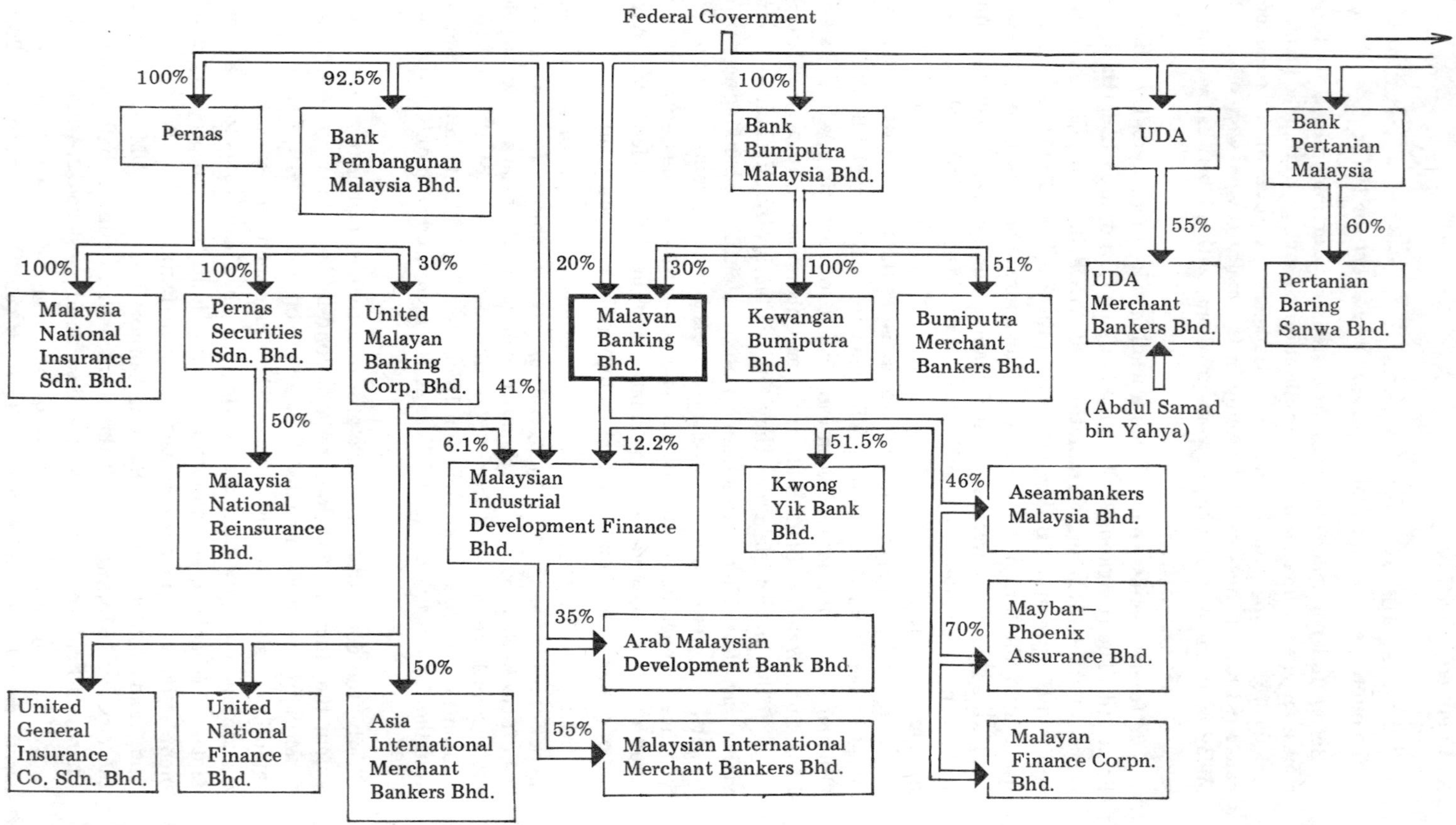

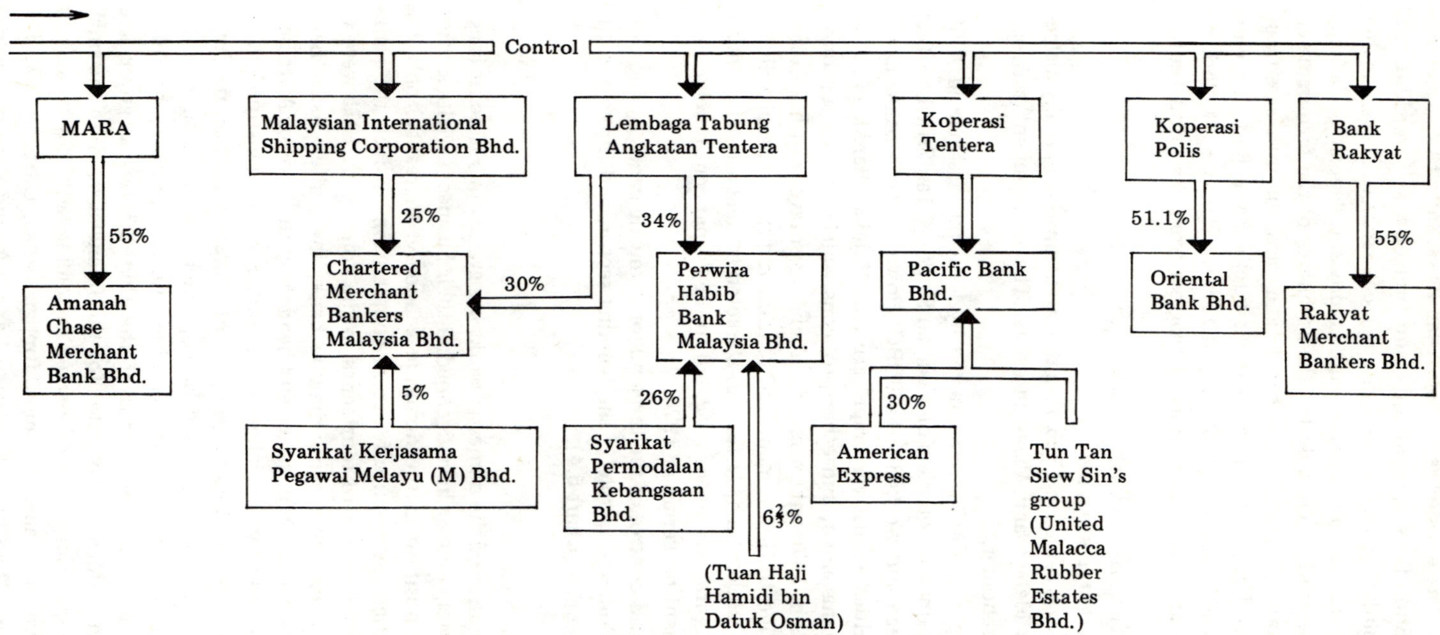

Note. Unless otherwise stated companies under control are 100% owned.

Apart from the big three, only five independent domestic banks had assets over $100 million.[62] These were the United Asian Bank Bhd., Hock Hua Bank Bhd., Public Bank Bhd., Development and Commercial Bank (Ltd.) Bhd., and Southern Banking Bhd. The rest of the eighteen local banks were even smaller, each with assets of less than $100 million and credits and deposits well below that.[63] Few of these banks were able to take advantage of the favourable environment in the post-Independence period, and blossom into significant financial power. The United Asian Bank Bhd., Public Bank Bhd., Development and Commercial Bank (Ltd.) Bhd., and Perwira Habib Bank Bhd. are the few which appear to be making steady progress from the mid-seventies.

(b) THE BIG THREE DOMESTIC BANKS AND THE GOVERNMENT'S ROLE

Bank Bumiputra was set up in 1965 with the intention of eventually distributing the shares to Malays and Malay interests. The Government was, and still is, the only shareholder.[64]

Malayan Banking and UMBC were started by local businessmen in 1960, though one of the principal founders of Malayan Banking, Tan Sri Khoo Teck Puat, is a Singaporean and worked with OCBC. However, both banks experienced some difficulties amidst very rapid growth: Malayan Banking in 1966 because of weak management and other problems which led to a run on its deposits, and UMBC in 1976 with rumours of lending in favour of bank directors.[65] The former led to Government intervention and the eventual majority control of Malayan Banking. The latter also attracted official attention which, together with the aspirations of the NEP, led to the 30 per cent purchase and control in management by Pernas in 1976.

The ownership and control of the three major domestic banks by the Government gives it a dominating role in the banking sector, and through it, the financial sector in general (Chart 5.4).

(c) THE FOREIGN BANKS

While the importance of the domestic banks has greatly increased, it is not the case that the foreign banks have declined in their business activities. They still occupy a key position in the domestic economy. In reality, only the three major domestic banks can offer them competition. In fact, the banks whose activities ranked eighth to fourteenth in the country in 1975 were all foreign-controlled. Even the seventh-ranking bank, the United Asian Bank which is majority-owned by Malaysians and headed by the Tengku Ariff Bendahara of Pahang, is basically controlled by the Indian banking institution.

The foreign banks can be loosely grouped into three categories: the traditional leaders, The Chartered Bank and HSBC, which mainly finance wholesaling, importing and exporting, estate planting, and tin dredging; the Singaporean banks such as OCBC, the banks of the United Overseas group and Overseas Union Bank which largely cater for the financial needs of the small and medium Malaysian Chinese businessmen in trading activities because of their close historical ties; and the 'new' foreign banks, Citibank NA, The Bank of Tokyo, Ltd., The Chase Manhattan Bank NA, and Bank of America NT & SA. The first two groups continued to expand their business slowly, whereas the third group has expanded aggressively despite a recent history in this country and a low deposit base. They are particularly important in the finance of manufacturing activities where the Americans and Japanese investors are among the leaders. It is the smaller and less influential foreign and domestic banks which have obliged and restructured in the last five years either to keep to the spirit of the NEP (Oriental Bank and Pacific Bank) or to conform with local banking regulations (United Asian Bank and Perwira Habib Bank). The trend of restructuring will probably continue and affect the major foreign banks.

B. Merchant Banks and Borrowing Companies

Merchant banking is really a new field of banking activity in Malaysia. Their activities, while expanding, are still only supplementary and complementary to those of the commercial banks. Their loan operations reached only $376.1 million at the end of 1975, $170.5 million of which were short-term in nature. Bank Negara has expressed some concern at their slow progress and the high proportion of long-term loans on short-term funds.[66] They have generally been set up by the big banks or financial institutions and one would therefore expect the structure of ownership and control to reflect that of the commercial banks with perhaps even more concentration of control. Their very recent history, coming after the launching of the NEP, also means that they have to conform with the NEP without fail. Indeed, this is the case. Nine of the twelve merchant banks, in fact, have the Government or one of its corporations as a major partner, two others have large Malay interests, and all but one has at least one commercial bank as a major partner.[67]

In the case of the borrowing companies, the commercial banks again play the leading role, with each bank owning at least one borrowing company. Apart from the Malaysian Borneo Finance Corp. (M) Bhd. and Central Malaysian Finance Bhd., which ranked sixth and tenth respectively amongst the top ten borrowing companies respectively,[68] the rest of the top ten borrowing companies are bank-affiliated. The bank-affiliated borrowing companies dominated the deposits and loans operation of the whole industry with shares of 82 per cent and 74 per cent respectively in 1974.[69] Yet they are the second most important source of funds after the commercial banks, specializing in hire purchase loans for consumer durables.[70] In so far as the Government and Malay interests dominate the commercial banks and the commercial banks dominate the borrowing companies, Government and Malay interests obviously dominate the activities of the borrowing companies, but less overwhelmingly than in the case of the merchant banks.

It is also interesting to note that most of the fifteen borrowing companies not affiliated to banks (out of a total of thirty-two) are either indirectly affiliated to a bank or are part of a major conglomerate.[71]

C. Insurance Companies

(a) RESTRUCTURING UNDER THE NEP

The share ownership structure in the insurance field is beginning to undergo changes too. The first trend is the Malaysianization of foreign-owned insurance companies. The Finance Minister, Y.B.M. Tengku Tan Sri Razaleigh, in his message to the British–American Insurance Company Ltd. (Nassau) upon its successful restructuring of its Malaysian operations, said,

. . . Under the restructuring agreement, 51% of the equity of this new Malaysian company will be owned by Malaysians by 1981, including 30% by Bumiputras. By 1990, the percentage of equity of the company owned by Malaysians will increase to 70%. In management the Company has recruited, trained and promoted Malaysian employees to top management positions. These policies and attitudes are in line with the government's New Economic Policy.[72]

Looking at the insurance companies' restructuring based on the British–American case as an example, control is still exercised by the parent foreign company since they hold the largest single block of shares whereas the 51 per cent Malaysian shareholdings are more dispersed. If Malaysian participation is eventually raised to 70 per cent via a public issue of shares, the foreign parent company will still own a controlling albeit minority shareholding. In fact, there are indications that this may be the trend, as the restructured company, Guardian Royal Exchange Assurance (M) Sdn. Bhd., is seeking a public listing.[73] Another, the Malaysian American Assurance Co. Bhd., is already listed on the Kuala Lumpur Stock Exchange.

In 1974, there were 17 domestically incorporated insurance companies with 73 foreign ones giving a total of 90. By 1975, with the restructuring of the Guardian Royal Exchange group and the deregistering of some dormant ones, the number of domestic and foreign companies became 21 and 60 respectively, giving a total of 81.[74] Of these 21 domestic insurance companies, at least 2 (Malaysian American Assurance Co. Bhd. and Guardian Royal Exchange) would be considered foreign-controlled under the categorization of this book.

There is a second related but more important aspect of this restructuring; it is the increase in Malay participation:

At the end of 1975, 27% of the total equity of $65 million paid up in 21 domestically incorporated companies belonged to Bumiputra companies, co-operative societies, institutions, organisations and individuals while other Malaysians held 44% and the foreign share was 29%. In eight of the domestic companies, Bumiputra interests reached more than 51% of equity, and in three more, it was 30% upwards. This shows the very significant progress achieved by the Bumiputras since 1970 in acquiring equity in insurance companies.[75]

Two of these Bumiputra companies are very important. The Malaysia National Insurance Sdn. Bhd. (MNI), a wholly-owned subsidiary of Pernas, occupied the fourth position in terms of endowment and whole life insurance, and held fifth place in general insurance in 1974 (Tables 5.5 and 5.6). In each case, it is one of the only two domestic companies to be placed among the top ten. The other Bumiputra company, the Malaysia National Reinsurance Bhd. (MNR), of which 50 per cent is owned by Pernas, is the only domestic reinsurance company. Its 1974 premium income of $6 million was 13.73 per cent of the $43.8 million received by underwriting companies outside Malaysia. Its growth has been very rapid since its incorporation in 1973.[76]

Nevertheless, how much impact has restructuring of foreign-owned insurance companies had on the real control structure of this industry? We discuss this question by sub-industrial breakdown.

(b) LIFE INSURANCE

In life insurance, the role of foreign-controlled firms is still strong. Apart from The Malaysian Co-operative Insurance Society Ltd. (MCIS) and the newly set up, but fast expanding, Malaysia National Insurance Sdn. Bhd., the foreign-controlled companies occupy all the other eight positions among the top ten (Table 5.5). In particular, the OCBC-controlled group of insurance companies, The Great Eastern Life Assurance Co. Ltd. (GEL), Overseas Assurance Corp. Ltd., and Wing On Life Assurance Co. Ltd., which were the second, fifth, and ninth most important companies respectively in 1974 in terms of number of policies, is the single most important entity in the life insurance industry. Not only do they possess the largest number of policies issued, total value of policies and total premium income, but the equity participation of these insurance companies, especially that by GEL, in the leading companies of Singapore

TABLE 5.5
LIFE INSURANCE POLICIES IN FORCE, 1974

Name of Company	*Controlled by*	*Number of Policies*	*Total Value in $ Million*	*Total Premium in $ Million*
1. The Malaysian Co-operative Insurance Society Ltd.	Malaysian	90,752	486.7	21,718
2. Great Eastern Life Assurance Co. Ltd.	Singaporean	84,813	935.5	42,145
3. American International Assurance Co. Ltd.	American	84,270	1,048.8	38,342
4. Malaysia National Insurance Sdn. Bhd.	Malaysian	26,332	211.9	2,256
5. The Overseas Assurance Corporation, Ltd.	Singaporean	18,113	151.4	6,718
6. The Prudential Assurance Ltd.	British	13,044	202.5	6,397
7. The Asia Life Assurance Society Ltd.	Singaporean	11,393	80.3	4,338
8. Life Insurance Corporation of India	Indian	8,696	42.4	1,917
9. Wing On Life Assurance Co. Ltd.	Singaporean	6,870	34.6	2,079
Total		344,283	3,194.1	125,910

Source. 13th Annual Report of the Insurance Industry for 1975 by the Director-General of Insurance, pp. 132—3.

and Malaysia also forms a key and integral part of the OCBC financial empire (Chart 5.5). American International Assurance Co. Ltd. (AIA) is the second most important life insurance company in the country, specializing in catering for the higher valued policies. Together, these two groups covered 195,066 or 54.18 per cent of all existing life policies with combined insured value of $2,206.3 million and premium of $89.284 million which were respectively 65.1 per cent and 68.0 per cent of the national total in 1974.

Strictly speaking, MCIS is a co-operative society with all the members as owners and controllers. Yet the vast dispersal of its membership and the long-standing management by Nadarajah Kularajah has made him and his associates the effective controller of the group. In addition to issuing insurance, Kularajah has developed MCIS into a conglomerate with major interests in oil palm estates, a hotel, and property development.

(c) GENERAL INSURANCE

Foreign dominance in this section of the industry is still evident (see Table 5.6) despite some expansion of the domestically incorporated insurance companies. The Director-General of Insurance reported:

> Again the highlight for the years 1974 and also 1975 was the considerable strength displayed by domestically incorporated companies which in the case of general insurance business, increased their share of the market from 27.4% in 1973 to 34.6% in 1974 and to 41.5% in 1975. These companies are most likely to continue to have an ever expanding share of the general insurance market in the years ahead, particularly as foreign insurers restructure themselves into domestically incorporated companies with significant equity ownership by Malaysians, particularly Bumiputras.[77]

The increase in percentage is really the result of the restructuring of the Guardian Royal Exchange group of companies rather than a significant expansion into the businesses of the foreign companies by the original domestically incorporated ones. Once a distinction is made, as has been done earlier for Guardian Royal Exchange Assurance (M) Sdn. Bhd., between ownership and control, one has to be less optimistic than the Director-General. Indeed, the first, third, fourth, and sixth to eleventh in the top twelve general insurance companies are all foreign-owned and/or controlled. Nevertheless, there is a more even distribution of market shares among the leading companies with no single clearly dominating one, unlike the case of life insurance. The only important locally-owned and controlled insurance company is Safety Life and General Insurance Sdn. Bhd., belonging to the Soon Seng conglomerate (Chart 5.6).

In home insurance, the foreign firm of British–American Insurance Co. (M) Sdn. Bhd. is the only important one.

(d) CONCLUSION

Clearly, while Government and Malay interests in the insurance industry have been growing, the recent effort at restructuring has left the foreigners with control of the companies involved. Foreign predominance in the insurance field is still very strong. Nevertheless, sufficient headway has been made to assure the Malays of an important minority position in the field and this will

CHART 5.5
THE LEE RUBBER–OCBC GROUP

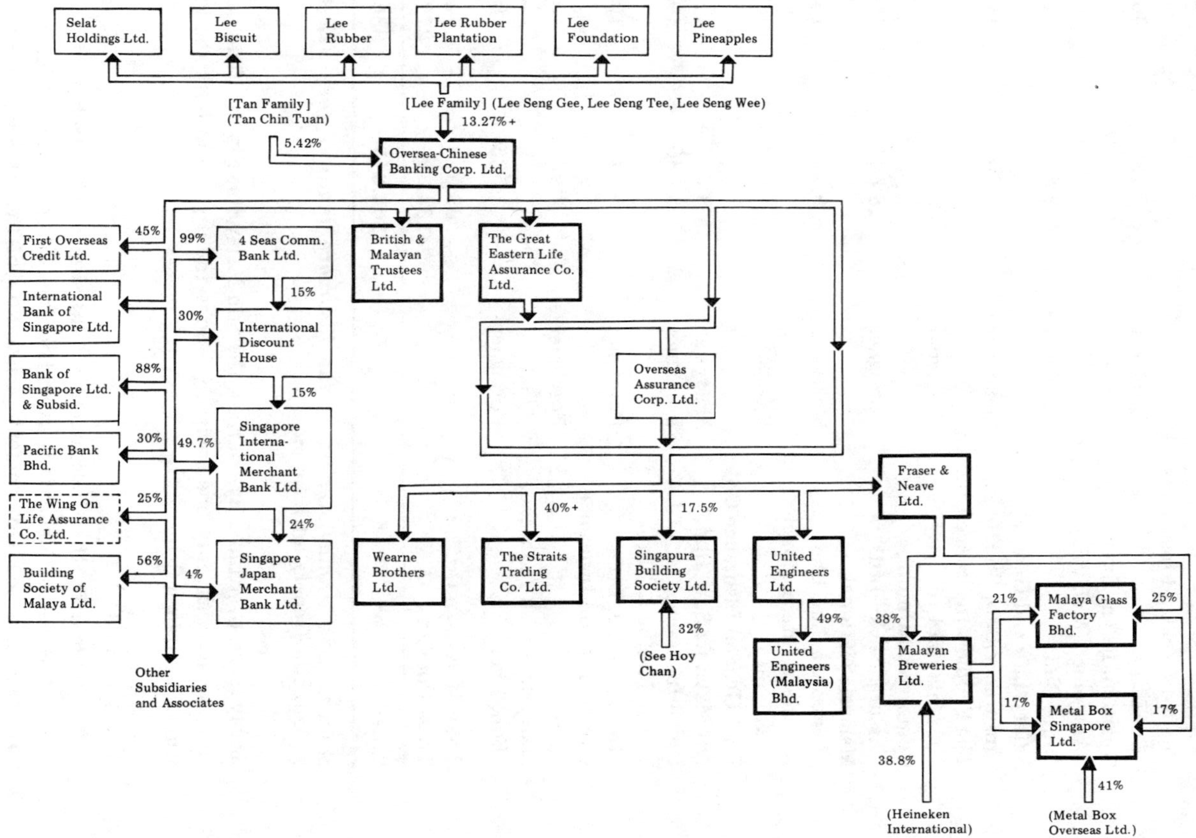

TABLE 5.6

GENERAL INSURANCE POLICIES FOR 1974

Name of Company	*Controlled by*	*Net Premium in $ Million*	*Total Income in $ Million*
The New Zealand Insurance Co. Ltd.	Foreigner	12.798	30.072
Guardian Royal Exchange Assurance (Malaysia) Sdn. Bhd.	Foreigner	9.852	22.738
Safety Life and General Insurance Sdn. Bhd.	Malaysian	12.204	19.993
The People's Insurance Co. of Malaysia Ltd.	Foreigner	9.647	18.688
Commercial Union Assurance Co. Ltd.	Foreigner	8.564	15.059
Malaysia National Insurance Sdn. Bhd.	Malaysian	9.343	15.058
American International Assurance	Foreigner	5.087	14.793
First General Insurance Co. of Malaysia Sdn. Bhd.	Malaysian	3.318	11.122
Royal Insurance Co. Ltd.	Foreigner	5.686	10.493
Taisho Marine & Fire Insurance Co. Ltd.	Foreigner	5.144	10.221
Overseas Union Insurance Ltd.	Foreigner	4.980	10.077
Malaysia British Assurance Sdn. Bhd.	Foreigner	7.525	9.675
Total Malaysian Co.		69.948	114.181
Total Foreign Co.		134.399	272.442
Total		204.347	386.623

Source. 13th Annual Report of the Insurance Industry for 1975 by the Director-General of Insurance, pp. 140—1.

slowly grow over time. By contrast, the non-Malay stake in this field has been quite small with only one company among the top ten in both the life and general insurance fields.

D. Conclusion

To summarize, the Government's ownership and control position in the financial sector of Malaysia is overwhelming. Chart 5.4, in particular, shows how extensive the Government penetration of the banking sector is, with direct control of the top two banks, and indirect control of the fourth largest bank in the country. Through these, it is able to control most of the merchant banks as well as the major borrowing companies. In addition, the Government also controls the other financial institutions such as Malaysian Industrial Development Finance Bhd., Malaysia Building Society Bhd., Bank Pembangunan

CHART 5.6
THE SOON SENG GROUP OF COMPANIES

Soon Seng & Co.	
Safety Life and General Insurance Sdn. Bhd.	
Safety Finance Co. Sdn. Bhd.	
Safety Development Co. Sdn. Bhd.	
Cheras Mining Co. Sdn. Bhd.	
Subang Mining Co. Sdn. Bhd.	
Soon Seng Wire Products Sdn. Bhd.	
Malaysia Steel Wire Sdn. Bhd.	
Malaysia Galvanised Iron Works Sdn. Bhd.	
Malaysia Galvanised Iron Pipes Sdn. Bhd.	
Malaysia Steel Works (K.L.) Sdn. Bhd.	
Soon Seng Asbestos Cement Products Sdn. Bhd.	
Soon Seng Plywood Sdn. Bhd.	
Dominion Rubber Company (M) Ltd.	
Golden Castle Realty Sdn. Bhd.	
'Peninsula' Service Station	These are fictitious names provided in May Tai's Master's dissertation with M.I.T., real names of the companies not known.
'City' Service Station	
New Malacca Garden Sdn. Bhd.	
'City' Omnibus Company Sdn. Bhd.	
'Express' Omnibus Company Sdn. Bhd.	
'Bandar' Omnibus Company Sdn. Bhd.	
'Eastern Lumber' Corporation	
'United' Rubber Company Sdn. Bhd.	

Malaysia and others. The hold of the Government over the financial sector is most impressive. The possibility of turning over this control to Malay businessmen, if the Government should so desire, is thus open.

The foreigners' role in the financial sector has been moderated somewhat by Government penetration. Despite that, their position in the insurance field, and to a lesser extent, in the banking sector, is still entrenched. In the case of banking, what they, as a group, may have been slow in picking up has been more than balanced by their leading role in the newer and expanding pastures of industrial financing and merchant banking. Not surprisingly, the actors playing the leading role switched from the British to the Americans.

By contrast, the non-Malays' role in this crucial sector remains unimpressive. Although they have been moving into this field since Independence, yet, with the exception of MCIS in life insurance, and Safety in general insurance, little headway has been made into the ranks of the industry's leaders.

5.5 THE MANUFACTURING AND OTHER SECTORS

A. General Background

Until the fifties, there was little manufacturing activity in Malaysia. Most of the manufacturing activities were performed by small-scale operators. They resembled cottage industries rather than bona fide industrial enterprises in nature.[78]

There were some very large-scale industrial organizations with more than 200 workers employed. But the numbers were so few that they can be listed with little difficulty, and the great majority were started and controlled by the British.[79] The earliest and most important of these were Syarikat Eastern Smelting Bhd., Straits Trading Ltd. (both in tin smelting), Fraser & Neave Ltd., Malayan Breweries Bhd., and Cold Storage (Malaysia) Sdn. Bhd. (all in the beverage business), United Engineers Ltd., Hume Industries (M) Bhd., and Metal Box Malaysia Bhd. Several others such as Malayan Cement Bhd. and Malayan Tobacco Bhd. began operations in the fifties. Of these, only Eastern Smelting and Straits Trading were started by Chinese tin miners in Penang and Singapore respectively; however, the predecessor to Eastern Smelting soon met with failure. It was taken over by the Europeans who have run it until now.[80] Some big industries were started by Singaporean Chinese businessmen, for example, Lee Pineapple Canning Sdn. Bhd., Lam Soon Oil and Soap Mfg. Co. Sdn. Bhd., and The Amoy Canning Corp. (M) Sdn. Bhd. Those started by the Malaysian Chinese were limited to the biscuit manufacturing of the Khong Guan group, several coconut oil mills in Penang, and a number of rubber remilling factories (again the Lee group owns many of these), as well as rubber products factories (such as Fung Keong Rubber Manufactory (M) Sdn. Bhd. and Shum Yip Leong Rubber Works Sdn. Bhd.).[81]

By the seventies, the Lee Rubber–OCBC group appeared to be in control of some of these (see Chart 5.5). The others like Hume, Cold Storage, Metal Box, Eastern Smelting, Malayan Cement, and Malayan Tobacco are still owned and controlled by their foreign parent companies, although the structure of their share ownership has invariably changed with increased local small shareholder participation, and some trend towards minority Malay participation under the NEP.[82]

Before we proceed to discuss the current pattern of ownership and control in this sector, it is necessary to provide a brief recapitulation of the role of manufacturing in the colonial era as a background. In those days, on the one hand, the return to investment in the rubber and tin sectors was very high, and, on the other, the size of the market was relatively small to make investment in the manufacturing sector unattractive. As a result, there were only a few British manufacturing establishments in this country at the time of Independence. Thus, when the Independent Government promoted and achieved a very significant expansion of the industrial sector,[83] the British capitalists were no longer so privileged as in the colonial era to dominate this field of activity by squeezing out other contenders, whether local Chinese or other foreigners. The result is that we witness an industrial sector where the ownership and control pattern is quite different from that of the traditional sectors. No doubt, the old-established British industrial firms flourished and expanded into other fields of industry and new firms came in and set up operations.[84] Yet, other foreigners and the Malaysian Chinese have been able to establish very important footholds in this new and most dynamic sector.

The Americans and the Japanese in particular responded to the drive for industrialization. The American investment was originally concentrated in the fields of petroleum and chemicals (Esso Malaysia Bhd., Chemical Company of Malaysia Bhd., Pacific Chemicals Bhd.). But from the mid-seventies, they have invested strongly in the electronics industry making that industry one of the leading manufacturing industries in Malaysia.[85] The Japanese have been active in a range of industries: iron and steel (Malayawata Steel Bhd., Federal Iron Works Sdn. Bhd., Steel Pipe Industries of Malaysia Sdn. Bhd.), shipbuilding (Malaysia Shipyard and Engineering Sdn. Bhd.), car assembly, electrical appliances (Sanyo, Matsushita, Toshiba) and, later on, electronics and textiles (Kanebo and, more importantly, the Pen group, by Toray Industries through their Hong Kong associate of Textile Alliance Ltd., see Chart 5.7). The interesting feature of these two groups of investors is that the Americans tend to be largely wholly-owned while the Japanese ones tend to have local non-Malay as well as Malay or Government partners.

Whereas the Americans and Japanese tend to invest in the larger and more modern manufacturing establishments, the local businessmen tend to be involved in the medium-sized ones. However, by virtue of their larger numbers, the local manufacturing investors play a no less important role than the foreigners. This can be seen from the data provided by the Financial Survey of Limited Companies for 1970. The locally-controlled manufacturing limited companies had a total equity capital of $648 million as against $567 million for the foreign-controlled companies.[86]

We shall consider the capital ownership pattern of local businessmen in the manufacturing sector together with the property development and other sectors jointly. Very few of the local industrialists started in manufacturing. Most of them were traders dealing in the various Malaysian raw material production or exporting activities; a minority were importers of consumer and/or intermediate merchandise. It was only after they had accumulated some wealth and entrepreneurial expertise that they were able to take advantage of the post-Independence investment climate and launch into industrial activities. The same motivation of diversification and expansion which led them into industrial activities also led them into other sectors such as hotels, housing development, finance, and others. Hence, it is hardly surprising that every group charted here is a conglomerate spanning a wide spectrum of activities.

B. The Leading Non-Malay Businessmen

In this section, we document the extensive business conglomeration of several leading industrialists. The exercise is not meant to be exhaustive, but serves to illustrate the extent of the spread in business activities and concentration of control of groups within some industries. This is also done to provide some insight into the process of evolution of some of these conglomerates, as well as their possible outlook and perspective, as a prelude to our analysis in Chapter 8.

The most important group of industrialists to have emerged in the sixties is probably that headed by the Kuok brothers (Chart 5.8). They originated as sugar and rice traders but developed into one of the leading sugar traders in Asia, if not the world.[87] From there, it was a logical step to backward integrate into the refining of sugar and then into sugar-cane plantations. This they did through setting up and, later, amalgamating Malayan Sugar Manufacturing Co. Bhd. and Perlis Plantations Bhd. They now have wide-ranging interests spanning shipbuilding, plywood manufacture, housing and com-

CHART 5.7
JARDINE MATHESON AND ASSOCIATED HONG KONG INTERESTS

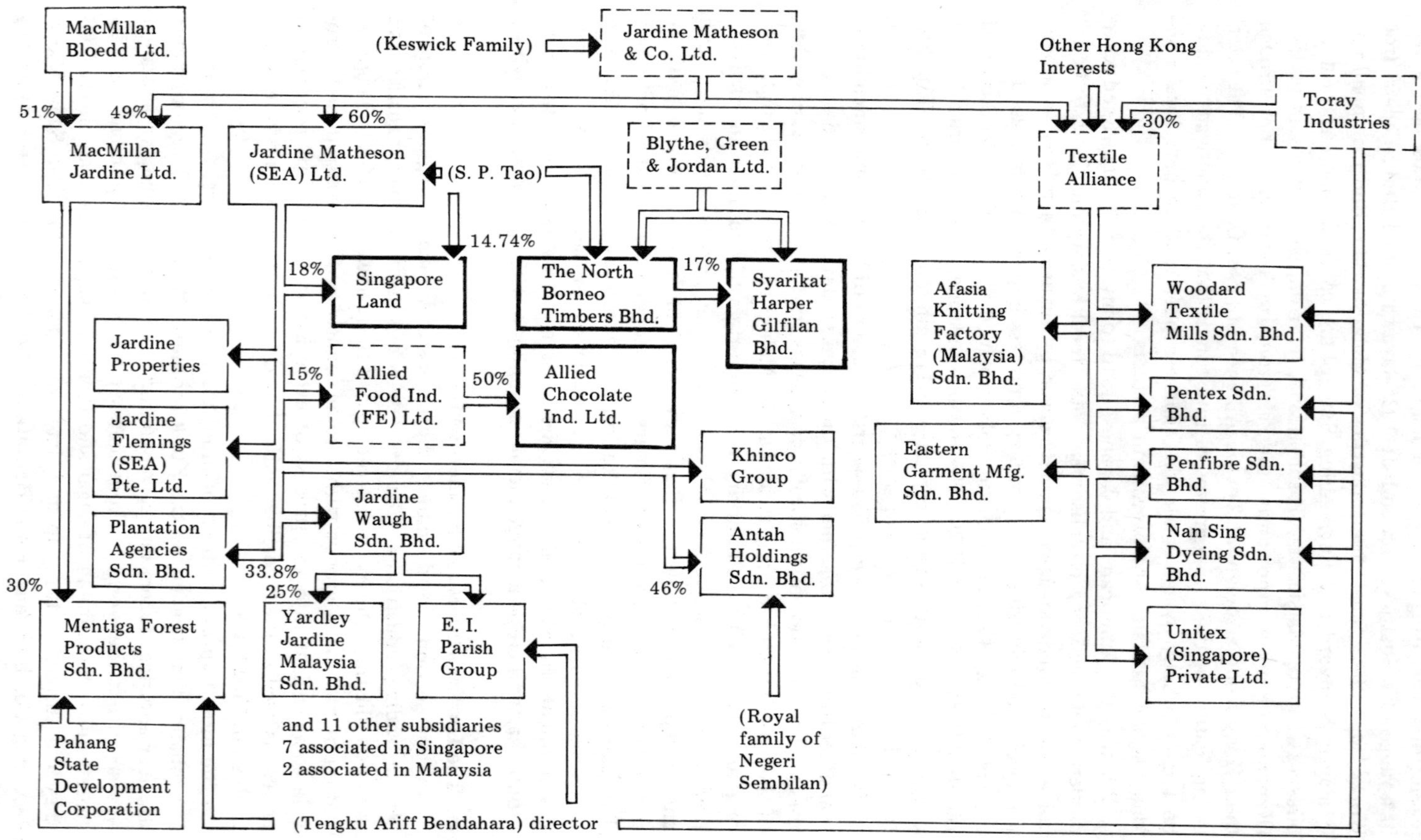

CHART 5.8
THE KUOK BROTHERS' GROUP

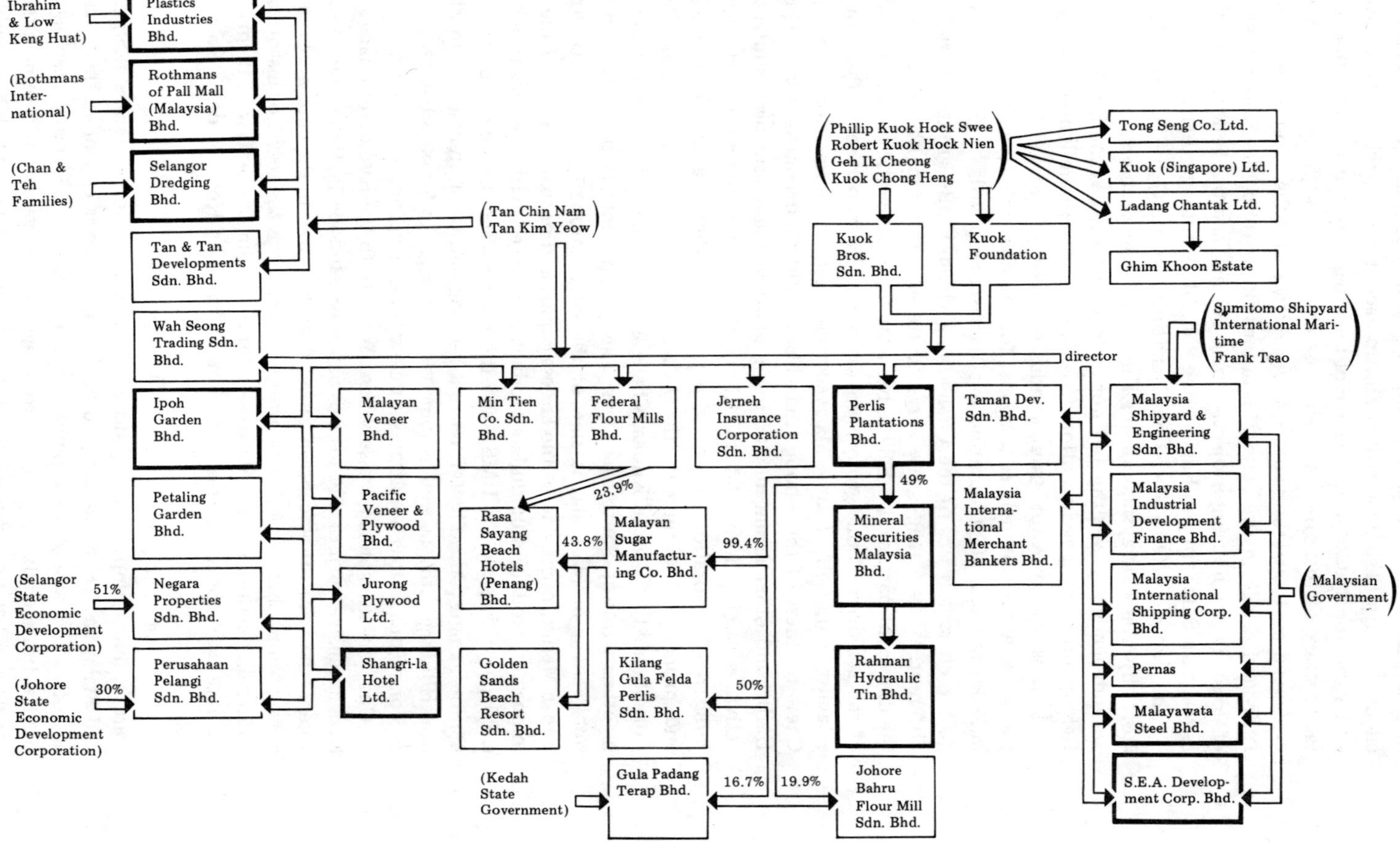

mercial property development, shipping, and hotels, not just in Malaysia but all over South-East Asia and in Fiji. In each industry, their establishment is either the undisputed leader or one of the most important.[88] The most important feature of this group is their close connection with the Government, as evidenced by their joint-venture arrangements with the State Governments of Perlis and Kedah in the Perlis Plantations Bhd. group, the State Government of Johor in the housing project, Taman Pelangi, and the Federal Government in Malaysia Shipyard and Engineering Sdn. Bhd., among others.

The Tan Kim Yeow–Tan Chin Nam brothers and Geh Ik Cheong[89] are the most important Malaysians among Kuok's business partners. The Tan brothers are independently wealthy but not in the same class as the Kuoks. They and Geh are probably a combination of senior executives-cum-junior partners.

In most of the Kuok group's industrial activities, major foreign industrial giants are always present as partners, for example, the Japanese participation in Malayan Sugar Manufacturing and Malaysia Shipyard.

The characteristics of the Chang Ming Thien–UMBC group (Chart 5.9) are different. While Chang is the nerve centre of this group, he is not necessarily the dominant partner. UMBC has been the financial centre around which most of the activities of this group were organized. Every partner in this group has established himself in some Malaysian raw material production,[90] except the Chew brothers of the Khong Guan biscuit and flour conglomerate. Through UMBC and other arrangements, this group owns and controls manufacturing activities ranging from food (the Khong Guan group), lumbering (Timbermine Industrial Corporation), plywood manufacture (Sentosa and Olympia), hotel and property development (the Faber Merlin group), and mining (Pahang Consolidated). Like the Kuoks, Chang also has substantial business activities in other parts of South-East Asia. This group controls the most important hotel chain in Malaysia, is one of the larger property developers through Faber Merlin, owns one of the largest banks, and probably is one of the more important producers of timber products. However, with the recent selling of a 30 per cent stake in UMBC and the forced disentanglement of the Faber Merlin–Pahang Consolidated mutual holding and the latter's stake in Plantation Holdings Ltd., as well as some reorganization in Chang's banking interest in Hong Kong,[91] it is not at present clear how this group will evolve.

One qualification is necessary here. While both the Kuok and Chang groups have extensive business interests in Singapore, Indonesia, Hong Kong, and elsewhere, they are the exception rather than the rule. In the course of research, it was found that while many groups, probably as the result of historical and continuing economic ties, do have interests in Singapore; few of them appear to have an important presence, if at all, in Hong Kong or other South-East Asian countries.

The Hong Leong group (Chart 5.10) originated from Singapore in the hardware business, importing and distributing construction materials in Singapore and Malaysia. They are yet another group that has expanded their business activities and wealth very rapidly in the sixties and seventies. Starting from the hardware trade, it is logical to integrate backwards into the manufacturing of construction raw materials (thus, for example, Steel Pipe Industries of Malaysia Sdn. Bhd., Fancy Tile Works Bhd., the minority stake in Tasek

CHART 5.9

CHANG MING THIEN AND ASSOCIATES

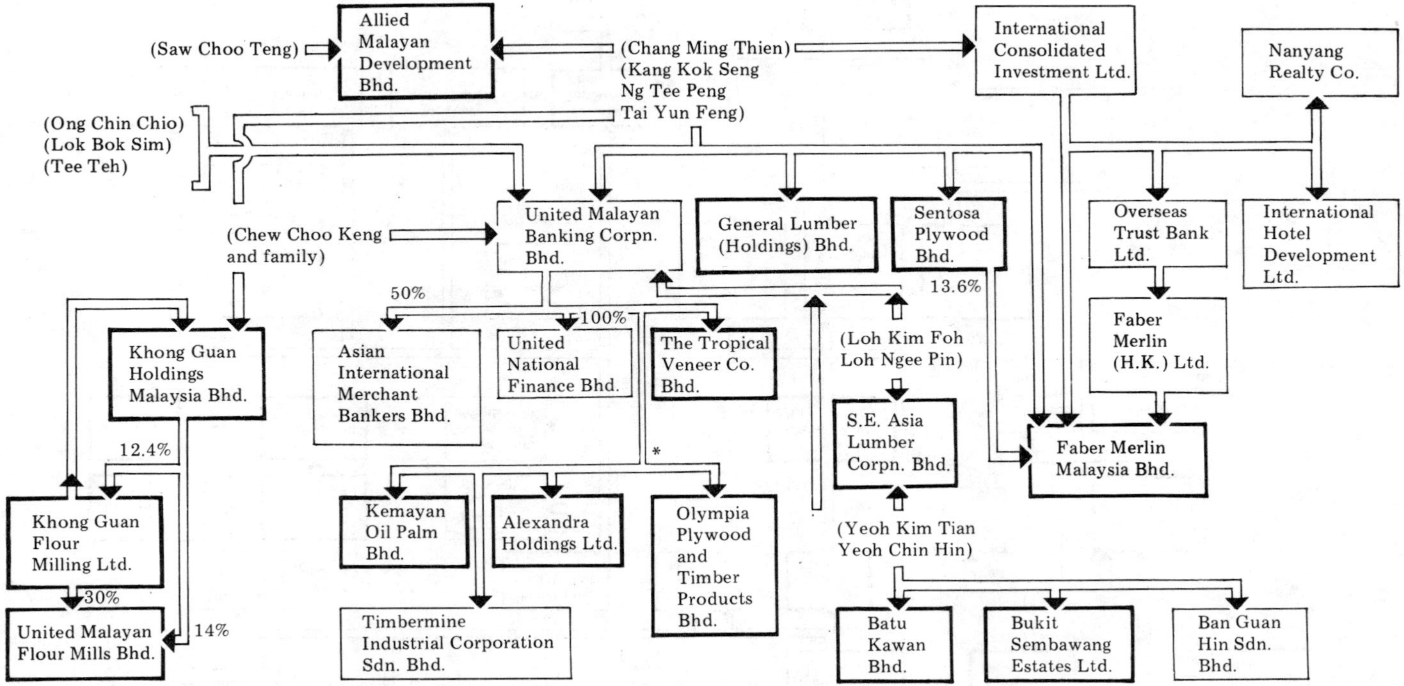

Note. *Exactly how these companies are controlled by the Chang–Kang group has not been traced. However, it is noted that at least one of these four UMBC executives sits on the boards.

CHART 5.10
THE HONG LEONG GROUP

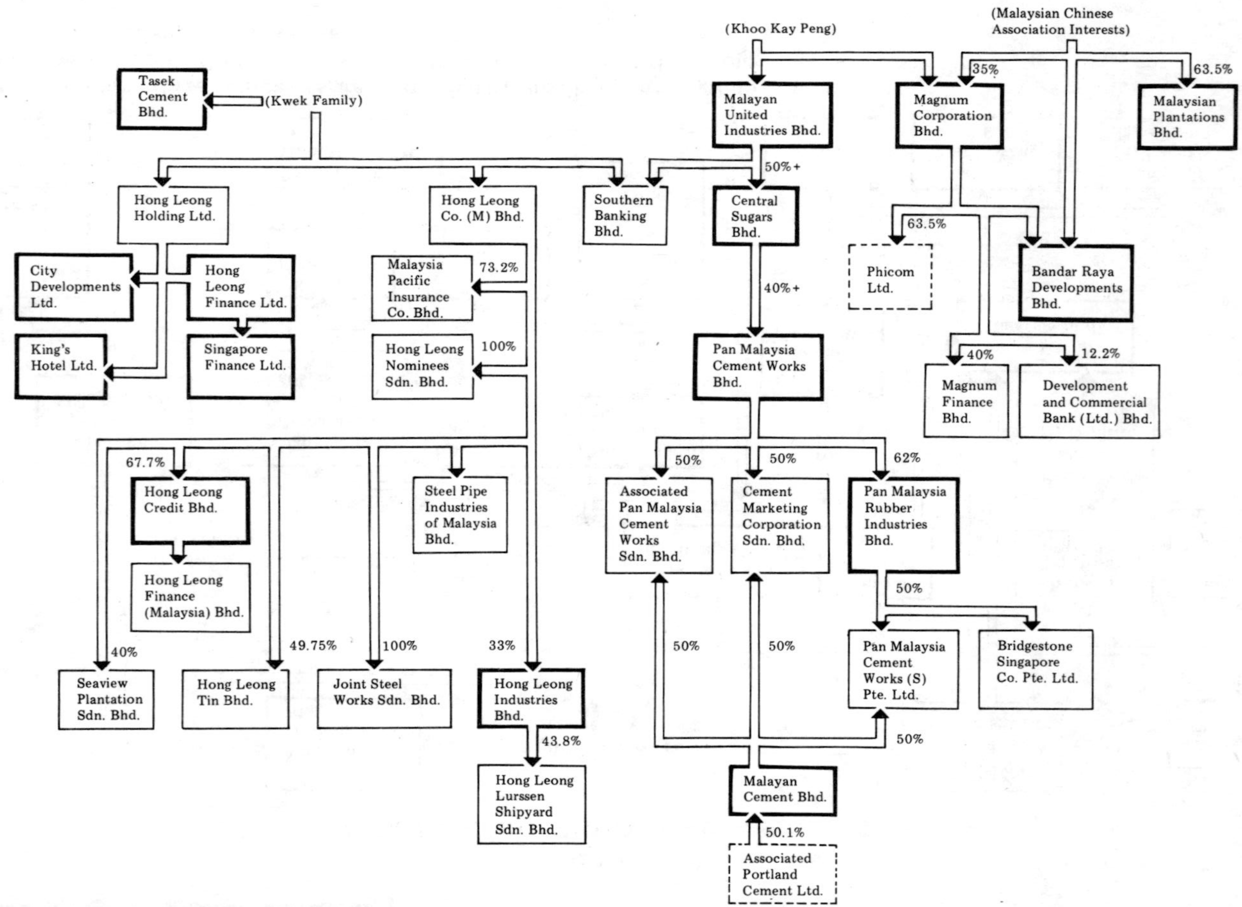

Cement Bhd.) or integrate forward into property development (through City Developments Ltd. and others). By now, they have also built up an important presence in the finance sector with Hong Leong Finance Ltd. (on both sides of the Causeway), Malaysia Pacific Insurance Co. Bhd., and a minority stake in Southern Banking Bhd., shipbuilding (Hong Leong–Lurssen Shipyard Bhd.), and other fields.

Not all the big enterprises and conglomerates are included among the publicly listed corporations, though most of them would have been. Unfortunately, researching into private limited companies would be too time consuming, as information is not so easily available as from the publicly listed corporations. The Soon Seng group is one exception where information has been relatively easy to obtain. In fact, it is one of the largest groups of private companies and one of the more important groups of industrialists in this country. Again starting from their hardware business, they have become one of the leading steel manufacturers, with the widest range of iron and steel products of any local producer, apart from having built up an interest in finance (through Safety Finance Co. Sdn. Bhd. and Safety Life and General Insurance Sdn. Bhd.), plantations, mining, and property development.

So far, we have provided some documentation of the origins and a brief account of the evolution of four of the largest conglomerates with a strong industrial base. It would have been desirable to repeat the process extensively and systematically to cover a representative range of enterprises. However, this would be too demanding a task for this book, in view of the difficulties in data collection for the private limited companies mentioned above, as well as the identification of all the medium-sized enterprises. Nevertheless, casual observations made in the course of research suggest that the pattern of evolution and conglomeration is no different—i.e., branching into a field of industrial activity usually associated with the original trading activity and diversification into a number of fields, including property development and raw material production. It is just that the scale of operations will be correspondingly smaller.

5.6 MALAY PARTICIPATION IN THE ECONOMY

In the earlier sections of this chapter, scattered documentation on the rising participation by the Malays in the corporate sector of the economy has been provided. It should be obvious by now that their participation in some sectors has been very strong and dominating since the NEP, while still extremely weak in others. This section proposes to provide a preliminary assessment of the rising Malay participation in the corporate sector. No distinction has been made between Malay and Government ownership and control in the discussion in this section. This is because Malay participation in this area of the economy has been insignificant historically, thus prompting the Government to formulate the strategy of acquiring shares and wealth by newly set up public enterprises and holding them in trust for the Malay general public.

The Government has had a long history of operating public enterprises. However, until the earlier years of Independence, this participation had been limited, by and large, to the statutory bodies, operating monopolies in the key transport, communication, and utilities industries, regulating/developing particular aspects of the economy such as Bank Negara, the Malayan Rubber Fund Board with the Rubber Research Institute (RRI), Rural Industry Development Authority (RIDA, which later became MARA), and the Federal Land Development Authority (then FLDA, now Felda).

Since the sixties, many more public enterprises have been set up, including statutory bodies such as MARA (Trust Fund for the Indigenous Peoples), UDA (Urban Development Authority), DARA (Pahang Tenggara Development Authority), and privately incorporated companies such as Bank Bumiputra Bhd., Bank Pembangunan Malaysia Bhd. (the Development Bank of Malaysia, BPM), Pernas, Food Industries Malaysia Bhd. (FIMA), Malaysian International Shipping Corporation Bhd. (MISC), Malaysia Shipyard and Engineering Sdn. Bhd., Petronas, and so on. In addition, there are also the State Economic Development Corporations (SEDCs) enacted by the individual State Assemblies, and the specialized financial institutions such as Bank Rakyat and Bank Pertanian, set up by Acts of Parliament. Some of these like MARA, its predecessor RIDA, together with Bank Bumiputra and the Selangor State Development Corporation (PKNS) were set up before the mid-sixties. But the rest were set up after 1969 as part of the implementation of the NEP to assist in the attainment of the goal of restructuring society by raising the level of Malay equity and managerial participation in the 'modern' sector of the economy via the twin routes of acquiring shares in existing and new companies, and financial and managerial assistance to the small Malay businessmen.[92] Therefore, the thrust and activities of these organizations differ sharply from the earlier organizations.

Utilizing capital and loans provided by the Government as well as some commercial loans, these newer corporations set out to make a major impact in the structure of ownership and control in the corporate sector of the economy. The importance attached by the Government to these public enterprises can be seen from the allocation of public expenditure to them under the Second and Third Malaysia Plans: 98 per cent of the $1,734.5 million allocated under the TMP (or 9.4 per cent of the total Government development expenditure) for commerce and industry goes to the public enterprises, especially the trio of MARA, Pernas, and UDA.[93] By 1977, this trio and the SEDCs had a network of 291 holding companies, subsidiaries and associates with a total paid-up capital in excess of $900 million;[94] the Pernas group alone accounted for nearly $300 million. These public corporations accounted for a little over 5 per cent of the corporate capital in Malaysia which, together with that owned by private Malay individuals and companies, amounted to a little over 8 per cent of the total, in contrast to the 57 per cent owned by the foreigners and 35 per cent by other Malaysians.[95] Yet, this achievement is well short of the 30 per cent target set by the Government and has thus become the target of many Malay criticisms of inadequate progress. Partly in response to such criticisms, the Bumiputra Investment Foundation was launched in 1978 to accelerate the acquisition of shares.

However, looking at it more objectively and considering that the NEP was started only in the early seventies, the progress made in increasing the Malay role in the economy has been phenomenal, especially if one looks beyond the percentage of corporate shares held by the Malays and those held in trust by the public enterprises. First of all, an increase of more than 6 per cent from a mere 2 per cent base in seven years is harder to achieve compared with an increase from a larger base. Secondly, the real significance of these share acquisitions goes far beyond that indicated by mere numbers as they have enabled these corporations to gain solid control of the financial and tin mining sectors, and are gaining in the plantation, manufacturing, and other sectors.

Take Pernas for instance. It was able to bring Sime Darby, one of the largest industrial and commercial conglomerates and one of the five largest estate owners in South-East Asia, under effective Malaysian control.[96] There are also signs that it may be aiming at control of Highlands & Lowlands, perhaps in co-operation with the K.L.–Kepong group,[97] not to mention the abundant rumours of a take-over attempt of H & C and/or Guthrie through Sime Darby or its subsidiaries. When and if a take-over of H & C and/or Guthrie materializes, Pernas will establish a dominating position in the estate sector, just as it has done in the mining and insurance fields. Neither of these two cases has been confirmed, yet they are not impossible.[98] Even without the acquisition of the latter two planting syndicates, the control of Sime Darby in itself is already of great significance. This complements the wide range of business activities that Pernas has picked up over the years (Chart 5.3). Apart from those commodities and insurance companies mentioned earlier, Pernas is also interested in a wide range of manufacturing industries through its participation in Johor Cement, Goodyear Malaysia Bhd., Malayawata Steel Bhd., Pernas NEC Multiplex Sdn. Bhd., Pernas Plessey Electronics Sdn. Bhd. and others; construction and property development through Pernas Construction Sdn. Bhd. and its control of Island & Peninsular Development Bhd., one of the largest local property developers; hotel business (its associate, Far Eastern Hotels Development (M) Bhd., owns the Kuala Lumpur Hilton); and of course trading, shipping, and investment activities.

These subsidiaries and associates of Pernas fall into two broad categories: those acquired from existing and prospering enterprises such as London Tin, Island & Peninsular, Far Eastern Hotels Development (M) Bhd., Malayawata; and those initiated with leading foreign firms such as Goodyear Malaysia, Pernas NEC, Pernas Plessey, BM Engineering Sdn. Bhd., etc. Relatively few enterprises have been initiated and built up from scratch by Pernas such as Malaysia National Insurance Sdn. Bhd. and Malaysia National Reinsurance Bhd. This distinction between major acquisition and initiating new projects is necessary because the former restructures wealth-holding with taxpayers' money without creating new opportunities whereas the latter can contribute to the growth of the economy and create new opportunities for the Malays and other races as well, assuming that private investments are not displaced. In the former case, depending on how the ownership of Pernas and/or its investments is eventually transferred to the Malay public, for instance whether it is an outright transfer or a sale of shares, and how the resultant revenue is spent on the Malaysian public, it may or may not involve a real transfer from one sector to another. In his book, Snodgrass has ably discussed this and related problems.[99]

Other Government public enterprises have also entered the private sector quite aggressively. MARA, which was set up primarily to assist the develop-

CHART 5.11
MARA'S GROUP OF COMPANIES

Name of Company	*Nature of Business*	*Holding (%)*	*Capital ($ million)*
Kompleks Kewangan Malaysia Bhd.	Finance	98.3	73.0
Amanah Saham Mara Bhd.			
Malaysia Discount Bhd.			
Amanah Saham Mara Nominees Sdn. Bhd.			
Amanah dan Arthurs International Sdn. Bhd.			
Pelaboran Amanah Nasional Bhd.			
Amanah Chase Merchant Bank Bhd.			
Amanah Butler Malaysia Bhd.			
Batik Malaysia Bhd.	Commercial and	99.5	4.5
Kayu Sedia Sdn. Bhd.	Industrial	100.0	1.5
Kulitkraf Sdn. Bhd.		100.0	4.96
Syarikat Ubiyu (Malaysia) Bhd.		100.0	7.0
Senama Sdn. Bhd.		100.0	1.2
Syarikat Mawar Sdn. Bhd.		100.0	0.45
Syarikat Jengka Sdn. Bhd.		88.5	26.0
Pamagrima Sdn. Bhd.		71.6	2.38
KIMA Sdn. Bhd.		70.0	4.0
Pulp & Paper Industries Sdn. Bhd.		48.0	
Raleigh Cycles (M) Bhd.		17.4	
Maltronics Sdn. Bhd.		20.0	
Limbangan Timor Sdn. Bhd.	Bus Services and	100.0	3.75
Lori Malaysia Bhd.	Transportation	100.0	7.3
Kenderaan Klang/Banting Bhd.		100.0	2.0
MARA Ekspress Sdn. Bhd.		100.0	1.74
USMETA Sdn. Bhd.		100.0	1.0
Kenderaan Labu Sendayan Sdn. Bhd.		100.0	0.216
Kenderaan Melayu Kelantan Bhd.		92.8	1.875
Kenderaan Sungei Manik Sdn. Bhd.		91.4	0.618
Syarikat Ikatan Setia Bhd.		94.5	0.329
Tanjung Kramat Temerloh Utara Omnibus Bhd.		95.5	0.251
Perusahaan & Pengangkutan Jelai Bhd.		86.1	0.146
Kenderaan Sri Kedah Sdn. Bhd.		83.7	0.25
MED-Bumikar MARA Sdn. Bhd.		40.0	1.0
Kontena Nasional Sdn. Bhd.		25.0	6.0

ment of small Malay entrepreneurs, has gone beyond that to set up a whole range of companies, especially in bus transport, commerce and manufacturing (batek, chemicals, wood-based products), and in financial activities, mainly through Kompleks Kewangan Malaysia Bhd. and the Amanah Chase Merchant Bank Bhd. (Chart 5.11). UDA has grown during the last five years into the major property developer in the country. It has developed several prime commercial skyscrapers in Kuala Lumpur and constructed over 10,000 houses in

CHART 5.12
THE MAJOR PROJECTS OF THE URBAN DEVELOPMENT AUTHORITY

Name of Project	*Partner*
Hotel Abad Century	
Hentian Pudu Raya	
Cahaya Suria	
Bangunan Bukota	
Bukit Bintang Plaza	
Daya Bumi	
Bangunan Datuk Zainal	Syarikat Fajar (M) Sdn. Bhd.
Kompleks Pertama Kompleks Sri Lokman	Datuk Wong Kee Tat
Kompleks Damai	Datuk Low Keng Huat group
Sungei Wang Plaza Regent Hotel	Tan Sri Chong Kok Lim group
Wisma Budiman	Budiman Sdn. Bhd.
Kompleks Udarama	Multi-Purpose Holdings
Hong Kong Bank Building	The Hongkong & Shanghai Banking Corp. Singapore Land
Wisma Chinda	Chin Brothers
Kompleks Kestana	Kumpulan Kemajuan Raya (of Syarikat Permodalan Kebangsaan Bhd.)
Mersing Holiday Motel Merdu Hotel Hotel Temenggong	Malay interest
Pantai Motel Hotel on Jalan Bayam, Kota Bharu Kompleks Ipoh	Other Government Agencies
Bandar Baru Tampoi	
Taman UDA, Alor Star	
Tanjong Tokong Project	
Taman Tun Dr. Ismail	SEA Park Development Sdn. Bhd.
Subang Jaya	Intercontinental Housing Development Ltd.
Ibraco-UDA	Ibraco
Taman Connally Taman Ouniaga Sentul Jaya	Malay interest
Sungei Petani Project	State Government of Kedah
UDA Wardley Merchant Bank	The Hongkong & Shanghai Banking Corp.
UDA-Redikon	
Sepang Sermic	

Note. Only the big projects are listed.

more than a dozen joint-venture housing development companies with the private sector in the last few years. It has even ventured into merchant banking (Chart 5.12). Bank Rakyat, then under Datuk Harun Idris, has also ventured beyond the confines of the co-operative society's activities and developed several prime office towers in Kuala Lumpur, initiated a merchant bank and some manufacturing companies, and invested in shares. The various SEDCs have also participated in this wave of joint ventures. However, only the two most important of these, the PKNS of Selangor and the Johor State Economic Development Corporation, which have also become two of the nation's most important housing and property developers, mining enterprises, and manufacturers, have been documented here (Charts 5.13 and 5.14).

Furthermore, public and private enterprises such as Bank Pertanian (with a merchant bank and significant holdings of planting company shares like Harrisons Malaysian Estates Ltd.), Syarikat Perusahaan Pegawai Kerajaan Bhd. (SPPK) (housing development for civil servants, one of the largest developers in the nation) and companies closely connected with the Government such as the Syarikat Permodalan Kebangsaan Bhd. (SPK) and the Fleet group have all played important roles in acquiring shares in the private sector. In addition, the Armed Forces Fund and the Police Co-operative Society are also venturing into financial and commercial-industrial companies, for example, the Armed Forces Fund into Perwira Habib Bank and Amalgamated Steel Mills Sdn. Bhd. among others, and the Police Co-operative Society into Oriental Bank Bhd. and Koperasi Tentera (Armed Forces Co-operative) into Pacific Bank Bhd. (Charts 5.15 and 5.16 provide partial documentation of the network of some of these organizations).

There has also been some activity by the Malay private sector to take advantage of the conditions created by the New Economic Policy. Since this is a relatively new phenomenon, and the bulk of it occurs in the realm of private limited companies, it is very difficult to document the details of the changes without making a full-scale study of company registers of shares and tracing all the linkages, as we have argued earlier for the non-Malay private limited companies. Nevertheless, several groups have come into the limelight to enable easier documentation and this has been done in Charts 5.17 and 5.19. These include the widespread interests of Datuk Ibrahim (Chart 5.17) and Mars Holdings Sdn. Bhd. that now controls the largest underground tin-mine and one of the larger independent tin mining companies, The Pahang Consolidated Co. Ltd., and the manufacturing conglomerate of Federal Cables, Wires & Metal Mfg. Bhd. (Chart 5.18). The Tengku Ariff Bendahara of Pahang (TAB)'s wide-ranging business interests have also been charted (Chart 5.19). This list is by no means exhaustive.[100]

Furthermore, a list of Malay directors of all the publicly listed companies on the Kuala Lumpur and Singapore Stock Exchanges (Table 8.1) has been compiled. While it is true many of them are directors as representatives of organizations such as Pernas, or the State Economic Development Corporations, the majority are probably acting as directors in their private capacity. No doubt, their positions within the Government and/or the ruling party afford them a very useful entry point. Anyway, it is apparent that there is also great concentration of wealth and control of corporations in the hands of a very

CHART 5.13
COMPANIES OF THE PERBADANAN KEMAJUAN NEGERI SELANGOR
(SELANGOR STATE DEVELOPMENT CORPORATION)

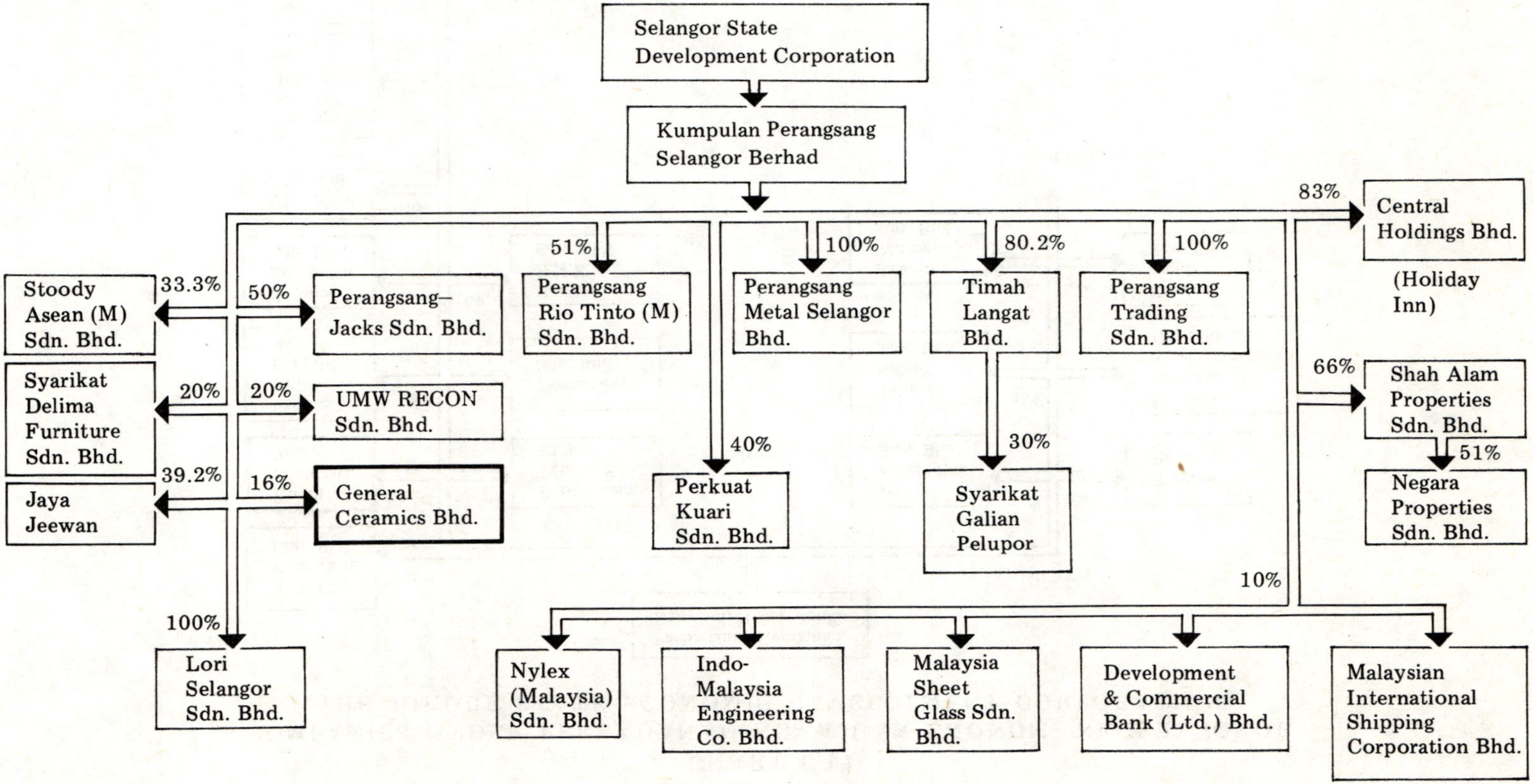

CHART 5.14
COMPANIES UNDER PERBADANAN KEMAJUAN EKONOMI NEGERI JOHOR
(THE JOHORE STATE ECONOMIC DEVELOPMENT CORPORATION)

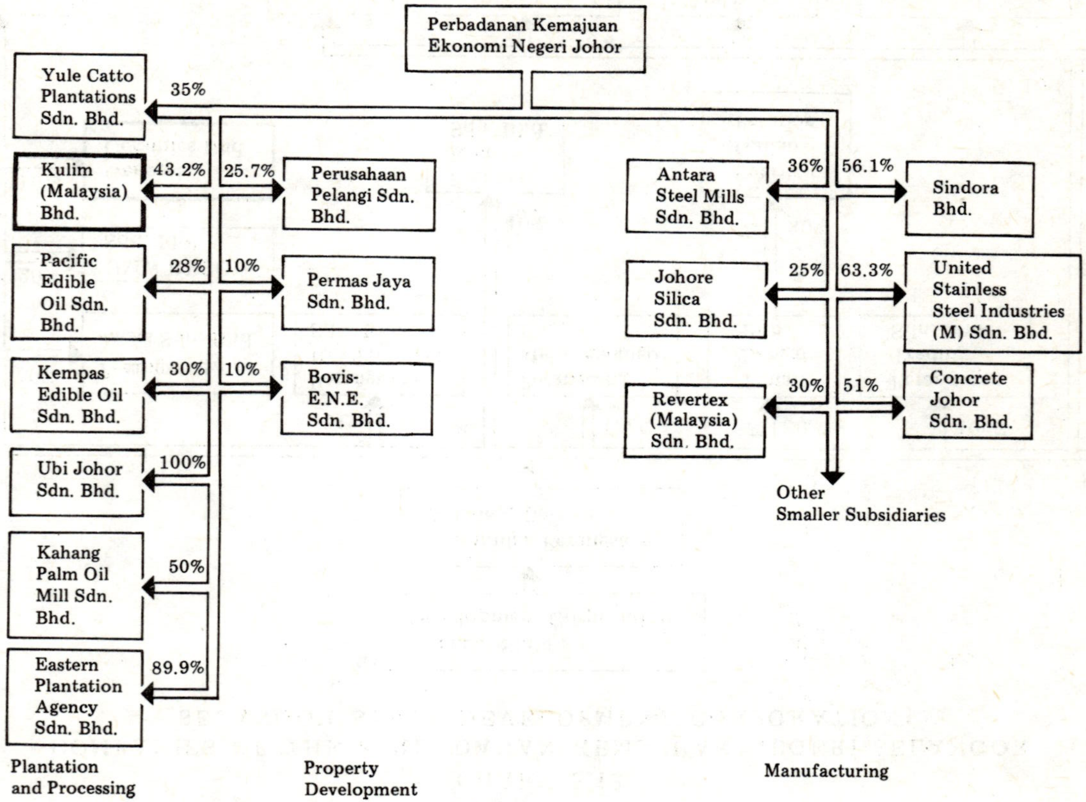

CHART 5.15

SYARIKAT PERMODALAN KEBANGSAAN BHD.

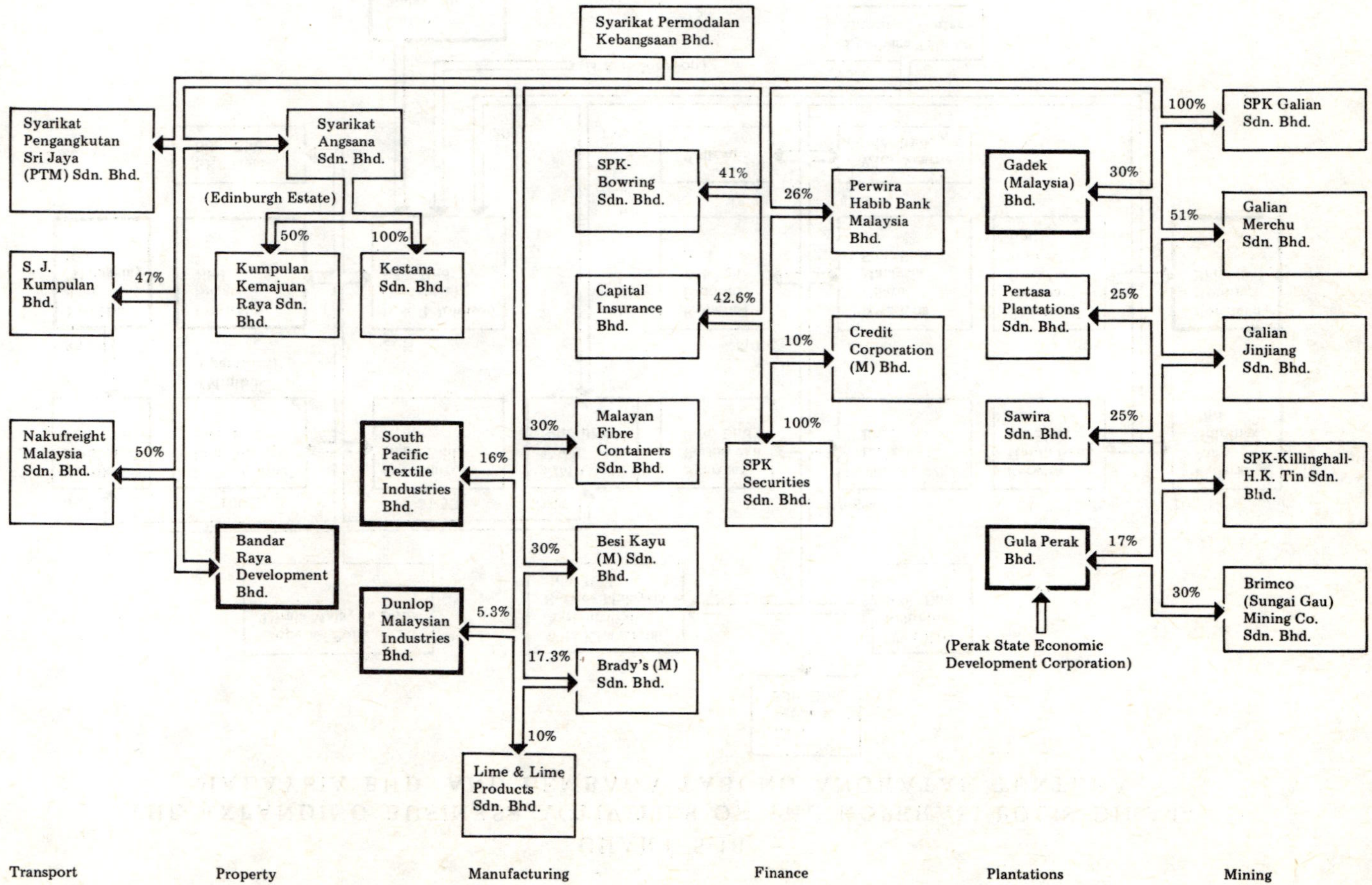

CHART 5.16

THE EXPANDING BUSINESS ACTIVITIES OF THE KOPERASI POLIS DIRAJA MALAYSIA BHD. AND LEMBAGA TABUNG ANGKATAN TENTERA

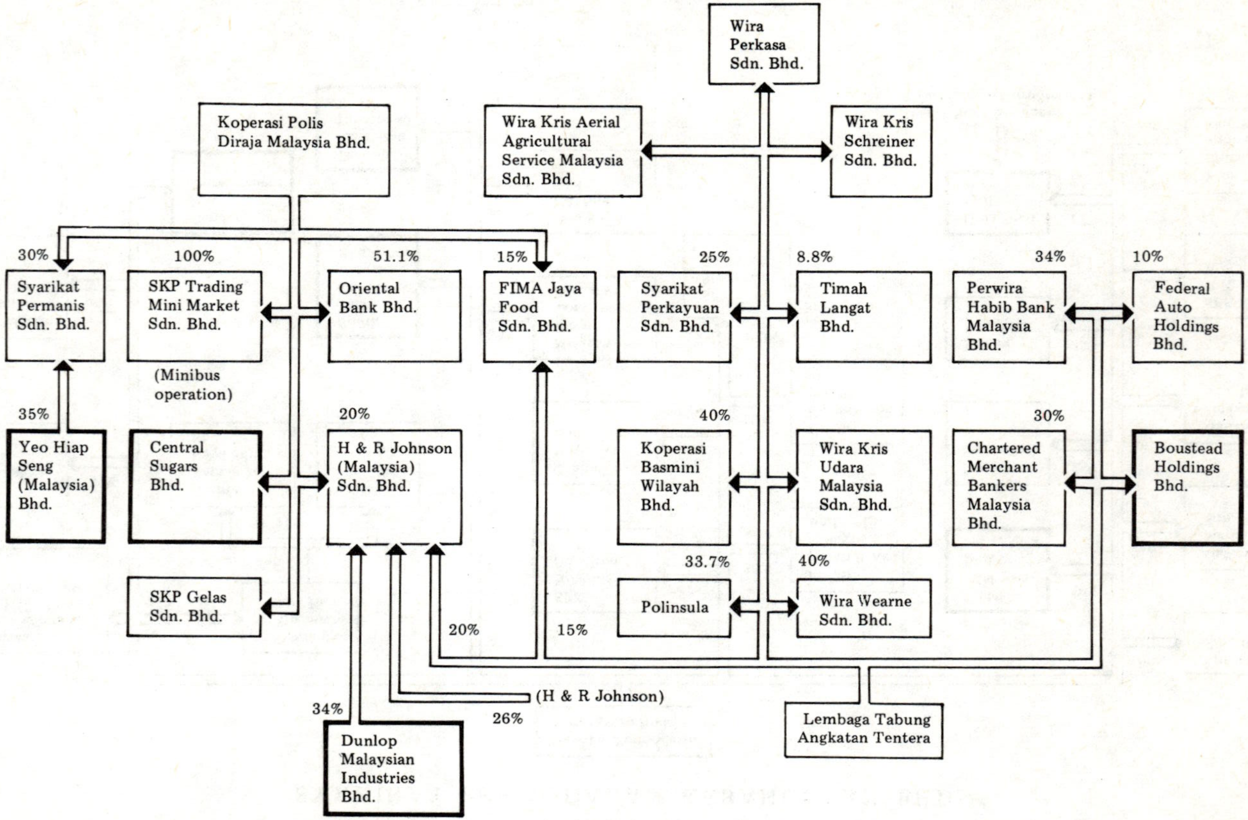

CHART 5.17
DATUK HAJI IBRAHIM BIN MOHAMED'S GROUP

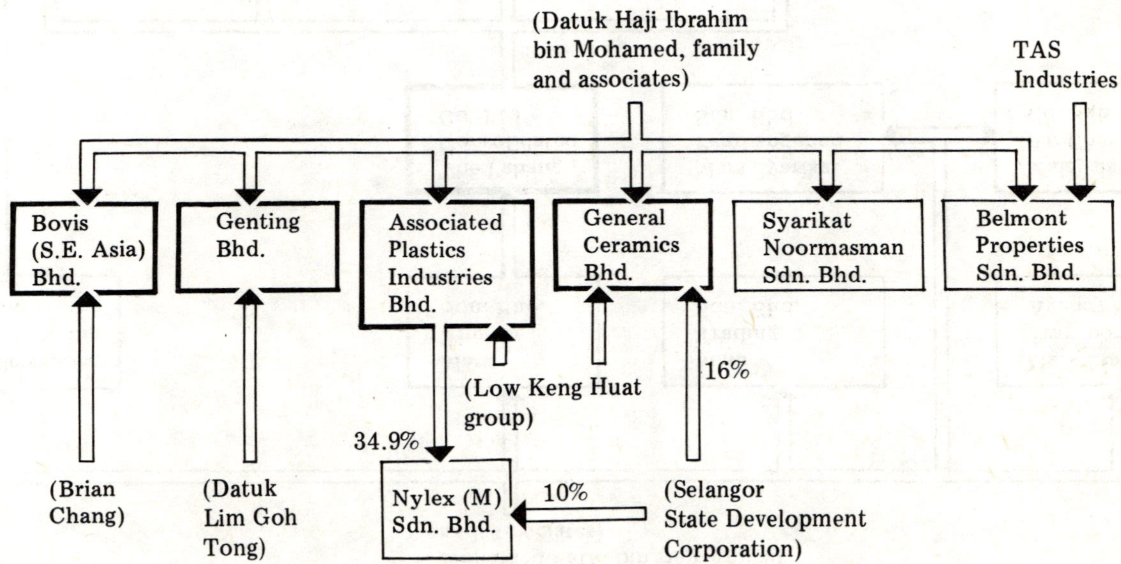

CHART 5.18
MARS HOLDINGS

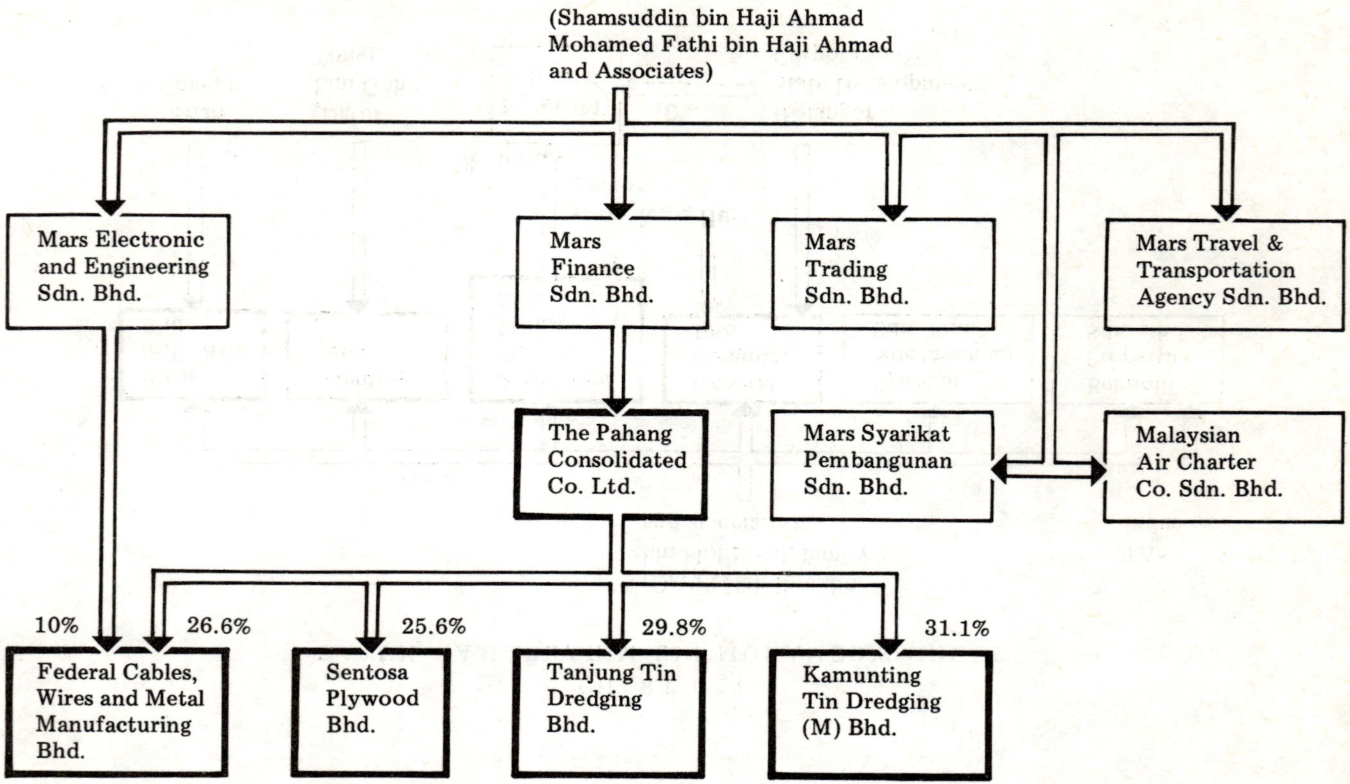

CHART 5.19

TAB AND HIS HOLDINGS

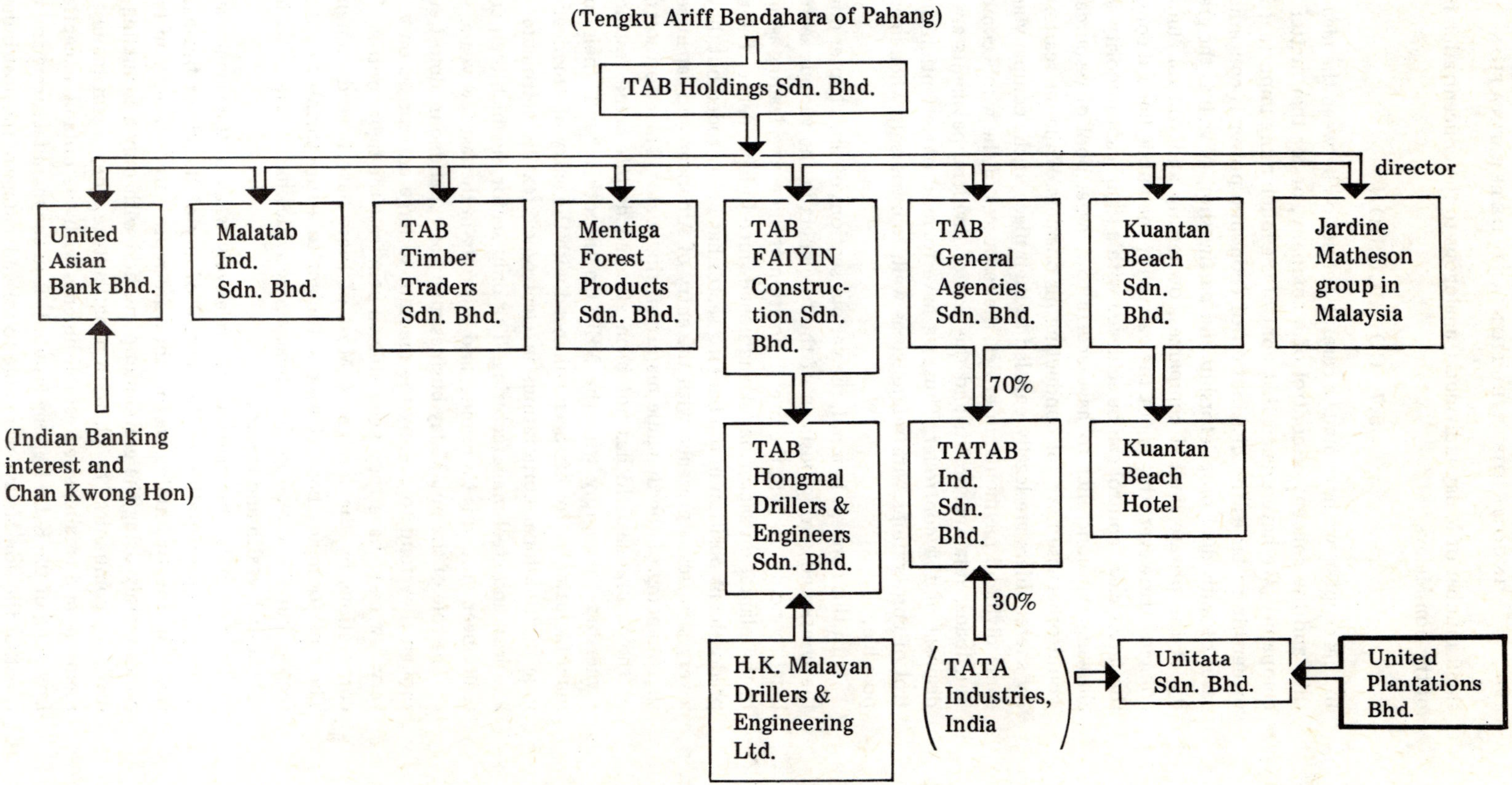

small number of Malay individuals, analogous to the concentration in the case of the non-Malays.

5.7 CONCLUSION

In this chapter, we have made a careful distinction between the idea of ownership and the concept of control of a company, or for that matter, group of companies. We have argued that control is a much more important issue than ownership as far as the distribution of economic power is concerned. In the cases of individual proprietorship and partnership, as well as the great majority of the private limited companies, ownership and control almost always coincide. However, this is not the case with the public limited companies. In the latter case, control can be achieved with a significant minority share, thus allowing the controller to have access to a larger pool of resources than he would otherwise have for conducting his business. While the scattered minority shareholders are legally entitled to their piece of the company and receive some dividend payments, in effect, the resources of the whole company, capital, loans, retained profit, and the size of dividend payments are all at the disposal of the controller. Thus, we have focused our attention on the control of corporations with reference as well, to ownership when necessary and possible.

With this concept in mind, the various sections of this chapter documented the continued strong position of the foreigners in the various sectors of the local economy. In fact, the overall position of the several leading agency houses in the plantation sector has strengthened since Independence. Their formerly predominant position in the banking sector has been eroded but they retained a very significant presence with the entry of American and Japanese banks in the financing of the dynamic manufacturing sector. Their position of control in the insurance field has not been affected despite some restructuring of ownership to comply with the NEP. On the other hand, their role in the manufacturing sector has been enhanced with the entry of American and Japanese multinational corporations in electronics, textile, petroleum, chemical, and iron and steel manufacturing. The only sector in which their control has really been eroded is tin mining, and this only in the last few years.

The role of the non-Malay businessmen has expanded in almost every field, though they tend to occupy the medium to large enterprises only. In only a very few cases have they been able to penetrate the tight control of the huge corporations by the foreigners. Most of these have been documented here. Their performance has not been sufficient to assure them of control of any sector, but the spread in their business activities has ensured for the owners substantial wealth and income.

The non-Malay businessmen are relatively weak in the finance sector with no major representation in the control of any of the major financial institutions. In the tin mining sector, they are represented strongly in the smaller mines mainly using the gravel-pump method with only a sprinkling of big tin dredging companies. In plantation agriculture, they again mainly own the medium- and smaller-sized establishments with the notable exception of Lee Loy Seng of the K.L.–Kepong group. It is in the manufacturing and other sectors that the non-Malays were able to take advantage of the post-Independence climate and the relative lack of penetration by the foreigners to become established. Yet most of them invariably end up in partnership with the foreigners.

As for the Malays who were very under-represented in the corporate sector until 1970, since then very significant headway has been made, especially by the Government on their behalf. While they still lag behind the non-Malays, and both groups lag substantially behind the foreigners, in terms of percentage of corporate shareholdings, they have made major and dominating acquisitions in particular sectors. In no other sectors is their control so strong as in the finance, tin mining, and petroleum sectors. Moreover, they are also making important inroads into the plantation, property development, manufacturing, trading, and services sectors. This is only the beginning of the trend. In years to come one can expect the Malays' role to expand sharply, mainly through the small number of present wealth holders and especially the Government via the various public enterprises. This process is most likely to occur through a combination of joint-venture projects with leading foreign and local non-Malay businessmen as well as a continual restructuring of existing old firms, especially the larger ones and those in commodity production and key manufacturing.

However, if precedents up to 1977 are any guide, most of the foreign firms are likely to restructure in such a way that they retain a significant minority shareholding, 30 per cent and upwards, together with control of the corporation. Moreover, since it has been envisaged that foreign investment will continue to expand and is indeed being actively solicited, we can expect the absolute amount of foreign investment to continue to increase, albeit in the context of a declining overall share of total corporate shareholdings. Once a distinction is made between ownership and control, it is to be expected that the relative decline of the foreigners' role will not be as dramatic as that envisaged under the TMP. On the contrary, control by them will remain quite strong.

Another striking feature that has emerged from this chapter is, of course, the great concentration of wealth and resources of the leading companies in the hands of a very few. The nineteen conglomerates drawn up, with their associates and subsidiaries not included, control close to half of the companies listed on the Kuala Lumpur Stock Exchange. And, no more than a few score families or groups control these conglomerates!

1. J. J. Puthucheary, *Ownership and Control in the Malayan Economy*, Singapore, Eastern Universities Press, 1960, p. 27.

2. For example, Sieh's study dealt with the question of ownership and control with very aggregated data looking at the distribution of shares by size group. This approach would have understated the extent of concentration as it is common practice for an individual or group to hold shares in a company under diverse names, whether of family members or associated companies. More importantly, this approach does not allow the researcher to identify the whole network of control by group(s) as we have done. Hirschman and Lindenberg have both tried to chart the companies within each group; however, their efforts have not been comprehensive enough, and Lindenberg has several important errors in the charting. In this chapter, we have presented only nineteen charts although many more have been done in the process of research.

3. R. K. Mamajiwala, 'Ownership and Control of Public Limited Planting Companies Incorporated in the Federation of Malaya', M.A. Thesis, University of Malaya, 1965.

4. For example, in one of the major groups that we discussed, one of the most important executives/partners of the Kuok brothers, Geh Ik Cheong, was a son-in-law of the Lee Rubber–OCBC founder, yet as far as we can tell, there are minimal business relationships between the two groups. Moreover, even when any two groups share the same non-executive director or even chairman, the actual business ties between the two groups of companies and the controlling directors may still be minimal, in which case using them as linkages is quite misleading.

5. The role of oil palm in the Malaysian economy did not become important until the seventies and should not be considered traditional. However, in so far as they are mainly tied up with the rubber estates, they have been classified as traditional. Actually, most of the rubber estates, especially the larger ones, have planted some oil palm following from the decision to diversify when they replanted in the sixties. This can be seen from Table 5.1. For more detailed figures on the number of estates with both crops, see the relevant tables in *Rubber Statistics Handbook* and *Oil Palm, Coconut and Tea Statistics* of various years published by the Department of Statistics.

6. At this level of operation, shares are tightly held because the controlling families may not be able to secure outside participation on the one hand, and on the other are very jealous of the benefits flowing into the hands of other people if shares are dispersed.

7. This is the impression gained from a general reading of local newspapers over the years, a comparison of the number of companies listed in the yearly *Stock Exchange Handbook* and in the various issues of Fraser & Co., *Facts and Figures*, Singapore (hereafter, FFF).

8. From the research leading to the construction of the charts in this chapter, control is frequently achieved with less than a 50 per cent holding of the company shares. This is especially true for the large publicly listed companies with widely dispersed shareholdings. One can also refer to the large quantity of literature on control in other countries for a general flavour of the definition of control. In fact, the ability of the large corporations to float bonds and shares to the public means that they have access to a larger pool of funds than they would otherwise have. This would definitely give them an added advantage compared to the smaller non-listed companies, with only their own capital for projects.

9. This is because some companies may have a minority percentage of shares in the hands of a controlling foreign interest with the rest of the shares well dispersed among Malaysians. Such companies would have been defined as being under local control by the Department of Statistics.

10. Bearing in mind that the 30 per cent or so of the share capital floated in the market is generally too widely dispersed in the hands of a large number of small investors for them to get organized and nominate a director to the Board.

11. In fact, for all the limited companies as a whole, the directors of the companies hold about 50 per cent of the shares (see *Financial Survey*, 1970). This estimate probably has not taken into consideration the shares held by family members, in trusts, and in nominee companies.

12. The choice of $10 million and $30 million is somewhat arbitrary. It is from a general impression of what is considered a large-sized company in the local economy.

13. For example, Chang Ming Thien is the original entrepreneur, Kang Kock Seng is his senior executive who has probably become an important shareholder by now (see Chart 5.9). In the case of the Kuok brothers, the

brothers are the major shareholders with the assistance of Geh Ik Cheong (Chart 5.8).

14. Puthucheary, op. cit., Chapter 2, especially Chart II, p. 88. Allen and Donnithorne, Bauer, and others have also looked into the role of the agency houses, but none of them in such detail as Puthucheary.

15. See Ungku Aziz, *Subdivision of Estates in Malaya*, Kuala Lumpur, University of Malaya, 1962.

16. See for example, the study of Mamajiwala, op. cit. For examples of the evolution of the major Chinese businessmen in the pre-war period, see 黃枝連，馬華社會史導論，星州，萬里文化出版社 1971 (Huang Chih Lien, *An Introductory Exposition into the Social History of the Malayan Chinese*, Singapore, Wan Li, 1971), and Song Ong Siang, *One Hundred Years History of the Chinese in Singapore*, London, J. Murray, 1923.

17. This is the conclusion one can draw from Mamajiwala's study. Furthermore, looking through the list of directors and the seat of control of the planting and mining companies listed in the *Stock Exchange Handbook* of various years, the very small number of locally-controlled planting and mining companies is an indication that few of the local directors/shareholders had picked up a substantial block of shares for nomination to the board or for control.

The notable exceptions were the Malacca planting syndicate of Tan Cheng Lock–Tan Hoon Siang–Chee Bay Hoon–Ong Chin Yam–Tan Swi Chay in United Malacca, Ayer Molek and Bukit Katil and Tee Teh–Gan Teck Yeow in Bukit Jalil. Mamajiwala, op. cit., *passim*.

18. *Monthly Statistical Bulletin of West Malaysia*, June 1976, Table 1.2, reported 1.430 million acres of rubber under estates. *Oil Palm, Coconut and Tea Statistics*, Table 11, reported 77,900 acres and 72,500 acres as the respective increase in oil palm estate acreage for 1972 and 1973, which have been used to project the oil palm acreage for 1974 to be 754,000 acres.

19. This can be seen from Boustead Holding Bhd.'s acquisition of the whole of the Heah Joo Seang Estates, K.L.–Kepong's purchase of significant minority interest in Yule Catto and H & L, and so on.

20. The information here is pieced together from the Stock Exchange of Singapore, *Company Handbook*, various years; company annual reports; interviews; *Malaysia and Singapore Who's Who*, various years; FFF, various years.

21. ibid., in fact, in 1953, Sime Darby owned/controlled/managed only thirty-two companies with 109,901 acres, Puthucheary, op. cit., p. 46; but by 1968, the number of companies under its wing had been amalgamated into nine with 110,692 acres. See company annual report and FFF, 1970.

22. In 1953, it had 226,072 acres, Puthucheary, Table X, p. 46. In 1968, it had 233,174 acres (FFF, 1970) and in 1974, 222,614 acres (Table 5.1).

23. In 1953, it had 156,306 acres, Puthucheary, op. cit., p. 46. The figure here refers to H & C's plantations in Malaysia. It also has extensive holdings in Indonesia and India.

24. Malaysian interests hold about 30 per cent, Stock Exchange of Singapore, *Company Handbook*, 1974.

25. Puthucheary, op. cit., p. 46, and FFF, 1970.

26. See report on Jardine Matheson (South-East Asia) Ltd. in the Stock Exchange of Kuala Lumpur, *Company Handbook*, 1978. Moreover, in 1980, Genting took over the three planting companies held by Hong Kong's Kadoorie interests managed by P.A.

27. Introduction to FFF, 1970, and the Stock Exchange of Singapore, *Company Handbook*, 1974.

28. ibid., and Table 5.1.

29. This can be seen by comparing the data given by FFF, 1970 and other

years as well as Zorn and Leigh-Hunt's *Manual of Planting and Mining Companies*, various years.

30. REA owned and managed 6,600 acres and Cumberbatch owned and managed 138,648 acres in 1953. Harper Gilfillan, Thomas Barlow, and Boustead–Buttery owned and managed 92,145 acres, 47,381 acres, and 169,555 acres respectively in 1953. See Puthucheary, op. cit., p. 46.

31. See Mamajiwala, op. cit., *passim*.

32. For example, to acquire 10,000 acres of estate land costing $2,000 per acre will require $20 million. This is not a sum many people can afford. Besides, a good piece of estate land usually costs more than $2,000 per acre.

33. For example, recently, H & C defeated the attempt by Genting Highlands to seize one of its three largest planting companies (Golden Hope) in 1977, and again defeated the attempt by other groups on its London Sumatra and Harcros Investment Trusts in 1978. See *Far Eastern Economic Review*, various issues in the relevant years for summary reports.

34. See for example, Mamajiwala, op. cit.

35. Lee began by acquiring K.L.–Kepong and Kepong with a total area of 115,006 acres from the control of the Meagl Sdn. Bhd. and Batu Kawan, Batu Lintang, and Duff Development from the control of Plantation Agencies. See FFF, various years, Singapore Stock Exchange, *Annual Company Handbook*, 1974. K.L.–Kepong first took a position in H & L to the tune of 13.19 per cent in 1974 when Sime Darby and Pernas picked up 13.86 per cent and 9.1 per cent respectively. In about the same period, the three Barlows, Hindson, and Hunter which had held 30.13 per cent of total shares in trust reduced this holding to less than 1 per cent. See 1974 H & L annual report. In 3/1975, K.L–Kepong announced a further acquisition of H & L shares bringing its total stake in H & L to 25 per cent (see *Gazette* 4/1975 published by the K.L. Stock Exchange) making it the single largest shareholder of H & L. In 1975, the K.L.–Kepong group announced the acquisition of the Escot and Allagar rubber estates (*Gazette* 11/1975). In 1976, K.L.–Kepong acquired 20 per cent of Yule Catto and built up the stake to 26 per cent, while Batu Kawan bought 50 per cent of Gadek (*Gazette* 5/1976). If all these acquisitions and controlled companies are added to those listed in Table 5.1, Lee would become the largest estate holder in the country.

36. See, for example, *Far Eastern Economic Review*, 24/12/1976.

37. See note 33.

38. For example, Chan Wing's vast estate has been absorbed by Kempas, a subsidiary of Sime Darby. Heah Joo Seang Estates was sold in two stages to Guthrie.

39. Associated Estate Agencies' estates were acquired following British withdrawal in the mid-fifties (see Mamajiwala) while that of Heah Joo Seang was taken over from the Japanese after their defeat in the war.

40. For example, Loh Boon Siew, the Tai family charted in this chapter, the Neoh Choo Ee family, etc., all purchased estates of thousands of acres.

41. See Ungku Aziz, op. cit., for a general exposition, and P. O. Thomas, *Malaysian Natural Rubber in the Seventies: A Forecast of Production Trends*, Kuala Lumpur, Rubber Research Institute, 1970, for the figures on acreage subdivided.

42. The wealth of Pillai can be seen from recent Government prosecution of his income tax evasion from estate income to the tune of $18,884,687 for the years 1953 to 1972 (*New Straits Times*, 15/4/1976). This example also highlights the profits that can be generated by huge estates which are tens of thousands of acres in size.

43. By right, there should be a distinction between Malay holdings and

Government holdings. However, in the case of Malaysia, especially in recent years, the Government penetration of the private sector has been for the expressed purpose of raising Malay participation in the industrial and commercial sectors. Government acquisitions have generally been conducted by one of the several Malay trust funds. Moreover, in the Third Malaysia Plan, the Government has also started to classify shares acquired in this manner as those of Malay interests. Therefore, the distinction is not important.

44. See the structure of shareholdings after some of the companies had moved their residences to Malaysia. Some examples are Kulim, *Far Eastern Economic Review*, 26/11/1976, Guthrie Ropel cited earlier, and H & L.

45. *Third Malaysia Plan 1976–1980*, p. 183. Note that the criterion here is ownership, probably in the sense defined by the Department of Statistics, i.e., 50.01 per cent ownership of total capital.

46. Stock Exchange of Singapore, *Company Handbook*, 1974.

47. ibid., also 1975 issue, 1974 Haw Par Brothers International annual report, *Far Eastern Economic Review*, 14/11/1975.

48. ibid., also *New Straits Times*, 2/4/1976.

49. However, given that land control is a state matter, and the State Governments are keen to share in the benefits, this has proved not to be the case, as the companies under the wing of the Pernas-controlled Malaysia Mining Corporation have been having problems in renegotiating lease arrangements with the Selangor State Economic Development Corporation which wants its subsidiary, the Perangsang Selangor, to participate. See the many announcements on related matters in various issues of *Business Times* in 1978 as well as the many statements by Rahim Aki, the chairman of the Malaysia Mining Corporation, on this matter.

50. It is difficult to estimate how much cash would be necessary for this acquisition. If CC alone were to strive for the acquisition of LT, it would probably have to be prepared to offer for all the shares of LT under the same terms as those forced upon Pernas by the London Stock Exchange under its take-over code. At the Pernas offer price of 197.5 pence per share, it would have cost £20.4 million if only 50 per cent of the shareholders decided to sell.

51. It is premature to attach any solid figure to this estimate because the real worth of the new company has not been published. However, if one can assume that the 42 per cent of the output of the industry produced by the new group takes 42 per cent of the total share capital of the industry to produce, then, Pernas with its 70 per cent stake in the company would account for 29 per cent of the share capital of the industry. This is, however, a conservative estimate in view of the capital intensity of the tin dredges. This estimate of the Malay share in the tin industry has not taken into account the new companies being formed by Kumpulan Perangsang with others such as Timah Langat launched in 1978.

52. Most of Rahim's speeches and announcements can be found in *Business Times*.

53. See Puthucheary, op. cit., and Huang Chih Lien, op. cit.

54. Bank Negara Malaysia, *Annual Report*, 1975, p. 17.

55. The other foreign banks were the Indian Bank, Indian Overseas Bank, United Commercial Bank (which amalgamated their Malaysian interests into the United Asian Bank with some local equity participation in the seventies), Bank of Canton, Mercantile Bank (since absorbed by The Hongkong & Shanghai Bank), Algemene Bank Nederland (then under a different name), Eastern Bank (taken over by The Chartered Bank), Lee Wah Bank (owned by the Eu family but taken over by the United Overseas Bank of Singapore), and Chung Khiaw Bank (owned by the Aw family and also taken over by the United Overseas Bank).

56. It was co-founded by Lee Kong Chian, the founder of Lee Rubber, and has been dominated by his family group since the post-war years, and to a lesser extent, descendants of other early founders such as Tan Chin Tuan, Tan Siew Sin/Tan Hoon Siang, and the descendants of the Four Seas Communication Bank following the merger in the mid-seventies. For the early history, see 星州十年 and 南洋年鑑 .

57. In the forties and fifties, Tan Cheng Lock represented the Malaccan interests on the Board. Tan Hoon Siang did so for more than ten years until Tun Tan Siew Sin's retirement as Finance Minister, when he took over the representation.

58. This has been the impression gained from reading the history and background of the banks, their founders, and their activities. See Putucheary, op. cit., Huang, op. cit., 馬星華人誌，墾荒四十年 , etc.

59. Bank Negara Malaysia, *Annual Report*, 1975, p. 17.

60. Malayan Banking was founded by Tan Sri Khoo Teck Puat with Goh Tjooi Kok (Singaporean, estate owner, industrialist, founder of Tat Lee Bank in the seventies), Loke Wan Tho (son and heir of the tin miner and property owner Loke Yew, founder of the Cathay Organization), Oei Tjong Ie (son of Indonesian 'sugar king', Oei Tiong Ham), Wang Teng Kiat (financier, now of Malayan Credit and Bandar Raya) among others. See Malayan Banking, *Annual Report*, 1962; FFF, 1964 and 1967. Kwong Yik Bank was founded by the Loke family. The major shareholders of UMBC include Chang Ming Thien, Yeoh Chin Hin (tin miner from Ipoh), Tee Teh (Selangor rubber trader-planter), Datuk Saw Choo Teng (Penang estate owner and rubber trader, co-founder of Southern Banking), Ong Chin Chio (Singaporean rubber trader), Lok Bok Sim (Singapore copra trader and financier), and Chew Choo Keng (of the Khong Guan biscuit group). Public Bank is part of the conglomerate of Datuk Teh Hong Piow and Seet Hong Kiat. Teh was formerly with OCBC, but left and eventually set up this bank in 1966. United Asian Bank's origins have been mentioned in note 55. Malaysian interests in this bank totalled at least 51 per cent with Chan Kwong Hon (tin miner), Y.A.M. TAB (Pahang's 'timber' Prince, Chart 5.19), P. P. Narayanan (probably representing the interest of the National Union of Plantation Workers), and Tan Sri K. T. Jethanand. Southern Banking was started by the Saw brothers with Datuk Loh Boon Siew (assembler and distributor of the Honda line of motor products, property developer), the Kweks of the Hong Leong group (Chart 5.10); and several other wealthy Penang businessmen. Development & Commercial Bank was founded by the wealthy tin miner and co-founder of the Malayan Chinese Association, former Minister of Finance Tun Colonel Sir Henry H. S. Lee. Gathered from *Who's Who*, *Biography of Directors*, referees.

61. Kassim and Chan, *SGV Survey of Commercial Banks 1974*, Table J, summary.

62. ibid., Kwong Yik Bank is now a subsidiary of Malayan Banking and therefore is not regarded as independent.

63. ibid.

64. Bank Bumiputra, *10 Years of Bank Bumiputra*, 1975.

65. FFF, 1967, p. 122; article by Solomon in *Malaysian Business*, June 1975, p. 53; *Far Eastern Economic Review*, 21/5/1976.

66. Bank Negara Malaysia, *Annual Report*, 1975, p. 81; 1977, p. 73.

67. Kassim and Chan, *SGV Survey of Commercial Banks 1974*, Table I.

68. Kassim and Chan, *SGV Survey of Finance Companies 1974*, Table G.

69. ibid., Tables E8 and E12.

70. For example, their deposits totalled $1,438.6 million while loans totalled $919.5 million in 1975, Bank Negara Malaysia, *Annual Report*, 1975, p. 78.

71. Hong Leong Finance, Boon Siew Finance, Malaysian Borneo Finance, and Sim Lim Finance are all part of conglomerates, that of the Hong Leong group, Loh Boon Siew group, Loy group, and Sim Lim group respectively, as are Chew Geok Lin Finance, Central Malaysian Finance, Eu Finance, and Tai Cheng Finance.

72. *New Straits Times*, 3/5/1976.

73. *Annual Report by the Director General of Insurance*, 1975, p. 47.

74. ibid., p. 44.

75. ibid., p. 50.

76. ibid., p. 68.

77. ibid., p. 69.

78. IBRD, *Economic Development of Malaya*, Singapore, 1955, p. 301, cited and elaborated by Puthucheary, op. cit., pp. 96—7.

79. ibid., pp. 97—9 and especially p. 102.

80. See Yeh Tai Heng, 葉痞痕，梹榔嶼大觀 , *An Overview of Penang.*

81. Puthucheary, op. cit., pp. 128—33.

82. For example, the Straits Times group has been split into a Singapore and a Malaysian operation. The latter is under the New Straits Times group which is controlled by the Fleet group of companies close to the ruling UMNO interests. The recently restructured Metal Box and Jack Chia Enterprises are further examples.

83. The manufacturing sector's value added has increased from less than $500 million (about 6 per cent of GNP) in 1957 to $1,970 million in 1973 (or about 17.1) per cent of the GDP of the peninsula). Treasury, *Economic Report*, 1973–4, Table 1.2; Department of Statistics, *National Accounts of the States of Malaya*, Table XII. By 1977, the pan-Malaysian manufacturing value added had increased to $3,748 million, Treasury, *Economic Report*, 1977–8.

84. The following are some examples of old firms that have expanded and diversified their operations: Wearne into auto assembly, Inchcape into auto assembly and parts manufacture, Rothmans into printing and plastics, Malayan Cement into Associated Pan Malaysian Cement and Ready-Mix Concrete, property development, Dunlop into big tyres. As for the new firms, the numbers are too numerous.

85. Bank Negara Malaysia, *Quarterly Economic Bulletin*, September 1978, Table on production in the manufacturing industries.

86. Department of Statistics, *Financial Survey of Limited Companies*, 1970, Table 2.1, pp. 17 and 19. However, the concept of control differs from the one we use in this book; more discussion on this can be found in Chapter 6.

87. See *Insight*, August 1978, feature article on the Kuoks.

88. For example, the Malayan Sugar Manufacturer was the first sugar refinery and remains the largest in the country. Perlis Plantation is the most profitable of the sugar planting and refining companies. Rasa Sayang and Shangri-la are among the best hotels in Penang and Singapore respectively. Ipoh Garden is one of the three largest private housing property developers in this country, the other two being the See Hoy Chan group and the Lee Yan Lian group. Pacific Veneer and Plywood is also among the larger plywood manufacturers, as is Federal Flour among the flour mills. Malaysia Shipyard and Engineering is certainly the dominant shipbuilder among the five in Malaysia.

89. Geh is a former son-in-law of the founder of Lee Rubber. However, there appear to be no current business ties between the two groups.

90. For a background of the partners, see note 60 to this chapter.

91. *Far Eastern Economic Review*, various issues in late 1977 and early 1978.

92. For further discussion see Mavis Puthucheary, 'Public Enterprise and the Creation of a Bumiputra Entrepreneurial Community', paper presented at the Fourth Economic Convention organized by the Malaysian Economic Association in Kuala Lumpur, 1977; and Chandra Muzaffar, 'Some Political Perspectives on the New Economic Policy', paper presented to the convention cited above.

93. See M. C. Puthucheary, op. cit., p. 4.

94. Estimated by Puthucheary, ibid., p. 11.

95. The figures for 1975 cited in the *Third Malaysia Plan* are 5.4 per cent for the Government enterprises and 7.8 per cent overall for the Malays including the public enterprises. By contrast, the 1970 figure was only 2 per cent. Since 1975, more acquisitions have been made by the Malays and the latest figure for 1977 cited in a speech by the Minister of Commerce and Industry in Parliament was close to 10 per cent.

96. The officially announced Pernas stake in SD amounted to about 10 per cent. However, Pernas may control it if other major minority shareholdings by other Government enterprises or groups sympathetic to the Pernas viewpoint vote with Pernas.

97. We have already summarized the K.L.–Kepong stake in H & L in note 35. In fact, Pernas–SD with close to 24 per cent and K.L.–Kepong with 25 per cent of H & L have already established control. It is unrealistic to consider the stakes as independently held with no co-operation. With the NEP, K.L.–Kepong itself needs to restructure to ensure 30 per cent Malay shareholding; it would clearly want to control jointly H & L with Pernas.

98. SD attempted to take over Guthrie in early 1979 but fell short. Nevertheless, it continues to hold just under 30 per cent of Guthrie. In addition, its purchases of minority stakes in H & C through open market operations certainly add fuel to the speculations. The following chart identifies the kind of

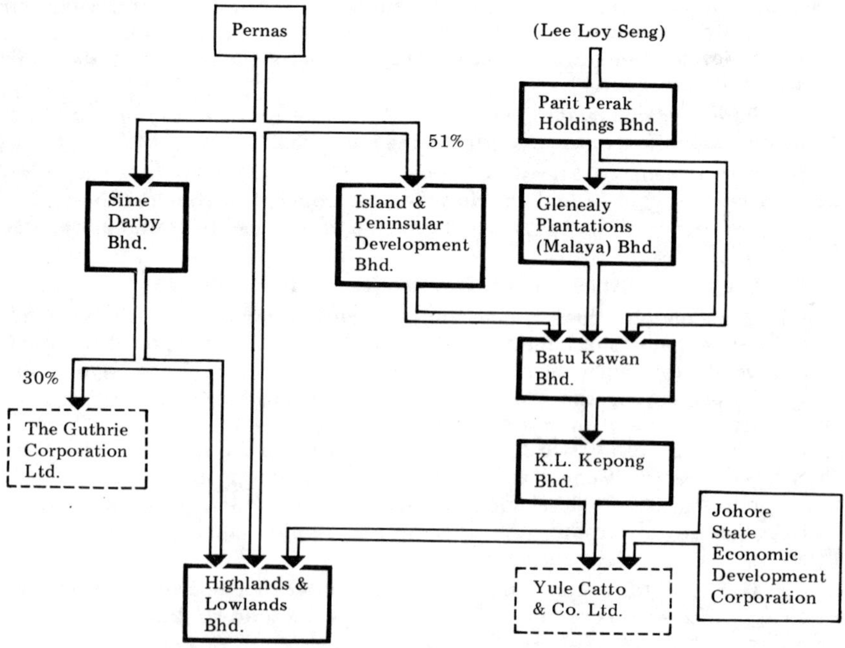

control the Pernas–SD–Lee Loy Seng group has in the plantation sector. If any more of the major plantations come under their wing, the influence in this sector would parallel that of Pernas–CC in tin mining.

99. Snodgrass, *Inequality and Economic Development in Malaysia*.

100. There are certainly other very rich Malays, for example, Datuk Syed Kechik, Datuk Seri Syed Nahar, Datuk Harris, Datuk Patinggi Abdul Rahman, the family of the late Tun Fuad, not to mention the Royal families. However, it is difficult and sensitive to try to document and chart their extensive business ties.

6 Earnings of Firms and Income of the Owners

6.1 INTRODUCTION

A. General

IN the last chapter, the discussion centred on the ownership and control pattern of the publicly listed limited companies. The claim was that these represented the largest, wealthiest, and most profitable operations. In this chapter, this point will be further substantiated by comparing the performance of the publicly listed limited companies with that of the private limited ones, as well as with that of the partnerships and individual proprietorships.

In the preceding chapter, the conglomerate was the unit of observation. The extent of conglomeration was used to highlight the concentration of wealth-generating activities in the hands of a very small minority. The more companies each conglomeration encompasses, the more concentration of wealth there is likely to be. The result is that a study at the company level only would grossly underestimate the wealth and income concentration in the hands of the rich. Analogously, each company may have more than one establishment, and each establishment may have more than one major field of activity. One expects the existence of multi-activity establishments and multi-establishment companies to be manifested most among the largest companies and establishments. On the other hand, the smaller the company and establishment, the less likely it is for such duplications to exist.[1] This reflects the greater amount of absolute wealth (profit) generated by, and the greater access to credit of, the larger operators and consequently the larger and faster accumulation of reinvestment capital for more expansion and consolidation.[2] It is with these considerations that the conglomeration was chosen as the unit of analysis in the last chapter.

However, when it is desirable to arrive at a picture of the general distribution of wealth covering the whole range of firms, it is almost impossible to repeat the detailed documentation undertaken in the last chapter. Instead, one has to resort to the census and survey data provided by the Department of Statistics which use the establishment as the unit of observation for the manufacturing and distributive trades, and analogously, the mine in the case of the mining industry. The use of profit distribution by size of establishment extracted from these surveys is bound to contain substantial distortion compared with profit distribution by conglomeration. *A priori*, one expects very little distortion for the smaller establishments, since at this level of operation an establishment and a firm are synonymous.[3] However, at the other end, as has been argued, it is more probable that the larger establishments are part of a conglomerate rather than independent entities. Therefore, treating establishments as independent entities necessarily leads to underestimation of the disparity in wealth between the rich and not-so-rich.

In this chapter, interest is centred on the urban and rural self-employed who participate in commercial, industrial, and service activities. The prime targets are the holders of stocks and shares as well as the directors of private and limited companies which span a whole range of activities from banking, insurance, and other financial services, manufacturing, wholesaling and retailing to estate planting, mining as well as others. While this would have covered $1,560 million in value added for the year 1970 out of a GNP of $9,758 million, or 15.99 per cent,[4] it would still have left large numbers of wealth-generating persons/organizations unaccounted for. The investigation would not be complete without a foray into the activities of the sole proprietors, partnerships, and public corporations.

The number of sole proprietors and partnerships is certainly large, yet no precise figure is available. A very crude estimate seems to be about 300,000 operators.[5] In so far as they include large numbers of retailers, caterers, and middlemen, spanning activities from buying agricultural produce (padi, rubber, coconut) from the smallholders and providing credit for their purchase of production inputs (fertilizers, insecticides) and everyday needs (sundry and food items), to the provision of consumer items to all urban and rural residents, they are the most numerous and visible economic agents. They have also borne the brunt of the charges of middlemen-monopoly-monopsony exploitation of the smallholders in general, and of the Malay peasantry in particular. As such, they have been accused of being the root cause of Malay rural poverty, and this image has had obvious implications on racial tensions in the country.

B. Definition of Measures of Income from Wealth

There are several possible candidates for the measure of income from wealth: shareholders' share, gross operating surplus, and net operating surplus. Ideally, data on shares for shareholders would provide the most revealing information because they reflect real wealth. Unfortunately, no data are available for such estimations. Figures on profit before tax are not acceptable for two reasons. Firstly, they cannot be reliably estimated because of the nature of the data provided by the Department of Statistics.[6] Secondly and more importantly, it has been argued in Chapter 1 that dividend income is definitely not an adequate reflection of the income flow and the subsequent wealth accumulation of the businessmen. This is because business executives derive other benefits, both material and intangible, from a big profitable organization.[7] In the same spirit, one can argue that there are other components in the cost column under the standard accounting practices which really benefit the major shareholders and should be re-classified to reflect entrepreneurial wealth. Therefore, it is necessary to seek alternative measures of wealth itself and the income arising from it.

Gross operating surplus (GOS) and net operating surplus (NOS) stand out as two possible alternative measures.[8] GOS, defined as the value added net of wage payments (but including interest payments, depreciation, duties, profit taxes, advertisements, and administrative expenditure), covers mainly the return to capital employed (i.e., the sum of paid-up and loan capital), taxation accruing to the Government and, probably to a smaller extent, administrative expenses.[9] The NOS differs from the GOS by the deduction of 'other business expenses' and depreciation. Moreover, if interest payment and indirect duties are included in the category of 'other business expenses' and deducted from GOS accordingly, NOS closely approximates profit before tax used in accounting practice.[10]

6.2 BIG FIRMS, SMALL FIRMS

In this section, firms of various sizes in selected industries are contrasted in terms of their relative performance. The main purpose is to highlight the relationship between the size differential and profitability. Using four main characteristics (legal organization category, nationality of majority control, size of sales, and size of employment), Tables 6.1 and 6.2 summarize the performances of the manufacturing and mining sectors respectively for 1968, Table 6.3 supplies the data for the construction sector in 1970 while Table 6.4 provides the corresponding data for the distributive trades for 1966, but for only two of the characteristics.

For the manufacturing sector (Table 6.1), the public limited companies owned the largest establishments with average sales of $9.223 million, average employment of 186, and an average GOS of $2.394 million per establishment in 1968. These three figures were respectively 4.4, 2.4, and 6.2 times larger than the corresponding figures for the next largest legal organization group, the private limited companies. The latter group's figures were in turn approximately 9, 5, and 10 times larger than those of the partnerships respectively. Numerically, the individual proprietors were the largest group with 5,785 establishments or 64.19 per cent of the total.[11] However, their average figures of $45,593 in sales, four full-time employees and $7,808 in GOS were completely dwarfed in comparison to those of the limited companies.

The same picture held for the mining and construction industries, though the contrasts were not as striking and the numerical distribution of establishments among the different legal organization categories was more even (Tables 6.2 and 6.3). In particular, among the local mining establishments, the variation in sales, employment, and GOS was very small (at most twice between the highest and the lowest). The average GOS for the individual proprietors of the mining and construction industries, at $58,389 and $49,326 respectively, were fairly substantial when compared with those of the individual proprietors in manufacturing.

In the case of the distributive trades, it was again the individual proprietors who were the smallest. Their total of 70,469 establishments was the most numerous (88.87 per cent of all distributive establishments), but their average turnover was the smallest at $37,702. This was also the smallest turnover throughout the four sectors under comparison (Table 6.4).

In fact, it is best to look at the distributive trades as three separate sectors with different characteristics: the caterers, the retailers, and the wholesalers,

TABLE 6.1

PERFORMANCE OF WEST MALAYSIAN MANUFACTURING INDUSTRIES BY VARIOUS CLASSIFICATION, 1968 ($ THOUSAND)

Number of Establishments		Average Sales	Av. Gross Operating Surplus	Av. Net Operating Surplus	Net/Gross Operating Surplus (%)	Av. Shareholder's Share before Tax
by Sales Size						
2,176	< $5.00	$ 2.4	$ 1.1	$ 0.8	78.50	$ 1.1
1,184	5.00— 9.99	7.2	2.7	2.2	81.18	2.6
1,162	10.00— 19.99	14.3	4.3	3.5	80.33	4.3
1,140	20.00— 49.99	32.4	7.4	5.4	72.90	7.2
917	50.00— 99.99	71.0	13.3	9.4	70.47	13.0
737	100.00— 199.99	142.9	27.5	19.7	71.67	27.0
685	200.00— 499.99	323.2	60.6	43.1	71.06	59.0
300	500.00— 999.99	713.8	121.6	86.5	71.14	117.1
351	1,000.00—4,999.99	2,131.7	351.5	233.4	66.40	336.0
101	5,000+	16,324.6	3,486.9	2,527.8	72.49	3,238.0
by Employee Size						
3,347	none	12.4	3.2	2.8	87.77	3.1
2,738	1— 4	39.0	7.3	5.7	78.50	7.1
957	5— 9	112.8	18.2	13.4	73.84	17.8
738	10— 19	263.9	35.9	26.2	73.02	34.9
394	20— 29	430.1	60.3	42.0	69.53	58.7
334	30— 49	766.4	131.4	87.1	66.27	125.9
275	50— 99	1,419.1	280.1	202.2	72.20	262.8
133	100—199	5,460.3	1,053.6	803.6	76.28	995.4
77	200—499	7,590.9	1,776.4	1,223.3	68.86	1,691.9
20	500+	25,048.8	5,543.7	3,621.3	65.32	4,996.3

(Continued)

TABLE 6.1 (Continued)

Number of Establishments		*Average Sales*	*Av. Gross Operating Surplus*	*Av. Net Operating Surplus*	*Net/Gross Operating Surplus (%)*	*Av. Shareholder's Share before Tax*
by Legal Organization						
5,785	Individual proprietorship	$ 45.6	$ 7.8	$ 6.1	78.50	$ 7.7
1,948	Partnership	230.1	36.9	29.6	80.26	36.4
791	Private limited company	2,078.8	381.6	267.1	70.00	356.2
77	Public Limited company	9,222.6	2,394.3	1,633.9	68.24	2,233.8
399	Co-operative	10.2	4.1	2.3	55.59	4.0
13	Others	767.5	155.0	51.0	32.92	155.0
9,013	Total	341.6	67.3	48.0	71.15	—
Controlled by						
8,468	Malaysian	192.4	34.2	—	—	—
260	Singaporean	1,683.8	312.7	—	—	—
94	British	6,219.6	1,527.2	—	—	—
16	American	9,171.9	2,482.8	—	—	—
3	Japanese	4,118.3	1,606.7	—	—	—
3	Dutch	2,208.7	315.3	—	—	—
61	Indian	50.3	12.2	—	—	—
108	Others	2,390.5	424.0	—	—	—

Source. Census of Manufacturing Industries 1968.

Note. The percentage of Net/Gross Operating Surplus may differ from Av. Net Operating Surplus ÷ Av. Gross Operating Surplus because of rounding of both the average net and gross operating surpluses.

TABLE 6.2

AVERAGE GROSS OPERATING SURPLUS FOR THE MINING INDUSTRIES, 1968 ($ THOUSAND)

Number of Mines		*Total Value of Output*	*Average Value of Output*	*Gross Operating Surplus*	*Average Gross Operating Surplus*
by Sales Size					
216	< $50.00	$ 5,027	$ 23.3	$ −288	$ −1.3
193	50.00— 99.99	14,193	73.5	3,102	16.1
343	100.00— 199.99	50,385	146.9	16,442	48.0
550	200.00— 499.99	171,602	312.0	76,668	139.4
95	500.00— 999.99	62,559	658.5	32,154	338.5
45	1,000.00—1,999.99	64,458	1,432.4	35,832	796.3
53	2,000.00—4,999.99	161,406	3,045.4	112,190	2,116.8
10	5,000.00+	144,566	1,456.6	107,453	10,745.3
by Legal Organization					
247	Individual	41,238	167.0	14,422	58.4
682	Partnership	137,359	201.4	45,227	66.3
422	Limited Company	156,188	370.1	67,726	160.5
Controlled by					
1,351	Malaysian	334,785	247.8	127,375	94.3
154	Foreigner	339,411	2,204.0	211,553	1,373.7
1,505	Total	674,196	448.0	338,928	225.2

Source. *Census of Mining Industries 1968*.

Notes. (1) Number of mines is greater than number of firms because many firms have more than one mine.

(2) Foreigners control 4.568 million of 5.124 million tons of iron ore (89.16 per cent) and 40,403 of 95,637 tons of tin (42.25 per cent).

TABLE 6.3
AVERAGE GROSS OPERATING SURPLUS OF THE CONSTRUCTION INDUSTRIES, 1970 ($ THOUSAND)

Number of Contractors		Average Value of Output per Contractor	Value Added	Salaries and Wages	Gross Operating Surplus	Net Operating Surplus	Average Gross Operating Surplus	Average Net Operating Surplus	Average after Tax Profit
by Sales Size									
656	$100.00— 499.99	$ 236	$ 60,536	$ 36,669	$23,837	$16,707	$ 36.3	$ 25.5	$ 15.3
125	500.00— 999.99	680	32,238	18.855	16,383	12,662	131.1	101.3	60.8
70	1,000.00—1,999.99	1,406	39,494	22,029	17,465	13,744	249.5	196.3	117.8
37	2,000.00—4,999.99	2,955	44,253	24,956	19,297	14,796	521.5	399.9	239.9
7	5,000.00+	6,695	17,037	7,759	9,278	8,326	1,325.4	1,189.4	713.7
by Employee Size									
39	1— 9	209	2,413	874	1,539	n.a.	39.5	n.a.	n.a.
178	10— 19	198	12,425	5,807	6,618	n.a.	37.2	n.a.	n.a.
162	20— 29	256	14,472	8,368	6,104	n.a.	37.7	n.a.	n.a.
126	30— 39	310	15,370	8,188	7,182	n.a.	57.0	n.a.	n.a.
87	40— 49	359	11,944	6,890	5,054	n.a.	58.1	n.a.	n.a.
182	50— 99	608	40,775	24,022	16,753	n.a.	92.0	n.a.	n.a.
53	100—149	1,122	23,022	14,427	8,595	n.a.	162.2	n.a.	n.a.
41	150—249	1,768	29,758	16,712	13,046	n.a.	318.2	n.a.	n.a.
27	250—999	3,583	43,379	25,010	18,369	n.a.	680.3	n.a.	n.a.

(Continued)

TABLE 6.3 (Continued)

Number of Contractors		Average Value of Output per Contractor	Value Added	Salaries and Wages	Gross Operating Surplus	Net Operating Surplus	Average Gross Operating Surplus	Average Net Operating Surplus	Average after Tax Profit
by Legal Organization									
503	Individual proprietor	$ 335	$ 66,951	$ 42,140	$24,811	$18,385	$ 49.3	$ 36.6	$ 21.9
241	Partnership	507	46,633	26,121	20,512	16,282	85.1	67.6	40.5
139	Private limited company	1,160	68,437	37,135	31,302	23,493	225.2	169.0	101.4
12	Public limited company	2,716	11,537	4,902	6,635	5,075	552.9	422.9	253.8
Controlled by									
841	Malaysian	520	173,099	100,491	72,608	n.a.	86.3	n.a.	n.a.
30	Singaporean	794	12,073	5,003	7,070	n.a.	235.7	n.a.	n.a.
13	British	1,979	5,458	3,149	2,309	n.a.	177.6	n.a.	n.a.
11	Others	696	2,928	1,655	1,273	n.a.	115.7	n.a.	n.a.
895	Total	552	193,558	110,298	83,260	63,253	93.0	70.7	42.4

Source. Survey of Construction Industries 1970, Tables 1.4—1.7, pp. 34—7.

TABLE 6.4

AVERAGE TURNOVER IN THE DISTRIBUTIVE TRADES, 1966 ($ THOUSAND)

	Individual Proprietor		*Partnership*		*Others (1)*		*Total*		*Those with Accounts*		
	Number of Establish-ments	*Average Turn-over*	*Number of Establish-ments*	*Average Turn-over*	*Number of Establish-ments*	*Average Turn-over*	*Number of Establish-ments*	*Average Turn-over*	*Number of Establish-ments*	*Average Turn-over*	*Net Turn-over (2)*
Catering											
Coffee shops, drink stalls	10,600	$12	656	$ 36	11	$ 26	11,267	$13	2,556	$ 30	$ 7
Bars	90	60	42	92	10	270	142	84	114	96	31
Food stalls, restaurants	4,883	15	460	85	28	412	5,371	23	1,121	75	19
Total Catering	15,573	13	1,158	58	49	296	16,780	17	3,791	45	11
Retailing											
Butchers' meat and poultry	2,558	32	122	125	6	573	2,686	37	387	99	10
Fish	3,557	15	128	105	*	*	3,685	17	191	116	11
Fruit and vegetables	5,019	11	155	63	*	*	5,134	12	286	63	8
Provisions (including rice)	22,405	32	1,459	142	152	310	24,016	40	8,240	96	7
Clothing and textiles	2,388	42	434	184	21	465	2,843	66	1,432	121	9
Total Retailing	50,549	28	3,895	136	629	273	55,073	38	18,668	90	9

(Continued)

TABLE 6.4 (Continued)

	Individual Proprietor		*Partnership*		*Others (1)*		*Total*		*Those with Accounts*		
	Number of Establishments	*Average Turnover*	*Number of Establishments*	*Average Turnover*	*Number of Establishments*	*Average Turnover*	*Number of Establishments*	*Average Turnover*	*Number of Establishments*	*Average Turnover*	*Net Turnover (2)*
Wholesaling											
Household and Personal Goods											
Fish	187	$ 191	95	$ 458	*	*	282	$ 281	192	$ 377	$156
Fruits	305	104	80	293	—	—	385	143	207	237	30
Rice, other grain, flour	222	756	250	1,299	44	4,929	516	1,375	509	1,393	87
Other food	246	361	199	902	69	1,664	514	745	440	864	58
Clothing and textiles	119	350	153	657	26	1,505	298	608	295	614	62
Business, Industrial, Agricultural Goods											
Vehicle parts accessories	204	152	155	288	59	808	418	295	371	326	18
Other building material	418	211	161	501	85	1,611	664	461	555	547	51
Rubber	1,278	206	339	769	51	5,898	1,668	494	1,284	625	37
Bags, bottles, scrap	159	266	91	207	5	600	266	158	187	220	17
Large general wholesalers	9	1,247	17	2,449	136	5,018	162	4,539	162	4,540	622
Total Wholesaling (3)	4,347	234	2,231	668	865	2,295	7,443	604	6,180	719	62

Source. *Census of Distributive Trades 1966*, Tables 5, 11, 17.1, 25, 31.1, and 39.

Notes. *'Other' combined with 'Partnership' to preserve confidentiality. For this reason the sum of figures in these figures differs slightly from the actual totals shown.

(1) They consist principally of private limited companies.

(2) Net Turnover = Value of Turnover – Value of Purchases – Stock Adjustments, i.e., it has not been netted of wages and salaries, rent, interest payments, and taxes.

(3) The number of establishments reported under 'Total Wholesaling' and 'Total Retailing' is larger than the summation of the individual lines because many other wholesaling and retailing trades have not been listed here.

with the caterers under individual proprietorship getting a mere $13,181 in turnover. Unfortunately, it is not possible to compile data on GOS, let alone NOS, profit, and shareholders' share. The only figure available is the net turnover which would be equivalent to the GOS with salaries and wages and such figures are available only for the establishments which kept accounts and these tend to be larger ones. As such, net turnover is really not comparable with GOS. Therefore, in view of the greater care needed to deal with the distributive trades, we shall discuss them in a later section.

While the public limited companies' establishments are, on the average, the largest in West Malaysia, not all of them are necessarily large; neither is it true that there are no other large companies. There were 101 manufacturing establishments with sales in excess of $5 million in 1968.[12] Among these were twenty-two public limited manufacturing establishments with an average of $28.829 million, seventy-four private ones with $14.047 million and five partnerships with $9.812 million.[13] Among the 1,505 mining establishments, there were only ten with output value in excess of $5 million. With an average sales value of $14.457 million, they achieved the very high GOS of $10.745 million.[14] As for the construction industry, only seven concerns had an average output value of more than $5 million; their average GOS of $1.325 million was also modest in comparison with the large manufacturing and mining concerns.[15]

Now we shall attempt to identify the 101 largest establishments within the manufacturing sector. In Table 6.5, the eighteen manufacturing industries with the highest average sales and GOS exceeding $200,000 each have been listed.[16] These eighteen industries had a total GOS of $292.140 million. That is to say, eighteen of the 112 (16.07 per cent) industrial classification, with 363 of the 9,013 (4.03 per cent) establishments produced 48.14 per cent of the total GOS of all manufacturing industries. Among these, thirty-one establishments in six industries had average sales exceeding $5 million and they accounted for $116.756 million (19.24 per cent) of total GOS.[17]

The extent of concentration of GOS (hence profit and wealth) in a very few industries is truly striking.

Furthermore, within each of these industries, a few establishments dominated. Table 6.6 lists the probable identity of all the 101 establishments which had average sales of more than $5 million in 1968. Once the sales value and GOS of these large establishments had been subtracted from the corresponding figures for the various industries in Table 6.5, the remaining larger numbered establishments had much smaller sales value and average GOS (less than one-third of the average of the 101 largest establishments). These 101 establishments provided $163.246 million (55.88 per cent of total GOS of these eighteen industries or 26.90 per cent of total manufacturing GOS in 1968).[18] The listing of companies with large establishments allows one to compare some of them with those in Table 6.7, which is a listing of the eighty largest publicly listed companies in Malaysia in 1974. The bulk of the 101 large manufacturing establishments in 1968 formed the parent and/or subsidiary companies of the larger of these eighty publicly listed companies in 1974.[19]

It is necessary at this point to ask if the picture described for 1968 still holds good for 1974 so that one can compare the two and perhaps extra-

TABLE 6.5

THE EIGHTEEN LARGE-SCALE MANUFACTURING INDUSTRIES IN WEST MALAYSIA IN 1968

Industry	Number of Establishments	(Value in $'000) Average Sales	Gross Operating Surplus	Average Gross Operating Surplus	Average Net Operating Surplus	Net to Gross Ratio (%)
Products of petroleum and coal	6	29,210	36,174	6,029	5,022	83.29
Other dairy products	4	21,723	21,095	5,274	4,433	84.05
Breweries	2	15,681	15,962	7,981	6,324	79.24
Hydraulic cement	4	15,182	31,162	7,791	6,324	81.18
Pineapple canning	4	12,436	6,881	1,720	508	29.50
Assembly of lorries and automobiles	11	6,053	8,482	771	374	48.48
Other food manufacturing	25	4,257	23,185	927	699	75.35
Chemical fertilizers	13	3,132	8,102	623	274	43.90
Compressed and liquefied gas	4	2,754	5,508	1,377	634	46.02
Other basic metals	9	2,588	5,789	643	261	40.58
Rubber footwear, tyres and tubes	45	—	30,006	667	475	71.24
Other iron and steel basic shapes	14	2,100	6,546	468	335	71.68
Tobacco	114	1,918	47,072	413	268	64.91
Plywood and particle board	17	1,916	12,218	719	578	80.49
Paints, varnishes and lacquers	13	1,843	7,877	606	455	75.13
Soap, washing and cleaning compounds	37	1,180	15,264	413	143	34.76
Other chemical industries	5	957	2,081	416	351	84.33
Perfume, cosmetic, and toilet preparations	36	543	8,736	243	158	65.06
Total	363	—	292,140	805	—	—
% of All Manufacturing	4.03	—	48.14	—	—	—

Source. Census of Manufacturing Industries 1968.

TABLE 6.6
THE 101 LARGEST ESTABLISHMENTS IN WEST MALAYSIAN MANUFACTURING INDUSTRIES, 1968 ($ MILLION)

Number of Estab-lishments in Industry	*Name of Industry*	*Probable Identity of Establishments**	*Characteristics of Identified Establishments*			
			Number of Estab-lishments	*Average Number of Workers*	*Average Sales*	*Average Gross Operating Surplus*
2	Tobacco	Malayan Tobacco Co. Bhd.	1	500+	$158.6	$35.5
		Rothmans of Pall Mall (M) Bhd.	1	355	39.0	8.4
2	Other grains	Malayan Flour Mills Bhd.	1	359	53.4	5.5
		United Malayan Flour Mills Bhd.	1	126	19.2	5.5
1	Soft drinks	Fraser & Neave Ltd.	1	88	5.6	3.0
2	Petroleum refining	Esso Malaysia Bhd., Shell Refining Co. (F. of M.) Bhd.	2	201	77.0	13.7
26	Rubber remilling	Lee Rubber group	16	—	—	—
4	Rubber smokehouses	Lee Rubber group	4	131	6.2	0.6
5	Coconut oil mill	Lee Oilmills Sdn. Bhd., Federal Oilmills Sdn. Bhd., Lam Soon Oil and Soap Mfg. Co. Sdn. Bhd., Perak Oil Mill Sdn. Bhd., Lever Brothers (Malaysia) Sdn. Bhd.	5	58	9.3	1.0
2	Electrical appliances	—	2	206	8.8	2.2
4	Textiles	Textile Corp. of Malaya Bhd., South Pacific Textile Industries Bhd., Malaysia Textile Industries Bhd., India–Malaysia Textiles Bhd., Min Ngai Knitting Factory (Malaya) Bhd.	4	612	13.9	2.2

TABLE 6.6 (Continued)

Number of Estab- lishments in Industry	Name of Industry	Probable Identity of Establishments*	*Characteristics of Identified Establishments*			
			Number of Estab- lishments	*Average Number of Workers*	*Average Sales*	*Average Gross Operating Surplus*
1	Clothing	—	1	889	$6.5	$0.7
3	Printing and publicity	The New Straits Times Press (M) Bhd.	1	592	15.6	6.4
		Nanyang Press (M) Sdn. Bhd., Sin Chew Jit Poh Malaysia Sdn. Bhd.	2	360	6.5	2.1
5	Rubber footwear and tyres	Dunlop Malaysia Industries Bhd., Bata (Malaysia) Bhd., Fung Keong Rubber Manufactory (M) Sdn. Bhd., Shum Yip Leong Rubber Works Sdn. Bhd.	5	732	13.0	4.6
3	Soap, washing, and cleaning compounds	Lam Soon Oil and Soap Mfg. Co. Sdn. Bhd., Colgate-Palmolive (M)	1	592	24.7	10.2
		Sdn. Bhd., Lever Brothers (Malaysia) Sdn. Bhd.	2	123	7.8	2.2
1	Perfume, cosmetics, and toiletries	Manufacturing Services Sdn. Bhd. (?)	1	75	8.4	4.6
1	Structural cement	Hume Industries (M) Bhd.	1	325	10.3	3.0
4	Hydraulic cement	Tasek Cement Bhd., Malayan Cement Co. Bhd., Pan Malaysia Cement Works Bhd.	4	478	15.2	7.8
1	Tin can	Metal Box Malaysia Bhd.	1	328	9.7	2.3
2	Breweries	Malayan Breweries (M) Sdn. Bhd., Guinness Malaysia Bhd.	2	203	15.7	8.0

(Continued)

TABLE 6.6 (Continued)

Number of Establishments in Industry	Name of Industry	Probable Identity of Establishments*	Characteristics of Identified Establishments			
			Number of Establishments	Average Number of Workers	Average Sales	Average Gross Operating Surplus
4	Pineapple	Lee Pineapple, Malayan Pineapple Co. Ltd., The Amoy Canning Corp. (M) Bhd., United Malayan Pineapple Sdn. Bhd.	4	706	$12.4	$1.7
1	Dry cell	Union Carbide Asia Ltd.	1	n.a.	—	—
(2)**	Compound and liquefied gas	Malayan Oxygen Bhd., Far East Oxygen Bhd.	2	n.a.	—	—
6	Animal feed	Sin Heng Chan (Malaya) Bhd.	1	132	12.3	1.2
		Zuellig Feedmills (Malaya) Sdn. Bhd.	1	74	6.8	0.7
1	Biscuit	Khong Guan Biscuit Factory Sdn. Bhd.	1	378	5.4	0.7
(5)**	Other food	Malayan Sugar Manufacturing Co. Bhd., Yeo Hiap Seng (Malaysia) Bhd., The Amoy Canning Corp. (M) Bhd., Central Sugars Bhd., Ajinomoto (Malaysia) Bhd.	5	n.a.	—	—
4	Other dairy products	Food Specialities Malaya Sdn. Bhd., Cold Storage (Malaysia) Sdn. Bhd., Beatrice Foods Sdn. Bhd., Nestlé Products (M) Ltd.	4	136	21.7	5.3

(Continued)

TABLE 6.6 (Continued)

Number of Estab-lishments in Industry	Name of Industry	Probable Identity of Establishments*	Characteristics of Identified Establishments			
			Number of Estab-lishments	Average Number of Workers	Average Sales	Average Gross Operating Surplus
(5)**	Other iron and steel basic shapes	Malayawata Steel Bhd., United Malaysian Steel Mills Bhd., Federal Iron Works Sdn. Bhd., Southern Iron and Steel Works Sdn. Bhd., Soon Seng Wire Products Sdn. Bhd.	5	n.a.	—	—
(5)**	Assembly of lorries and cars	Cycle & Carriage Industries (Malaysia) Sdn. Bhd., Associated Motor Industries (M) Sdn. Bhd., Asia Automobile Industries Sdn. Bhd., Assembly Service Sdn. Bhd., General Motors (M) Sdn. Bhd.	5	n.a.	—	—
(1)**	Fertilizer	Chemical Co. of Malaysia Bhd.	1	n.a.	—	—

Source. Various Tables, *Census of Manufacturing Industries 1968*.

Notes. * The data in the Census are presented in aggregated form. Therefore, the identification of firms is done by checking the company reports whenever they are easily available. For those whose company reports are not available to gather sales figures, educated guesses have to be made of the identities based on a general familiarity.

** The numbers in parentheses signify that they have not been identified with certainty.

TABLE 6.7
FINANCIAL DATA AND ORIGINS OF CONTROL OF THE LEADING PUBLICLY LISTED LIMITED COMPANIES IN WEST MALAYSIA[1] ($ MILLION)

	Country of Control	Country of Registration	Name of Company[5]	Market Value[2]	Consolidated Total Assets		Gross Profit before Tax		Paid-up Capital	
					Rank[3]	Value	Rank[4]	Value	Rank[4]	Value
1	S	S	Oversea-Chinese Banking Corporation Ltd.	$422.9	1	$2,365.8	7	$ 24.3	3	$113.7
2	M	U.K.	Sime Darby Bhd.	232.4	—	1,386.6	1	134.9	5	94.0
3	U.K.	U.K.	Highlands & Lowlands Bhd.	209.2	—	364.2	11	21.6	6	89.6
4	M	U.K.	Consolidated Plantations Bhd.	199.8	—	352.2	2	69.0	8	63.7
5	U.K.	S	Inchcape Bhd.	175.5	5	486.3	3	59.6	2	118.6
6	S	S	United Overseas Bank Ltd.	159.9	2	2,135.1	21	15.1	7	86.9
7	U.K.	U.K.	Cold Storage Holdings Ltd.	154.3	—	120.0	14	19.9	9	56.5
8	M	M	Malayan Banking Bhd.	145.8	3	1,761.3	23	14.6	14	45.0
9	U.K.	M	Malayan Tobacco Co. Bhd.	141.8	25	113.2	9	22.8	14	45.0
10	S	S	The Straits Trading Co. Ltd.	140.4	13	162.6	11	21.6	14	45.0
11	M	M	K.L.–Kepong Bhd.	122.4	10	184.9	19	15.6	1	147.5
12	S	S	Fraser & Neave Ltd.	122.4	20	135.3	21	15.1	14	45.0
13	S	S	Haw Par Bros. International Ltd.	110.0	6	484.0	13	20.8	4	106.8
14	U.K.–M	M	Berjuntai Tin Dredging Bhd.	97.7	58	71.1	5	28.4	39	25.4
15	U.K.	M	Dunlop Malaysian Industries Bhd.	82.5	45	80.7	17	17.5	28	30.0
16	F	M	North Borneo Timbers Bhd.	80.4	41	82.5	9	22.8	27	32.2
17	D	M	United Plantations Bhd.	80.0	63	66.3	46	7.7	25	32.5
18	M	M	Genting Highlands Bhd.	69.8	73	49.4	29	11.8	18	40.1

(Continued)

TABLE 6.7 (Continued)

	Country of Control	Country of Registration	*Name of Company*[5]	*Market Value*[2]	*Consolidated Total Assets*		*Gross Profit before Tax*		*Paid-up Capital*	
					Rank[3]	*Value*	*Rank*[4]	*Value*	*Rank*[4]	*Value*
19	M	M	Kempas (M) Bhd.	$66.9	30	$107.1	32	$10.9	18	$40.1
20	S	S	Wearne Brothers Ltd.	66.7	18	140.3	16	17.9	13	45.1
21	M	M	Kepong Plantations Bhd.	66.3	51	75.0	48	7.3	79	8.5
22	M	M	Batu Kawan Bhd.	62.9	65	63.6	55	6.4	52	16.6
23	H.K.	S	Straits Steamship Co. Ltd.	62.7	9	199.9	57	6.0	53	16.1
24	M	M	Malayawata Steel Bhd.	62.6	33	102.6	19	15.6	21	38.9
25	U.K.	M	Datuk Keramat Holdings Bhd.	61.2	38	84.4	44	8.3	45	20.0
26	U.K.	M	Syarikat Harper Gilfillan Bhd.	61.0	12	150.0	40	9.2	67	13.4
27	M	M	Tractors Malaysia Bhd.	60.0	12	167.7	4	36.8	12	48.0
28	S	S	Great Eastern Life Assurance Co. Ltd.	58.9	7	294.0	50	7.0	75	9.2
29	U.K.	M	Guinness Malaysia Bhd.	58.8	78	44.6	31	11.2	42	24.0
30	U.K.	M	Dunlop Estates Bhd.	54.4	27	111.8	37	10.1	20	40.0
31	U.K.	S	Guthrie Bhd.	52.5	32	103.5	37	10.1	26	32.4
32	M	M	Island & Peninsular Development Bhd.	52.4	42	81.8	33	10.6	32	29.9
33	S	S	Cycle & Carriage Ltd.	50.1	15	152.0	6	28.0	28	30.0
34	U.K.–M	U.K.	Malayan Tin Dredging (M) Bhd.	47.1	—	103.8	35	10.2	64	13.2
35	U.K.	M	Guthrie Ropel Bhd.	47.0	55	72.1	54	6.7	10	56.0
36	U.K.	M	Shell Refining Co. (F of M) Bhd.	46.5	48	78.3	28	12.0	28	30.0
37	M	M	Selangor Properties Bhd.	46.2	72	50.4	60	4.5	34	28.9
38	S	M	Tasek Cement Bhd.	44.5	57	71.6	66	3.8	36	26.3
39	U.S.A	M	Esso Malaysia Bhd.	43.7	17	145.0	15	18.1	11	54.0
40	U.K.	M	Malayan Cement Bhd.	43.5	96	31.0	30	11.3	35	27.2

(Continued)

TABLE 6.7 (Continued)

	Country of Control	Country of Registration	Name of Company[5]	Market Value[2]	Consolidated Total Assets		Gross Profit before Tax		Paid-up Capital	
					Rank[3]	Value	Rank[4]	Value	Rank[4]	Value
41	U.K.	U.K.	Kulim (M) Bhd.	$43.4	—	$ 74.4	49	$ 7.2	33	$29.8
42	U.K.	M	Boustead Holding Bhd.	41.1	29	110.5	45	8.1	58	15.1
43	U.K.	H.K.	Jardine Matheson (S.E.A.) Ltd.	39.8	—	139.3	50	7.0	68	12.2
44	M	M	The New Straits Times Press (M) Bhd.	38.8	100	29.3	39	10.0	65	13.8
45	M	M	Empat Nombor Ekor Bhd.	37.2	69	53.9	42	8.5	44	20.9
46	M	M	Glenealy Plantations (M) Bhd.	36.8	136	18.6	75	1.3	54	16.0
47	F	S	United Engineers Ltd.	36.3	37	87.2	42	8.5	37	25.7
48	M	M	Malaysia Building Society Bhd.	35.5	11	183.1	41	8.9	38	25.5
49	U.K.–M	M	Aokam Tin Bhd.	35.0	98	30.1	26	13.7	60	14.0
50	F	M	Hume Industries (M) Bhd.	32.1	76	45.8	47	7.5	40	25.3
51	M	M	Faber Merlin Malaysia Bhd.	30.6	35	92.0	78	1.1	22	37.3
52	M	M	Pan Malaysia Cement Works Bhd.	29.6	79	43.4	24	14.3	43	21.9
53	U.K.	M	Selangor Coconuts Bhd.	28.1	64	63.7	61	4.4	24	33.0
54	S	S	Hong Leong Finance Ltd.	26.3	22	120.0	71	3.2	57	15.4
55	M	M	Benta Plantations Bhd.	25.2	99	30.1	65	3.8	60	14.0
56	U.K.–M	U.K.	Ayer Hitam Tin Dredging Malaysia Bhd.	24.4	—	36.6	37	13.2	76	9.1

(Continued)

TABLE 6.7 (Continued)

	Country of Control	Country of Registration	Name of Company[5]	Market Value[2]	Consolidated Total Assets		Gross Profit before Tax		Paid-up Capital	
					Rank[3]	Value	Rank[4]	Value	Rank[4]	Value
57	M	M	Selangor Dredging Bhd.	$23.3	103	$ 27.9	70	$ 3.5	68	$12.2
58	U.K.	S	Metal Box Co. of Malaysia Ltd.	23.1	53	74.2	50	7.0	66	13.5
59	U.K.–M	M	Austral Amalgamated Tin Bhd.	23.0	105	27.3	56	6.3	72	10.0
60	S	M	Petaling Tin Bhd.	20.6	120	22.4	79	–0.2	80	7.1
61	U.K.	M	United Asbestos Cement Bhd.	19.7	116	24.9	53	6.8	60	14.0
62	M	M	United Motor Works (M) Holdings Bhd.	19.2	35	106.3	33	10.6	49	18.4
63	M	M	Tan Chong Motor Holdings Bhd.	19.1	44	81.6	35	10.2	50	18.0
64	M	M	Public Bank Bhd.	19.0	8	202.1	76	1.2	52	16.0
65	M	M	Central Securities (Holding) Bhd.	19.0	68	56.8	62	4.3	47	19.8
66	M	M	United Malacca Rubber Estates Bhd.	17.6	122	21.8	63	3.9	71	10.7
67	M	M	Duff Development Bhd.	17.4	110	26.5	76	1.2	60	14.0
68	M	M	Perlis Plantations Bhd.	17.0	138	18.6	80	–0.7	45	20.0
69	M	M	Oriental Holdings Bhd.	16.9	149	16.7	71	3.2	77	9.0
70	U.K.–M	U.K.	Tronoh Mines Malaysia Bhd.	16.5	—	11.1	74	2.4	56	15.5
71	M	M	Malayan Flour Mills Bhd.	16.5	91	34.4	65	3.8	59	15.0
72	M	M	Federal Cables Wires & Metal Mfg. Bhd.	16.4	97	31.0	63	3.9	72	10.0
73	T	S	Jack Chia-MPH Ltd.	16.3	75	46.1	71	3.2	41	25.0
74	U.K.	M	Malayan Containers Bhd.	16.1	80	43.3	58	5.6	70	11.9

(Continued)

TABLE 6.7 (Continued)

	Country of Control	Country of Registration	Name of Company[5]	Market Value[2]	Consolidated Total Assets		Gross Profit before Tax		Paid-up Capital	
					Rank[3]	Value	Rank[4]	Value	Rank[4]	Value
75	C	M	Bata Malaysia Bhd.	$15.3	139	$ 18.4	69	$ 3.6	77	$ 9.0
76	U.K.	M	Chemical Co. of Malaysia Bhd.		54	72.6	8	23.8	28	30.0
77	S	S	Malayan Breweries Ltd.		21	134.7	18	16.8	23	36.0
78	S	S	Sim Lim Investments Ltd.		23	119.8	63	3.9	51	17.9
79	U.K.	M	Rothmans of Pall Mall (M) Bhd.		47	78.4	25	13.8	48	19.1
80	U.K.	M	William Jacks & Co. (Malaysia) Bhd.		49	77.0	59	5.0	72	10.0

Source. Ronnie Duclos, comp. and ed., *Information Malaysia 1975/76*, pp. 270—82, and own assessment.

Notes. M = Malaysia S = Singapore F = Foreign
D = Netherlands T = Thailand C = Canada

(1) The quantitative data refer to the financial year 1973/4; however the country of control has been updated to 1977. Such reclassification is bound to introduce some distortions, but the changes refer mainly to the Sime Darby group of companies and the tin companies that Pernas gained control of in 1977, accounting for $243.9 million and $73.6 million in profit respectively which would have been classified under foreign controlled if the same year of control as the results are referred to.

(2) The ranking by market value follows Duclos, but re-adjusted to eliminate ranking for the companies operating mainly in Singapore.

(3) The ranking by consolidated total assets is the one given by Duclos with no change, i.e., the size of companies not listed in this table has been taken into account.

(4) Rankings by size of profit and size of capital have been done by this author for the eighty companies only.

(5) The names of some companies have since been changed, largely because of restructuring.

polate from 1968 to the present. In the absence of similar data for 1974, one cannot answer this question conclusively. However, based on a general familiarity with industrial development in Malaysia, there appears to be no new factors which could have fundamentally altered the ownership and control structure of industries as observed in 1968.[20] Since then, many new factories have gone into production. The more important of these additions have been heavily concentrated in a few industries, mainly electronics and textiles. Most of the new additions have been large factories which should further increase the extent of concentration.[21]

Two inferences are possible. Firstly, the few largest among these eighty companies hold and control a very substantial part of the wealth generated in the manufacturing sector though their manufacturing establishments constitute less than 4 per cent of all manufacturing establishments. Secondly, these manufacturing establishments and/or firms are invariably part of a conglomeration that encompasses other economic activities. Most of these conglomerates are listed as public companies. The identification of these establishments and companies shows that the linkages drawn in the last chapter make good sense and we are able to identify which are indeed the largest and most profitable conglomerations in this country through tracing such links. Although this exercise is done for the manufacturing sector alone, their overall control of the corporate wealth of this nation is illustrated vividly when taken together with the discussion of the financial, planting, and mining activities in the last chapter.

In fact, concentration goes even further than the above data can show. A few examples of multi-establishment ownership within an industry by a conglomerate will illustrate this.

To start with an extreme example, of the 74 establishments in rubber remilling and smokehouses, 26 are rubber remillers, and 4 are rubber smokehouses with sales of more than $5 million. Among these 30, the Lee Rubber group from Singapore (which also controls the OCBC group) is known to own 16 remilling factories each with sales in excess of $5 million, and 5 smokehouses (probably 3 or 4 of these have sales in excess of $5 million).[22] In addition, the Lee–OCBC conglomerate holds more than 10,000 acres of rubber plantation and Lee Pineapple (which has a factory with over $5 million in sales and a supporting pineapple estate) (Chart 5.5). No other rubber remiller is known to operate more than one factory although some of them do operate other businesses.

Another outstanding example is the interest of the original directors of the UMBC group in a chain of hotels, and lumber and plywood factories (Chart 5.9). In tin mining, the interest of Pernas–Charter Consolidated and in the plantation sector, the holdings of SD, Guthrie, H & C, etc., are further examples.[23]

At the other extreme, it is also important to understand the performance of the small establishments. Table 6.8 identifies a group of fourteen industries which are small-scale operations but important in terms of their numbers. These industries were chosen to represent a spectrum of industrial activities. However, sophisticated statistical techniques were not used in selecting them. Thus, it must be emphasized that the results are not meant to be conclusive

TABLE 6.8

PERFORMANCE OF FOURTEEN SELECTED MANUFACTURING INDUSTRIES, 1968 ($ THOUSAND)

	Number of Establish-ments	*Gross Operating Surplus*	*Net Operating Surplus*	*Net/Gross Operating Surplus (%)*	*Average Net Operating Surplus*
Rubber remilling	82	$ 46,664	$40,659	87.13	$496
Small rice mills	910	3,068	2,117	69.00	2
Bakeries	412	4,555	3,779	82.96	9
Ice factories	51	4,048	2,649	65.44	52
Textile	60	13,081	9,650	73.77	161
Sawmills	384	36,378	27,515	75.64	72
Furniture and fixtures	660	6,017	4,581	76.13	7
Printing and publishing	371	29,418	21,410	72.78	58
Tin smithing	496	1,363	1,199	87.97	2
Industrial machinery	224	7,334	5,497	74.95	25
Electrical appliances	37	8,975	7,109	79.21	192
Motor vehicle bodies	44	726	573	78.93	13
Plastic	76	5,871	3,976	67.72	52
Meehoon	238	1,761	1,486	84.38	6
Total	4,045	169,259			
% of Total Manufacturing Industries	44.88	27.90			

Source. Census of Manufacturing Industries 1968, various Tables.

from a statistical point of view but to enable a good understanding of the structure and performances of:

(1) the large number of small-scale producers,
(2) the several new manufacturing activities which are gaining in importance in the Malaysian economy,
(3) the several important traditional manufacturing activities which have provided some of the initial accumulation for entry into larger and more modern manufacturing activities.[24]

Since the fourteen industries represent such a mixed bag of activities, any comparison among them by industry would be uninteresting and misleading. The one notable feature common to most of them is the smallness of their scale of production: average industrial sales started from $6,000 for the small rice mills, while most have average sales not exceeding $200,000.[25] However, their importance is underlined by the fact that they represented 4,045 (44.88 per cent) of the 9,013 manufacturing establishments in 1968. Since the traditional manufacturing activities were mainly cottage industries, it is not surprising to find that these establishments have very low average industrial NOS. The 910 small rice mills have an average NOS of $2,326; the 496 tin-smithing factories averaged $2,427, the furniture makers $6,941, the meehoon and noodle producers $6,244, the bakers $9,172.

The disposable income of these establishments would be very small if we took into account the fact that interest payments have yet to be deducted. In the case of the small rice millers and tin-smithing operators, the figures are likely to be less than $1,500 which would put them in the same category as the farmers and unskilled workers. In fact, 60 per cent of the small rice millers have a GOS of less than $1,000.[26]

In Table 6.9, the frequencies of these small establishments by their GOS have been tabulated. This is the GOS distribution[27] for the fourteen smaller industries in aggregate, but not that of the manufacturing industries as a whole though the distribution should not be too far off the latter. 1,434 or 35.45 per cent of these 4,045 establishments were very small, with gross operating surplus of less than $3,000. 1,244 or 30.75 per cent were the small ones with GOS of less than $10,000 but more than $3,000. 1,038 or 25.66 per cent can be considered medium-sized with a GOS from $10,000 to $99,999. Notice that the large ones with GOS greater than $100,000 numbered only 302 or 7.47 per cent; these included thirty-five really profitable ones with a GOS of over $1 million.

While one may not be very confident about the representativeness of this distribution, nevertheless, one can be reasonably sure that the contrast drawn here between the two extremes is accurate.[28] This is particularly clear when it is recalled that the eighteen largest industries are dominated by the 101 establishments of the largest firms, and the remaining ones within those industries are truly small.

There is another way to check this distribution. From Table 6.10, 2,933 or 32.54 per cent of the establishments averaged less than $3,000 in GOS; another 2,537 or 28.15 per cent had less than $10,000 but more than $3,000. In short, about 60.69 per cent had less than $10,000 in GOS.[29]

From the preceding discussions, it is clear that there is a dramatic difference

TABLE 6.9
DISTRIBUTION OF ESTABLISHMENTS BY SIZE OF GROSS OPERATING SURPLUS WITHIN THE FOURTEEN SELECTED MANUFACTURING INDUSTRIES IN WEST MALAYSIA, 1968

Average Gross Operating Surplus	*Number of Establishments*	*Percentage of Total*	*Cumulated Percentage*
< $1,000	603	14.91	14.91
1,000— 1,999	579	14.31	29.22
2,000— 2,999	252	6.23	35.45
3,000— 3,999	422	10.43	45.88
4,000— 5,999	451	11.15	57.03
6,000— 7,999	341	8.43	65.46
8,000— 9,999	30	0.74	66.20
10,000— 19,999	437	10.80	77.00
20,000— 29,999	149	3.68	80.68
30,000— 49,999	136	3.36	84.04
50,000— 99,999	316	7.81	91.85
100,000— 199,999	150	3.71	95.56
200,000— 299,999	37	0.91	96.47
300,000— 499,999	59	1.46	97.93
500,000— 999,999	21	0.52	98.45
1,000,000—1,999,999	26	0.64	99.09
2,000,000—2,999,999	6	0.15	99.24
3,000,000+	3	0.07	99.31
Sub-total	4,018	99.31	
Left out for Irregularities	27		
Total	4,045		

Source. Computed and compiled from *Census of Manufacturing Industries 1968.*

in profits between the large and small manufacturing firms. Tables 6.2 to 6.4 show that the same vast differences existed between the large and small establishments in mining, construction, and distributive trades. The individual proprietors were also the smallest operators and the limited companies the largest. However, while the majority of the individual proprietors were the smallest operators, a very few of them and the partnerships had attained a quite high GOS. We should note that the smallest operators in mining and construction tended to have higher GOS than their manufacturing or distributive trade counterparts. Their averages of $58,389 and $49,326 in 1968 respectively put them into the range of performance of the medium-sized manufacturing and distributive establishments.

The most telling indication of the dominance of large companies is shown by the financial surveys of limited companies for 1967 and 1970. In 1967, 6 per cent of all limited companies had sales of more than $5 million and

TABLE 6.10

POSSIBLE AVERAGE INCOME DISTRIBUTION OF THE WEST MALAYSIA MANUFACTURING ESTABLISHMENT, 1968

Number of Establishments	*% of Total*	*Characteristics of Establishments*			*Average Gross Operating Surplus*
		Legal Organization	*No. of Employees*	*Sales Group*	
6		Public	500+		$11,142,833
16		Public	200+		3,625,000
14	1.21	Public	100+	$5,000,000+	3,377,357
14		Private	500+		3,144,071
5		Partner	50—499		1,963,400
54		Private	200+	average sales = $6,693,910	1,315,870
97		Private	100+	4,795,830	860,423
6	1.14	Public	30— 49	1,958,170	739,333
164		Private	50— 99	1,732,960	357,360
16		Public	50— 99	1,529,560	353,813
8		Public	20— 29	1,042,000	217,250
6		Private	none	1,533,670	211,500
82	4.90	Partner	50—499	500,000—5,000,000	179,976
141		Private	30— 49	av. sales = 1,034,870	178,568
25		Individual	100+	500,000+	123,400
89		Private	20— 29	av. sales = 689,460	84,461
99	2.09	Partner	10— 49	500,000—5,000,000	83,414
3		Individual	50— 99	500,000+	76,667
5	1.40	Public	10— 19	av. sales = 239,800	63,400
118		Private	10— 19	av. sales = 451,340	60,212
46	0.51	Individual	10— 49	500,000+	57,326
99	1.10	Partner	0— 9	100,000—499,999	44,889

(Continued)

TABLE 6.10 (Continued)

Number of Establishments	% of Total	Characteristics of Establishments			Average Gross Operating Surplus
		Legal Organization	No. of Employees	Sales Group	
550	6.10	Partner	10— 49	$100,000—499,999	$43,367
70	0.78	Private	5— 9	av. sales = 130,560	36,929
107	1.19	Individual	1— 9	100,000—499,999	36,075
394	4.37	Individual	10— 49	100,000—499,999	32,848
38	0.42	Private	1— 4 }	50,000—99,999	29,778
339	3.76	Partner	0— 9 }	50,000—99,999	16,006
4	—	Public	5— 9	av. sales = 115,250	16,000
516	5.73	Individual	1— 9	50,000— 99,999	12,626
333	3.69	Partner			8,973
999	11.08	Individual	1— 9	20,000— 49,999	7,351
154	1.71	Partner			4,987
933	10.35	Individual	0— 9	10,000— 19,999	4,164
118	1.31	Partner }	0— 9	5,000— 9,999	3,127
947	10.51	Individual }	0— 9	5,000— 9,999	2,627
2	—	Public	< 5 }	< 5,000	1,500
1,815	20.14	Individual	none }	< 5,000	1,202
169	1.88	Partner	}	< 5,000	935
412	4.57	Co-ops and other organizations			
9,013					

Source. Tables in Appendix to Chapter 6, Tan, 'Income Distribution and Determination in West Malaysia'.

Notes. Public = Public Limited Co. Private = Private Limited Company
Partner = Partnership Individual = Individual Proprietorship
500+, 200+, etc., indicate the average number of employees/establishment.

accounted for 76 per cent of total sales while 80 per cent of the companies had sales of less than $1 million and accounted for only 6 per cent of total sales.[30] As for 1970, 9.3 per cent of the companies sold 76.0 per cent of the total value, while 68.5 per cent of the companies sold 6.7 per cent of the goods.[31] Table 6.12(b) on page 230 contrasts the profits of these companies in the two years.

6.3 FOREIGN VERSUS LOCAL FIRMS

The role of foreigners was documented on a company and/or conglomerate basis, when the question of control was discussed in the last chapter. In this section, the relative profitabilities of the local- and foreign-controlled companies are compared for the whole range of the corporate sector. To provide for some continuity with the last chapter and to put the discussion into perspective, the top eighty publicly listed companies are first classified and compared according to whether they are foreign or locally owned. Thereafter, the aggregate performances of the foreign versus local companies are discussed using materials gathered for the earlier section as well as the financial surveys of limited companies.

In Table 6.7, companies numbered 2, 4, 19, 27, and 55 as well as 14, 34, 49, 56, 59, and 70 were under foreign control in 1974 when the data were gathered, but came under Government control in 1977 when the SD board was substantially changed, and Pernas and CC merged their tin interests in 1976.[32] The importance of these two Government 'take-overs' can be seen from the following summary based on Table 6.11(a). In 1974, actual Government-controlled companies amongst the top eighty numbered only four with less

TABLE 6.11(a)
1974 PROFIT AND PAID-UP CAPITAL SHARE OF THE TOP EIGHTY PUBLICLY LISTED COMPANIES IN MALAYSIA BY NATIONALITY OF CONTROL

	Capital		*Profit*		
	Value ($ Million)	*Share (%)*	*Value ($ Million)*	*Share (%)*	*Rate (%)*
Foreign controlled					
Singaporean	610.1	23.67	185.8	17.38	30.45
Others	965.4	37.46	377.9	35.35	39.14
Malaysian controlled					
Government C	347.7	13.49	329.6	30.84	94.79
Government A	123.2	4.78	49.1	4.59	39.85
Private local	530.7	20.59	126.5	11.83	23.84
Total	2,577.1	99.99	1,068.9	99.99	41.48

Source. Compiled from Table 6.8.

Notes. A refers to the companies actually under Government control in 1974.
C refers to companies then under foreign control but subsequently came under Government control in 1977.

than 5 per cent share of their total paid-up capital and profit. By contrast, the foreigners controlled fifty-five of the companies with more than 74 per cent and 84 per cent of the total paid-up capital and profit respectively. However, had the Government then controlled the companies under SD and the tin group, it would have controlled fifteen of the companies with total paid-up capital and profit of $470.9 million and $378.7 million or 18.3 per cent and 35.4 per cent of all the eighty companies respectively. Even after subtracting the share of these eleven companies, the foreigners would still have controlled forty-four of these companies with paid-up capital and profit amounting to $1,475.5 million and $563.7 million, or 61 per cent and 53 per cent of the total, respectively. On the other hand, only twenty-one of the eighty were under local private control with total paid-up capital and profit of $530.7 million and $126.5 million, or 20.6 per cent and 11.8 per cent of the total respectively.

From the above discussion and Table 6.11, the importance of the clustering of companies among the major conglomerates is also very apparent, echoing the argument in the last chapter. Certainly, the impact of the switch in control of the two conglomerates discussed above highlights the importance of clustering. Looking at it in another way, the SD conglomerate, for example, made a profit (at $134.9 million) which is the equivalent of more than 13,490 small manufacturing enterprises put together, and there are at most 35,000 small firms in Peninsular Malaysia each making less than $10,000 profit a year.[33] Little wonder that Pernas was determined to bring SD under its control and the former foreign controller of SD was equally determined to contest the challenge.

Tables 6.11(b) and (c) also highlight other interesting features. The foreign-controlled companies tend to have larger paid-up capital and profit. There is a more even spread in the paid-up capital of the foreign-controlled companies

TABLE 6.11(b)
DISTRIBUTION OF THE TOP EIGHTY PUBLICLY LISTED COMPANIES IN MALAYSIA BY SIZE OF PAID-UP CAPITAL IN 1974

Paid-up Capital in $ Million	*Malaysian Controlled*			*Foreign Controlled*		*Total*
	Private	*Government*		*Singaporean*	*Others*	
		A	*C*			
5.0— 9.99	2	0	1	2	1	6
10.0—19.99	11	1	5	2	9	28
20.0—29.99	5	1	1	2	6	15
30.0—39.99	1	1	0	2	7	11
40.0—49.99	1	1	2	3	2	9
50.0—99.99	0	0	2	1	4	7
100.0+	1	0	0	2	1	4
Total	21	4	11	14	30	80

Source and *Notes*. As for Table 6.11(a).

TABLE 6.11(c)
DISTRIBUTION OF THE TOP EIGHTY PUBLICLY LISTED COMPANIES IN MALAYSIA BY SIZE OF PROFIT IN 1974

Size of Profit in $ Million	*Malaysian Controlled*			*Foreign Controlled*		Total
	Private	*Government*		*Singaporean*	*Others*	
		A	*C*			
< 1.0	1	0	0	1	0	2
1.0— 1.99	4	0	0	0	0	4
2.0— 4.99	7	0	2	3	3	15
5.0— 9.99	3	1	1	2	13	20
10.0—14.99	5	2	4	0	6	17
15.0—19.99	1	1	0	4	3	9
20.0—29.99	0	0	1	4	4	9
30.0—49.99	0	0	1	0	0	1
50.0+	0	0	2	0	1	3
Total	21	4	11	14	30	80

Source and *Notes.* As for Table 6.11(a).

among the various sized companies with a concentration of their profits in the range of $5—10 million. By contrast, the local privately-controlled firms tend to cluster in the size group of $10—20 million in paid-up capital and $2—5 million in gross profit. These are of course firms dominated by the Malaysian Chinese. As for the companies controlled by the Malaysian Government, it is hardly surprising that they have distributions skewed towards the larger paid-up capital and higher gross profits; after all, as discussed in the preceding page, eleven of the fifteen companies under their orbit were formerly foreign-controlled corporations.

We will now look beyond the large publicly listed companies in order to get an overall view of Malaysian companies under foreign control.

From Tables 6.1 to 6.4 we can see that the foreign establishments consistently out-perform the local ones in average gross operating surplus and average sales value. This is true in manufacturing, mining, and construction as well as the distributive trades.

The 113 manufacturing establishments controlled by the British, Americans, and Japanese in 1968 had average sales of at least $4 million and an average GOS of at least $1.5 million. The Dutch and Singaporean companies were next with averages of more than $1.5 million in sales and $300,000 in GOS. The Malaysian ones by contrast averaged only $192,390 and $34,248 respectively (Table 6.1). Large Malaysian-controlled companies did exist but their small number relative to the large number of small-scale establishments has meant that the Malaysian averages had to be small. This dichotomy in characteristics between foreign- and locally-controlled firms reflects that foreign control was dominant mainly at the level of the large and very large establishments and corporations.[34] In mining, 9 of the largest 10 mines, 44 of the next

TABLE 6.12(a)
NUMBER OF FIRMS IN DIFFERENT SALES SIZE GROUPS IN 1967 AND 1970

Sales Size in $ Million	*Locally-controlled Company*				*Foreign-controlled Company*		*Branches of Foreign Company*	
	1967		*1970*		*1967*	*1970*	*1967*	*1970*
	No.	%	*No.*	%				
<1	2,929	85	3,033	73	130	372	425	266
1–5	448	13	862	21	69	177	141	151
5+	69	2	249	6	89	155	77	93
Total	3,446	100	4,144	100	288	704	643	510

Sources. Financial Survey of Limited Companies 1967, Table 1, p. 2; *Financial Survey of Limited Companies 1970*, Table A, p. 1; Table 6.1 of Tan, 'Income Distribution and Determination in West Malaysia'.

largest 53, and 29 of the third largest 45 are all foreign controlled. The average GOS of $1.37 million for the foreign mines is more than 4.5 times the average for Malaysian mines (Table 6.2). The construction industry is the only one in which the GOS of the foreign-controlled companies is only slightly higher than that for the locally-controlled companies (Table 6.3).

There are few foreign business activities in the form of individual proprietorships and partnerships except perhaps in the professional groups (such as

TABLE 6.12(b)
AVERAGE PROFIT BY SALES SIZE OF THE LIMITED COMPANIES IN 1967 AND 1970 ($ THOUSAND)

Sales Size in $ Million	*Locally-controlled Company*		*Foreign-controlled Company*		*Branches of Foreign Company*	
	1967	*1970*	*1967*	*1970*	*1967*	*1970*
<1	3.4	13.9	24.9	18.9	22.3	42.8
1–5	71.1	113.8	140.9	132.8	145.7	301.7
5+	712.3	859.2	1,675.0	1,773.0	1,662.0	3,762.0

Sources. As for Table 6.12(a).

Note. The average profit per firm in Table 6.12(b) has been calculated by assuming that there is no difference in the profitability of the firms by sales sizes. Hence, if the sixty-nine local companies with sales of $5 million sold 54 per cent of the total sales, we assume that these companies made 54 per cent of the profit as well, i.e., the average profit per company is equal to 54 per cent of profit divided by 69.

TABLE 6.12(c)
AVERAGE GROSS OPERATING SURPLUS BY SALES SIZE GROUP OF THE LIMITED COMPANIES IN 1967 AND 1970 ($ THOUSAND)

Sales Size in $ Million	*Locally-controlled Company*		*Foreign-controlled Company*		*Branches of Foreign Company*	
	1967	*1970*	*1967*	*1970*	*1967*	*1970*
<1	11.7	26.1	45.8	33.8	58.4	60.4
1–5	243.0	213.8	258.3	237.8	381.7	425.7
5+	2,435.0	1,614.0	3,071.0	3,174.0	4,335.0	5,308.0

Sources. As for Table 6.12(a).

accountants, lawyers, and others) which are not under consideration here. Thus Table 6.12, dealing only with limited companies, can provide a good overall picture of foreign business activities in Malaysia: they formed about 20.63 per cent and 22.66 per cent of the total number of limited companies in West Malaysia in 1967 and 1970 respectively, yet they made $424.4 million or 75.14 per cent and $712.1 million or 66.78 per cent of total profits in 1967 and 1970 respectively. Their level of average profit in each size group was at least twice as large as that of their local counterparts. This is not surprising as most of them were concentrated at the higher end of the profit scale; 166 of the 235 firms (70.64 per cent) with sales in excess of $5 million in 1967 were foreign controlled and 210 of the 658 firms (31.91 per cent) with sales in the range of $1–5 million were also foreign controlled. In 1970, the percentages of foreign firms in the above two sales groups fell somewhat to 248 of 497 (50 per cent) and 328 of 1,190 (27.56 per cent) respectively. This was probably a reflection of the continually increasing participation of local businessmen in the generally improved investment climate for them after Independence.

There is another interesting aspect. While the foreign-controlled firms were at least twice as profitable as their local counterparts, their GOS were not twice as much in some cases (Table 6.12(c)). The GOS of the intermediate-sized foreign and that of the locals were about the same and that for the large companies in 1967 differed little. Why then did the local companies make smaller profits? One important reason is the much smaller proportion of interest and rent payments that the foreigners paid compared with the locals. Therefore, the higher cost of credit cuts into the profitability of the local firms which may not be any less efficient in generating GOS which can then be used for reinvestment, regardless of their choice of technology. It will be interesting to understand the reasons for the higher payment of interest and rent by the local companies.

Although the foreign companies made more profit, they ended up paying less tax on profit:

	Direct Taxes/Gross Profit (in %)		
	1966	*1967*	*1970*
Locally-controlled Company	51.39	51.25	50.25
Foreign-controlled Company	34.02	43.56	46.15
Branches of Foreign Company	36.14	39.85	38.49

Source. Table 6.1 of Tan, 'Income Distribution and Determination in West Malaysia'.

A further note about the profitability of the foreign-controlled firms seems in order. The possibility of transfer pricing in addition to their already higher profitability has not been taken into account.

6.4 THE DISTRIBUTIVE TRADES

It is necessary to discuss the distributive trades separately as the measurement and estimation of GOS and profit are different from those of the other sectors. In this sector, only figures on turnover, and in some cases net turnover which is the difference between gross turnover and the cost of merchandise sold, are available. Unlike the GOS figure for the other sectors, the cost of labour has not been excluded while the indirect taxes have been excluded from net turnover figures.[35] This distinction provides some feel of the difference in magnitude between GOS and net turnover.

From Table 6.13, the net turnover as a ratio of GOS ranged from 55 per cent to 75 per cent for the wholesaling establishments in 1967 and 1970,[36] while that of the retailers ranged from 130 per cent to 220 per cent.[37] Thus, using net turnover to approximate GOS understates the latter's value by between a quarter and nearly one-half for the wholesalers. On the other hand, for the retailers in 1967, using net turnover overstates GOS by 30 per cent to 120 per cent! The most important factor in this difference in bias is the presence of immense indirect tax payments by the wholesalers, but relatively minor payments by the retailers. It should be kept in mind that the figures we are interested in measuring are the shareholders' share which should have netted out the indirect tax payment had data permitted it. In the case of the manufacturers, miners, and construction establishments, the proportion of indirect tax payments is either small or has been excluded from the sales figures,[38] i.e., it should not cause major distortion if GOS is used to approximate shareholders' share. However, in the case of the wholesalers, the indirect tax payments have to be netted out in view of their size.[39] At any rate, the most important point in this exposé for us to keep in mind in later discussion is that net turnover and GOS both overstate the actual value of the shareholders' share, regardless of their relationship to one another. In the case of wholesaling, the net turnover is a bit closer to the shareholders' share than GOS and vice-versa in the case of retailing. Therefore, as far as possible, the amount of wage and other payments ought to be netted out from net turnover before the figures can be

TABLE 6.13

FINANCIAL DATA OF LIMITED COMPANIES IN DISTRIBUTIVE TRADES IN 1967 AND 1970 ($ MILLION)

	Locally-controlled Company		*Foreign-controlled Company*		*Branches of Foreign Company*	
	1967	*1970*	*1967*	*1970*	*1967*	*1970*
(a) *Wholesale*						
Revenue	$1,062.7	$1,947.9	$969.2	$1,827.0	$782.8	$641.2
Wages	33.5	61.1	56.0	63.6	39.9	24.1
Interest and rent	10.0	18.2	12.3	17.5	9.6	9.0
Depreciation	5.6	11.5	16.6	8.9	7.9	4.4
Indirect taxes	24.8	151.5	108.7	109.2	111.8	60.8
Gross profit	22.0	50.0	17.7	46.4	29.9	30.9
Profit tax	10.7	27.0	12.2	20.5	12.5	11.4
Dividend	7.5	13.6	9.7	—	—	19.5
Retained earnings	3.8	9.4	−4.1	12.3	n.a.	n.a.
Local equity	119.5	228.3	28.6	8.5	—	—
Foreign equity	11.6	8.8	147.0	156.4	n.a.	n.a.
Total equity	131.1	237.1	175.6	164.9	n.a.	n.a.
Profit/Equity (%)	16.78	21.09	10.08	28.14	—	—
Profit/Revenue (%)	2.07	2.57	1.83	2.54	3.82	4.82
Gross operating surplus	62.4	231.2	155.3	182.0	159.2	105.1
Net turnover	71.1	140.8	102.6	136.4	87.3	68.4
Net turnover/Gross operating surplus (%)	114	61	66	75	55	65
Shareholders' share	27.6	61.5	34.3	55.3	37.8	35.3

(Continued)

TABLE 6.13 (Continued)

	Locally-controlled Company		Foreign-controlled Company		Branches of Foreign Company	
	1967	*1970*	*1967*	*1970*	*1967*	*1970*
(b) *Retail*						
Revenue	$290.0	$664.5	$177.5	$353.0	$ 67.7	$ 66.5
Wages	16.8	36.5	13.3	17.3	8.1	5.1
Interest and rent	3.2	12.3	3.4	4.8	1.5	1.2
Depreciation	2.0	3.1	0.9	2.4	0.3	0.4
Indirect taxes	3.3	21.2	4.4	9.1	1.4	0.7
Gross profit	3.8	15.6	6.0	11.4	2.4	3.6
Profit tax	2.7	8.9	2.7	4.9	1.0	1.0
Dividend	1.4	3.9	1.4	—	—	2.7
Retained earnings	—0.4	2.8	1.9	2.4	n.a.	n.a.
Local equity	47.5	117.9	2.0	3.4	—	—
Foreign equity	6.0	5.8	17.3	21.3	n.a.	n.a.
Total equity	53.4	123.7	19.3	24.7	n.a.	n.a.
Profit/Equity (%)	7.12	12.61	31.09	46.15	—	—
Profit/Revenue (%)	1.31	2.35	3.38	3.23	3.55	5.41
Gross operating surplus	12.3	52.2	14.7	27.7	5.6	5.9
Net turnover	25.9	67.5	23.6	35.9	12.3	10.3
Net turnover/Gross operating surplus	211	129	161	130	220	175
Shareholders' share	5.8	18.7	6.9	13.8	2.7	4.0

Sources. *Financial Survey of Limited Companies 1967.*
Financial Survey of Limited Companies 1970.

used to approximate the flow of income arising from ownership of capital for the distributive sector.

Before we go on to estimate the sizes of wage and other payments and net them out from our net turnover figures for the various sub-sectors within the distributive trades, a slight digression is of some interest. Table 6.13 highlights the differing fortunes of the owners of the trading establishments *v.* the wage earners. Whereas the gross profit for both the wholesalers and retailers had generally increased by more than 100 per cent, their wage bills had increased by less than that in the period from 1967 to 1970. This divergence in the growth in profit and wage bill is added evidence to the assertion in Chapter 4 that the higher-income bracket has gained relative to those in the lower-income brackets.

We now return to estimating the size of earnings of the distributive establishments. An attempt is made to estimate the sizes of wages, rent, and interest payments to arrive at the shareholders' share. Those with accounts probably hired at least two full-time employees as against the industry average of one to two employees.[40] Their higher turnover could be associated with better location, hence higher rent or higher depreciation if they owned their own premises, and higher working capital. The rents and working capital have been estimated at $1,200 and $5,000 respectively for catering, and $1,200 and $19,100 respectively for retailers.[41] If it is further assumed that all of the working capital of the caterers and half in the case of the retailers was borrowed at a 10 per cent interest rate,[42] then the interest payments could be $125 and $1,000 respectively. From Table 6.4, the coffee shops (which constitute 66 per cent of the caterers) had an average net turnover of $7,354 and the retailers, $9,000; these were for establishments with accounts. Netting out the wage, rent, and interest payments, the average shareholders' share for the caterers and retailers with accounts could be $3,415 and $3,334 respectively for those who rented their premises. Those who owned their own premises received similar gross profit, but an average shareholders' share of $4,615 and $4,534 respectively.

The smaller coffee stalls (not shops) and retailers without accounts, with even smaller turnover but concomitantly smaller expenditure,[43] are not likely to exceed the above level of gross profit. In fact, the average coffee shops and retail shops had a gross turnover of only $13,217 and $38,000 respectively. If a proportionate relationship holds they should have a net turnover averaging only $3,300 and $3,800 respectively. After deducting $600 for rent for both, as well as $55 and $317 for interest payment for catering and retailing respectively,[44] the average coffee shops and retail shops netted less than $2,645 and $2,600 respectively. For the 8,711 (or 77.31 per cent) coffee shops and drink stalls, and 36,405 (or 66.10 per cent) retailers which did not have accounts, their average gross and net turnover was $8,209 and $1,993 respectively for coffee shops, and $12,124 and $1,212 for retailers.[45] After accounting for rent and interest payment, their shareholders' share would be below $1,500 and $1,000 respectively.

With this discussion as a basis for grasping the relationship between net turnover and shareholders' share, we can now turn to Tables 6.14—6.16 to get an idea of the distribution of the caterers, retailers, and wholesalers with a

TABLE 6.14
AVERAGE TURNOVER OF CATERING ESTABLISHMENTS BY SALES SIZE IN 1966

Sales Size	*Individual Proprietor*		*Partnership*		*Total*	
	Number of Establishments	*Average Turnover*	*Number of Establishments*	*Average Turnover*	*Number of Establishments*	*Average Turnover*
< $5,000	4,747	$ 2,807	35	$ 3,571	4,782	$ 2,813
5,000— 9,999	4,591	7,065	n.a.	n.a.	4,732	7,077
10,000— 19,999	3,461	13,957	197	14,467	3,658	13,984
20,000— 49,999	2,307	29,444	415	32,807	2,732	29,927
50,000— 99,999	354	65,480	n.a.	n.a.	580	66,828
100,000—249,999	100	147,780	113	153,009	225	152,027
250,000+	13	408,692	36	463,556	71	477,296

Source. Census of Distributive Trades 1966, Table 12, p. 30.

TABLE 6.15

AVERAGE TURNOVER OF RETAILING ESTABLISHMENTS BY SALES SIZE IN 1966

Sales Size	*Individual Proprietor*		*Partnership*		*Others*		*Total*	
	Number of Establish-ments	*Average Turnover*	*Number of Establish-ments*	*Average Turnover*	*Number of Establish-ments*	*Average Turnover*	*Number of Establish-ments*	*Average Turnover*
< $5,000	12,732	$ 2,566	123	$ 3,171	3	$ 1,333	12,858	$ 2,572
5,000— 9,999	9,472	7,177	134	7,955	—	—	9,606	7,188
10,000— 19,999	11,107	14,207	447	14,143	19	7,684	11,573	14,194
20,000— 49,999	10,510	31,299	976	33,004	84	34,012	11,570	31,462
50,000— 99,999	4,163	69,509	753	73,803	141	76,014	5,057	70,330
100,000—249,999	1,964	148,937	891	154,911	231	143,494	3,086	150,254
250,000—499,999	458	337,131	353	347,637	46	339,109	857	341,564
500,000+	143	773,979	218	808,468	105	1,043,105	466	850,751
Total	50,549	28,376	3,895	136,727	629	273,447	55,073	38,838

Source. Census of Distributive Trades 1966, Table 26, p. 49.

TABLE 6.16
AVERAGE TURNOVER OF WHOLESALING ESTABLISHMENTS
BY SALES SIZE GROUP IN 1966

Sales Size	Individual Proprietor		Partnership		Others		Total	
	Number of Establish-ments	*Average Turnover*	*Number of Establish-ments*	*Average Turnover*	*Number of Establish-ments*	*Average Turnover*	*Number of Establish-ments*	*Average Turnover*
< $20,000	779	$ 10,910	71	$ 10,789	7	$ 8,571	857	$ 10,882
20,000— 49,999	751	33,510	231	33,745	21	34,190	1,003	33,580
50,000— 99,999	756	73,078	165	72,897	37	78,000	958	73,236
100,000— 249,999	920	159,922	452	169,604	121	174,157	1,493	164,008
250,000— 499,999	663	354,370	552	349,620	134	388,149	1,349	355,781
500,000— 999,999	314	693,732	346	691,766	149	703,430	809	694,679
1,000,000—4,999,999	160	1,838,619	392	1,921,176	295	2,342,898	847	2,052,465
5,000,000+	4	8,977,250	22	9,511,636	101	11,021,990	127	10,695,952
Total	4,347	234,393	2,231	668,736	865	2,295,883	7,443	604,164

Source. Census of Distributive Trades 1966, Table 40, p. 67.

cross classification of legal organization by sales category. The same polarization in the performance of big versus small establishments, with the bulk of them in the small-sized categories as discussed earlier for the other sectors, is observed.

At this juncture, it is desirable to single out three types of retailers—the general provisions (i.e., sundry shops), fish retailers, and fruit and vegetable retailers—for more detailed analysis. The profit margin and average return figures estimated here will be used in Chapter 7 for analysis, and are preparatory towards our discussion on the question of the monopoly-monopsony status of middlemen in relation to rural poverty.

For the whole of Peninsular Malaysia, there were 24,016 provision shops in 1966. From Table 6.17, a little more than one-third of these (8,240) were bigger than the rest with an average turnover of $95,662. These 8,240 stores kept accounts and we have an accurate assessment of the net turnover which amounted to $7,094 per establishment. It is probably accurate to assume that almost all of the 24,016 establishments were owned and operated by one family as there were 24,718 owner-operators reported.[46] Using the net to gross turnover ratio of 7.42 per cent for those with accounts,[47] it is possible to estimate the net turnover value for the other establishments without accounts and for all establishments taken as a whole.[48] On this basis, those without accounts had an average net turnover of $908. One-sixth (4,289) were from the East Coast states and averaged only $475 in net return; those from the northern states of Kedah, Perlis, and Penang (totalling 2,907) averaged $738 in net turnover; even the most affluent area of the central region (Selangor and Negeri Sembilan) could provide these small operators with a net turnover of only $1,404. This is an extremely low level of income even if one assumes that they pay no rent or interest; it is a level of income no higher than that of the farmers.

One qualification to the above observation is necessary. The income estimated refers only to income from the business operations of the small traders. Some of these traders have other income to raise their total income to a higher level, probably because of a family member having an outside job. For example, the small rural provision stores in the Muda area received overall household incomes of a little over $3,000 on the average despite a business income of only about $1,700.[49] This is a level still quite low but not as low as the average farmer's income in 1973. However the semi-urban and semi-rural and the urban provisions stores which have higher business incomes have relatively small other income.

The above discussion does point to possible underestimation of the household income of the small traders, but not their profit level, i.e., income from middlemen activities. It is important to keep this distinction in mind. Given their low profit level, perhaps one can speculate that the motivations for the smaller traders to seek alternative sources of income are not unlike those which lead the small padi farmers and small rubber smallholders to seek supplementary off-farm income.

As for those with accounts, they had a net turnover ranging from $5,037 for the northern states to $8,877 for the central states (see Table 6.17). The shareholders' share ranged from $1,584 for the north to $5,424 for the

TABLE 6.17
PERFORMANCE OF THREE RETAILING ACTIVITIES IN 1966

	All Establishments			*Establishments with Accounts*			*Establishments with No Accounts*		
	Number	*Average Gross Turnover*	*Estimated Average Net Turnover*	*Number*	*Average Gross Turnover*	*Estimated Average Net Turnover*	*Number*	*Average Gross Turnover*	*Estimated Average Net Turnover*
(a) *Fruit and Vegetables*									
South	1,025	$16,141	$2,019	66	$ 74,970	$ 9,379	959	$12,093	$1,513
Central	1,170	17,353	2,919	67	79,149	13,313	1,103	13,599	2,287
Central-North	997	11,412	1,650	68	41,794	6,044	929	9,188	1,329
North	751	14,744	1,381	77	60,312	5,649	674	9,539	994
East	1,191	4,119	370	8	68,125	6,125	1,183	3,686	331
Total	5,134	12,506	1,646	286	63,923	8,413	4,848	9,473	1,247
(b) *Fish*									
South	754	21,462	1,857	50	130,620	11,300	704	13,709	1,186
Central	655	28,417	3,002	42	194,071	20,500	613	17,067	1,802
Central-North	559	21,868	1,920	55	67,291	5,909	504	16,911	1,485
North	739	14,456	1,448	33	98,030	9,818	706	10,550	1,057
East	978	8,281	354	11	51,091	2,182	967	7,794	333
Total	3,685	17,856	1,690	191	116,126	10,990	3,494	12,485	1,181

(Continued)

TABLE 6.17 (Continued)

	All Establishments			*Establishments with Accounts*			*Establishments with No Accounts*		
	Number	*Average Gross Turnover*	*Estimated Average Net Turnover*	*Number*	*Average Gross Turnover*	*Estimated Average Net Turnover*	*Number*	*Average Gross Turnover*	*Estimated Average Net Turnover*
(c) *Provisions*									
South	5,244	$47,958	$3,343	1,943	$102,249	$7,128	3,301	$16,002	$1,115
Central	4,872	60,274	5,027	2,362	106,432	8,877	2,510	16,837	1,404
Central-North	4,638	37,669	2,865	1,869	75,598	5,750	2,769	12,068	918
North	4,300	28,590	2,131	1,393	67,574	5,037	2,907	9,910	738
East	4,962	27,907	1,595	673	152,700	8,725	4,289	8,325	475
Total	24,016	40,859	3,030	8,240	95,662	7,094	15,776	12,235	908

Source. Census of Distributive Trades 1966, Table 17, pp. 36–41.

Note. South: Johor and Malacca; Central: Selangor and Negeri Sembilan; Central-North: Perak; North: Kedah, Penang and Perlis; East: Kelantan, Pahang and Trengganu.

central region with an average of $3,541 for the whole peninsula.[50] This would represent the combined return to the owners' investment in capital (mainly the working capital), labour and management. It is a little difficult to compare the performances of the five regions as four of them had a higher proportion of establishments keeping accounts, thus giving a lower average gross turnover and a higher rate of net turnover to gross turnover, assuming that the higher the volume, the more likely it is for the establishment to charge a lower margin. On the other hand, the fact that only the largest among the establishments in the eastern region seemed to have kept accounts probably explains why it had a much lower net to gross ratio. Not surprisingly, this region also had a very high net turnover value of $8,725. Therefore, in effect, one is comparing those establishments at the higher range of performance in the four other regions against the highest turnover establishments in the eastern region. Similarly, since the net turnover of those without accounts has been estimated on the net to gross ratio, it is clear that there may be some underestimation for the four regions and a much bigger underestimation for the eastern region. Nevertheless, even allowing the net to gross ratio for those without accounts in all five regions to be raised to a very high percentage of 10 per cent,[51] their net turnover would still range only from $833 to $1,584, hardly affecting the earlier conclusion that these establishments have low incomes.

Table 6.17 also provides the estimated average net turnover of the fish retailers as well as that of the fruit and vegetable retailers, using the same procedure of estimation as that for the provisions shops. The level of net average turnover and hence the profit level was comparable with that of the provisions shops. In some cases, the average net turnover (and hence profit level) of the fish retailers and the fruit and vegetable retailers of the East Coast was at the appallingly low level of $330. The exceptions to the generally low middlemen-incomes were the fish retailers with accounts in the central region who made an average net turnover of $20,500, putting their income, after other expenses, into the category of the professionals!

It is of interest to examine the profit level of these three trades because they are the three most numerous groups of retailers forming the bulk (about 60 per cent) of all retailing establishments. Moreover, they form part of the chain of middlemen who handle agricultural and fishing produce on transit to the consumers, with the sundry stores taking on the added role of selling provisions to the rural small producers. As such, they have been looked upon as a key link in the exploitation of the small rural producers. And our analysis has shown that most of them made a surprisingly modest level of profit from their trading activities. Table 6.18 summarizes the performance of three types of wholesaling activities: fish, rubber, and rice. As the wholesalers are the persons who set the prices for the retailers for ultimate purchases from the small producers and disposal to the consumers, it is clearly of interest to study their margins and profit levels, especially since the earlier analysis seems to indicate that the retailers themselves are almost as poor as the farmers whom they are supposed to be exploiting.

The question of who is in the position to exploit whom is reserved for Chapter 7 where there will be a more detailed analysis of these wholesalers together with the marketing structure.

TABLE 6.18

PERFORMANCE OF THREE WHOLESALING ACTIVITIES IN 1966

	All Establishments			*Establishments with Accounts*			*Establishments with No Accounts*		
	Number	*Average Gross Turnover*	*Estimated Average Net Turnover*	*Number*	*Average Gross Turnover*	*Estimated Average Net Turnover*	*Number*	*Average Gross Turnover*	*Estimated Average Net Turnover*
(a) *Fish*									
South	30	$ 230,400	$ 19,889	23	$ 275,000	$ 23,739	7	$ 83,857	$ 7,237
Central	110	297,455	23,387	68	400,074	31,456	42	120,595	9,479
Central-North	43	376,326	35,988	42	384,667	36,786	1	26,000	2,486
North	50	385,520	34,408	49	392,612	35,041	1	38,000	3,393
East	49	87,714	7,509	10	344,600	29,500	39	21,846	1,870
Total	282	281,518	24,281	192	376,927	32,510	90	77,978	6,729
(b) *Rice*									
South	206	856,252	54,030	203	867,064	54,793	3	124,667	7,866
Central	103	2,469,544	161,340	102	2,491,794	162,794	1	200,000	15,180
Central-North	69	1,192,594	61,304	69	1,192,594	61,304	—	—	—
North	100	1,677,400	119,810	100	1,677,400	119,810	—	—	—
East	38	761,184	6,757	35	817,486	7,257	3	104,333	929
Total	516	1,375,397	85,752	509	1,392,570	86,823	7	126,714	7,894

(Continued)

TABLE 6.18 (Continued)

	All Establishments			*Establishments with Accounts*			*Establishments with No Accounts*		
	Number	*Average Gross Turnover*	*Estimated Average Net Turnover*	*Number*	*Average Gross Turnover*	*Estimated Average Net Turnover*	*Number*	*Average Gross Turnover*	*Estimated Average Net Turnover*
(c) *Rubber*									
South	227	$738,811	$42,459	216	$ 774,560	$44,514	11	$36,818	$2,117
Central	307	951,866	54,950	240	1,192,929	68,867	67	88,209	5,090
Central-North	649	302,815	15,897	502	383,849	20,151	147	26,088	1,370
North	183	461,235	37,483	120	617,625	50,192	63	163,349	13,280
East	302	279,272	19,586	206	399,583	28,024	96	91,719	6,429
Total	1,668	494,728	29,616	1,284	625,186	37,426	384	58,508	3,505

Source. *Census of Distributive Trades 1966*, Table 35, pp. 63—8.

Note. North: Kedah, Penang and Perlis; Central: Selangor and Negeri Sembilan; Central-North: Perak; South: Johor and Malacca; East: Kelantan, Pahang and Trengganu.

6.5 CONCLUSION

In so far as the company is dominated by one family, the GOS/shareholders' share of that company reflects the income of that family. This poses no problem for the family enterprises; their GOS is their family income. However, for the publicly listed companies, the controlling family is legally entitled to whatever portion its shareholding entails, which will be only a portion of the GOS of that company. In reality, because major decisions of expansion, dividends, retained earnings, etc., rest in the hands of the controlling shareholder, all the company resources are, in some loose sense, his. He may choose to retain part of this as stock instead of realizing it as a flow via dividend payment. If this line of argument is acceptable, the GOS of a conglomerate reflects the real income from wealth of the major shareholder. At any rate, 30 per cent of a huge sum like a million dollars in comparison with the $1,500 a small farmer or unskilled worker makes is still very large.

Armed with this measure (GOS), Sections 6.2 and 6.3 highlight the very large differences in the financial characteristics between the small number of big firms and the very large number of small firms, and between foreign and local firms. The presence of the two dichotomies is striking.

The small establishments are usually organized as individual proprietorships. We have seen that the average sales and GOS for this form of business organization were very modest. For example, among the manufacturing establishments, possibly one-third received an average GOS of less than $3,000 and another one-third made $3,000 to $10,000 in GOS. At the other end, a little more than 100 large establishments (less than 4 per cent of the total number of manufacturing establishments) made about 30 per cent of the total GOS; some of the larger ones in this category averaged more than $1 million and even tens of millions. This did not take into account the increasing incidence of duplications of establishments within one firm and duplications of firms within a conglomerate as the size of the operation increases.

The foreign-controlled firms tended to be the largest ones. Until Pernas took over Sime Darby and London Tin in 1976–7, only twenty-five of the top eighty publicly listed companies in terms of market value were Malaysian controlled. The rest were all foreign controlled, primarily British. It is also significant to point out that the foreign-controlled firms paid more than 10 per cent less profit tax than their local counterparts, despite a higher profit level.

The differences have also been discussed using data from the companies listed on the Stock Exchange, and a link-up is made between the large companies discussed in Chapter 5 and in this chapter, using the various census data.

Section 6.4 described in detail the earnings of the proprietors in the catering and retailing trades. It is surprising to find that the great majority received income in a range not much higher than that of the farmers and wage earners described in Part I of the book. This sets the stage for an analysis of the monopoly-monopsony middlemen in the next chapter.

1. For example, for the small manufacturing industries with 0—4 employees, only 7.2 per cent of the establishments had other activities whereas 20.3 per cent of those with more than 50 employees had other activities. Chee Peng Lim, 'Survey of Small-Scale Industries in Peninsular Malaysia', Ph.D. dissertation, University of Malaya, 1976, Table VIII-18, p. 327.

For specific industries such as coconut oil mills, soft drinks, sawmills, and structural shapes, which are all larger industries within the group of small enterprises Chee surveyed, 21.4 per cent, 36.8 per cent, 30.0 per cent, and 40.0 per cent respectively had other activities. On the other hand, the foundry owners and the blacksmiths saw only 5.0 per cent or less of their ranks picking up other activities, ibid., Table VII-19, p. 328.

2. See Section 6.3 on big firms *v.* small firms for verification.

3. See the introductory paragraphs of Chapter 5 for a brief discussion of this.

4. The figure for value added of the corporate sector came from the *Financial Survey of Limited Companies 1970* and the GNP figure came from the *Third Malaysia Plan 1976–1980*.

5. Tan Tat-wai, 'Employment and Labour Utilisation in West Malaysia'.

6. This is because there is no detailed breakdown of cost data in the published results of the Department of Statistics surveys. See also note 8.

7. See argument presented in Chapter 1, pp. 9—10.

8. Actually, it is the shareholders' share of a company's income that we are interested in. It is the proportion within the total amount of surplus generated that belongs to the shareholders directly, overtly as in profit before tax, or in disguise such as depreciation and depletion allowances. The next note provides a pictorial definition of the shareholders' share, the gross operating surplus, and the net operating surplus. It is only because of the constraints imposed by data limitation which make it difficult to derive shareholders' share under most circumstances that we have resorted to the GOS and NOS for analytical purposes.

9. The following is a pictorial definition of the several measures used in this chapter:

	Value of Sales of Goods
–	Costs of Materials
	Value Added
–	Salaries and Wages
	Gross Operating Surplus (GOS)
	Advertisement*
	Insurance*
–	Expense Account and Benefits*
	Shareholders' Share@
–	Depreciation & Depletion Allowance*
	Net Operating Surplus (NOS)
–	Interest & Rent Payments@
–	Indirect Duties on Products (if any)@
	Profit before Tax

Note. Items with * denote those included under 'Other Business Expenditure' in the Department of Statistics Survey results which we have used to derive the GOS and NOS. Strictly speaking, items with @ are cost items which should have been subtracted from the GOS to arrive at the shareholders' share. Unfortunately data constraints prevent that exclusion. For a detailed discussion about the empirical relationships among these major items and the three measures we are using, see Tan, 'Income Distribution and Determination in West Malaysia', Chapter 6.

10. As we can see from the definition in the note above, when indirect taxes and interest payments are not major, the NOS and profit before tax are almost the same.

11. While the individual proprietors were the most numerous small operators, they were not the smallest. The 399 co-operatives were even smaller.

12. See Table 6.1. The number of establishments with sales averaging more than $5 million per year has not increased much since 1968. By 1971, 41 public limited establishments, 98 private limited ones, 3 partnerships and several individual proprietorships belonged to this category. See *Survey of Manufacturing Industries 1971*, Table 11.

13. Computed from background tables prepared (using figures from the *Census of Manufacturing Industries 1968*) to construct Table 6.1.

14. Table 6.2.

15. Table 6.3.

16. The only omission from the ranking of the GOS is the rubber remilling industry off-estates because of the presence of substantial indirect taxes. This industry will be dealt with separately later on.

17. Computed from the *Census of Manufacturing Industries 1968*.

18. Tables 6.1 and 6.6.

19. The remainder of the 101 have also by and large been included in one of the conglomerates presented in the charts in Chapter 5 of Tan, 'Income Distribution . . .'.

20. While as rigorous an analysis for the later years has not been carried out as has been done for 1968, preliminary and less systematic analysis of later-year surveys have tended to support this contention.

21. For example, the Textile Alliance–Toray Industry group has set up a number of large textile factories in Malaysia to become the single largest textile group in this country. Each of the four factories they built in Prai, Penang, has a capital expenditure of over $100 million (see annual company reports filed with the Registrar of Companies, also Chart 5.7).

22. The impression is gained from combining the reports in *Straits Times Directory*, telephone directory, and J. Puthucheary, *Ownership and Control in the Malayan Economy*, and information provided by referees.

23. There are other examples from other industries. For example, many of the sawmillers owned and controlled a chain of timber concessions and sawmills; see for example the *Straits Times Directory*, and also the interlocking relationships of the Sarawak timber industry charted out by this author, but not presented here, based on 墾荒四十年 published by the Hock Chiew clan association of Sarawak. In tin mining, well-known individuals like Tun H. S. Lee, Foong Seong, the Yong family, the Yeoh family, Chin Pek Soo, Chung Sum, etc., are all known to possess multiple mines. Again, one can look up the *Straits Times Directory* for some up-to-date information on some of these holdings. For a general historical exposition of the ownership structure of Chinese mines, see Yip Yat Hoong, *The Development of the Tin Mining Industry of Malaya*, Kuala Lumpur, University of Malaya Press, 1969.

24. They have been chosen for a variety of reasons. Small rice mills, meehoon, furniture and fixtures, tin-smithing, and industrial machinery have all been industries with a long history, small scale in their operation but among the most numerous. Textile, electrical appliances, and plastic products are newer industries with a moderate range of sales averages. The other industries

also have a fairly long history, but there is a greater range in their scale of operations. Rubber remilling and sawmilling have also been chosen because they will be used for further analysis in Chapter 8 on the origins and bases of the local businessmen.

25. Rubber remilling is the exception within the group. Its very high gross operating surplus can be explained by the presence of substantial indirect duties, see Chapter 8.

26. Based on tables prepared but not presented here.

27. GOS distribution is used here as a proxy for profit distribution.

28. As explained in note 24, the range that these fourteen industries represent in size of operation is quite large. The only significant section of the manufacturing industries not represented in this distribution is that of the largest enterprises. As a result, there is an under-representation of the industries with large establishments and high GOS. However, since their number is so small, if their representation is provided by adding a percentage consistent with their proportion of the total number of manufacturing establishment, it is not likely to alter the average very much. Their small number also enables us to visualize the impact of their absence in the distribution and how the distribution may change with their inclusion.

29. This finding is consistent with that of Chee, op. cit., in his survey of small-scale industries of Malaysia in 1974. In a limited sample of 399, he found that 111 or 27.8 per cent received gross profit of \$7,738; 149 or 37.4 per cent received an average of less than \$77,150 and 40 received an average of \$77,150. Using a conversion rate of 2 : 1 from gross profit to GOS worked out in Chapter 6 of Tan, 'Income Distribution . . .', that would imply an average GOS of about \$140,000 and some of the 40 must have a GOS of less than \$100,000. Summing up, between 60 and 68 per cent would have a GOS of less than \$100,000. The relevant data from Chee have been summarized in Table 6.13 of Tan, op. cit.

30. *Financial Survey of Limited Companies 1967*, Table 1, p. 2.

31. *Financial Survey . . . 1970*, Table A, p. 1.

32. There is, however, one qualification necessary here. As we use a broader definition of control, whereas the Department of Statistics uses the 50 per cent ownership as a criterion for control, an educated guess would be that the Department of Statistics would report a picture of less foreign control than we would here.

33. The figure of 35,000 has been estimated based on the figures of Tables 6.1 to 6.4. About 5,500 small manufacturing establishments had less than \$10,000 in average NOS, 400 mining concerns had less than \$10,000 in average NOS and perhaps close to half of the 65,000 caterers and retailers made less than that.

34. In 1967, eighty-nine foreign subsidiaries (or 31 per cent of the total) sold 92 per cent of the total sales generated by the subsidiaries of foreign companies operating in Malaysia. Seventy-seven foreign branches (or 12 per cent of the total) sold 81 per cent of total sales generated by all foreign branches in Malaysia. Among the local companies, 2 per cent of the locally-controlled ones sold 54 per cent of total sales generated by the locally-controlled companies. See *Financial Survey . . . 1967*, Table 1, p. 2. Analogous data for 1970 can also be obtained from Table A of the 1970 survey.

35.

Gross Turnover		Gross Turnover
− Cost of Goods Sold	Cost of	− Cost of Goods Sold
− Indirect Taxes	Merchandise	− Wage Payment
Net Turnover		Gross Operating Surplus

36. The net turnover/GOS ratio for the locally-controlled companies in 1967 is the only exception falling outside this range. There is one peculiarity in the trend. While the ratio for the foreign-controlled companies and branches of foreign companies has risen from 1967 to 1970, that for the locals fell drastically. One possible explanation is the drastic increase in indirect taxes paid by the locally-controlled companies, perhaps implying that the nature of business activity of the local wholesalers may have changed.

37. Here again, the ratio for local retailers fell sharply and we can trace it to the big increases in wage payment and indirect taxes. Thus, there again appear to be possible changes in the business activity. It is also noteworthy that the local retailers enjoyed the largest absolute and relative increase in the value of their turnover, unlike the wholesalers when the subsidiaries of the foreign companies were the largest beneficiaries of the increase in turnover.

38. In the case of the tin miners, export duties have already been netted out of their sales receipts as they generally obtain their proceeds from the tin smelters who pay the duties at the point of export.

39. If this is not done, the ratio of net turnover to GOS would rise to between 157 per cent and over 200 per cent.

40. The small establishments are assumed to hire no employees as they cannot afford them. The assumption of two employees per establishment with accounts is consistent with the industry average once a weighted average is taken.

41. The rent of the caterers is assumed to average $100 per month. Their average working capital is assumed to be the equivalent of $1\frac{1}{2}$ months' worth of turnover. The corresponding figures for the retailers are actual, but rounded off, average figures obtained from the *Census of Distributive Trades 1966*.

42. The actual interest rate that a small trader has to pay is frequently more than 10 per cent. This can be gathered from the difficulties some of the hawkers have in getting short-term trade credit as reported by Hara, 'Hawkers in Penang', and the report by Chee, op. cit., on the small-scale industries.

43. These probably have only unpaid family helpers rather than paid employees. Their level of rent payment is also likely to be more modest in smaller premises located in less choice spots.

44. For those with accounts, stock works out to be approximately half month of sales value for the coffee shops; while that for the retailers is approximately $2\frac{1}{2}$ months' worth of turnover. Here, for those without accounts, an assumption is made that the coffee shops stock about $\frac{1}{2}$ month's worth of turnover of materials, while the retailers stock for one month. Both are conservative estimates. It is also assumed that these do not hire employees.

45. See Table 6.4 and *Census of Distributive Trades 1966*, p. 25, and Table 17.1

46. Table 6.4.

47. The 7.42 per cent is obtained by dividing the actual figure for net turnover by that of gross turnover. Those reported in Table 6.4 have been rounded to the nearest thousand.

48. For those who are concerned with the possibility of differing net to gross turnover ratio with turnover size, there is no empirical basis. On the contrary, data seem to indicate that the ratio is more a function of the level of competition. For example, the eastern region in Table 6.17 has very high volume but low net to gross turnover ratio and high net turnover. In the central region, the volume and net to gross turnover ratio are both high and the dealers in that region received the highest net turnover. However, in the southern region with the largest number of establishments, probably implying greater competition since the southern region has less population than the

central region, both the volume and net to gross turnover ratio were more modest.

49. See FAO–IBRD Programme, *The Muda Survey—A First Report.*

50. These figures have been estimated by assuming that they hired one worker per establishment and either pay a higher rent or owned their own premises. These assumptions can be supported by data from the 1966 Census, op. cit., Table 21, p. 45: there were 9,411 employees for the 24,016 establishments; however, it seems most likely that the 8,240 firms with accounts were the establishments that hired employees, giving about one employee per establishment. Higher rent has been assumed for probable locational advantages these more prosperous establishments may have. Thus, taking the average wage of $1,733 reported in Chapter 4 for one worker and assuming a rent of $60 per month or $720 per year and an interest rate of 10 per cent on a stock of one month's turnover and netting these from the net turnover figures, we obtain the shareholders' share.

51. Ten per cent is undoubtedly a very high ratio, going by the ratios implied by the figures reported in Tables 6.4 and 6.17.

7 Monopoly-monopsony Middlemen: Truth or Fantasy?

7.1 INTRODUCTION

ECONOMISTS throughout the world have often pointed an accusing finger at the presence of monopoly-monopsony in the marketing of agriculture produce and consumer goods as the characteristic cause of rural poverty. Malaysia is no exception; writers have written at great length about the existence of middlemen and how they exploit Malay peasants. Unfortunately, in the case of Malaysia, this is a particularly sensitive issue as there is a racial angle to it.[1]

Ungku Aziz is one of the earliest modern exponents of such a view—his charges date from 1957, and he remains its most persistent champion today. The following statement made by him is typical:

> Malay farmers and fishermen are exploited in four different ways. First they are exploited by the merchants who charge excessive margin for their services. Very frequently, a shopkeeper is in a monopolistic position vis-à-vis the farmers. . . . The second form of exploitation is through high rates of interest charged by money-lenders and shopkeepers who supply the farmers with credit in kind or loan in cash. It appears to be quite normal for the rate of interest on loans to be between 100 to 200% per year.[2]

Munro and Chee (1976) have summarized the charges against the middlemen as follows:

> . . . (a) being drones performing no useful function. Thus, by definition *any* payment they receive represents unlawful gain at the expense of the customer and/or fishermen.
> (b) enslaving fishermen through the operation of a peculiar credit system. Middlemen make loans to fishermen who in turn are required to deliver the entire catch to their creditors. The middleman, it is alleged, is thus free to exploit the fishermen at will for (the middleman) can set any price he wishes. . . . It is alleged further that under such a system, the fishermen have no incentive to save and invest, for any returns accruing from the investment will be appropriated by the middlemen.
> (c) engaging in price collusion, both for the purpose of strengthening their hand against the fishermen and for the purpose of exploiting the consumers.[3]

Other renowned social scientists on Malaysia have also written on middlemen monopoly-monopsony in all walks of farm production.[4] There is certainly no lack of similar postulations and expositions despite the fact that those making the assertions invariably point to the lack of sufficient empirical data for verification.[5] But it is unreasonable to continue making assertions on this question while neglecting empirical evidence by claiming that data are non-existent and research difficult. There is actually an abundance of data as we shall illustrate in this chapter. Yet no one has tried to piece together a complete picture with the available empirical data to substantiate the extent of imperfect competition. Such an attempt is made in this chapter.

Some good studies are available on the profit margins that the retailers and wholesalers receive in these trades, for example, the studies by Lim (1968), Cheam (1971), Elliston (1967), Ooi (1970), Agarwal (1966), and others. These studies can provide data on the income and profit level of some of the middlemen. We also have the estimated profit levels and the estimated gross income figures, especially Tables 6.17 and 6.18, of some of the middlemen derived from Chapter 6. All this information, together with considerations about the number of dealers in each region, the ease of entry, the marketing margin, and other factors including credit services provided by the middlemen, is integrated to evaluate the extent of competition and hence the prevalence of imperfect competition in Malaysian marketing channels.

Four different groups of trading activities, the provisions stores, the rubber dealers, fish dealers, and vegetable and fruit dealers, form the backbone of rural to urban (and vice-versa) trading activities. They are discussed at the different levels of retailing and wholesaling.

7.2 THE EXTENT OF COMPETITION

A. Provisions Stores

Provisions stores are central to the everyday life of the populace of Malaysia. In the rural areas, they are not infrequently the only, or at best one of the few available, suppliers of daily consumer items in the village. In addition, these items are usually sold on credit. In fact, they are the major source of credit for their customers, frequently accounting for over 60 per cent of the credit a farmer can receive.[6] Therein lies the root of the charge of high margins and exorbitant interest rates on credits.

There seems to be little doubt that the interest rates charged are fairly high.[7] One main reason for this seems to be the high risk involved as defaults are common. Unfortunately, there are inadequate data on the extent and magnitude of bad debts. Thus the net return and profit figures given here and elsewhere have not taken into account the necessary subtraction arising from bad debts.

The more central question is the degree of competition that exists at the village level. This largely hinges on whether the farmers have alternative sources for the purchase of goods and sale of produce, for one can expect the prices the farmers face to be more favourable under the pressure of competition.

Rosemary Barnard (1970) in her study of a Kedah village observed,

> As is often the case among small-scale trading concerns, supplier credit is limited, and the margin of profit is so small that by the time harvest is due,

stocks are visibly depleted. A number of larger stores at nearby [towns] . . . serve as alternatives to the village shopkeeper. Nearly every household has a bicycle so that accessibility to a shopkeeper outside the village for the daily small purchases presents little problem.[8]

Even in the deep interior occupied by the Orang Asli, the Chinese shopkeepers have to face competition. Maeda (1971) wrote:

> They [the shopkeepers] sell . . . at prices 10% to 20% higher than those in the town. Part of the reason for this is that the Chinese dealers in Padang Enday seldom give the shopkeeper any reduced prices unless he buys wholesale. . . . The village shopkeepers are in competition not only with the Chinese merchants in the town, but also with a Malay peddler who passes there on occasion.[9]

It is difficult to conceive that in other rural or semi-urban villages there is even less competition than in such remote villages. Thus, there is an upper limit on the price increment that can be added on because of competition from pedlars and neighbouring shops. In general we can conclude that the shops do charge a higher price, because they (especially the smaller ones) cannot get special prices from their suppliers with the small volume they handle.

Another indication of the degree of competitiveness comes from the recent findings of the Muda survey. With the completion of the Muda irrigation scheme and more farms turning to double cropping, the summed gross turnover of all provisions stores increased from $35.327 million in 1966 to $62.067 million in 1972. However, this increase has not resulted in any significant increase in the average turnover value or profit of the average provisions shops. Most of the increase in total sales has been absorbed by an increase in the number of establishments—from 1,167 to 2,109, while the average gross turnover has remained at roughly the same level—$30,272 in 1966 and $30,741 per establishment in 1972.[10] This is hardly surprising. Entry is easy as the initial capital requirement for opening a sundry shop is quite small.[11] The high unemployment and under-employment existing in this country means that there is a pool of persons willing to undertake this venture when the opportunity arises.[12]

Table 7.1 summarizes other data from the FAO survey. The general level of profit to gross turnover ratio and the profit level is consistent with that derived in Table 6.17(c) for the provisions stores in general.[13] The 10—12 per cent profit margin for the rural areas is consistent with that reported in the preceding pages. The trend of the profit-sales ratio supports the earlier hypothesis about higher sales supporting a lower profit rate or conversely, the smaller the shop, the higher is the gross profit margin necessary to sustain it. It is interesting to note that the semi-rural, semi-urban shops have larger sales, profit, and income than even the urban shops. This is perhaps due to the relatively smaller concentration of shops in these semi-urban areas compared with the urban areas as well as their role in serving as the middlemen between the rural provisions shops and the urban wholesalers. Their customer base may also be wider in the sense that the villagers who cannot find their merchandise at the village shops or are dissatisfied with the prices charged there would turn to the semi-urban shops.

TABLE 7.1
PROFIT AND INCOME LEVEL OF SUNDRY SHOPS IN MUDA (IN $)

	Rural Areas			*Semi-urban*			*Urban*		
	1968	*68 in 72 Prices*	*1972*	*1968*	*68 in 72 Prices*	*1972*	*1968*	*68 in 72 Prices*	*1972*
Average sales	$13,895	$16,118	$14,450	$103,255	$161,000	$111,027	$62,680	$56,882	$50,710
Net profit	1,346	1,763	1,774	6,051	7,278	5,524	3,220	4,490	3,945
Total income	2,196	3,494	3,431	6,344	8,317	6,194	3,485	4,669	4,046
Savings	n.a.	1,195	1,046	3,311	4,457	3,122	1,633	2,277	1,779
Profit/Sales	9.69%	10.94%	12.28%	5.86%	4.52%	4.98%	5.14%	7.89%	7.78%

Source. FAO–IBRD Programme, *The Muda Survey—A First Report*, Table 76.

B. Agricultural Produce Purchasing Agents

(a) PADI

The investigation is now shifted to the profit margin of, and prices offered by, the agricultural produce purchasing agents: the padi purchasing middlemen, the first-level rubber dealers, etc. There is little unclassified material to draw on. However, the Muda Project farm survey of 1966 showed that the price differential between the middlemen and co-operative societies amounted to only 4¢ per *gantang*, giving rise to a possible income loss of about $58 per average farmer, a significant absolute amount to the poor farmers, but a small amount compared to the burden of rent.[14] Narkswasdi and Selvadurai reported even better prices paid by the middlemen in Tanjong Karang, and the same reason of higher price caused 58 per cent of the farmers in Malacca to sell to the middlemen, while 35 per cent sold to the co-operative societies.[15] In Kemubu and Province Wellesley, 70 per cent and 84 per cent of the farmers respectively sold to the middlemen,[16] probably for the same reason.

(b) RUBBER

(i) Marketing Margin. As for the rubber dealers, Lim (1968) computed the marketing margins for smoked and unsmoked sheets to be 4.7 per cent and 14.6 per cent of the rubber f.o.b. price respectively, using a f.o.b. price of 78¢ per *kati* or 129¢ per kilo. Of the 150 dealers surveyed, 34 per cent received a surplus of less than $1,400, another 37 per cent received $3,605, only 8.0 per cent received $11,586 and 6.0 per cent made in excess of $20,000 per year.[17] Thus he concluded,

> The above evidence shows that the proportions these marketing margins form of the market price are certainly not as high as has commonly been asserted. It may be questioned whether the big decline in rubber price since 1964 has reduced margins below the levels in Table 13. All evidence available, however, indicates that they are very much the same today.[18]
>
> The above analysis indicates that the marketing of smallholders' rubber can probably be considered satisfactory in so far as Ribbed Smoked Sheets are concerned. Indeed it is doubtful whether other systems could perform similar services, including the provision of credit, so efficiently at such low a cost [*sic*]. In respect of Unsmoked Sheets, however, it cannot but be doubted that the marketing margin charged by the dealers is excessive, even though there is a clear case for income compensation between different types of rubber.[19]

Cheam (1971) has further refined Lim's work. From the following framework:

> The mere magnitudes of the various margins are no indication of the efficiency or inefficiency of the present marketing system. Higher marketing margins may be the result of more marketing services provided. . . . However, the breakdown of margin at each trade level into costs and surplus will provide some indication as to whether the margin is reasonable.[20]

He went on to establish the conclusion that the marketing margin for the purchase of scrap rubber is unsatisfactory, despite the fact that the greater uncertainty involved in the buying of scrap rubber partly accounts for the higher margin.[21] Using Wharton's theoretical model to study the existence of monopsonistic conditions, Cheam attempted to test several hypotheses. He argued that there would be a one-to-one relationship between the f.o.b. price and each of the three trade level prices (exporter—middle-level dealer—first-level dealer) which would imply a constant margin if marketing cost remains constant. On this basis, he concluded from the evidence available that the market among the middle-level dealers for all areas and that of the first-level dealers in the developed areas are competitive, whereas first-level dealers in remote areas and the remillers seem to be somewhat upwardly rigid in the price they provide to their clients in times of rising prices.[22]

The one-to-one correspondence between the f.o.b. price and those prevailing at each of the three trade levels is a very stringent demand. This condition will be satisfied if, but only if, there is perfect competition prevailing in the market-place and this is not the case for rubber dealing. In fact, perfect competition is a utopian condition existing only in the theoretical realm of classical and neo-classical economists. Therefore, to show that there is no one-to-one correspondence in these prices is only to show a very trivial result: i.e., the rubber market is not perfectly competitive, but this also applies to every other market in Malaysia and abroad! The existence of imperfect market conditions does not automatically imply a monopoly-monopsony hold on the smallholders. However, it does of course illustrate some amount of exploitation of the smallholders.

If there is no one-to-one transmission of f.o.b. price increments by the dealers to the smallholders, how much transmission is there? And what is an 'acceptable' level of transmission?

From Table 7.2 it is quite clear that the dealers at all three levels (first level—middle level—remiller-exporter) did not absorb the bulk of the increase in prices; they accounted for less than 40 per cent of the price increase. On the

TABLE 7.2
PRICE TRANSMISSION BY THE DEALERS TO THE SMALLHOLDERS (FOR SELANGOR IN 1964)
(IN ¢/*kati*)

	F.O.B. Price	*Dealer Margin*	*% of Price Increment to Dealers*	*% of Price Increment to Smallholder and Increased Taxation*
Highest week	81.6¢	12.3¢		
Lowest week	71.2	9.9		
Price increase	10.4	2.4	23	77
October average	80.8	13.1		
January average	71.9	9.8		
Price increase	8.9	3.3	37	63

Source. Lim Sow Ching, *A Study of the Marketing . . .*, Table E.

other hand, it would be ridiculous to claim on the basis of Table 7.2, which is very partial and crude, that there is adequate price transmission. One needs to isolate the margin and the surplus (i.e., margin minus cost) of the dealers at different levels to determine what their income is, before jumping to any conclusions about price transmissions.[23]

The average margin for the middle-level dealers from 1962 to 1964 fluctuated between 3.6¢ to 3.8¢ weekly, regardless of how big the actual price fluctuations were, with the overall average for 1960–4 standing at 3.6¢ per *kati*.[24] This constancy in the middle-level margin is consistent with Cheam's contention that there is adequate price transmission from the middle-level dealers to the first-level dealers.

Cheam's finding that the first-level dealers and the remillers seemed to be somewhat upwardly rigid in their buying price in times of rising export price warrants a more careful analysis. On the surface, this seems to fit the behaviour of a monopsonistic buyer.[25] In reality, there may be other reasons which account for part or all of the upward rigidity in price. In particular, the export duty is assessed on a two-week average price of the grade 1 Ribbed Smoked Sheets and the exporters of the lower grades of rubber have to pay the same amount of tax. Proportionately, the tax rate would be greater the lower the grade of rubber exported, resulting in a smaller percentage of the price increase being transmitted to the smallholders, the lower the grade. In so far as Cheam's study has not taken this into consideration, we should be cautious in accepting his conclusion with regard to the remilling and exporting level. However, his observations on the first-level dealers in remote areas stand.

(ii) Ease of Entry. Lim in his study of the competitiveness of the market also considered several other factors, including the density of dealers and the ease with which changes in daily prices are transmitted to the smallholders. On both counts, he found the level of competition and the availability of information adequate.[26] In fact, competition was deemed to be fierce enough to force twelve dealers into closing down in 1964.[27] Is this reasonable? Judging from Lim's information on the necessary initial investment for a first-level dealer, entry should be no problem since the smallest dealer needed only a $2,100 initial investment.[28]

In a later study, Lim computed the density of dealers in all the states and deemed that the averages of 4.26 dealers per thousand metric tons and 2.32 dealers per thousand hectares are roughly acceptable levels of dealer concentration to provide close to a reasonably competitive market. In fact, in the states of Kelantan and Trengganu, where production is more scattered, the number of dealers per thousand metric tons and hectares is also relatively larger. This is before taking into consideration the sizeable number of unlicensed buyers.[29] Their activities would make trading more competitive.

Another indication of the possible level of competition is the amount of excess capacity existing in different locales. Substantial excess smoking facilities seemed to exist in all states except Kelantan and Malacca, as measured by the ratio of capacity to production: Johor 138.3 per cent, Trengganu 141.2 per cent, Kedah 156.5 per cent and Selangor as high as 163.6 per cent.[30]

The level of net turnover reported for rubber in the central area in Table 6.18(c) is consistent with that reported by Lim and provides an independent check. The major difference is that the figures in Table 6.18(c) include both first- and middle-level dealers while Lim dealt with only the first-level dealers in Selangor. Many features observed by Lim and Cheam can also be observed here.

A curious feature to note is that of all the regions, the central-north had the lowest net to gross turnover ratio and net turnover, only $1,370 for those without accounts, in contrast to the ratios for the less developed and more remote northern and eastern regions, which are the two highest. A possible explanation is that the relatively larger number of dealers in the northern and eastern regions bid down on the volume each handled, giving rise to lower absolute average gross and net turnover. However, their smaller volume also demanded a higher margin to sustain their business which was probably facilitated by a higher proportion of unsmoked sheets produced. Incidentally, these regions have proportionately more Malay dealers, though they are still in the minority.

(*iii*) *Credit Provision.* Turning to the question of whether the provision of credit and other facilities assisted the dealers in spreading their monopolistic hold, Lim claimed:

> . . . the provision of loans, whether in cash or in kind, with smoking and processing facilities did not significantly influence the marketing margins. There was some evidence, however, that those dealers who were also grocers might have had a 'hold' over smallholders selling Unsmoked Sheets only, in that prices somewhat below the average were paid for such rubber. It should be noted that the dealer-grocers usually have much smaller businesses than dealers without provision shops. The evidence gathered suggests that the combination of dealer and grocer into one firm is economically necessary in situations where the trade volume or size of the market is small. . . . To the extent that a dealer has no guarantee that his debtors' rubber will be sold exclusively to him, the market cannot really be considered to be restricted by dealers' money-lending and other activities.[31]

(*iv*) *Other Factors.* Lim also evaluated other factors affecting market competition. The spread of price information is adequate because of the daily broadcasts by Radio Malaysia in local languages. Many smallholders sell regularly to one dealer mainly for 'convenience' and 'friendly relations' and they get relatively higher prices and a consistent moisture content deduction.[32] The last point is important since moisture content is evaluated visually, leaving room for manipulation by the dealers. A consistent deduction with relatively higher prices probably implies a consistent and relatively fair criterion of evaluation as opposed to an arbitrary and excessive one.

(*v*) *Profit-cum-Income Level.* It is possible to estimate the range of the shareholders' share of the rubber dealers by netting out the estimated wage, interest, and rent payments. On the average, these dealers hired 1.5 workers per establishment, necessitating a wage payment of $3,800 per establishment.[33] Most of them rented their premises at $600 per year[34] and since the average credit extended per dealer was $6,450, with 37 per cent bad debt, it is fair to assume that they needed at least that amount plus their monthly purchase as working capital, giving rise to an interest payment of $4,600.[35] Taking all these costs into consideration, the average shareholders' share for the rubber dealers in West Malaysia worked out to $20,616 each per year.[36] This was the average for all the rubber dealers, and maybe for some of the packers-exporters as well. If Lim's tabulation of the profit of the first-level dealers in Selangor is any guide, only a very small number of big first-level dealers could obtain a gross profit of this magnitude. This will then imply that the overall surpluses of the middle-level dealers could be quite large (greater than $25,000 on the average) compared with the first-level dealers and smallholders, but still small when compared with the large companies discussed in Chapters 5 and 6.

(c) FISH

From Table 6.17(b), the net to gross turnover ratio as well as the net turnover for the fish retailers were very modest. In particular, the East Coast fish retailers received a net turnover averaging only $333! At any rate, the average for 3,494 of the 3,685 (98 per cent) fish retailers was only $1,181. After deducting wages (an average of one worker for every six establishments), their income would have been below $1,000. The fish wholesalers, of course, operated at a different level. Their average net turnover was $24,281 and after deducting $4,200 for labour costs, $2,400 for interest, and perhaps some rent,[37] their shareholders' share was about $17,000 a year each. This is a comfortable income but not overwhelmingly huge. The net to gross turnover ratio was about 9 per cent, a margin not higher than that of other middlemen. Thus, the wholesalers achieved higher returns as a result of a larger volume of business.

On the question of the density of middlemen dealing with the fishermen, Munro and Chee, Elliston, and Ooi all came away with the conclusion that the fishermen were not bound to sell and deal with particular middlemen within the same village.[38]

Munro and Chee further raised an interesting point by arguing that if profit maximization is the goal, collusion becomes much less plausible. They show this by formulating the relation between the margin and volume which the middlemen face and proving that the reduction of net margin will raise profit because the percentage fall in net margin is less than the percentage rise in quantity.[39]

(d) RICE

The wide range in performance of the rice wholesalers as indicated by Table 6.18(b) makes it more difficult to arrive at any generalization about them. The figures show that their profit was generally one level above that of the fish and even rubber wholesalers, again the only exceptions being those from the East Coast. The relationships among the rice wholesalers, the provisions shops, and the rice millers are not well established. The data provided in Table 6.18(b) have been furnished as a matter of record to facilitate future study, but are insufficient to obtain any clear conclusion. Hence, unlike the case of the rubber dealers, it is difficult to form any hypothesis about their role in the exploitation of the padi farmers and/or customers.

(e) FRUIT AND VEGETABLES

The one business among those dealing with rural produce which was clearly exploitative of the producers was the fruit and vegetable sector. From Table 6.18, one can see that their net to gross turnover ratio exceeded 10 per cent, and for retailers in the central region, reached levels as high as 16.8 per cent. This is consistent with evidence claiming that the vegetable retailers' and wholesalers' profit margin as a percentage of final consumer price was over 40 per cent and 10 per cent respectively.[40] Ironically, both the vegetable farmers and middlemen are mainly ethnic Chinese. The most serious middleman exploitation documented from our discussion so far is not one between non-Malay middlemen and Malay farmers but between non-Malay middlemen and non-Malay farmers! Of course as the number of non-Malay vegetable farmers is much smaller compared with the Malay padi farmers and rubber smallholders, less importance has been attached to them. However, one should keep in mind that many of the new villagers are vegetable farmers when circumstances permit, and the Third Malaysia Plan has in fact identified the new villagers as one group with high unemployment and living in poverty.[41]

C. Conclusion

All in all, from the preceding discussion, it is felt that the level of competitiveness was not too unreasonable in most of the trading areas, the major exception being vegetable trading. Another possible area of unsatisfactory marketing arrangements was identified by Lim and Cheam as trading in rubber in the form of unsmoked sheets. But by raising some important points they have missed out, we have raised some doubts about their conclusion. The presence of a high margin in the case of the unsmoked sheets, especially in remote areas, is not necessarily an indication of the lack of competitiveness. On the contrary, once the whole marketing structure is taken into account, the high margin usually charged by the smaller dealers can be seen to be the result of fierce competition driving down the trading volume which in turn necessitates the presence of a higher margin in those areas and with those customers that they have some power to affect. As such, encouraging more competition may not be the solution to the problem. We will attempt to clarify this situation in the last part of this chapter.

7.3 GENERAL STRUCTURE OF MARKET DISTRIBUTION

A. Introduction

The evidence amassed so far suggests a very important question: if the lower-level middlemen (the provisions shops, first-level rubber dealers, etc.) charge a higher margin than their higher-level equivalents (the middle-level dealers, the exporters, importers, and agency houses), why is it that they receive a smaller average absolute surplus and thus profit and income? The answer implied throughout this chapter is that they cater to a small community and hence have a very modest trade volume. The high margin is not adequate to overcome the small volume of trade in order to give the grassroots-level middlemen a high level of income. On the other hand, the wholesalers, the agency houses and the like can operate on a smaller margin but still come up with very hefty profits because of a high trade volume.

This contrast in performance by the big and small trading units poses some very interesting and important questions. What gives rise to this polarization in trading characteristics, and who sets the margin and/or determines the sales volume at the different levels? Who are the really exploitative middlemen in the system: the small middlemen with high margin but low income, or the wholesalers with small margin but high income, or both? If it is both, who should shoulder the greater part of the blame of exploitation? Can this question be answered independently or must it be tied to the issue of who sets the margin?

While it may not be possible to document a very detailed answer here, it is possible to offer some insights which may suggest directions for future research.

One obvious answer is the way in which the distribution system has been set up. The many handlings necessitated by the system mean that there is bound to be a large gap between the manufacturer outlet price and the final consumer price and, analogously, between the price received by the smallholder and the exported price. Each additional handling implies one more cost to be maintained and one more profit margin to be made by the handler. As a result, even if the margin at each level is modest, the summation of all the cost and profit margins at the different levels results in a total increment in price (faced by the local consumers) or reduction in price (faced by the small producers) that is quite substantial.

Stead, in his general report on the Malayan fishing industry, is one of the few who recognize this possibility. He wrote in 1955:

> . . . The fact is that there is very large margin between the price paid to the fishermen and that price charged to the ultimate consumers. This is largely due to the many handlings which the product receives. . . .
> . . . It is therefore not necessary to argue any great profit on the part of any particular agent to see how the many handlings may cause the price that the consumers will have to pay to mount higher and higher.[42]

Although there are several studies on the marketing structure of Malaysia at the industry level, there is, as yet, no study that pieces them together into an overall picture of the marketing structure for the country. Lee (1974) writing on historical Singapore, Puthucheary (1960) on the agency houses, and Huang (1971) on the Malaysian Chinese are some attempts in this direction. The main drawbacks of these studies are that they have not studied the whole economy as a unit, how the economy has been tied up with foreign interests which have been oligopolistic in their own fields world-wide, how such ties may in turn dictate the system of distribution and wealth-holding in the economy, and how the terms of trade and hence the livelihood of the people are determined as a result of such a system.

B. The Structure of Market Distribution

The system of distribution is a pyramidal structure with the largest wholesaler (he is usually the importer-exporter as well) sitting on top of the pyramid.

Beneath him are several layers of different-sized middlemen. At the village level, the general provisions stores sell food and general consumer items and purchase some agricultural produce from the farmers: credit is offered out of necessity[43] and as a lubricant to the system. The provisions store procures its supplies from the retailer and/or wholesaler at the next level up, with some credit (usually short-term and at high interest) and may also sell the farm produce to him. This is usually a trader located in the semi-urban, semi-rural towns. These traders in turn purchase from several urban large retailers and/or wholesalers, each specializing in the importing or distribution of a particular line or lines of products. Again, they would provide some short-term trade credit.[44] These may or may not be the ultimate sources of the products in this country, as there may be a sole importer of a product or a sole distributor on behalf of a manufacturer that these wholesalers have to deal with.[45]

The basic price of any item is usually set at the level of the import price according to some 'international' price or cost-plus basis if it is from a domestic producer. Frequently, the wholesaler constrains his retailers to sell the products at a fixed price or allows only a small percentage of increase in price. However, when it comes down to the village level, 'price control' may or may not be in force. The village provisions stores are subjected instead to other competitive and financial constraints. As they have to accept the price set and the shorter-term credit provided by the next level of dealer as well as pay out high interest, they themselves are being exploited by the next level of dealers, resulting in modest income and fairly frugal living standards. It is difficult to imagine that the present Government or some other distribution agents can offer comparable services at a lower cost.[46]

Another frequent mistake is to assume that the merchants (foreign and local) sitting on top of the pyramid are just traders. While they may have started out as traders, they usually or almost inevitably build up a conglomerate with interests in manufacturing, trading, finance, and possibly in property development. This is essentially the point highlighted by the charts in Chapter 5. This system has emerged from historical roots: the agency houses have evolved over the years to become the chief representatives of the foreign interests in Malaysia.

Puthucheary, using data based mainly on information of the late thirties and forties, is the only one so far who has investigated this. His study outlined, in a very limited way, how the agency houses sat at the apex of the pyramid with their links to British financial interests,[47] and their ability to dominate a wide range of activities from the export of raw materials to the import of consumer and producer goods, to the provision of infrastructure services such as insurance and shipping. These themselves are, however, middleman activities by nature.

The question that arises is—can these activities really be carried out independently of the manufacturing and/or financial interest in the imperial country involved in the production of the commodities and the procurement of the raw materials?

It is impractical for us to explore here the full details of this link but some examples of such links are selected for discussion.

(a) THE BRITISH CONNECTION

The most interesting aspect of Chart 7.1 is that two of the three major tin-mining agency houses are linked to the same very important international mining group (Anglo-American Group of South Africa), while two of the five major planting agency houses and three other major general agency houses are linked to four of the five most important British banking interests.[48] The fourth major planting agency house, Guthrie, is also part of a British industrial and commercial conglomerate. While it may be far-fetched at this point to claim on the basis of so few details that the agency houses have always been, in part, the tools of major British business interests in penetrating and controlling Malaysia, such linkages are too important to be treated as mere coincidences. At the very least, Chart 7.1 justifies further research into the international linkages and hence the real source of strength and control of the agency houses.

The connection between the groups controlling mining operations in Malaysia with the major international financial interests is particularly impressive. It is well documented that the Lloyd-supported Patino interest held an overwhelming position in the world's tin mining and smelting activities with their ownership and control of London Tin and Eastern Smelting (about 30 per cent of world capacity) among other tin interests throughout the world.[49] Even after its curious withdrawal from London Tin and hence Malaysian tin mining activities it retained its strong control of the world smelting industry. Charter Consolidated, already itself a major force in tin mining, enhanced greatly its control and access to the world supply of tin through its merger-joint take-over of London Tin with Pernas. It too has impressive 'credentials'. To quote the London Stock Exchange *Official Yearbook 1975*, Charter Consolidated's principal shareholder, the Anglo-American Corporation of South Africa, is: 'Largely interested in South Africa gold mining companies, Zambian copper undertakings, the diamond industry, finance and investment companies and in coal mining and industrial enterprises in South Africa and elsewhere'.[50] It is the most important mining and industrial concern in southern Africa and is probably one of the most important mining conglomerates in the world.

Chart 7.2 is a summary of the major British industrial interests which have established themselves in Malaysia between the two World Wars and prior to Independence. Each is a major force in its own field in the United Kingdom, if not in Europe or the world as well. It is difficult to imagine that local businessmen, and especially the small retailers and middlemen, are indeed in a position to challenge the pricing and marketing set-up of such conglomerate giants.[51]

It is perhaps possible to speculate about the stages of British economic penetration of the Malaysian economy. Initially, the commercial arms of the British trading and industrial interests came East with the setting up of the agency houses. They took advantage of local acquaintances to push for British control of the mining sector and subsequently the plantation sector. Their domination ensured British industrial interest in the procurement of raw materials and disbursement of industrial products.[52] In this manner the agency houses rose to the apex of the Malaysian marketing pyramid. Subsequently,

CHART 7.1
THE LINKAGES OF THE AGENCY HOUSES WITH THE MAJOR BRITISH INTERESTS

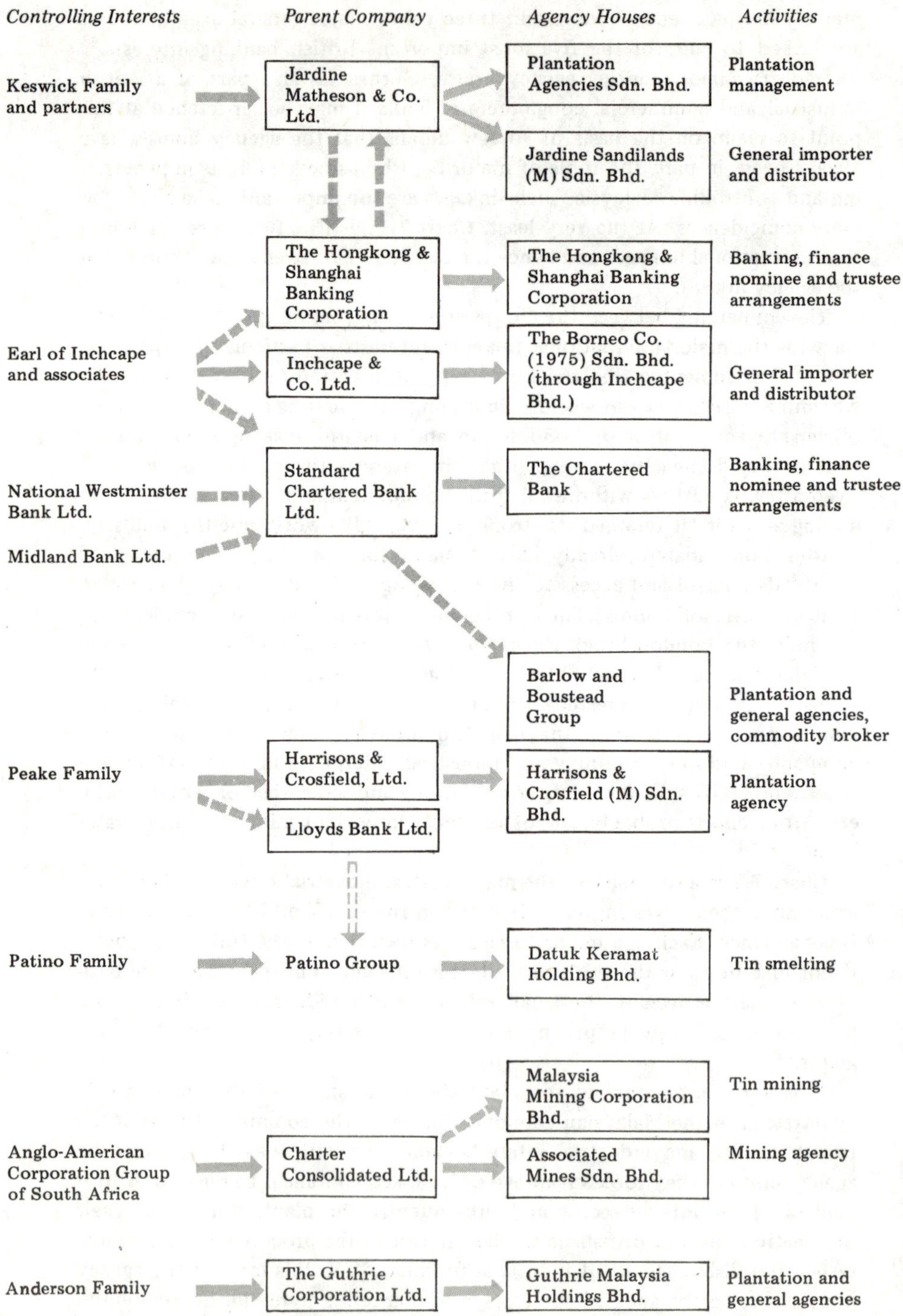

CHART 7.1 (Continued)

Controlling interest

Minority interest or represented on board

Financial ties

Sources. Stock Exchange of London, *The Stock Exchange Official Yearbook 1975–76*; *Jane's Major Companies of Europe*, 1974.

Note. (1) Linkages in this figure are based primarily on reported shareholdings whenever possible. However, in the absence of such information, the interlocking of directorates is used as a criterion. The latter is done with as much care as possible and fully explained in the following notes.

(2) The Hongkong and Shanghai Banking Corporation (HSBC) is probably the most difficult business organization to trace the origins of ownership and control given the nature of Hong Kong's corporate disclosure law. However, it is a fact that it and Jardine Matheson (J–M) hold significant minority shareholdings in one another, which explains the mutual appointment of directors (for example, on J–M board). In other cases, Pao's group of shipping companies, by HSBC's own report, is the largest single group of debtors of the Bank, and the Bank in turn is the largest shareholder in some of Pao's companies, which is clearly why Pao has been appointed to the Board. It is not known how much shareholdings the Bank has in Hutchison International (HI) and Wheelock Marden (W–M). Though all the evidence points to a traditionally close relation, recent difficulties suffered by the two companies have resulted in HSBC becoming the overt largest shareholder of HI and bidding for overt take-over of W–M (see *Far Eastern Economic Review*, 5 November 1976). Therefore, it is hardly surprising that the chairmen of both companies sit on the Bank's board. As a result of such observations, it is not far-fetched to speculate that the Inchcape group is closely tied up with the Bank as well since there is an Inchcape director on HSBC's board (or is it vice-versa?). Moreover, the close ties between W–M and Inchcape can be seen from the fact that W–M's Malaysia and Singapore operations merged with other units of Inchcape Bhd. to form the enlarged Inchcape's Malaysian and Singapore operations.

(3) The connection of the Inchcape group with Standard and Chartered has also been established by the same procedure. While they are not one of the three largest shareholders, the appointment of two Inchcape directors on a board of thirteen is certainly a clear indication of their influence within the group.

(4) The Peake family is probably the most important shareholder in Harrisons and Crosfield as there have always been at least two Peakes on the board of H & C. Besides, H. O. Peake has been made the life President of H & C, which is very unusual if he is only a hired executive. The connection of this group with Lloyds Bank came about with Peake sitting on the board of Lloyds as well.

(5) The Patino connection with Lloyds has been updated by Pacific Imperialist Notebook, May 1976. The data there have been cross-checked by this author looking at the *London Stock Exchange Handbook*, 1975, and the *Singapore Stock Exchange Handbook*, 1975.

CHART 7.2
LINKAGES OF NEWER BRITISH INVESTMENT IN MALAYSIA WITH THE MAJOR BRITISH INDUSTRIAL INTERESTS

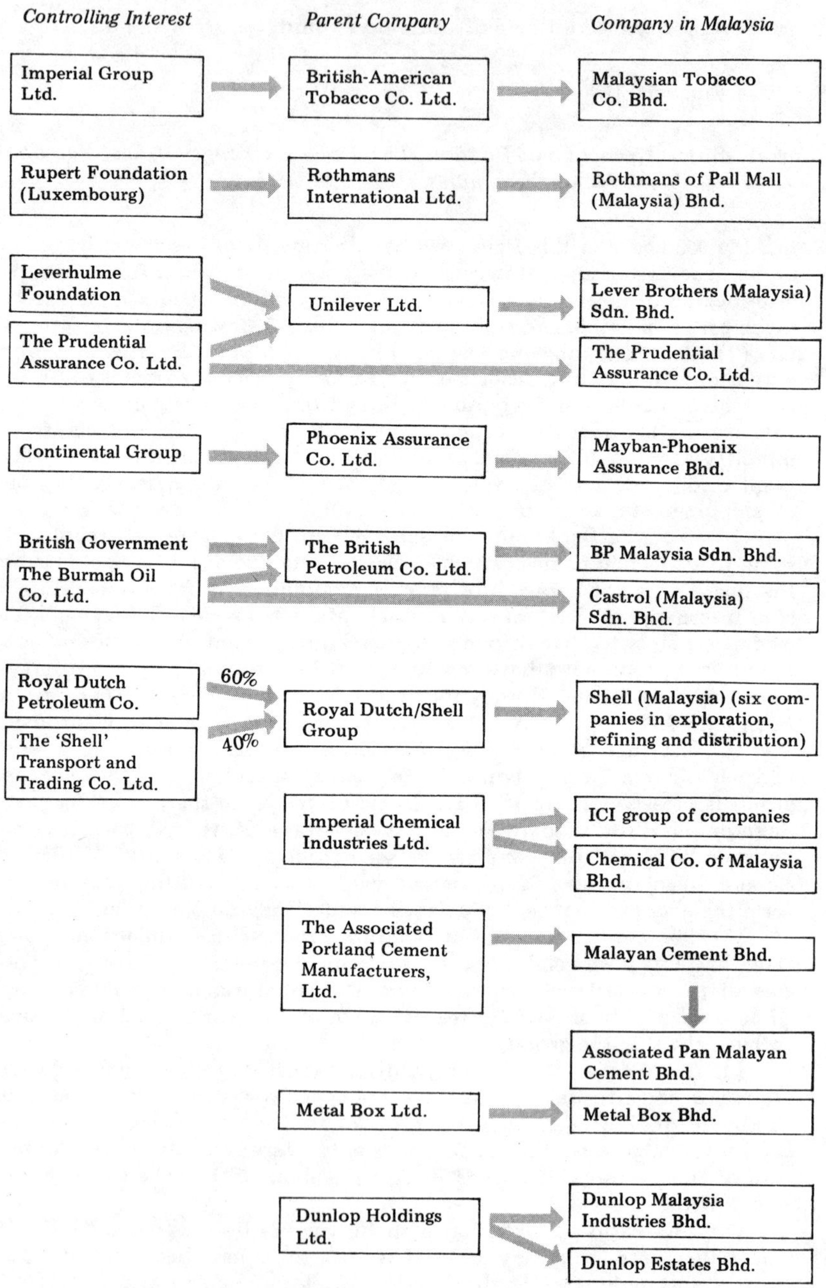

Sources. Stock Exchange of London, *The Stock Exchange Official Yearbook 1975–76*; Stock Exchange of Singapore, *Company Handbook*, 1975; *Jane's Major Companies of Europe, 1974*.

when local demand rose to a significant level, the agency houses were in an excellent position to set up manufacturing concerns, which they did.[53] Meanwhile, some of the industrial interests also decided to manufacture locally themselves, accounting for the movement by the companies listed in Chart 7.2 and others to set up factories in Malaysia.

So long as the parent companies were important forces in the United Kingdom and the British capital most influential in the world economy in general, none, or very few, outside business interests could penetrate into the Malaysian economy. This explains the relative lack of American or Japanese interest in Malaysia until after Independence.[54]

Our intention here is not, of course, to create the impression that there is only one single pyramid structure for the whole economy. There are probably many—at the very least there is one European and one Chinese structure. There are also probably different pyramid structures for each major sector with substantial ties at the top level,[55] and some degree of interwoven relationship at each level, all coming together to form one complex but definable major pyramid.

(b) THE LOCAL MARKETING PYRAMIDS

It is a well-documented fact that the Chinese in the Straits Settlements financed and controlled the early spice-planting and mining activities in Peninsular Malaya.[56] Their established position as holders of capital through years of trading activities in this area, their ties with the Malay Rajas,[57] their ability to ensure and control a steady and cheap supply of labour[58] through their interests in shipping and connections with secret societies' leadership were the basis of their business penetration.

These initial favourable factors gave the Chinese in the Straits Settlements the necessary counterweights to the early British challenge, and enabled them to dominate the first stage of the Malayan tin industry.[59]

Competition between Chinese and European economic interests, where their pyramids have extended into the same sectors, has been very intense at times. The groups representing British interests who held (and hold) the credit line, the source of supplies, marketing outlets, and more advanced technology and business organization were able eventually to win supremacy in the twentieth century with the help of systematic Colonial Government efforts at strengthening the position of the European capitalists by eroding Chinese control over labour and by enacting all kinds of regulations unfavourable for the Asians.[60] The economic supremacy of the major business conglomerates has been largely maintained to this day.

The Chinese in the Straits Settlements were not annihilated but lost their supremacy. They continued to possess the capital and some sources of supply, the marketing outlets, and the control of labour which gave them the basis to play a complementary role at the middle and lower level of the main pyramid, as well as to sit at the apex of some individual industrial or trade pyramids. This picture continued until Independence after which the Chinese businessmen were able to regain some of their roles in the structure. Since the late sixties, the Malay politician-bureaucrats have also increased their participation (see Chapters 5 and 6).

CHART 7.3
THE MARKETING PYRAMID OF MALAYSIAN ECONOMIC ACTIVITIES

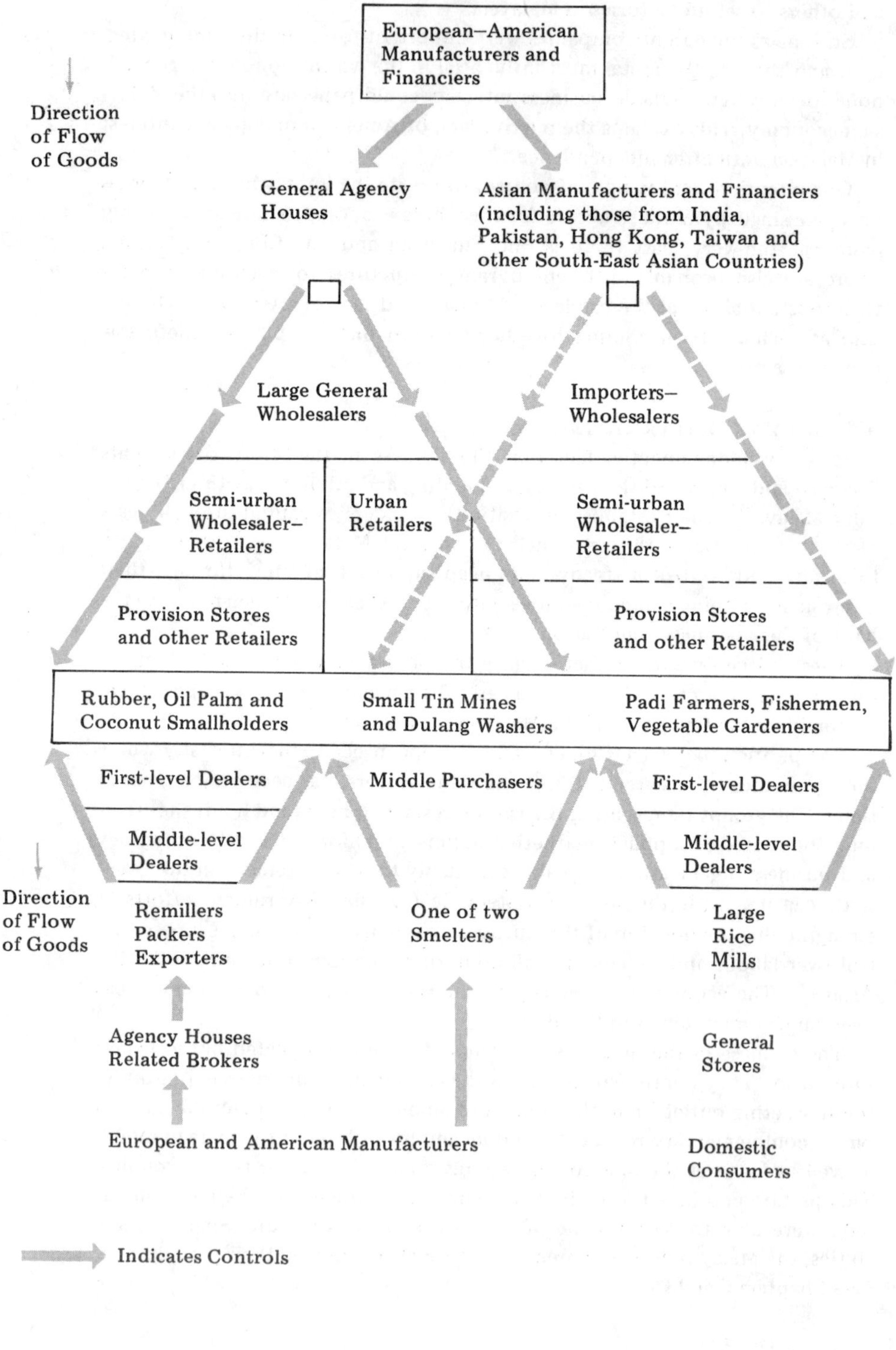

CHART 7.4
PRESENT MARKETING CHANNEL FOR SMALLHOLDERS' RUBBER

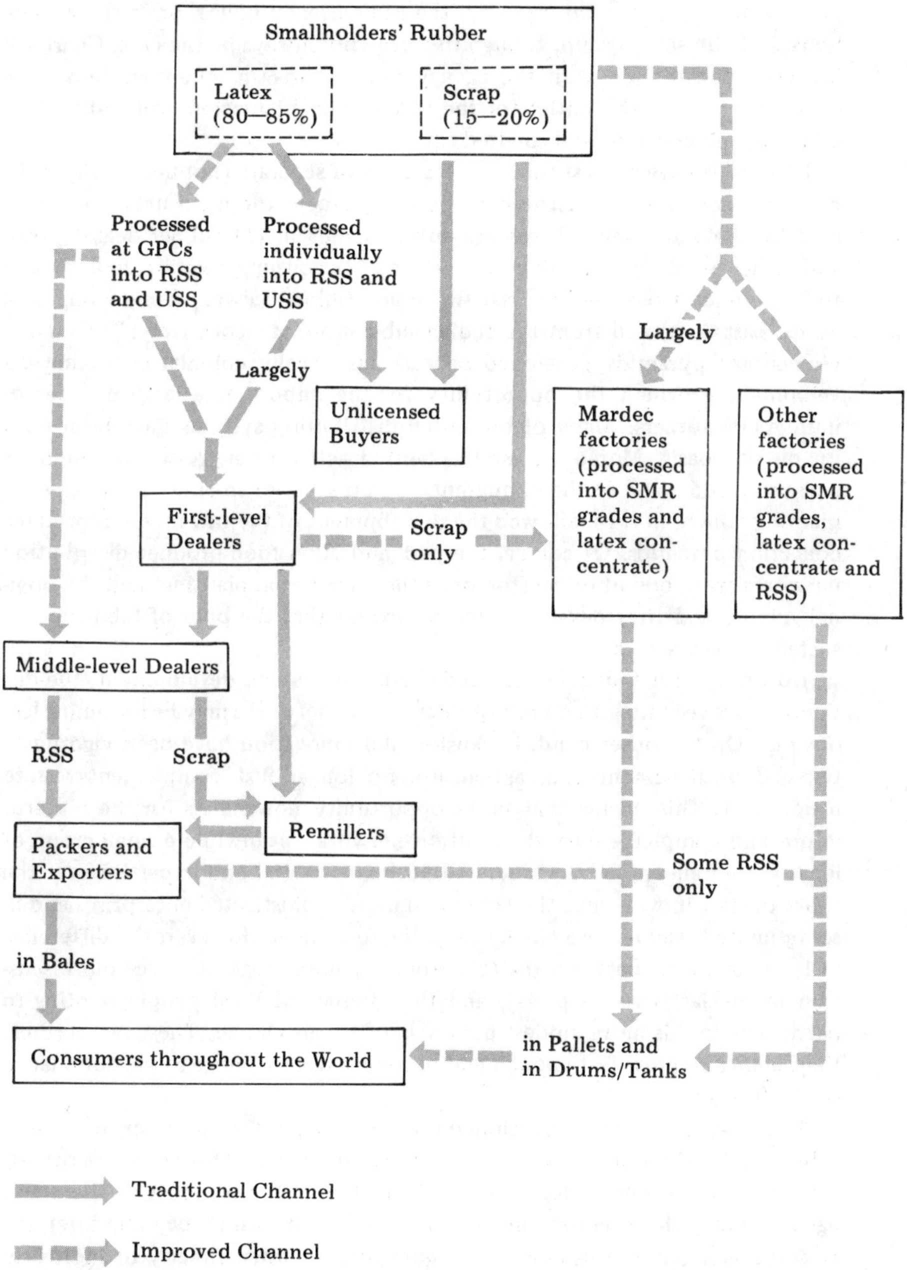

Source. Lim Sow Ching, 'Marketing of Rubber by Smallholders in Peninsular Malaysia', in UN, *Economic Bulletin for Asia & the Pacific*, Vol. XXVI, No. 2/3, 9/12/75, p. 60.

Chart 7.3 illustrates a possible modern scenario of the interaction and organization of the main marketing pyramids while Chart 7.4 is the specific example for the rubber marketing structure.

It is important to recognize that in many instances the importing and exporting apexes may converge with the same agency house, or in the agency houses of the same group, though this need not always be the case. Chart 7.3 has been constructed with the agency houses directing the main importing channel as well as the outlet for the three major plantation crops of rubber, oil palm, and coconut, and smelted tin ores.

The locals have at least four broad groups of separate (not necessarily independent) networks of distribution to complement the main network organized by the Europeans. These are sub-pyramids in (1) rubber dealing, padi and other rural food produce collection, (2) consumer goods, and general food produce from the Far East (including China, Taiwan, Hong Kong, and South-East Asia) and from the Indian sub-continent respectively. These complementary pyramids developed because historically colonial economic development provided the opportunity for the import of a large number of immigrant workers. Many of the initial distribution systems have been built up on this basis. Moreover, estate planting activities suggested to the local peasantry and some of the immigrants the prospect of smallholding cash-crop planting which, in turn, allowed the development of the raw material produce collection pyramids. Of course, the padi and other food-produce distribution networks were bound to develop once these cash-crop plantings and the original mining activities developed to the extent that the pool of labour could sustain these markets.

However, with Independence and further economic development, the distinction between major and minor distribution networks may be becoming less obvious. On the other hand, expansion and innovation have been vigorously pursued until smallholding agriculture no longer just complements estate production. This means that more opportunity now exists for the hitherto minor and complementary distribution network. Meanwhile a small group of local entrepreneurs has accumulated adequate capital and expertise over the years to start moving into the larger and more sophisticated enterprises and in some limited way poses a challenge to the foreigners. However, the difference in levels of profit between the two groups is quite substantial (see our discussion in the last two chapters), and the number of local people wanting to participate in this more modest pool of profit is also larger. These factors limit their ability to grow fast enough and become a real challenge to the dominance of the foreigners.

It has been previously mentioned that credit plays the all-important role of lubricant for these distribution networks or pyramids. This enhances the significance of the impression portrayed in Chart 7.1: that most of the major agency houses have close connections with major British banking interests. Unfortunately, how this convenient coincidence either directly or indirectly facilitates the setting up of the distribution pyramid has not been researched in detail.

Actually, there is one other small but important group of business interests in the rural production activities. This is the group of Chettiar money-lenders who were and still are probably the major suppliers of larger amounts of credit to the peasantry and smaller estate planters. They, unlike the other non-Malay middlemen, should not be considered local as the initial capital was brought in from South Indian-based Chettiar firms[61] and they probably are also the source of the fairly large repatriation of money to India. Very little work has been done on their exact role, Kratoska (1975) being the only exception. Therefore, it is very difficult to construct their exact place in this system and that task will be left for a later effort.

7.4 CONCLUSION

In this chapter, substantial effort has been put into investigating the validity of the charge that the provisions stores and rural produce purchasers are highly exploitative monopolistic-monopsonistic middlemen. This was done by documenting the ease of entry, the marketing margin, the presence of alternative suppliers and buyers and other trade practices. In each case, we found that competition was frequently quite keen. However, they did charge a fairly high margin. Despite that, the profit and consequently income of the majority of the middlemen (especially those who come into contact with the small producers/ purchasers) were modest, being generally at a level little higher than the income of the villagers with whom they conducted the transactions. While the 10 per cent or so margin could only provide them with a modest income, it was already a burden to the poor villagers. In that sense there was exploitation. Yet the problem of exploitation is not so simple, and the usual stereotype that middlemen exploit rural producers has to be more carefully analysed.

In reality, there are many levels of middlemen. Section 7.4 outlines the multi-tier marketing system in this country. That is one of the major reasons for the unfavourable prices faced by the villagers. The many handlings necessitated by the distribution system means that many deductions have to be made to support the cost of each handling. Though the margin at each level is frequently modest, the summation of all handling costs is quite substantial. Moreover, the lower the level, the smaller is the volume handled, and this requires a higher margin.

A second and particularly important point in stressing the multi-tier distribution system is the difference in control or economic power of the different levels. It is the marketing structure as a whole that makes it inevitable that there is a large gap between the income of the rural farmer and the prices he should be getting. We can document an obvious difference between traders most in contact with rural producers and those with international links at the top of the pyramid. The point is that the lower-level middlemen really have little freedom in dictating the price, as they are tied by their supplier/purchaser price, the number of their customers, as well as the credit and other binding factors imposed on them by the next-level dealer.

The higher one moves up the pyramid, the more flexibility one has. This is because of the size of one's market, the range of customers, the relatively more oligopolistic condition. Ultimately, at the top of the pyramid, the agency houses/wholesalers/mining companies and so on have been shown to have very strong ties with the important industrial and financial conglomerates in Europe.

In the case of tin, for example, the controlling group sitting on top easily controls close to 50 per cent of world output. While it still has to bargain with the major users to reach a price level mutually satisfactory, the control of such a large proportion of a material must enhance tremendously one's bargaining power. Indeed, in the notes to Section 7.4, a preliminary attempt was made to document how such oligopolistic positions have facilitated the arm-twisting process in the international cartels set-up and the consideration of minimum or maximum prices for particular commodities.[62]

Another significant consideration is the role played by credit in the distribution system. Little effort has been made to document its importance, except for some cursory inquiry in the notes. Nevertheless, it is important to point out the bargaining power of the large wholesalers/importers/exporters in using a combination of the threat of credit reduction and the bait of more credit, suspension/provision of dealerships, the addition/deletion of new agents to determine the size of market, and hence margin and profit each level of agent in each locality faces. By contrast, this is not within the realm of control of the smaller middlemen.

In short, the higher up the pyramid, the greater is the possibility of price-fixing and control, the greater is the flexibility in helping to construct the distribution channel, and the greater is the overall level of profit and income.

Unfortunately, to the average rural farmer, the realities of the multi-tier distribution system are not easily visible. Naturally, the mechanism of price-fixing and the seat of economic power are even more obscure. It is thus hardly surprising that he sees the one closest to him—the provisions store or the first-level dealer—as the exploiter, even if he observes that the latter's livelihood is not all that much better. It is when the social scientists and politicians fail, or choose not, to see the real roots of the problem and instead propagate the simplistic, stereotype view of middleman exploitation, highlighting in particular its racial aspect, that the whole issue becomes even more clouded.

1. '. . . It was emphasized by officials to peasants that Chinese middlemen producers were responsible for their poverty, and appeals were made to peasant racial loyalties to eliminate this class of trader.' Lim Teck Ghee, 'Peasant Agriculture in Colonial Malaya', pp. 238—9, citing from his research into the files of colonial records, specifically Monthly Report Lower Perak, September 1898, and Perak Government Gazette, 1893.

2. Ungku Abdul Aziz, 'The Interdependent Development of Agriculture and Other Industries', paper presented at the Tenth Conference of Agricultural Economists, reprinted in *Malayan Economic Review*, 4, 1959, p. 25.

3. Munro and Chee, 'Fishermen and Fishing Development in Penang and Kedah', p. 80. The authors, however, do not subscribe to this view.

4. For example, Gamba in his paper on savings and indebtedness claimed: '. . . The shopkeeper-cum-moneylender, and the merchant agent, took advantage of the cash needs of the native producer, and granted him loans at exorbitant rates of interest—interest to be repaid in cash or in kind. . . . The lender saw to it that the debt was difficult of redemption, so that eventually he came

to have monopoly powers over the disposal of the produce and over the cultivator's land and even over his chattels' (p. 44).

He went on to construct a hypothetical case of *padi kuncha* (i.e., credit for future padi arrangement) and presented a gross profit of $700 on a promised loan of $1,400 disbursed throughout the year. This is based on an assumed interest rate of 100 per cent on loans over an eight-month period (p. 45). While the paper in general provided a good summary of the various modes of saving and lending arrangements among the rural and urban poor, the particular example is clearly a misrepresentation of the typical case from the materials presented in this thesis. First of all, the average indebtedness reported by the various padi farm surveys seldom amounts to over $500, let alone $1,400. Secondly, the typical turnover and income of the shopkeepers are simply not high enough to sustain single loans of such magnitude. Their level of income and profit would also be many times higher if they could make a single-loan profit of $700 rather than the estimated $3,000 per year.

C. Gamba, 'Poverty and Some Socio-Economic Aspects of Hoarding, Saving and Borrowing in Malaya', *Malayan Economic Review*, 3, October 1958, pp. 33—62. It is also possible to quote substantially from others.

5. For example, C. R. Wharton, 'Marketing, Merchandising and Money Lending: A Note on Middlemen Monopoly in Malaya', *Malayan Economic Review*, 7 (October 1962).

6. In Selangor and Malacca, provision stores provided 61.6 per cent and 64.2 per cent of total loans respectively, amounting to $350.7 and $617.9, almost all in kind (see Narkswasdi and Selvadurai, *Economic Survey of Padi Production in West Malaysia*). In Kelantan, they provided 22.9 per cent (Selvadurai, Ani Arope and Nik Hassan, *Socio-Economic Study of Padi Farms on the Kemubu Area of Kelantan, 1968*) and in Province Wellesley, 29.6 per cent, mainly in kind (Selvadurai and Ani Arope, *Padi Farms in Province Wellesley, 1968*). In Kedah, they provided twenty-one surveyed households with an average of $269 per household or 31.1 per cent of total credit (Barnard, 'Organisation of Production in a Kedah Rice Farming Village').

7. Selvadurai, *Padi Farming in West Malaysia*, p. 119, claimed that interest is as high as 60 per cent but provides no substantiation for this claim. Bailey and Carter, pp. 8—9, describe the system of credit provision by the shops, claiming that the interest rate ranges from 30 to 200 per cent. They estimated the no-profit cost of credit lending by the co-operative societies to be about 50 per cent, not allowing for bad debts. However, shops provide better services such as spot credit and consumption credit (consumption credit is rather important, see Kuchiba and Tsubouchi, 'A Padi Farming Community in Kedah, Malaysia'. See also Kratoska, *The Chettiar and the Yeoman . . .*, pp. 14—15.

8. Barnard, op. cit., pp. 109—11.

9. N. Maeda, *Economic Activity among the Orang Hulu*, pp. 52—3.

10. FAO–IBRD Programme, *The Muda Survey—A First Report*, Tables 72 and 73.

11. The capital requirement is probably the fund for stocking up one or two months' turnover worth of merchandise, probably about $2,500, judging from the turnover reported in the last chapter.

12. There is no direct evidence for this, but one can infer it from the case of the hawkers reported in Chapter 4, although the unemployed may not find it so easy to enter the field, as the capital requirement for entrance is higher for provision stores than for hawking.

13. Net turnover in this case is a fairly close approximate to profit because other costs are relatively small.

14. The 4¢ per *gantang* price differential and the amount of marketed surplus (147 *gantang*) have been obtained from the Farm Economic Survey of

the Muda River Project, 1966, Table 29. Cost to the farmers of this price differential = 4¢ × 147 *gantang*.

15. Narkswasdi and Selvadurai, op. cit., pp. 238—9, 308.

16. Selvadurai, op. cit., on Province Wellesley, Table L, p. 69; Selvadurai, Ani Arope and Nik Hassan, op. cit., p. 100.

17. Lim Sow Ching, *A Study of the Marketing of Smallholders' Rubber at the First Level in Selangor*, Table 13, p. 28, and Table 19, p. 34.

18. ibid., p. 28.

19. ibid., p. 36.

20. Cheam Soon Tee, *A Study of the Marketing of Smallholders' Lower Grade Rubber*, Kuala Lumpur, Rubber Research Institute, Economic Report No. 8, 1971, p. 51.

21. ibid., p. 53.

22. ibid., pp. 66—7.

23. However, Table 7.2 does indicate one possible means by which this question of price transmission can be researched, although some care should be taken to allow for the possible existence of time lag between the fluctuation of the marketing margin and the fluctuation of prices, as well as other factors.

24. Lim Sow Ching, op. cit.

25. The general theory behind this line of thinking is based on Paul Sweezy, 'Demand Under Conditions of Oligopoly', *Journal of Political Economy*, XLVII, 1939, pp. 568—73.

26. Lim Sow Ching, op. cit., pp. 50—2.

27. ibid., p. 32.

28. ibid., Table 19, p. 34.

29. ibid., pp. 12—13; Cheam, op. cit., p. 10; Lim Sow Ching, 'Marketing of Rubber by Smallholders in Peninsular Malaysia', *Economic Bulletin for Asia and the Far East*, XXVI, September/December 1975, pp. 58—71, Table 4, p. 63.

30. Lim Sow Ching, *A Study of the Marketing . . .*, Table A. But of course excess capacity exists in most industries, its mere existence is not enough evidence of the existence of competition. One really has to look into how it is defined, the size of the excess capacity taken in conjunction with other factors, to decide.

31. Lim Sow Ching, 'Marketing . . .', p. 64.

32. ibid., pp. 64—5.

33. The wage payment has been worked out based on the payment reported in Table 33, p. 61 of the *Census of Distributive Trades 1966*. However, if one were to take the average monthly wage rate reported by Lim, *A Study of the Marketing . . .*, Table B in Appendix, then it will be much lower at $106 per month per person.

34. Rent payment is assumed to be $50 per month.

35. Working capital requirement is assumed to be funds for one month's turnover stock ($40,000) + $6,000 (the average credit provided per dealer), or a total of $46,000. Interest payment is 10 per cent of this.

36. Table 6.18(c) reports that the average net turnover is $29,616. This, minus the interest payment, minus the rent, minus the wage payment, works out at $20,616.

37. Three workers are assumed to be hired at the rate of $1,400 per year (wage rate is based on the industrial average as reported by the *Census of Distributive Trades 1966*). Interest payment is taken to be about 10 per cent of the monthly turnover, which is the assumed level of credit.

38. See Munro and Chee, op. cit., and their citations from Elliston and Ooi; G. R. Elliston, 'The Role of the Middlemen in the Fishing Industry in West Malaysia', *Review of Agricultural Economics*, 1, 1967, pp. 16—33; Ooi Sang Kuang, 'A Study of the Fishing Industry in Penang', unpublished B.E. graduation exercise, University of Malaya, 1970.

39. Munro and Chee, op. cit., footnote 148.

40. See for example, M. C. Agarwal, 'Marketing Margins for Malayan Cabbage', *Journal of Agricultural Economics*, XVII, May 1966.

41. *Third Malaysia Plan 1976–1980*, p. 166.

42. Stead, *General Report of the Malayan Fishing Industry*, p. 124 and p. 12.

43. This is because the income of the farmers is often seasonal and too small. Padi farmers, in particular, need credit due to the planting of one crop which brings in income only during harvesting.

44. Credit has always been the necessary ingredient in the marketing system. Swift noted that 'Lack of capital is another factor which limits the cash lending activities of the Chinese rural shopkeepers since they themselves are dependent on the town suppliers for the supply of their trading capital'. M. G. Swift, 'Capital, Saving and Credit in the Malay Peasant Economy', in R. Firth and B. S. Yamey, eds., *Capital, Saving and Credit in Peasant Society*, London, Allen and Unwin, 1964, pp. 33—56. Mokhzani bin Abdul Rahim, 'Credit in a Malay Peasant Economy', made analogous observations for the seventies. Yip, *The Development of the Tin Mining Industry of Malaya*, pp. 24—5, 89—94 discusses the credit given by Eastern Smelting and Straits Trading to the tin dealers for purchases, and on the system in earlier times. As for the early Chinese planting of agricultural products, it was also dependent on the system of credit for expansion. This is true whether it was pepper, nutmeg, or tapioca in the Straits Settlements. For example, on nutmeg planting: '. . . This extension of Chinese planting activities was undertaken by individual squatters dependent on the advances provided by the Chinese merchants and shopkeepers of Georgetown. In the first instance, the "squatter" obtained an advance to enable him to clear a small patch of land on which he began by raising "plantains, indigo, nilam and kitchen vegetables, which at once supported him and (kept) his ground clean". He also planted nutmegs. When cultivation of these began to interfere with his other activities he obtained further, larger advances from his financier in town who also provided him with provisions. . . . The rates of interest charged on the advances were therefore high, generally varying between 18—24%.' Jackson, *Planters and Speculators*, p. 109. On pp. 100 and 109, Jackson describes analogous processes for the other crops' cultivation among the new immigrants. See also Puthucheary, *Ownership and Control in the Malayan Economy*, pp. 64—6.

45. Puthucheary, *Ownership and Control in the Malayan Economy* (pp. 23 and 24), describes how the agency houses sat at the top of the distribution pyramid, and he also describes (pp. 62 and 63) the funnelling and fanning-out process in the system of distribution from the top down.

46. See for example comparison in Narkswasdi and Selvadurai, op. cit.; Kratoska, op. cit., also has a comparison of the co-operative system introduced by the government with that of the existing one. It is hard to conceive of the government hiring someone with less than a secondary education to be the officer-in-charge at the village level, yet it is also hard to conceive that any high school graduate will be willing to accept the yearly wage of $1,500 offered to employees of one of the middlemen stores (see Chapter 4). From this consideration alone, it does not appear that the overhead cost of the government-provided service would be lower than that of the middlemen.

47. Puthucheary, op. cit., pp. 56—7 and 60—6.

48. A couple of notes are necessary here. Before the joint Pernas–Charter Consolidated take-over of London Tin and then amalgamation of Malaysian operations, Anglo–Oriental and Datuk Keramat (then Eastern Smelting) were both controlled by the Patino group. The four are the Hongkong & Shanghai Bank, National Westminster Bank, Lloyds' Bank, and Midland Bank. The only absentee among the big five is Barclays.

49. Puthucheary quoting U.S. Senate Preparedness Sub-Committee's 6th Report, see Puthucheary, op. cit., pp. 86—91. For a more recent development of this, see *Fraser's Facts and Figures*, various years, in conjunction with the *Stock Exchange Handbook* of London for more up-to-date information about this interlock.

50. *Stock Exchange Handbook*, London, 1975, p. 767.

51. However, with the decline of British economic power, and the rise of Malaysian businessmen, some of the latter have been able to begin to challenge the domination of the former. Lee Loy Seng, Chang Ming Thien, Pernas, discussed in Chapter 5, are all examples of this. Nevertheless, the recent attempt by Genting Highlands to bid for the shares of one of Harrisons & Crosfield's big planting companies failed. So did later challenges to other H & C plantation companies, and Sime Darby's attempt for Guthrie.

52. There has not been any solid evidence or documentation, though one indication of this is the list of sole agency arrangements made by the agency houses.

53. For example, Sime Darby, Inchcape, Harper Gilfillan, all went into substantial manufacturing activities.

54. There was some Japanese investment in rubber estates and iron ore mining. See Yuen Choy Leng, 'Japanese Rubber and Iron Investment in Malaya 1900–41', *Journal of South East Asian Studies*, March 1974, pp. 102—14. Other than that, there was no significant foreign participation in the economy with the exception of several American, French, and Dutch plantations. Following Independence, the Americans and Japanese have moved into the manufacturing sector and the financial sector.

55. While the Chinese planting system in the nineteenth and twentieth centuries was independent of the European planters *per se*, the economic system they operated under was not independent. It could not be as there was no independent marketing outlet and almost all products were sold to the European market. This led Jackson to remark: '. . . The production of these crops put the Chinese planters at the mercy of the economic situation in Europe. Prices fluctuated noticeably during the nineteenth century producing immediate responses among the Chinese planters . . .'. Jackson, op. cit., p. 6. This ultimate dependence greatly affected the system and structure of the Malayan economy. The system and its dynamics were topics of great concern to Huang, *An Introductory Exposition into the Social History of the Malayan Chinese*, and Lee Poh Ping, 'Chinese Society in Nineteenth and Early Twentieth Century Singapore: A Socioeconomic Analysis', Ph.D. dissertation, Cornell University, 1974, especially pp. 56—7, 100.

56. An early proponent of the idea of a South-East Asian Chinese commercial pyramid of distribution is that in 滿鉄東亞經濟調查局：英屬馬來，緬甸及澳洲的華僑, cited by Huang in his *Social History*. . . . Huang himself provided a comprehensive discussion of what he termed the 'tri-level' economic system（三重經濟結構）, which is the basis of the pyramid system presented here. (See his Figures 4 and 5, pp. 26 and 28, and discussion on p. 66 in particular.)

57. For example, on early tin mining ventures:

'. . . In these settlements, the Chinese and Western merchants were the only people who could provide the capital. These accumulated their wealth mainly from the profits of the ever-expanding trade, but the Chinese also had a great source of income in the excise farms, . . . it was almost wholly the Chinese who responded to the offers of the Malay chiefs'. Wong Lin Ken, *The Malayan Tin Industry to 1914*, Tuscon, Arizona, University of Arizona Press for Association for Asian Studies, 1965, pp. 21—2. Pages 22—3 gave some examples of prominent Malay chiefs-cum-tin miners.

'. . . Without exception known, the early Chinese miners came at the invitation of the Malay chiefs, . . . It was inevitable that when the Malay chiefs wanted to improve their revenues by exploiting their resources, they had to import both labour and capital from the flourishing Straits Settlements.' J. M. Gullick, *Indigenous Political Systems of Western Malaya*, Chapter 7.

58. This is not the place to document the Chinese merchants' access to a ready and cheap source of labour supply from southern China. See writers like R. N. Jackson, Chen Ta, Purcal, etc., on aspects of this. It is the question of how much control these merchants actually had over the 'pig' labour via their ties with the secret societies that has not been conclusively established. On the importance of a cheap source of labour, see Wong, op. cit., pp. 216—27, 237—8; Yip, op. cit., pp. 150—1, for tin mining. The supply of cheap labour is also important in the plantation sector of the economy. This is what prompted the planters' associations to push for the importation of Indian labourers under subsidy. See Jackson, op. cit., for accounts related to pepper, nutmeg, and tapioca planting, pp. 73, 110, and 145—8. As for the importance to sugar planting, see Philip Loh Fook Seng, *The Malay States 1877–1895*, Oxford University Press, Kuala Lumpur, 1969, pp. 154—5.

59. Wong, op. cit.; Yip, op. cit.

60. To quote Jackson again:

'. . . To facilitate the growth of commercial agriculture in Malaya, three fundamentals were essential: capital, labour and accessible land on easy terms: all three were in relatively short supply during the 19th century, and it was the ability of the Chinese to overcome this shortage in their own particular ways that enabled them to achieve considerable success in the production of export crops at an early date. By the end of the century, however, the Government had accepted the principle that if the desired expansion of European planting activities was to occur then some official effort to provide these essentials of development was necessary.' Jackson, op. cit., p. 235.

As for the official actions, see Yip, op. cit., pp. 20—1; Wong, op. cit., p. 237 for tin mining; Drabble, *Rubber in Malaya 1876–1922*, pp. 26—7, 102 for rubber.

61. Kratoska, op. cit., p. 11.

62. The issue of international price-fixing by the few companies/groups is very controversial and difficult to document. It is not the intention to make this claim here for the markets of the major produce items of Malaysia, neither has enough research been done for such a purpose. However, it suffices to show contrast in the prospect of price-fixing and control faced by the small middlemen on the one hand and the huge international conglomerates on the other. If any one group has a more realistic chance of fixing prices, margins, and distribution networks, it has to be those several huge enterprises controlling significant portions of the market of particular raw materials/products who have the potential. In particular, the importance of the international tin cartel in achieving some degree of price collusion and market discrimination in the thirties has been quite well documented. For example, see Elizabeth Ray, 'The International Tin Cartel', in William Y. Elliot, ed., *International Control in the non-Ferrous Metals*, New York, Macmillan Co., 1937. Pages 315—25 documented the Anglo-Oriental-London Tin group's dominant interest to impose a price floor for tin through the creation of international restriction schemes over the objection of lower cost independent producers such as Gopeng Consolidated. Pages 307—10 gave an account of the initial effort by

this group at consolidating its world-wide tin mining and smelting interest as well as the many intricate ties it has with other major mining and tin consumption groups.

See also Donald Smith, *Tin Producers' Collusive Cartel Under Oligopoly*, unpublished Harvard College Honours thesis, 1966.

From the research done for Chapter 5, it does not appear that the extent of concentration has decreased since the thirties, hence there is some reason to think that the dominant group should still be able to pull its weight. However more research is obviously needed.

Unfortunately, no such study exists for rubber or the other raw materials that Malaysia produces. At a superficial level, it appears that control of the rubber market is more dispersed than that of tin.

8 The Origins, Nature, and Outlook of Malaysian Businessmen

8.1 INTRODUCTION

In Chapters 5 and 6, the structure of ownership and control in Malaysia has been outlined. Particular attention was drawn to the small and modest profit levels at which the bulk of the businesses in Malaysia operate in contrast to the spread and depth of operation of the hundred or so huge conglomerates with profit levels in the millions. In Chapter 7, the marketing structure in Malaysia was outlined, highlighting the necessary but dominated role played by the large number of middlemen who fill the bottom and middle echelons of the various marketing pyramids. It would appear that the probability of a large number of small enterprises evolving into huge conglomerates is not very high, given their modest profit level. In this chapter, we further address the question of the extent of mobility from the bottom of the pyramid to the top by looking into the origins and bases of the local businessmen (Section 8.2) and tracing their path of development (Section 8.3). This question of upward mobility is interesting not only in itself, but also in relation to one of the aims of the NEP: the creation of a group of Malay entrepreneurs, as well as the various responses to this new thrust in policy.

The objective of 30 per cent Malay ownership of capital is a relatively easy one to achieve given a very conscious and persistent Government drive. The restructuring of ownership can be achieved by either of two methods or a combination of both: the Government purchasing shares on behalf of the Malay community and/or the creation of a class of Malay entrepreneurs capable of surviving in competition with the local and foreign capitalists. Data from the Third Malaysia Plan on ownership of share capital in the limited companies show that the share of Malay interests in the total has increased from 2.4 per cent in 1970 to 7.8 per cent in 1975.[1] The discussion in Chapters 5 and 6 has shown that these increases have come essentially from the more important sectors and companies, making the true impact of the increase perhaps larger than the numerical increase may indicate. If this trend continues, and it has,[2] there is no reason to doubt the probable attainment of 30 per cent ownership by 1990. In particular, control of these key commodity companies, which are invariably cash rich, means that the Government now has a huge pool of funds and further credit facilities in the private sector with which to make further acquisition. Indeed, it is such possible snowballing effect which makes these acquisitions critical on the one hand and the attainment of the 30 per cent target probable on the other. However, this will not by itself bring about the creation of a class of Malay businessmen.

To eradicate identification of race with economic activities, the creation of a Malay commercial and industrial community is more difficult, but more important. Once the origins and bases of the local businessmen are identified, perhaps one can analyse and isolate the factors essential to the development of a Malay business élite. In this chapter, some basic data and tentative observations are presented.

The implementation of the NEP creates a new situation and there are bound to be responses from the various races. Section 8.4 examines the outlook and characteristics of local businessmen by race and by level of operation, keeping in mind their social origins and the bases of their economic strength, and anticipates their responses to the wealth-restructuring prong of the NEP.

8.2 THE ORIGINS AND BASES OF LOCAL BUSINESSMEN

A. The Indian Traders

Indian[3] businessmen tend to be associated with the Chettiar financing activities mentioned in earlier chapters and also trading activities such as importing textile products, food, and other consumer items from India. One of the largest Indian trading concerns, Manilal and Sons (M) Sdn. Bhd., deals in Indian textiles and other commodities.[4] Some manage large departmental stores based in Kuala Lumpur.[5] Few of them amass their riches from activities based on local raw materials. Fewer, if any at all, are engaged in mining. Those involved in plantations (on a smaller scale) seem to have started out, by and large, from provision of credit and perhaps from land foreclosure after loan default.[6] One of the biggest Indian planters, Arumugam Pillay, owned over 4,000 acres of prime rubber estate land. It has been suggested that he too made his initial wealth from the provision of credit.[7]

In the past ten years, the National Union of Plantation Workers and the Malaysian Trades Union Congress which are dominated by Indians have emulated their American counterparts by using union funds to engage in business activities, building up a conglomerate with the establishment of Bank Buruh, several estates, and at least one textile factory.[8] Another Indian-managed conglomerate built up with funds from their members is the Malaysian Co-operative Insurance Society which, in addition to being the leading local insurance company, has also moved into hotel, land and property development, and other businesses.[9]

Two concluding remarks. First, Indian businessmen have a different orientation from that of Chinese and Malay businessmen. Their activities are based less on raw material processing and manufacturing, and more on trading and credit capital. While the capital of most Malaysian Chinese enterprises has been generated locally, the capital of many Indian enterprises originates from India. Secondly, despite the existence of conglomerates based on co-operative ownership, there is as much concentration in ownership and control as is true in general for the other races. This can be seen by recalling the low level of income received by the great majority of the Malaysian Indian estate workers, Government casual workers, and general unskilled workers outlined in Part I, as well as the fact that the rate of unemployment among the Indians is the highest.

B. The Malay Élite

It is necessary to go back into history to gain a perspective on the origins of the small group of Malay businessmen. When the traders and miners first became active in Malaya, they often had to seek the co-operation and partnership of the local Malay chiefs,[10] for the Rajas held the land rights and in fact had some modest accumulation of wealth. This gave the aristocracy an opening into business, though it should be noted that some small Malay traders and landowners have always existed. Following British colonization, it was the colonial masters' conscious policy to educate the sons, and to a much lesser extent daughters, of the aristocracy to play the intermediate administrative role.[11] It was this group of 'well-bred' middle-echelon civil servants who became the top civil servants and leading politicians in the country after Independence. It is not surprising therefore that the foreign and non-Malay businessmen seek out this élite as their partners.

The Malay businessmen whose business conglomerates have been charted in Chapter 5 fit this description. Tengku Ariff Bendahara, for example, is second in line to the throne of the Sultan of Pahang. Having received a good education, he started his business career by securing a large timber concession.[12] With due recognition of his entrepreneurial capabilities, it is obvious that his aristocratic background and the possible resultant political and business connections were a great help in aiding him to arrive at his present position. He provides an illustrative example of how a man can take advantage of his privileged position and combine it with his own initiative to advance his business career. On the other hand, while Datuk Syed Kechik bin Syed Mohamed was not born an aristocrat, for a man of his generation to be able to become a lawyer would rule out a poor peasantry background. He started as an UMNO politician in Kedah working closely with the first Prime Minister, Tengku Abdul Rahman Putra Al-Haj, before becoming former Sabah Chief Minister Tun Mustapha's right-hand man and Chairman of the Sabah Foundation.[13] His political career could be an asset in assisting his business career.

The royalty of the various states are fairly active in business, in addition to being substantial property owners. However, because of the possible sensitivity of documenting their detailed holdings, it suffices to point out here the examples of the Antah Holding group representing the royal interests of Negeri Sembilan, and Jomalina Sdn. Bhd. and Pahang Properties among others representing the royal interests of Pahang as evidence of their business activities. In Table 8.1, there are several more examples of members of the royal households who sit on the boards of publicly listed companies.

Table 8.1 lists thirty-two more important Malay directors on the boards of the publicly listed companies. All but one of them originated from very respectable social backgrounds. If they are not actually connected with the traditional aristocracy, they have an upper-class economic status. Thus, one would expect them to wield significant local or regional political influence. The ten

TABLE 8.1
BACKGROUND AND COMPANY AFFILIATION OF THE LEADING MALAY DIRECTORS

Name of Director	*Background*	*Company Affiliation*
1. Tan Sri Haji Mohamed Noah bin Omar	American University graduate, former Speaker of the Dewan Rakyat (Parliament), father-in-law of Tun Razak and Datuk Hussein Onn	Malayan Flour Mills Bhd. Malaysia Rice Industries Bhd. Malex Asbestos Cement Bhd. Matsushita Electric Co. (Malaysia) Bhd. Malayan United Industries Bhd. United Malayan Banking Corp. Esso Malaysia Bhd. Genting Bhd. Federal Cables, Wires & Metal Manufacturing Bhd. Hock Hua Bank Bhd. Johor Sugar Plantation Bhd. Kien Huat Realty Sdn. Bhd. K.L. Klang and Port Swettenham Omnibus Co. Bhd. Selangor Dredging Bhd. Supreme Corporation Bhd. Taiping Textiles Bhd.
2. Tan Sri Nik Ahmad Kamil*	Barrister, former Mentri Besar of Kelantan, High Commissioner to Australia, United Kingdom, U.S.A., and United Nations, Deputy Speaker and then Speaker of the Dewan Rakyat	Metal Box Co. of Malaysia Bhd. Boustead Holdings Bhd. Dunlop Malaysian Industries Bhd. Faber Merlin Malaysia Bhd. General Lumber (Holdings) Bhd. George Kent (Malaysia) Bhd.

*Passed away in 1977.

(Continued)

TABLE 8.1 (Continued)

Name of Director	*Background*	*Company Affiliation*
		Kinta Kellas Tin Development Co. Ltd. Petaling Tin Bhd. Public Bank Bhd. Rothmans of Pall Mall (Malaysia) Bhd. Shell Refining Co. (F.O.M.) Bhd. The Straits Trading Co. Ltd. South East Asia Development Corp. Bhd. United Engineers (Malaysia) Bhd. Utusan Melayu Bhd.
3. Y.M. Tunku Tan Sri Mohamed bin Tunku Besar Burhanuddin	formerly State Secretary of Selangor, High Commissioner to Pakistan, Chief Secretary to the Government, now with The Chartered Bank	Ajinomoto (Malaysia) Bhd. India–Malaysia Textile Bhd. Pegi Malaysia Bhd. Aluminium Company of Malaysia Bhd. Carlsberg Brewery Malaysia Bhd. Chartered Merchant Bankers Chemical Company of Malaysia Bhd. George Kent (Malaysia) Bhd. Malaysia American Assurance Co. Bhd. Supreme Corporation Bhd. Timuran Holdings Bhd. Bristow Helicopters Malaysia Sdn. Bhd. Pudu Ulu Mines Sdn. Bhd. Scott & English Sdn. Bhd. J & P Coats (Malaysia) Bhd. Wood & Allied Ind. Holdings

(Continued)

TABLE 8.1 (Continued)

Name of Director	*Background*	*Company Affiliation*
4. Tan Sri Taib bin Haji Andak	Barrister, former Registrar, Supreme Court, Chairman of Federal Land Development Authority	Associated Plastic Industries Bhd. Malayan Banking Bhd. S.E. Asia Development Corp. Bhd. Malaysian Industrial Development Finance Bhd. Malaysian International Shipping Corp. Bhd. Hume Industries (Far East) Ltd. Hume Industries (Malaysia) Bhd. Sime Darby group of companies (including Kempas Plantations, Benta Plantations, Taiping Consolidated, Tractor Malaysia) I.A.C. (Holdings) Ltd.
5. Dato' Syed Nahar bin Tun Syed Sheh Shahabuddin*	Bristol University graduate, member of UMNO Supreme Council, Mentri Besar of Kedah	Malayan Banking Bhd. Federal Land Development Authority Berjaya Kawat Bhd. United Motor Works Bhd. Faber Merlin Malaysia Bhd. Perlis Plantations Bhd. United Malayan Insurance Co. Bhd. Rahman Hydraulic Tin Bhd. National Savings Bank

*The publicly listed companies here are those with which he was associated before his election as the Mentri Besar of Kedah.

(Continued)

TABLE 8.1 (Continued)

Name of Director	*Background*	*Company Affiliation*
6. Y.M. Raja Tun Uda Al-Haj bin Raja Muhammed	former Mentri Besar of Selangor, High Commissioner to United Kingdom, former Governor of Penang	Great Eastern Life Assurance Co. Ltd. Overseas Chinese Banking Corp. Ltd. Malayan Breweries Ltd. Kent (FMS) Ltd. Killinghall Tin Ltd. Kinta Kellas Tin Development Co. Ltd. Hong Kong Tin Ltd. Renong Tin Development Co. Ltd.
7. Tan Sri Hussain bin Haji Mohamed Sidek	formerly Deputy Inspector-General of Police, Chairman of Malayan Railway	Oriental Bank Bhd. Genting Bhd. India–Malaysia Textiles Bhd. Paper Products (Malaysia) Bhd. Ban Seng Plastic Bhd. Federal Flour Mills Bhd. Hong Leong–Lurssen Shipyard Bhd. Merlin Hotel Malaysia Bhd. Malaysia Metal Industries Bhd. K.L. Kelang and Port Swettenham Omnibus Co. Bhd. Overseas Lumber Bhd. United Pulp and Paper Ltd.

(Continued)

TABLE 8.1 (Continued)

Name of Director	Background	Company Affiliation
8. Y.M. Tengku Tan Sri Razaleigh Hamzah*	son of former Mentri Besar of Kelantan, Economics graduate, former Chairman of Petronas, currently Minister of Finance	Bank Bumiputra Bhd. Malaysian Industrial Development Finance Bhd. Batu Kawan Bhd. K.L.–Kepong Bhd. Kepong Plantations Bhd.
9. Junus Sudin	Chartered Accountant, former Petronas executive director	Bolton Properties Bhd. Malaysia Mining Corporation Bhd. group of companies New Straits Times Bhd. National Electricity Board Perak State Economic Development Corp. Garam Malaysia Sdn. Bhd. Bajakimia Sdn. Bhd. Syarikat Dewan Bhd. Bian Chiang Bank Bhd.
10. Y.M. Tengku Ahmad Nerang bin Tengku Abdul Rahman Putra Al-Haj	son of former Prime Minister of Malaysia	Sanyo Industries Bhd. Mahawangsa Holdings Sdn. Bhd. Tropical Veneer Bhd. Min Ngai Knitting Sdn. Bhd. Pesama Timber Corp. Maha–Ehsan Sdn. Bhd.

*The companies listed here are those with which he was associated before his appointment as Minister of Finance.

(Continued)

TABLE 8.1 (Continued)

Name of Director	Background	Company Affiliation
		NGK Spark Plugs Sdn. Bhd. Dredging Malaysia Sdn. Bhd. Parry's Confectionery Sdn. Bhd.
11. Y.M. Tunku Ahmad bin Tunku Yahaya	B.A. (Economics), Kedah royalty, director of Bank Negara Malaysia	Dunlop Malaysian Industries Bhd. Dunlop Estates Bhd. Malaysian Industrial Development Finance Bhd. now deputy managing director of the Sime Darby group
12. Y.A.M. Tengku Ibrahim ibni Al-Marhum Sultan Sir Abu Bakar	son of late Sultan of Pahang	Central Securities (Holdings) Bhd. group of companies Bajakimia Sdn. Bhd.
13. Y.A.M. Tunku Abdullah ibni Al-Marhum Tuanku Abdul Rahman	son of late Yang Dipertuan Besar of Negeri Sembilan, former Assistant Secretary of Ministry of Works, member of Parliament	Malayan Cement Bhd.
14. Y.M. Tunku Imran ibni Tuanku Ja'afar	son of Yang Dipertuan Besar of Negeri Sembilan	Island & Peninsular Development Bhd. Austral Enterprises Bhd. Kumpulan Perusahaan Antah Sdn. Bhd. Haw Par Brothers International Ltd. London Tin Ltd. Anglo-Oriental Ltd.
15. Y.M. General Tunku Osman bin Tunku Mohamed Jewa	former Chief of Armed Forces Staff	Fusan Fishing Net Manufacturing Bhd

(Continued)

TABLE 8.1 (Continued)

Name of Director	*Background*	*Company Affiliation*
16. Y.M. Raja Dato Shahriman bin Raja Abdul Hamid	Chief of Dindings district of Perak	Kinta Electricity Distribution Co. Bhd. Malayan Flour Mill Bhd. Taiping Textiles Bhd.
17. Abdullah bin Datuk Haji Abdul Rahman	former Senator, lawyer	Cold Storage Holdings Ltd. Roxy Electric Industries Bhd.
18. Datuk Haji Ibrahim bin Mohamed	lawyer	Genting Bhd. General Ceramics Bhd. Associated Plastic Industries Bhd.
19. Tan Sri Datuk Syed Jaafar bin Hassan Albar*	member of Parliament, UMNO Youth leader	Tasek Cement Bhd.
20. Tan Sri Abdul Aziz bin Haji Mohamed Zain	former Solicitor-General, Judge of Federal Court, Chairman of National Electricity Board	Hume Industries (Malaysia) Bhd.
21. Tan Sri Nik Daud bin Haji Nik Mat	member of Public Service Commission	Central Sugar Bhd. United Asbestos Cement Bhd.
22. Tan Sri Datuk Bendahara Chik Mohamed Yusuf bin Sheik Abdul Rahman	lawyer, former Speaker of the Dewan Rakyat	General Lumber (Holding) Bhd. Malayan Flour Mills Bhd. United Malayan Banking Corp. Bhd.

*Passed away in 1977.

(Continued)

TABLE 8.1 (Continued)

Name of Director	Background	Company Affilation
23. Tan Sri Dato Haji Mohamed Ariff bin Darus	former Inspector-General of Police, now member of Public Service Commission	Sin Heng Chan Bhd. Tan Chong Motor Holdings Bhd.
24. Tan Sri Abdul Aziz bin Yeop Al-Haj	lawyer, High Commissioner to United Kingdom, Permanent Secretary to Ministry of Agriculture, now member of Parliament	Guthrie Bhd. Malayan Cables Bhd. Malaysia Rice Industries Bhd.
25. Datuk Laksamana Haji Mohamed Razali bin Mohamed Ali Wasi	former Deputy Mentri Besar of Perak, Mentri Besar of Perlis, Chairman of Penang Port Commission	Island and Peninsular Development Bhd. United Malayan Banking Corp. Bhd. United Malayan Flour Mills Bhd.
26. Tan Sri Dato' Seri Haji Osman bin Talib	former State Secretary of Perlis, Perak, Deputy Mentri Besar of Perak, Chief Minister of Malacca, Chairman of RISDA and National Electricity Board	Datuk Keramat Holdings Bhd. Wearne Brothers Ltd. Malaysia National Insurance Bhd.
27. Dato Hussein bin Mohamed Noordin	former member of Parliament, now Director of Muslim Pilgrims' Savings and Management Authority (Tabung Haji)	S.E. Asia Lumber Corp. Bhd. Tasek Cement Bhd. Utusan Malaysia Bhd.
28. Datuk Haji Abdullah bin Sahat	former Acting Mentri Besar of Perlis, Permanent Secretary to Ministry of Education	Public Bank Bhd. Sentosa Plywood Bhd. Champion Motors Sdn. Bhd. Aviation Services Sdn. Bhd.

(Continued)

TABLE 8.1 (Continued)

Name of Director	Background	Company Affiliation
29. Dato Mohamed Yusoff bin Haji Ahmad	Raffles graduate, former State Secretary to Perak	Guinness Malaysia Bhd. Sharikat Harper Gilfillan Bhd. Mentakab Rubber Co. (Malaya) Bhd.
30. Dato Setia Jaya Abdullah bin Ibrahim	landowner and miner	Austral Enterprises Bhd. Olympia Plywood and Timber Product Bhd. Selangor Properties Bhd. Supermarkets Malaysia Bhd. Lion Dentifrice Sdn. Bhd. Syarikat Lombongan Kundang Patah Sdn. Bhd.
31. Datuk Abdul Rahman bin Haji Musa		Bovis S.E. Asia Bhd. The New Serendah Rubber Bhd. South Johor Amalgamated Holdings Bhd.
32. Khalid Ahmad	former UMNO executive secretary	Sovran Industries Bhd.

Sources. *Straits Times Directory*, various years.
Who's Who in Malaysia and Singapore, various years.
Directory of Bumiputra Businessmen.
Kuala Lumpur Stock Exchange, *Annual Company Handbook*, various years.

or so most active directors are particularly prominent. For example, Tan Sri Haji Mohamed Noah bin Omar was Speaker of the Dewan Rakyat, UMNO leader, and is the father-in-law of both the late Prime Minister Tun Abdul Razak bin Dato' Hussein as well as the present Prime Minister Datuk Hussein Onn. The late Tan Sri Datuk Nik Ahmad Kamil was the Mentri Besar (M.B.) of Kelantan and later Speaker of the Dewan Rakyat before he passed away in late 1977. Dato' Syed Nahar bin Tun Syed Sheh Shahabuddin is a nephew of the former Prime Minister, Tengku Abdul Rahman, son of a former M.B. of Kedah and is himself a member of the Supreme Council of UMNO and the new M.B. of Kedah. Raja Tun Uda was a former M.B. of Selangor, former Governor of Penang, and was also once the High Commissioner to the United Kingdom. Tunku Tan Sri Mohamed bin Tunku Besar Burhanuddin was the State Secretary of Selangor, High Commissioner to Pakistan, and Chief Secretary of the Government. Tan Sri Taib bin Haji Andak is a lawyer by training and became the Registrar of the Supreme Court and then the Chairman of the Federal Land Development Authority. Tan Sri Haji Hussain bin Haji Mohamed Sidek was the Deputy Inspector-General of Police and Chairman of the Malayan Railway. Tengku Tan Sri Razaleigh Hamzah has of course resigned from his directorships since his appointment as the Minister of Finance, though his brother, Tengku Robert Hamzah, has taken over some of the directorships. They are from the royal family of Kelantan and their father was M.B. of Kelantan. Tengku Razaleigh has been an influential member of UMNO and is of course now one of its Vice-Presidents. Tengku Ahmad Nerang bin Tengku Abdul Rahman Putra Al-Haj is the son of Malaysia's first Prime Minister. Junus Sudin, a chartered accountant by training, is the only one without an impressive string of political or civil service credentials.[14] But he is reputed to be a close associate of Tengku Razaleigh.

Among the rest, there are those who have served, or are still serving, as Permanent Secretaries to major ministries, Chief of Armed Forces Staff, M.B., Inspector-General of Police, Speaker of the Dewan Rakyat, Deputy M.B., State Secretary, UMNO leader, Senator, Solicitor-General, and member of the Public Service Commission. In addition, there are at least three Tunku/Tengku directly descending from, or related to, the various royal households and a chief of a major district. Only two are without this type of credential although they both carry the title of Datuk/Dato.[15]

The exact amount of the holdings of each of these directors and their families is not known unless one can go through the files of the Registrar of Companies and cross-check with the holding and nominee companies of each of these people and their family and associates. Nevertheless, it is possible broadly to divide them into three groups: (1) Those who are independently wealthy and/or represent wealthy families or groups; (2) Those who represent the interests of Government-controlled corporations; and (3) Those who have been invited to join the board and hold a small percentage of the shares. In the first two cases, the directors would sit on the boards with real executive power and influence. The shareholdings they have or represent are likely to be controlling, or at the very least of a large enough minority to have a say. On the other hand, it is unlikely that the third category of directors exercises real decision-making and executive power. In each case, the presence of these

Malay shareholders-directors is probably reflective of a recognition of post-Independence reality. The advent of the NEP in particular necessitated the selling of shares and transfer of some decision-making and executive power to some Malay interests. At any rate, the psychological and political advantage of having influential members of the Malay élite sitting on the board and holding minority shares has been obvious for some time now. It is with this background that the aristocrats, influential politicians, and civil servants have been invited to the boards and may even have been sold shares at very favourable prices to facilitate transactions involving Government grants, permissions, or concessions.

C. The Chinese Businessmen

(a) A HISTORICAL RECAPITULATION

Historical records indicate that Chinese traders settled in Malacca several hundred years ago. Some of the early settlers married Malay women and their descendants form the 'babas and nyonyas' of Malacca.[16] Some of the wealthy traders with relatively stronger ties with China went back to their village to marry and/or sent their children to China for education. Some who were more adaptable to Western business and mode of life even sent their children to England for education after British colonization. It is probably these sons and daughters who became the prominent traders, financiers, miners, and planters in the late nineteenth and early twentieth centuries. While inadequate documentation on this part of the Malaysian Chinese socio-economic history exists to allow a definitive statement, nevertheless, research by Huang (1971) showed that almost all of the Chinese community and business leaders in that period came from relatively affluent backgrounds and had some education.[17] From other accounts, the new arrivals usually were too poor to initiate business ventures and they were almost always indentured labourers opening up new agricultural land for spices in the early days, on behalf of the city traders-cum-financiers in Penang or Malacca. Even if they were able to pay off their debts and proceed to open up land for themselves, the credit burden and profit-sharing arrangements were such that few of these cultivators could have become wealthy.[18] When tin mining became important later on, much the same arrangement was in operation, although the conditions were probably even harsher for the labourers and the possibility of the new migrants becoming miners even more slim.[19] The advent of rubber planting was no exception. The point is that the uncertainty of new tin ventures and the waiting time needed for rubber cultivation all worked against the migrant-labourers rising to the ranks of businessmen. During the late Ching Dynasty when the bulk of the waves of Chinese immigration to Malaysia took place, China had been in turmoil and economic difficulties necessitated the out-migration. Few of the immigrants would have come with money to initiate businesses, not to mention the lack of necessary contacts.

In short, while exceptions are possible, it is most likely that the wealth-holders of that and subsequent periods generally came from the sons and daughters or relatives and friends of the earlier successful trader-settlers.

It is therefore hardly surprising to find that Yap Ah Loy, one of the most prominent early miners and the founder of Kuala Lumpur, was a Taiping Rebellion officer who came with some of his men to take refuge; or that Tan Chay Yan and Tan Cheng Lock, who were amongst the first rubber planters, came from well-established families in Malacca whose vast riches remain till this day; or that the founder of Lee Rubber, Lee Kong Chian, built up his empire from the nearly ruinous, but nonetheless vast, business base of his father-in-law, Tan Kar Kee, who had been a prominent community and business leader; or that the Kuok brothers came from a well-to-do family and had tertiary education in the United Kingdom.[20]

Nevertheless, as more Chinese immigrants resided in Malaya and as more contact was made with the Malays, more and more opportunities opened up for small businesses to service the everyday needs of the various races. It was then that more realistic opportunities occurred for the new migrants and the labourers for establishing tiny businesses as an alternative to waged employment. Even though the size of turnover and profit was generally small, as it is now (see Chapters 6 and 7), yet the few lucky, hard-working, and skilful persons were given the chance of upward mobility and acquisition of wealth.

In the next section, attention is turned to hypothesizing on the basic businesses which can support upward movement and the possible paths of expansion and diversification.

(b) THE ORIGINS AND PATHS OF EXPANSION AND DIVERSIFICATION

Once the Malayan economy began to develop in such a way that many Malay and non-Malay socio-economic sub-systems developed all over the peninsula complementing and supporting the concentrated and efficient British colonial economy, the number of businessmen needed to service the system grew by leaps and bounds.[21] It was no longer a situation when few businesses were needed and only the élite, wealthy traders could negotiate. Now, with non-Malay mining and planting enclaves springing up over most of the West Coast and with the Malay peasantry participating in rubber planting activity, there was great need for an extensive network of retailers and wholesaler/retailers to transmit the goods to the places where production of raw materials was located, and transmit the commodities back to the major ports. The immigrant non-Malay Chinese, and to a lesser extent, the Indians, had the natural advantage to step into these roles. First of all, the need to service the enclaves was greater and more immediate. Secondly, the working conditions of the miners and labourers were very rough and uncertain, gravely affected by the many ups and downs of the Western economy[22] in contrast to the relative self-containment and stability of a peasant society, thus providing the non-Malays with an incentive to seek better employment. Thirdly, the pressure of having to support the extended household in China meant that they were more willing and found it more necessary to take risks and participate in new ventures to break out of economic difficulties. Retailing provided the basis and formed the entry point of business activities for the non-Malays. Once some groups of Chinese traders succeeded in establishing their trade contacts, they were in a position to use their advantages of contact, language and social groupings to

CHART 8.1
TYPICAL PATHS OF CORPORATE DEVELOPMENT

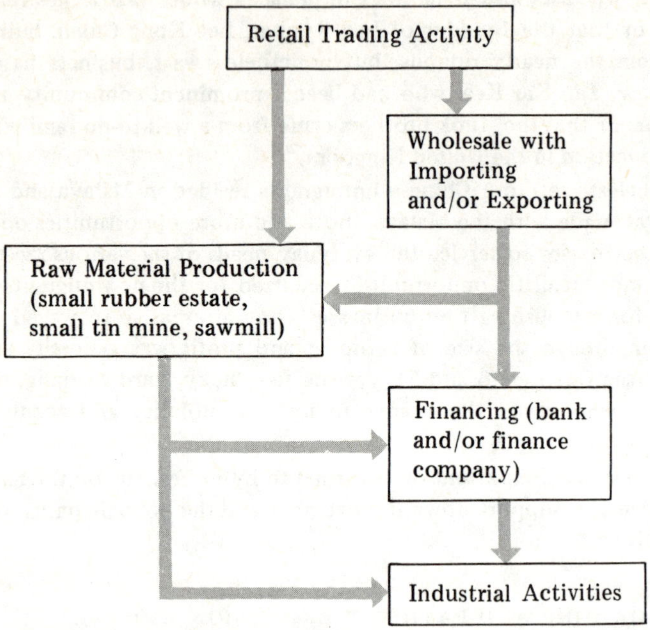

prevent others from similarly gaining an entry point, or alternatively, to assist someone in the same clan or family.[23]

The hypothetical scenario for the development of Malaysian conglomerates is as follows: the initial activity was usually retailing evolving into wholesaling, importing, or exporting. With larger surpluses accumulated and the development of broader experience and outlook, the traders could then move into resource-based activities related to their trading and/or some manufacturing. Chart 8.1 portrays some plausible paths of conglomeration.

To verify the above hypothesis rigorously would be too involved and beyond our present scope. Nevertheless, it is necessary to provide some rudimentary evidence of its plausibility. From the conglomerates charted in Chapter 5, the presence of all these various aspects of business activities in each is enough proof of the desire and success of diversification, regardless of origins and bases. Next, one should establish that diversification is a sound business policy born out of necessity and prudent business considerations. Finally, it is also necessary to show that the original sources of activity can generate adequate funds for further activities and that the sequence of expansion/diversification fits generally into the pattern outlined in Chart 8.1.

(*i*) *Origins*. From the discussions in Chapters 6 and 7, it is clear that about 500 retailers were big enough to have turnovers of $\$\frac{1}{2}$ million or more with a GOS of about \$40,000 per year, and about 1,000 wholesalers had sales in excess of \$1 million and a GOS greater than \$100,000, although most of

TABLE 8.2
GROSS OPERATING SURPLUS OF RUBBER REMILLERS AND LATEX PROCESSORS IN 1968 (IN $)

	Number of Establishments	*Average Sales*	*Average Gross Operating Surplus*
by Sales Group			
< $5,000	—	—	—
5,000— 9,999	1	$ 10,000	$ 4,000
10,000— 19,999	1	13,000	2,000
20,000— 49,999	3	34,000	15,000
50,000— 99,999	3	62,667	23,000
100,000— 199,999	1	187,000	13,000
200,000— 499,999	5	334,600	81,600
500,000— 999,999	5	887,200	6,000
1,000,000—4,999,999	37	2,471,054	241,595
5,000,000+	26	12,200,000	1,428,962
Total	82	5,063,878	569,078
Controlled by			
Malaysian	40	3,469,100	380,650
Singaporean	25	5,105,640	499,088
British	15	9,228,067	1,190,867
Others	2	5,206,000	549,500

Source. Census of Manufacturing Industries 1968.

these retailers and wholesalers were small in size.[24] Such a level of surpluses is adequate to cover a decent living as well as saving for expansion.

In mining, there were more than 100 mines with sales larger than $\$\frac{1}{2}$ million which could generate a GOS in excess of $200,000 (Table 6.3).[25]

Comparable data for estate owners do not exist,[26] but it is assumed that they do generate enough funds.[27] As for the remillers, sixty-three of them with sales over $1 million and GOS greater than $240,000 should presumably be in a position to expand as well (Table 8.2). However, one important qualification is in order. Unlike the tin miners, export duty as well as the replanting and research cess have not been deducted from the GOS;[28] therefore, these have to be deducted to arrive at the amount of funds which could be reinvested. After such deduction, these funds for remillers turned out to be negative for the year 1968![29]

Is this reasonable? Firstly, prices were bad in 1968, and the level of export duty and other cess may already be at too high a rate, especially at the lower ranges of rubber prices, to afford surplus accumulation and reinvestment.[30] Secondly, the figures have been computed by taking averages, thus not distinguishing between those who still profited and those who did not. Thirdly, speculative forward trading has already become a standard feature in the activities of the remillers, given the highly volatile rubber market with sharp

TABLE 8.3
GROSS OPERATING SURPLUS OF SAWMILLERS IN 1968 (IN $)

	Number of Establishments	*Average Sales*	*Average Gross Operating Surplus*
by Sales Group:			
< $5,000	1	$ 1,000	$ −2,000
5,000— 9,999	2	6,500	−6,500
10,000— 19,999	5	16,200	−4,400
20,000— 49,999	14	32,286	6,071
50,000— 99,999	31	78,290	12,677
100,000— 199,999	57	151,368	24,368
200,000— 499,999	149	342,611	59,960
500,000— 999,999	81	722,309	134,173
1,000,000—4,999,999	44	1,634,500	335,159
5,000,000+	—	—	—
Total	384	502,805	94,734
Controlled by			
Malaysian	371	494,598	94,256
Singaporean	13	737,000	108,385

Source. Census of Manufacturing Industries 1968.

fluctuations in prices.[31] Therefore, profit from the forward market trading might have compensated for production losses for some of the remillers. Fourthly, if the interest is on whether the remilling activity could have provided the funds for expansion in a historical context, it suffices to suggest that the burden of duties in earlier days may not be as great and the prices have registered a very high level in cycles. Enough surpluses might have been retained in these good times.

At any rate, according to industry sources, a profit margin of ½—1 per cent of total sales value is the norm that successful remillers receive in an average year, assuming reasonable performance in the futures market.[32] In short, adequate funds could be generated by the larger remillers for reinvestment.

For the sawmillers, again there were slightly more than 100 larger ones with sales greater than $½ million and a GOS of $130,000 or more (Table 8.3).

Hence, using data from the late sixties, one can surmise that the larger firms in trading, mining, rubber planting, and remilling and sawmilling can all generate adequate funds to reinvest for expansion activities. The number of these summed up to less than 2,000 and once account is taken of variations in size and profitability as well as the extent of duplications amongst themselves, it is unlikely that there would be more than several hundred firms/groups who would be in a position to expand.[33] If data from an earlier period (in the forties and fifties) were available, then one could have conducted an analogous exercise to determine the number in these categories of business organizations which would have been poised for expansion. That number would have been more reflective of, and could be used to cross-check against, those who have 'made it' in the sixties.

(*ii*) *The Case against Vertical Integration.* Some brief discussion on the up- and down-stream reinvestment possibilities for the three resource-based industries is now in order.

For the mining sector, the next step after mining is the smelting of ore. Both the two existing tin smelters were in fact started by local tin miners;[34] but control of Eastern Smelting soon passed to foreigners when it ran into difficulties, while the founders and subsequent major owners of Straits Trading became Singapore-based. Between them, these two smelters represent a very significant portion of world smelting capacity[35] and have been smelting not just Malaysian but Australian, Thai and Indonesian ore as well. It is therefore unlikely that other miners can successfully set up new smelting works.[36]

After the smelting stage, the tin concentrates are used mainly as an ingredient in the making of alloys consumed largely in the industrialized countries of the West. It is seldom the main component of the product in terms of volume, weight, or cost. In addition, since Malaysia has a small industrial base and is far from the main industrial centres, further down-stream activities in Malaysia would be highly uncompetitive, quite apart from whether the local businessmen have access to, and can master, the technological requirements.

Turning to rubber, much the same situation exists. The main use of rubber lies in the manufacture of tyres. Again, the small local market, the economies of large-scale production and the much lower cost of shipping rubber as opposed to tyres mean that Malaysian businessmen would not find it competitive to go into this most important down-stream activity for the export market. However, in terms of other rubber products, some local businessmen such as Fung Keong, Shum Yip Leong, and a few others have had a fairly long history in the manufacture of rubber shoes, boots, gloves, and even some production of tyres and tubes.[37]

Sawmilling is a more recent field of activity. But since it did not develop into an economic activity of major importance until the late sixties, it is only in the last decade or so that enough surplus funds have been accumulated for down-stream activities. However, the sawmillers have started to move into veneer and plywood manufacture, and in some limited cases into other wood-products manufacturing.

In the case of other more traditional cash-crop produce such as coconut and pineapple production, it is significant to note that several coconut oil mills existed to process the copra into coconut oil for export and for domestic use; several factories also exist to process coconut oil into soap and other products, and two pineapple canneries were built to can pineapples for export.[38]

In the light of this brief discussion on the constraints imposed by economic and technological considerations, we can understand why for the businessmen engaged in Malaysia's most important economic activities, tin and rubber, down-stream manufacturing activities were neither viable nor sound business projects. By contrast, diversification into another field, whether another resource-based activity, property holding or trading, usually entailed less capital requirement, specialized expertise, and risk. Foolish is the businessman who opts for down-stream investment. However, while the general point holds it did not prevent local businessmen from investing in down-stream activities when the opportunity did arise. Earlier, the cases of the sawmillers, coconut oil millers, and pineapple canneries were cited. Lately, with the growing importance of oil palm planting, local businessmen have also gone into palm oil refining and the making of olein, stearin, and edible oil.

8.3 THE PATH TO CONGLOMERATION

In the last section, the approximate paths for diversification and the underlying reasons were outlined. In this section, some details are given on the changing organizational structure of the business groups with their expanding variety of businesses as they grow in size and influence.

The earliest merchants started in small retailing enterprises. As their funds accumulated, some evolved into wholesalers and importers/exporters while others branched into small rubber estates or a partnership in a mining venture. Those dealing in copra or rice would go into coconut oil milling or rice milling respectively. A few would venture into financing or other manufacturing, usually related to food processing or modified handicrafts making.

In general, the smallest firms, which are the most common, tend to be organized along the line of individual proprietorship. Duplication of holdings in the sense of owning multiple firms is probably rare.[39]

As surpluses accumulate and expansion occurs, the smaller firms may change from individual proprietorships to partnerships and small limited private companies by pooling the resources of two, three, or four families depending on the size of operation and on the wealth accumulation. Such initial cooperative efforts, if successful and harmonious, may lead to an expansion in the size of operation; and as adequate accumulation materializes, will form the basis of the core grouping to even larger-sized companies. Eventually, this

CHART 8.2
CONTROL STRUCTURE OF SMALL AND MEDIUM-SIZED FIRMS

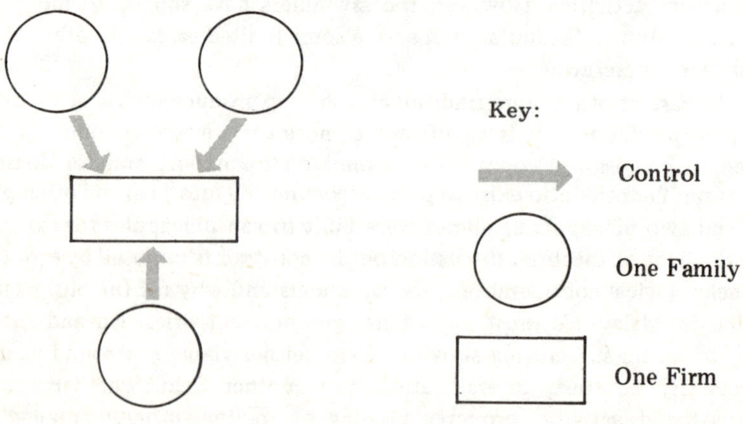

CHART 8.3
CONTROL STRUCTURE OF SMALL CONGLOMERATES

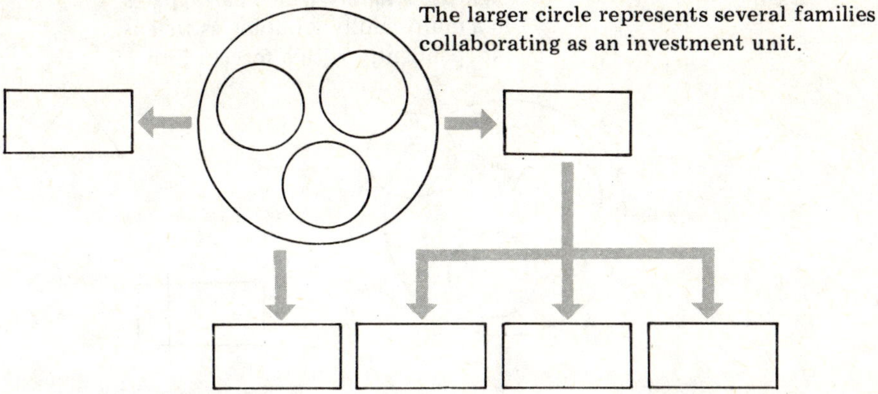

CHART 8.4
CONTROL STRUCTURE OF THE LARGE LOCAL GROUP WITH A FOREIGN PARTNER

(a)

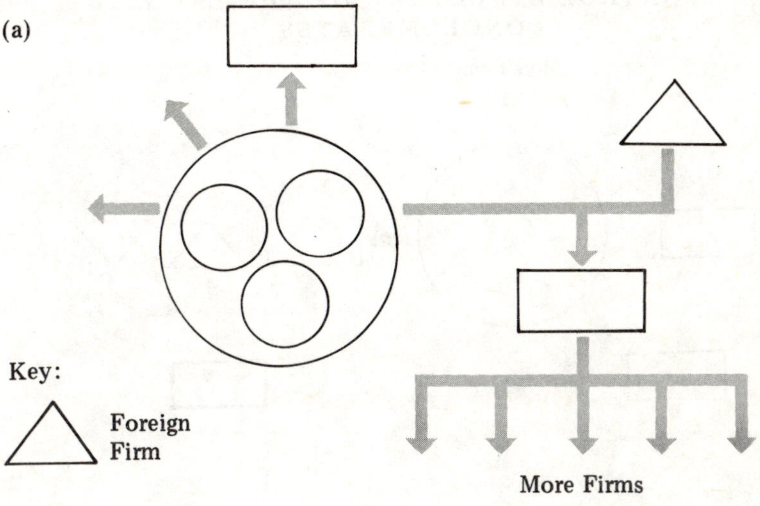

amalgamation of partners may diversify into several companies with more than one firm and may be in more than one industry. Charts 8.2 and 8.3 represent possible holding structures at different sized levels in this evolution.

At the bigger levels, it becomes necessary and attractive for the business group to seek Government and/or Malay partners. By now, the operation would be fairly big with holding companies, pyramid and crossed structures of control of the group companies. Some of the companies within the group would probably be listed on the Stock Exchange. The group would also have branched out into a range of manufacturing activities, some of which would be in partnership with foreigners' assistance in technology and/or marketing.

CHART 8.4 (Continued)

(b)

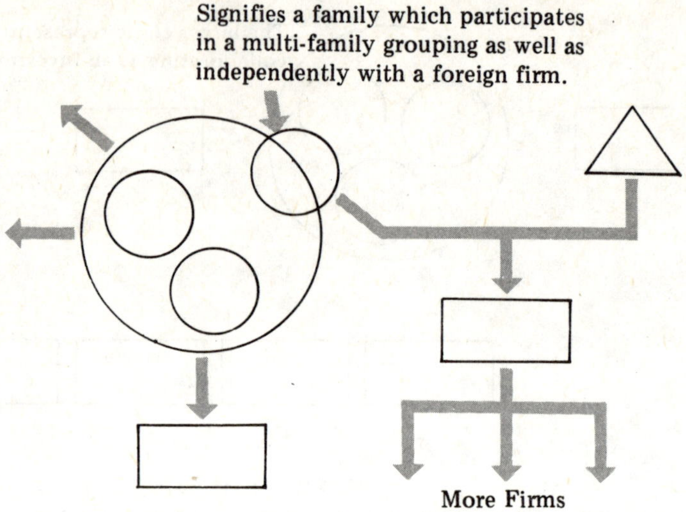

CHART 8.5(a)
CONTROL STRUCTURE OF THE LARGE CONGLOMERATES

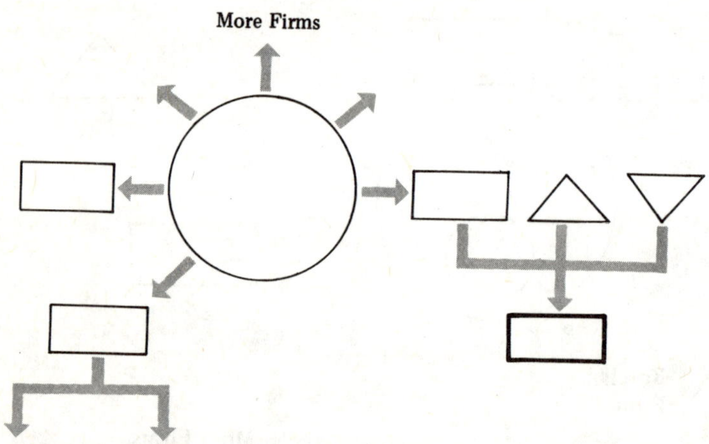

A financial institution may have been added to the fold to supplement their business activities, usually a finance company or an insurance company, while the very privileged few participated in a commercial bank. Charts 8.4 and 8.5 illustrate these possibilities.

8.4 THE PERSPECTIVES AND EXPECTATIONS OF MALAYSIAN BUSINESSMEN

In the preceding chapters and the three earlier sections of this chapter, a comprehensive picture of the distribution of wealth, ownership, and control among the Malaysian businessmen has been outlined; so have their origins

CHART 8.5(b)
CONTROL STRUCTURE OF THE LARGEST CONGLOMERATES WITH A BANK/FINANCE COMPANY AT THE TOP

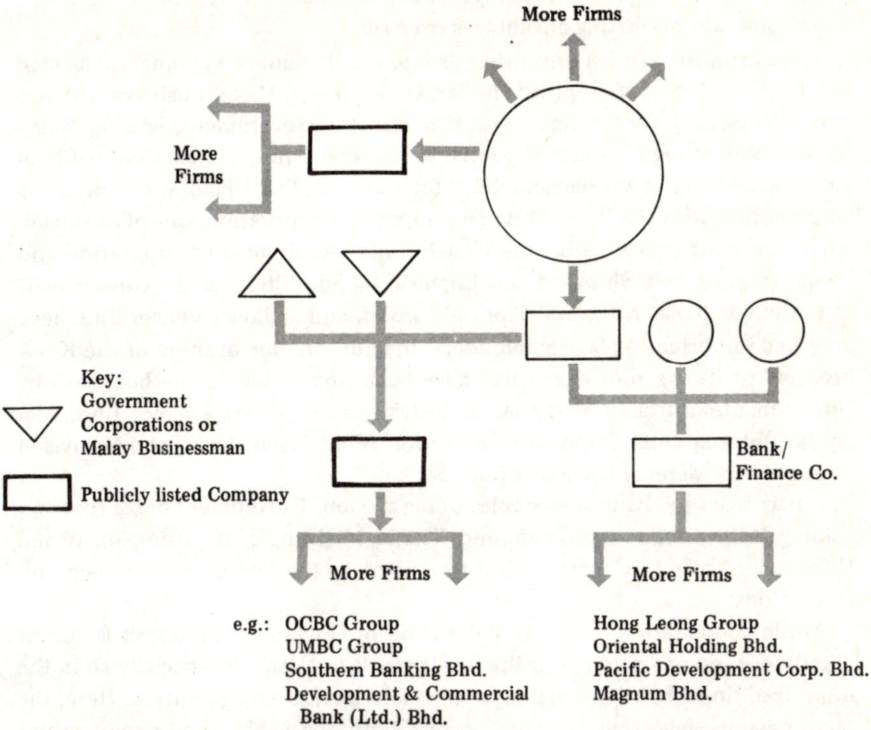

and bases of economic power. In this section, their perspectives and expectations of the distribution of future economic power are discussed *vis-à-vis* the present distribution of economic power and the changes with the new political realities dictated by the advent of the NEP. This is done by distinguishing between the Malays and non-Malays as well as subdividing within each racial category by their scale of operation.

A. The Non-Malays

(a) BIG BUSINESS

Among the big non-Malay entrepreneurs, co-operation with important Government officials and/or leading Malay political figures (or their families and friends) as well as foreign multinationals has occurred for some time. Initially, from Independence till the sixties, seeking Malay partner(s) was not mandatory. Rather, for those more far-sighted, it was an investment in the future as well as a means of expediting any necessary transactions with various Government agencies. The nature and size of Malay participation ranged from token shareholdings to significant minority stakes. The exact size of Malay participation hinged on the influence of the Malay partner and the outlook of the non-Malay businessmen. However, with the advent of the NEP, partnership with Malays has become almost a necessity. Of course, the nature of the partnership would also have to be changed progressively in the direction of bona fide partnership with real decision-making power and a significant if not a majority stake in ownership.[40] On the other hand, partnership with foreign companies is less a reflection of the lack of capital on the part of the local partners, but more an acknowledgement of the need for technological transfer and perhaps marketing advantages overseas.

Perhaps more so than any other group, the dynamic conglomerate headed by the Kuok brothers typifies the largest local non-Malay businessmen who have successfully forged very close ties with the Government, leading Malay figures, and foreign industrial giants. All their big projects charted in Chapter 5 have Government participation; for example, Perlis Plantations Bhd. is a joint venture with the Perlis State Development Corporation, one of its subsidiaries is a joint venture with the Kedah State Development Corporation and Felda, the Malaysia Shipyard and Engineering Sdn. Bhd. has the Government as the major partner. Federal Flour Mills Bhd. and Malayan Veneer Bhd. have long had important Malay shareholders. In addition, one or more of the Kuok brothers or their senior executives have been nominated to the board of the Government-controlled Malaysian Industrial Development Finance Bhd., Malaysian International Shipping Corporation Bhd., Malayawata, and Malaysian International Merchant Bankers Bhd.[41]

Apart from the Kuoks, examples of big tycoon–Government or big tycoon–leading Malays collaboration abound. The highlighting of the rising Malay and Government role in Chapter 5 is a testament to the importance of such collaborations.

While co-operation with the Malays and/or Government interests is almost mandatory, co-operation with the foreigners is not. This is especially so in the more traditional activities such as mining and plantation agriculture. Here, the big-time non-Malay businessmen possess both the capital and expertise not only to dispense with co-operation with the foreigners, but also to wrest control from them. Starting from the years immediately before Independence, control of the smaller planting and mining companies has been gradually passing into the hands of local businessmen.[42] However it was not until the early seventies that the most significant changes in the control of major planting companies began with Lee Loy Seng's group consolidating its plantation acquisition under the Batu Kawan Bhd.–K.L.–Kepong Bhd. grouping. The recent abortive attempt by Genting Bhd. to bid for Golden Hope Plantations Ltd. is another example of local businessmen not wanting to take a back seat to the foreigners in areas where they are competent. Another example of the wresting of control from foreigners is the amalgamation and subsequent expansion of the Faber Merlin group under Chang Ming Thien, which included control of Pahang Consolidated Co. Ltd. and a significant stake in Plantation Holdings Ltd. at its peak.[43]

The salient feature in these examples is of course the scale of operation of the local entrepreneurs. It is unlikely that anyone but the wealthiest and most competent businessmen would be able to aim at control of major foreign-owned companies. At their level of operation, partnership with the Government, Malays, and foreigners is not a problem; nor, for that matter, is the contest for control. Not only do they have the financial power, experience, and business expertise to handle the relationship, the profitability of their business would also enable them to absorb the cost of supporting 'sleeping' Malay partners if necessary. While they may not be overjoyed with making increasing concessions to the Malays under the NEP, the cost to them is probably relatively more bearable, especially since partnership with Malays in the past has most likely proved to be mutually beneficial. Moreover, their wealth and influence make them more attractive targets as partners of Malay leaders and the Government. In short, they are not likely to be overawed by, or too resistant to, the NEP.

(b) SMALL BUSINESS

At the other extreme, the small businessmen do not face the problem of taking in Malay partners. It is of course possible to require these small firms to acquire a Malay partner or partners,[44] but this makes little sense. In Chapter 6, they have been shown to be functioning on too small a scale, and with levels of profit which are too low, for them to support additional partners. Nor would the Malays, or for that matter any other partners who could afford it, be interested in buying or acquiring an interest in such concerns. Therefore, they would feel threatened only by policies which encouraged and supported the entry of other small operators of whatever race.

Their fortunes have been mixed in current development. Some of them no doubt benefited in an indirect manner from Government policies. A case in point is of course the doubling of retailing shops in the Muda region following the introduction of double cropping reported in Chapter 7. While the original retailers in the region appear to have raised their trading volume, and thus income, only very marginally, the increase in the number of retailers indicated expanded opportunity for those who were unemployed or in less desirable professions. On the other hand, pockets of these small businessmen may have been coming under increasing pressure from Government policies. For example, Government initiative in setting up rice mills and Group Processing Centres for rubber under co-operative arrangements may affect the turnover and hence income of the small businessmen engaged in these middleman activities. If indeed the alternatives provided by the Government can provide greater income through better prices and easier credit to the farmers, then this is a price that has to be paid. On the other hand, judging from the statements made by the guilds and associations representing the interests of the small retailers, the greatest threat to their livelihood appears to come from the development of chains of supermarkets and department stores.[45]

(c) THE DILEMMA OF THE MIDDLE-LEVEL BUSINESSMEN

In this section, we are dealing with the middle to sizeable, but not really large, operators. These generally include businesses capable of generating at least $100,000 in GOS[46] up to those with perhaps close to a million. These are the businessmen who are beginning to generate and accumulate enough surplus funds towards the goal of larger businesses as well as those who are poised for expansion into the huge conglomerates. These people would definitely come under the provisions of the Industrial Co-ordination Act (ICA) if they were engaged in manufacturing or are intending to go into it. For those who are not covered by the ICA, their future can still be potentially affected by other implementations of the NEP.[47]

At their level of operation and profits, it is both competitive and profitable enough for them to be unreceptive to giving up some share capital (implying a chunk of future profits)[48] unless they can see some tangible benefits. Their position and perspectives differ from the really large businessmen. First of all, as these middle-level businessmen are generally newer to the ranks of the affluent, the difficulties of amassing wealth are still more deeply imprinted in their minds. Secondly, the absolute level of their surpluses is much more modest than that of the big businesses; to them, 30 per cent of say 100,000 or 200,000 ringgit may make a greater dent in their livelihood than would 30 per cent of $1 or $2 million. It is unlikely that any of them would instead compare their livelihood with that of the poor and realize that 70 per cent of $100,000 is still far better than the average. The combined result of these two reasons is to make the sense of loss greater than that felt by the big businessmen for a proportionate surrender of share capital, or so it seems to them anyway.

The third factor is the selling price of the share capital reserved for Malays or Malay interests. Are the shares to be reserved at cost, at net asset value, or at a value which allows for future income stream? Are the shares to be purchased with cash or are they to be held in trust till the mutually agreed price has been covered by dividend payment? All these questions have an important bearing on the real cost of restructuring borne by the original shareholders and the extra burden that the non-Malay shareholders would have to shoulder in a new venture.[49]

The fourth and perhaps most important factor is the lack of suitable Malay partners. If restructuring is inevitable, and especially if the real cost of restructuring is high in the sense of low selling price and/or no cash payment on the acquisition of shares, then the non-Malay businessmen would naturally prefer influential or rich and capable Malays to be their partners. Yet, it is probably true that at this level of operation, the medium-sized non-Malay businessmen may not have an adequate opportunity to know and cultivate such potential Malay partners; neither would those in whom they might be interested consider them to be of sufficient potential. The dilemma is obvious.

Couple the above four factors with the practical difficulties these ambitious, up-and-coming medium-sized businessmen encountered in their business operations due to over-zealous implementation of the restructuring objective by civil servants,[50] it is small wonder that stiff resistance to the ICA comes from this group of medium to big businessmen. The objections of these medium to big businessmen have come about largely through the auspices of the Associated Chinese Chamber of Commerce which culminated in the recent Chinese Economic Conference in April 1978.[51] This is a problem to which they can find no satisfactory solution, as they perceive every practical foreseeable solution as being only second best.[52]

Contrary to common belief, the Chinese Chambers of Commerce are not led by, and do not represent, the interests of the biggest Chinese businessmen. The largest and most dynamic Chinese businessmen are seldom active in the offices of the various Chinese Chambers of Commerce.[53] It is usually the medium to large businessmen who play the leading role in defending their own interests, and to a lesser extent, that of the smaller operators. This is so because they are not adequately well connected on an individual basis and need an organization to represent their interests. By contrast, the huge businesses usually already have access to whatever influence that may be necessary.

An analogous dilemma confronts the medium-sized operators with respect to co-operation with foreign investors. Overwhelming British control before Independence had stymied their development for a long time but post-Independence development has given them the opportunity to grow to the present scale. The possibility of further growth and consolidation would be considerable in the absence of policies in favour of Malays and foreign investors. Naturally, foreign investors are viewed with some apprehension.[54] However, on an individual basis, some of them no doubt do consider partnership with foreigners.

B. The Malays

From the discussions in Sections 7.4 and 8.2, the constraints imposed by the marketing pyramids and the small number of Malay businessmen in any of the resource-based industries means that few Malays would have been able to enter the big league of businessmen in a short time without active Government intervention. We have seen that the few who do 'make it' usually come from an affluent background, are well connected, and have a high probability of being part of the aristocracy and/or civil service. Even with active Government intervention, it is more likely that most of the 30 per cent share capital to be owned by the Malays will be held in trust by Government-related companies (such as Pernas, MARA, UDA, Bank Bumiputra, the various funds, the State Economic Development Corporations, etc.) rather than be generated and acquired by Malay businessmen independently.[55] From this point of view, the most important group of Malays will be the politicians, civil servants, or civil servants turned executives who acquire and maintain these shares in trusts. The fact that they are receiving expert foreign advice[56] and the Government has intensified its programme to train executives[57] not only facilitates the acquisition of shares and the wresting of control, but also serves to educate these people in the fine art of corporate take-overs and management.

Apart from the Government-related companies which will hold the shares in trust for the Malays, the small number of privileged Malays described earlier and those few who are joining them as new politicians, leaders, and families rise to the fore are naturally the second most important group who will be acquiring shares. Since they are the group that possesses the wealth, knowledge, and influence, they are naturally poised to participate in new ventures and the restructuring of old ones. In reality, there is substantial overlapping between this group and those who are the major decision-makers in the Government and Government-controlled corporations.

In so far as the Government corporations and the group of Malay privileged monopolize between them the bulk of the Malay share of the new and restructured, big, and profitable companies, few of the benefits of the wealth restructuring aspect of the NEP will trickle down to the average Malay. And this is not the intention. As long as the creation of a Malay business community is perceived as the key link in the fostering of national unity, it is necessary to concentrate wealth and economic power in the hands of a small minority. Yet, the promises of the NEP raised the expectations of the Malays, especially the young, well-educated and ambitious, so high that they naturally and justifiably expect to share in the restructured wealth. Unfortunately, when the restructured wealth is widely distributed, the concentration of wealth and economic power necessary for maintaining a Malay business community would dissipate.[58] Therein lies a potential tension as a result of the NEP.

The best strategy to resolve such tension from the point of view of the Malay leaders is clearly to concentrate as much of the restructured wealth as possible in trust and eventually distribute the ownership of the trusts to the Malay general public. However, to ensure control of the trusts as a Malay counter-weight to the foreign and non-Malay business community, it is necessary to concentrate at least a workable controlling minority-holding of the trust in the hands of a few élite and to build up a whole echelon of Malay executives in the various trust organizations. This is a second reason why it may be necessary to perpetuate the concentration of Malay shares in trusts.

Before the Government began to implement more aggressive policies of share acquisition and corporate take-overs, it is possible that these young men could still have entered the business field or might have been trained as executives. However, the numbers would be smaller. More significantly, they would have been in a subordinate position as their existence and position would be subject to the calculations and goodwill of their bosses—the big local and foreign businessmen. They would have had relatively little prospect of changing this very dependent relationship. Now, with the policy of trust management on behalf of the Government and with funds provided by the Government, these young men have the opportunity to alter the dynamics to one of less dependency. In their role as trust managers, they are an equal, if not dominant, partner. The more they acquire in trust, the more power and initiative is likely to rest in their hands. The salary, bonus, fees, and other payments that they receive in executing their duties would rise proportionately, not to mention the higher executive positions they can create for their peers. These considerations are especially important if, as we have argued in preceding paragraphs, the chances of these young people striking it rich independently or in partnership with big non-Malay and foreign businessmen are slim.

Therefore, it is likely that one can observe more and more economic nationalism on the rise, reflecting the desire of these young professionals-politicians-civil servants-executives to establish an independent economic base in juxtaposition to the foreign and big local businessmen. Examples would be actions such as the Petroleum Development Act, pressure for the legislation and the speedy and thorough implementation of the ICA, the take-over of London Tin and Sime Darby.

They will continue to exercise great influence and acquire high income and eventual wealth, so long as the trusts are not broken up or so long as they are broken up in such a way that the positions of trust managers are retained. Hence the interest of this group will lie in perpetuating the existence of these trusts. This is precisely what Snodgrass means in speculating that there is a built-in bias of trust management working towards perpetuation of the trust set-up and against the distribution of the shares held in trust.[59]

On the other hand, another factor has to be borne in mind. At this stage of Malaysia's economic development and given the system of free enterprise economy, the main motivating force of growth still lies with the foreign and local businessmen. It will probably be quite a while before enough Malay executives are trained to be in a position continually to initiate and implement new business ventures on their own. Yet, too rapid acquisition by the trusts may impede the foreign and local business interests in their investment decisions. The slowdown and slow recovery in private investment since 1975 is at least in part due to investors' discomfort at the implementation of the NEP and ICA.[60] Thus, one would also expect those in the more senior ranks, those more far-sighted, and perhaps also with more benefits to gain outside of the trust arrangement among this group of politicians-civil servants-executives to pursue a more careful balance in restructuring the growth of the economy.

Meanwhile, with the rapidly expanding number of Malay college graduates, it is unlikely that all, or most of them, can share in the fruits of this restructuring, however fast it can be pursued. Those left behind and those who are more equity-minded are likely to become increasingly vocal about the inequity of the wealth restructuring. A recent very defensive speech by the Deputy Prime Minister is a reflection of the weight of such critics.[61]

What are the attitudes of these Malay executives towards co-operation with local businessmen? *A priori*, there should be no resistance to co-operating with them. In reality, local businesses tend to offer a lower level of surplus and profitability than the foreign ones (Chapter 6). Secondly, they can offer a more modest potential of growth since they tend to be in need of technology and perhaps access to international markets as well. The implication is that only the really large non-Malay businessmen can overcome these handicaps and be attractive to the Malay executives as partners.

At another level, we have discussed earlier the difficulties encountered by the medium- to large-sized non-Malay businessmen in fulfilling the restructuring objective and their consequential resistance to it. Their resistance may be seen by the Malay executives as being unco-operative and may even be viewed with resentment. This does not improve their lack of attractiveness as potential partners to the Malay executives. Yet, at this stage of economic development, these middle to large non-Malay businessmen still have an important role to play in terms of expanding the productive capacity of the nation to absorb the growing labour force and to take in an increasing proportion of Malay workers at all levels. In recognition of this role, a little more sympathy for, and some accommodation of the problems of, this level of businessmen would appear necessary.

1. *Third Malaysia Plan, 1976–1980*, Table 9-9, p. 184.

2. Chapters 5 and 6 have documented some of the more important changes in the control of major corporations by the Malays and the Government on their behalf. Since the restructuring of Sime Darby and UMBC in 1977, and

the tin group in 1976, more moves have been announced in 1978. The setting up of the Bumiputra Foundation in 1978 is probably the most important as it has a massive initial fund ($200 million) to acquire shares and has obtained significant minority interests in Sime Darby, K.L.–Kepong and other corporations. Subsequently, Pernas gained majority control of Island and Peninsular, and through it, a stake in K.L.–Kepong through Batu Kawan. In addition Pernas, SD and KLK have joint control of H & L, SD bought close to 30 per cent stake in Guthrie and a small stake in Harrisons & Crosfield. These are quite apart from the tin interests of the Selangor State Economic Development Corporation through the Perangsang Selangor, not to mention the buying of the majority ownership of a coastal shipping company by Datuk Syed Nahar from Straits Steamship, the setting up of a new bank in East Malaysia by a Malay group, the acquisition of controlling interest by the Fleet group of companies which owns the New Straits Times group in Bian Chiang Bank and others.

3. By Indians, here, we are referring to all the peoples originating from the Indian sub-continent including the Ceylonese, but who are now residing in Malaysia.

4. The group turnover was in excess of $100 million in the years 1974 and 1975; see company file with the Registrar of Companies.

5. For example, Doshi's, Green Silk Store, Globe Silk Store, Gian Singh, etc.

6. Most of the few Indian estate-owners listed in the *Straits Times Directory* of the various years are in fact Chettiars. This is of course not solid evidence but is an indication. Moreover, Kratoska (*The Chettiar and the Yeoman: British Cultural Categories and Rural Indebtedness in Malaya*) has talked about the Chettiar money-lenders foreclosing on land for loan repayment default. The author has also checked with a few small estate owners who claimed to have borrowed at high interest from the Chettiars.

7. This is according to a referee.

8. Interview with Dr P. P. Narayanan, leader of the National Union of Plantation Workers, in *Malaysian Business*, November 1975.

9. Their insurance activity has already been discussed in Chapter 5. The development of the Jaya Puri Hotel and the adjacent commercial property is one of their larger projects.

10. See note 57 of Chapter 7 for some historical sources.

11. See for example Milton Esman, *Administration and Development in Malaysia*, Ithaca, Cornell University Press, 1972.

12. Interview with Tengku Ariff Bendahara in *Asia Business and Industry*.

13. See his biography in *Who's Who in Malaysia*, various years.

14. Gathered from a combination of *Who's Who in Malaysia*, various years, *Information on Malaysia*, 1975/76, *Biography of Directors*, Singapore, Stock Exchange of Singapore, 1974.

15. 'Tunku', 'Tungku', 'Tengku', 'Tuanku', and 'Raja' are all equivalent to the title of 'prince'. Hereditary 'Datuks' are usually noblemen who have performed services for royalty. In modern days, the conferment of a Datukship has become more prevalent but it is not hereditary. 'Tan Sri' is a title given by the Yang Dipertuan Agung (King) of Malaysia to citizens who have performed distinguished services to the nation. 'Haji' is the title that Malaysian Muslims assume once they have performed the haj to Mecca. The number of people who have performed the pilgrimage has risen sharply in modern days due in part to the relatively cheaper cost of travelling, the higher standard of living, and well-organized trips for the faithful. However, in the olden days until as recently as the Second World War, it was not easy to pay for the pilgrimage.

Hence, they were likely to be from a relatively upper-class background which means that their sons would probably stand to benefit from relative prosperity.

16. Tan Chee Beng, 'Baba and Nyonya: A Study of the Ethnic Identity of the Chinese Peranakan in Malacca', unpublished Ph.D. dissertation, Cornell University, 1979.

17. Huang, *An Introductory Exposition into the Social History of the Malayan Chinese*, Tables.

18. See for example, Jackson, *Planters and Speculators Chinese and European Agricultural Enterprise in Malaya 1786–1921.*

19. The chances are slimmer because mining operations cannot be conducted anywhere. Mining sites are usually far away from urban centres and mining operations require the support of the local Malays who know the area, the control of a group of labourers and ability to arrange for a minimal supply of essentials to maintain the troop in the exploration and early mining process. On the other hand, it is possible for a planter and perhaps his family to try to open up a small tract of land which is naturally less costly and demanding. See Wong Lin Ken, *The Malayan Tin Industry to 1914*, on early mining.

20. For history of Lee Kong Chian, see article and book written by Tan Ee Leong; for Kuok, see write-up in *Insight*, September 1978.

21. For those who are interested in this development, see Huang, op. cit., writing on the development of the three-tier distribution system, and Lee Poh Ping, 'Chinese Society in Nineteenth and Early Twentieth Century Singapore', on the supplementary and competing role played by the Chinese businessmen to the British.

22. Whenever there was a downturn, retrenchment always occurred. The most severe retrenchment probably occurred during the depression of the thirties. Many historical writings have documented this.

23. The organization of Chinese businesses from the time they first set foot in Malaysia till quite recently has always been based on clan related concepts. Huang, op. cit., provides a documentation of the socio-economics of this development. The clannishness meant that Chinese from different provinces and dialect groups would have been discriminated against by one another, let alone non-Chinese trying to penetrate the business world.

24. For the data on distribution by size of turnover, see Table 6.4. Here, our interest is not so much GOS or shareholders' share but the amount of funds for reinvestment available to the company. In Chapter 6 of Tan, 'Income Distribution and Determination in West Malaysia', it has been pointed out that profit is about half of GOS. Since the profit tax is 40 per cent and interest payment is about 5 to 10 per cent of the GOS, the amount of funds for reinvestment works out to be the GOS – (profit tax + interest payment) = about 70 to 75 per cent GOS. It is just that GOS and shareholders' share are used as proxies for indicative purposes.

25. It was observed that the larger the mine, the higher the GOS, ranging from 39 per cent for the smallest to 62 per cent for the very large foreign mines (Table 6.3). Thus, the sixteen local mines with sales from \$1—2 million, nine with \$2—5 million and one in excess of \$5 million can generate enough GOS and funds for reinvestment to venture into another field. In addition, when ownership of multiple mines is taken into consideration, some of the eighty-six mines with sales between \$0.5 and 1 million can also generate enough surpluses if the whole group of mines belonging to one business group is taken as one unit. Indeed, many of the miners in this category have reinvested in other business activities, for example, Low Yat and Sons into hotels (the Federal Hotel chain), cement manufacturing and property development; Eu Tong Sen's family into finance, drugs, properties and manufacturing; Loke Yew's family into banking, property development, film making and distribu-

tion, and estate holding (see Charts 5.17, 5.22 and 5.25 in Tan, 'Income Distribution . . .'), Chong Kok Lim and Sons into hotel (Regent of K.L.) and property development (Sungei Wang Plaza), both with UDA.

26. Although we do not have precise figures on the number of estate owners who can generate such levels of surplus, it is possible to make estimates. This can be done by using the distribution of acreage operated by the estate owners summarized in Table 5.2 in conjunction with known data on yield and cost of production, as well as price level and the corresponding export duty.

27. This can be seen by the number of very wealthy rubber estate owners, for example the late Lim Lean Teng, the Saw brothers, Heah Joo Seang, etc.

28. The export duties should be deducted as they are not available to the remillers-exporters for reinvestment or other purposes. 1968 was a bad year in terms of rubber prices of between 110¢ and 120¢ per kilo with total tax duties of about 13.5 per cent. In fact, export duties collected that year were $52 million out of a total export value of $1,353.2 million or 3.84 per cent; to this add 11¢ per kilo of replanting and research cesses or about 9.52 per cent giving a total of 13.36 per cent. See Treasury, *Economic Report*, 1973–4, Table 4.3a, pp. 114—15.

29. This is obtained by subtracting 13.36 per cent of the sales value from the estimated GOS.

30. This example clearly illustrates the severity of rubber cess and duties and its disincentive impact on estate owners to replant with rubber and encouragement to the remillers-exporters to shift out of rubber. This is especially true in view of the attractive profit offered by planting oil palm.

31. Because of the price fluctuations, the smallholders, dealers, and remillers/exporters all watch the market closely. For example, the dealer may not be able to control the time when rubber will be transported to his premises for sale. It may arrive when the price level may not be to his liking and he may in turn not be able to reach a mutually satisfactory price with the next level of dealer. As a result, he may decide to participate in forward selling or buying. If every dealer and importer/exporter participates in this futures market, the amount of speculation is bound to increase.

There is another driving force towards speculation. The export duty the exporter has to pay is calculated by the Government based on the average price of the two weeks preceding the loading of cargo on to the ship itself. On the other hand, the rubber being exported may have been bought from dealers at least a month in advance for reprocessing, packaging, and so on. When the market is volatile, the difference in price in that one month can be very substantial and the delay of loading by one or two days or the speeding up of loading may result in a lower tax payment with the averaging of prices. To gain added protection (or due to greed for that matter), the exporter may feel compelled to trade on the futures market as a hedge against big fluctuations. Furthermore, in the régime of currency uncertainties (most of the rubber is sold on the British £ or US$ contracts), there is added uncertainty to worry about.

32. This refers to a price level in excess of 150¢ per kilo.

33. This is because the bigger the operation becomes, the more likely is the existence of duplication, i.e., the owning of multiple establishments or mines or estates, each one of which is of a large size. Therefore, it is highly unlikely that the 2,000 or so establishments would all be independent of one another. This is also not to say that the small and medium-sized establishments and firms cannot, and do not, expand and diversify; it is just that they will end up being involved in small and medium-sized activities on a modest scale of operation compared with the giants.

34. See Yeh Tai Heng, 葉痁痕，梹榔嶼大觀 *An Overview of Penang*.

35. A conservative estimate would be 40 per cent. The world smelting capacity in 1965 was 360,000 tons, the two smelters in Malaysia totalled 150,000 tons. In addition, it is reported that the parent company of Eastern Smelting (as it was then known) controls smelters in U.K. with a capacity of 55,000 tons. From the same source, it is possible to infer from London Tin control of Nigerian mines that its then parent company, the Patino-controlled Consolidated Smelters (also the holding company of Eastern Smelting and the U.K. smelters) probably has control of the smelter there too. For smelting capacity by country, see International Tin Council, *Report on the World Tin Position with Projections for 1965 and 1970*, by W. Robertson, London, 1865, Table II. For the tin conglomerate, see account by Puthucheary, *Ownership and Control in the Malayan Economy*, and the updating in Chapters 5 and 7 of this book.

36. Moreover, both the Thais and the Indonesians have set up their own smelters and there has been decreasing smelting of ores from the two countries of late. In fact a third smelter was set up in Ipoh a few years ago by some Japanese interests and the venture failed due to the difficulty of obtaining an adequate supply of ore.

37. Horizontal integration however has occurred. Local planters have established plantation agencies to complement their planting activities once their estate holdings reached an economic size. The earliest example is probably the Malacca planting syndicate headed by the late Tan Cheng Lock which set up Unitac. Thereafter, the Loke family and Tee Teh–Gan Teck Yeow set up the Associated Estate Agency. More recently, Lee Loy Seng has set up the Taiko Plantation Agency to manage his vast acquisitions.

38. Most of the coconut oil mills existed in Penang, for example Ban Teck Bee, Ban Hin Lee, etc. Lam Soon was among the earliest to process coconut oil into soap products and vegetable oil. Lee Pineapple Cannery was one of the two earliest pineapple canneries.

39. The size of duplications can be estimated by comparing the number of individual proprietorships and partnerships with the number of working proprietors in each trade and industry. If an owner works full time in his individual store, he will not have time to participate in alternative activities, apart from some financial investment in another solely-owned store with hired help, or in partnership with other people where he is no more than a sleeping partner. To make this possible, his original shop has to generate enough savings and surpluses for him to afford this. From previous discussions most of the small-scale enterprises, especially the individual proprietors, have too modest a level of GOS to provide for very quick accumulation of capital. The number of part-time working owners and absentee owners can be another reflection of the holding of multiple establishments by the individual proprietor. Thus, of the 5,785 manufacturing establishments run as individual proprietorships, there were 5,346 full-time owners and 293 part-time owners; for the mining sector, there were 127 full-time working proprietors among 247 individual proprietorships (see *Census of Manufacturing 1968* and *Census of Mining Industries 1968* or summary in Table 8.4, Tan, 'Income Distribution . . .'). That is to say, there were 146 manufacturing establishments and 120 mining establishments without a working proprietor. This represents the upper limit of duplication of ownership of establishments at the small-scale level.

40. However, it is not uncommon to see the Malay partner acquiring the shares without the cash payment of capital but with the future earnings of the allotted shares, i.e., the Malay partners under such arrangements use the dividend payment or accumulated earnings of the shares to repay the loan granted them to acquire the shares.

41. The size of their shareholdings in these companies has not been traced, but is likely to be small.

42. This point has already been documented in Chapter 5.

43. Chang set up the Merlin Hotel with Lim Foo Yong but merged it with Faber Union controlled by Raper to form Faber Merlin. After a few turbulent years and bitter struggles, Chang managed to gain control of Faber Merlin with Raper pulling out. Thereafter, the Faber Merlin group wrested control of Pahang Consolidated from the foreigners and through the latter built up a significant minority stake in Plantation Holdings, another foreign-controlled company in the orbit of Hutchison International of Hong Kong. However, in the process, Faber Merlin and Pahang Consolidated built up a cross holding with one another which together with other factors caused the Stock Exchange to demand a disentanglement of these mutual holdings. See *Straits Times*' Business section in 1972, *Far Eastern Economic Review*, various issues, especially 13, 20 and 27 June and 14 November 1975. Plantation Holdings has since been taken over by the Malaysian Chinese Association's economic arm and renamed Malaysian Plantations Bhd.

Nevertheless, it should not be misconstrued that Chang's group is anti-foreigner as he has gone into partnership with Toronto Dominion Bank to control the Overseas Trusts Bank in Hong Kong.

44. Under the Industrial Co-ordination Act, it is theoretically possible to force all firms with more than $500,000 in shareholders' fund to restructure 30 per cent of the share capital for the Malays. Under the original terms of the Act, $250,000 was the cut-off point. This would still leave most of the firms we have analysed outside the scope of the Act, although from the perspective of analysing corporate wealth, firms with paid-up capital of less than $1 million generally should not be considered big.

45. In general, for researchers who are interested in the opinions of the small traders and small manufacturing establishments, the Chinese press has good coverage of the activities and statements of the organizations representing these small businesses. The English and Malay press, on the other hand, have ignored these people. In 1978 alone, there were many statements in the Chinese press about threats of supermarket and departmental store chains to the small retailers. As an example, please refer to a speech by Mr Lim Kim Joo, President of the Penang Chinese Traders' Confederation, in 1977 (*Kwong Wah Yit Poh* and *Penang Sin Poh* 光華日報, 4 March 1977).

46. This will cover those firms with a paid-up capital of $\$\frac{1}{2}$ million and above, up to several million (probably no more than 5 million), i.e., slightly above the minimal covered by the Industrial Co-ordination Act.

47. The Industrial Co-ordination Act covers only the industrial enterprises. However, the mining companies have to renew their leases, property development companies have to seek permission for the conversion of land titles and the subdivision of land for housing development, transport companies need licences to purchase vehicles, all of which means that the Government can choose to apply pressure and has done so. See *Economic Quarterly* 經濟季刊 11, for a summary of some of the difficulties the Chinese businessmen encountered and perceived. In fact, the economic convention of the Malaysian Chinese itself is much more interesting and useful in that many actual examples of difficulties came up in the course of discussions.

48. We talk of giving up a chunk of future profit in the following sense: had there been no restructuring requirement, the proponent(s) of the venture could afford to finance and operate the project totally and could therefore reap 100 per cent of the profit generated. Now, however, the need to sell 30 per cent of the venture means that 30 per cent of whatever profit generated has passed into the hands of others. In addition, if there is a need to finance the 30 per cent acquisition for the Malay partner(s), the cost becomes greater.

49. Perhaps an example can best illustrate. Company *A* is expanding. It has paid-up capital of $1.0 million, fixed and net asset value of $2.0 million.

It is planning an expansion of $2.0 million which will be financed by $1.0 million in retained earnings and $1.0 million in loans. If 30 per cent of the capital has to be reserved since the company is undergoing expansion (the arithmetic is only slightly different if the equivalent of 30 per cent of the new expansion has to be restructured, presumably using some percentage of the value of new and old assets as a guide in allocating the percentage of share capital to be restructured), what would be a fair price? The true worth of the company at this point is $3.0 million ($1.0 million in paid-up capital, $1.0 million in retained earnings, and $1.0 million in hidden earnings, since the book value of the fixed assets is only $2.0 million when it is worth $3.0 million in the market). It is easy enough to argue for a price of $2.0 per share but it may be difficult to get Government approval for $3.0 per share. Further, once 30 per cent of the capital is reserved and the price is agreed upon, say $2.50, it makes a difference whether the Malay partners sign over $750,000 for the 300,000 shares, or whether they choose, or have to owe, to be indebted by that amount which would be covered by future dividends coming from the owning of 300,000 shares. In the former case, the original shareholders presumably can utilize the $750,000 in alternative ventures or otherwise, while in the latter they end up effectively giving away 30 per cent of their capital. If interest is charged on the outstanding loan, the situation is of course better.

In the case of a new venture, Malay partners may be additionally reluctant to undertake the initial investment because of the risky nature of new ventures. A non-Malay businessman who can undertake new ventures but is not wealthy enough to have plenty of surplus funds may need to peddle the 30 per cent share to some other non-Malays for the capital and would resent having have to reserve 30 per cent for capital that may not be immediately forthcoming. Of course he can seek to raise the paid-up capital to allow for the short-term shortage of capital and invite other non-Malays, but that would have the effect of diluting the profit per share, hence the attractiveness of the venture, not to mention his own decreased share of the profit.

50. A couple of examples raised by businessmen in the 1978 Malaysian Chinese Economic Convention can help to illustrate the problem. One industrialist complained that he was asked to surrender his freehold land title for one with a negotiable five-year lease title as a condition for approving his plan for the erection of a brick factory. Another complained that he sold 30 per cent of his shares in a transport company at par and below market value to Malay interests who immediately sold them at three times par value to other non-Malays and he had just received notification that he needs to restructure. No doubt these may have been the worst examples, but they nevertheless represent part of a widespread complaint.

51. *Nanyang Siang Pau*, *Sin Chew Jit Poh*, and other Chinese dailies provide good coverage of the objections raised by the Chinese businessmen in their various meetings in drafting proposals to amend the Industrial Co-ordination Act. In particular, see *Economic Quarterly* 經濟季刊 11, and press coverage in March and April 1978. Milne, 'The Politics of Malaysia's New Economic Policy', also contains some documentation of this.

52. It is a second-best position because they get squeezed by complying, as pointed out in notes 48 and 49. On the other hand, if they do not comply, not only would they face difficulties in expanding, the threat is always there that other difficulties can be thrown in the way of their existing operations, or new legislation drawn up to force even the restructuring of existing operations.

53. This can be ascertained by checking the business background of the leaders of the Chinese Chamber of Commerce in the different areas. For example, the Kuoks, Chang Ming Thien, and the Kweks of Hong Leong have never

been actively involved in the affairs of the Chambers.

54. See for example the various issues of *Economic Quarterly* 經濟季刊 for writings with regard to the role of foreign and local non-Malay investments.

55. This can be seen from the fact that less than 2 per cent of the corporate shares were held in the hands of Malay individuals while 6 per cent were in the hands of the Government trust operations in 1975. This is hardly surprising as the small number of Malay businessmen means that the number of those who can initiate and generate new projects will be limited in the short and medium run.

56. For example, N. M. Rothschild was the adviser to Pernas in the take-over of London Tin and in the fight for control of Sime Darby as well as a partner in a local bank. Now Morgan Grenfell is also playing the same advisory role and investing as a partner in a local bank. By contrast, hardly any local non-Malay businessmen are seeking such expertise.

57. This can be seen in the rapidly expanding number of Malay students the Government has been sending to the U.S. for further education under various programmes, the bolstering of the role of Intan, Institut Tadbiran Awam Negara or the Public Servants' Training Institute, the emphasis placed on pushing for business education in local tertiary education and so on.

58. The speech by the Deputy Prime Minister, Dr Mahathir, in late October 1978, at the Bumiputra Economic Convention at Universiti Kebangsaan Malaysia, attacking critics who are hostile to the idea of creating concentration of wealth in the hands of a minority of Malays is in fact an implicit acknowledgement of this problem.

59. Snodgrass, *Inequality and Economic Development in Malaysia.*

60. The prolonged slowdown in the private investment in Malaysia since the end of 1974 can be caused by three factors that are probably mutually reinforcing. The first and widely proclaimed reason in official circles is the world-wide problem with stagflation and its aftermath which has generally slowed investment in the industrial and developing countries. The second and widely proclaimed reason in the private sector is the adverse impact of the Industrial Co-ordination Act and the Petroleum Development Act which shook investor confidence. The third reason may be due to the changing structure of the Malaysian manufacturing sector. In the years after Independence, the thrust of industrialization was import substitution, giving rise to a fairly broadly-based industrial sector. However, by the seventies, the amount of investment in the import-substitution field may have climaxed, given the limited market size of a small country like Malaysia. On the other hand, the new growth industries such as electronics and textiles are very dependent on the international economy. Thus, the transition from import substitution into export promotion in a period of international economic uncertainties may have compounded the problem of investment.

At any rate, by late 1975 and definitely by 1976, investment recovery in neighbouring ASEAN countries such as Singapore and Thailand had become very strong, as had that of Taiwan and Hong Kong. Therefore, the prolonged stagnation in the recovery of Malaysian private investment cannot be simply explained by world trends. In the case of market saturation, the situation is not static either. In the last three years, Malaysia has generally enjoyed good commodity prices and the national income of the country has grown significantly, probably by a larger amount than indicated by the growth in real GNP. In the context of a growing national income, it is a matter of time before the purchasing power of the people and hence the market becomes attractive again to the import-substitution kind of industries. Therefore, neither can the third reason of market saturation stand on its own to explain the sluggishness in private investment.

61. See note 58.

9 Conclusion

THIS book set out to document the distribution of income and wealth in Malaysia. First we tried to determine who are the poor and who are the rich and trace the trend of inequality, especially since Independence. An equally important concern was the attempt to identify the determinants of this inequality. One aspect of this involved the analyses of the causes of poverty among different groups of people as well as within the society as a whole. The converse of it—what is responsible for the concentration of wealth among groups of individuals and to what extent is upward mobility possible for the majority of the population under the present conditions—was given equal attention. In the process, some methodological problems in the study of income distribution and determination and the attempt to integrate the two were highlighted. The preceding chapters have set out the necessary data and documentation for our concluding observations in this chapter.

9.1 DETERMINANTS OF INCOME INEQUALITY

The basic approach on income determinants of this book was outlined in Chapter 1. It has been advanced that the income of an individual is dependent on three related factors: the effort he puts in, the skills he has, and the opportunities available to him. Let us now briefly review our observations on this question.

A. Effort of the Individual in Determining Income

Many people, both laymen and social scientists, subscribe to the view that individualistic and subjective factors such as attitudes to work which affect effort put in by the individual are paramount in determining objective economic status and well-being. In the Malaysian context, this view often takes on a racial hue—the common stereotype is that the Malays are poor or less well off because they are resistant to change, or they are lazy, or they just make less effort. This is then contrasted with the opposite stereotype of the Chinese as hard-working, highly adaptable, and resourceful.

When comparisons are drawn between two groups of people, it is important to ask whether there is any proper basis for doing so, otherwise one is bound to come up with erroneous and biased analyses. This is even more likely to happen when the comparisons are being drawn between two ethnic groups, as the fallacious comparisons are bolstered by, and further reinforce, common racial stereotypes. It may be meaningful to compare Chinese and Malay farmers in one region, but rural Malays and urban Chinese are obviously going to be different, just as rural Chinese smallholders will differ from urban Chinese. Even when one is comparing farmers in the same place, it is still important to isolate factors such as agricultural practices available to one group but not to another.

In Chapter 2, we discussed an example where the Malay and Chinese padi farmers in the Tanjong Karang region were found to have put in similar efforts as reflected in man-days of work in a year. In fact, some of the Malay farmers had put in more. The difference in their yields was consequently small. Where there were differences, these were accounted for by differences in agricultural practices. The Chinese smallholders brought with them traditional practices from China where vegetable farming is an integral part of their general cultivation. This is a skill of production much less familiar to the Malays and their practice of fruit planting (coconuts, bananas, durians, and others) has not been developed to an equally productive and profitable level as yet. Clearly, lower income in the same occupation is not simply a matter of less effort deserving less pay. And, effort in any case is not an independent characteristic, it is a function of opportunity and hence can be induced or discouraged. When the opportunity is clearly illustrated to farmers in terms they value, effort will be forthcoming.

A second example is in Wikkramatileke's study of the performances of the Malay and Chinese settlers on an adjoining FLDA scheme. His conclusion, that the Chinese settlers worked harder and paid more attention to their farming, resulting in higher incomes, is objectively true. However, the reason for the Malays' relative lack of success may not be *simply* a case of laziness. One reason for the Chinese success was again their flourishing vegetable gardening.[1] Consequently, the success of the Chinese and their knowledge that vegetable gardening is productive spurs them to work harder; and success breeds more effort and more success. The contrary is also true.

These two examples illustrate the point that effort is not an independent variable and it is pointless to research into it as if it were so. The lively debate between Parkinson (1967, 1968) and Wilder (1968) on the non-economic factors in the economic retardation of the rural Malays illustrates that even when a sympathetic attempt is made to explain lack of effort in terms of socio-cultural factors, it is not much more successful. The most salient point which emerged from the exchange was the contradictory nature of the question itself.

It is claimed that the Malays are resistant to change for a variety of reasons social, cultural, religious. But so are other people, including the Malaysian Chinese. Yet, when the advantages of change can be illustrated in a meaningful way, they have been adopted. In reality, Malay modes of production have changed, however slowly or painfully. In Chapters 2 and 3 we documented the gradual but nevertheless significant conversion to double cropping, rubber planting and replanting, adaptation to oil palm growing under Felda, and the motorization of fishing boats. Hence for every point one social scientist raises on Malay resistance to change, another can easily put forward a counter-example and the exchange goes on indecisively. This illustrates the futility of a debate based only on partial observations. Change, effort, and skill must be motivated by a combination of reward, sensitivity, and a recognition and appreciation of the influence of socio-cultural background.

B. Skills and Upward Mobility

The only group of Malaysians with significant upward mobility are the university and college graduates who form the bulk of the upper- and high-income brackets. Apparently, tertiary education either trains or affords the necessary entry point into on-the-job training for higher paying jobs. But it has been established that the offspring of the rich have almost eight times as high an enrolment rate in tertiary education as those from the poorest income bracket.[2] The people in the middle class are largely those who have at least secondary school education. The sons and daughters of the rich also have a higher incidence of enrolment in secondary schools than those from the poorest households, though the difference is only 1½ times.[3]

The implication is that the opportunity for upward mobility or even the ability to maintain social status is definitely biased in favour of the higher income brackets. This is particularly significant because a change in the level of education is felt by those in the next generation of any given household. Consequently, the relative lack of opportunity for receiving higher levels of education by the children of the poor will confine their households to their respective income groups for at least one whole generation, if not more.[4]

At the level of wealth and property holding, Part II documented the extent of concentration of holdings, and how this limits upward mobility by the smaller traders and businessmen to the top of the business pyramid.[5] If the small traders find it difficult, how would it be possible for the non-traders, especially the workers and farmers, to aspire to wealth? A study on Malay entrepreneurship has shown that it is the offspring of businessmen who have the greater probability of success.[6] Perhaps this is an indication that 'on-the-job training' acquired from background and upbringing is important. The same would be true for the other races. The odds against upward mobility are indeed great.

It is now necessary to re-address the question of skill. The skills of the farmers and wage workers are clearly not items students learn in the existing school system. Indeed, most of such skills are picked up on the job. A farmer's child learns from helping in cultivation from his youth, while a worker learns his job in the factory or on apprenticeship to a skilled craftsman. A primary or even secondary school education generally does not provide any added skill to the income-earning ability of a farmer or worker in the short run. It is even doubtful whether their schooling is adequate to help them to pick up new methods from reading magazines and pamphlets. These levels of education are probably also insufficient to offer their recipients the necessary entry point into higher paying jobs. Therefore, until such time as adequate formal training programmes are implemented to raise the level of skills of the lower-income brackets, their skill level and the skill levels of their offspring can be considered as largely static. Of course, a more definite statement can be made only after a study of the effectiveness of Government agricultural extension work and the job training programmes (formal and informal) carried out by the private sector.

C. Structure of Income Determination

Apart from considering the effort put in and the skill level attained, it is necessary to evaluate the opportunities open to people; this is related to the structure of production and market.

At the village level, it is the structure of landholding and the use of traditional farming techniques. These limit productive capacities. It is also the prices that are received for agricultural produce and the prices paid for consumer items, especially the former.

In so far as the structure of production—organized around the family and utilizing old techniques—cannot enable the farmers to generate enough income and savings to be propelled into higher income brackets and different modes of production, it blocks improvement in the income of the farmers.

Farming techniques can be changed through Government initiatives—for example, irrigation projects for double cropping and replanting with new clones. Theoretically these changes should benefit all the relevant agricultural producers. However, those who are relatively more affluent (say the landlords, or the larger cultivators) have the resources to be among the first to take advantage of the proposed changes, and to benefit at a faster pace. Naturally, this will further enhance their already advantageous position *vis-à-vis* the smaller and/or tenant producers. Thus introducing improvements in farming techniques may increase inequality amongst the group of people the changes affect. This is when the structure of landholding becomes important, for it defines who benefits most from these Government policies.

As summarized in Chapter 2, the land tenancy system appears to be in transition from one dominated by kinship relations to one affected more by economic motivations. The former type of land tenure arrangement would render less important the projected unequalizing effect of a change in farm technique. However, since nearly half of the tenancy arrangements in the major padi areas (where the change in farming is implemented) is non-kinship-oriented and this proportion may be increasing, it does call for some concern about the unequalizing aspect.

Villagers receive prices less than the retail value of their produce (sometimes only a very small share of it), which depresses their income, because the multi-tier marketing system absorbs a significant portion of the prices along the way to support the operation cost and profit margins of the dealers at different levels. If every level of dealership is competitive, none of the dealers can dictate the terms of distribution, whether it is the number of times a product is handled, the prices at each level, the profit margin, or the volume each dealer handles. However, if monopolistic and/or monopsonistic conditions were to prevail at any one level, these terms will be affected and more manipulation will be possible by the dealers concerned, presumably to the detriment of the villagers. Figure 9.1 depicts the effect of the marketing structure on the price that the villagers receive.

The question of monopolistic-monopsonistic competition can be addressed at two levels: domestically among the different levels of dealers, and internationally including the major wholesaler-importer-exporter at the apex of the marketing pyramid within the country. Chapter 7 outlined the domestic marketing pyramid and analysed the level of competition at each level. It was ob-

FIGURE 9.1
EFFECT OF MARKETING STRUCTURE ON THE PRICES RECEIVED BY THE FARMERS

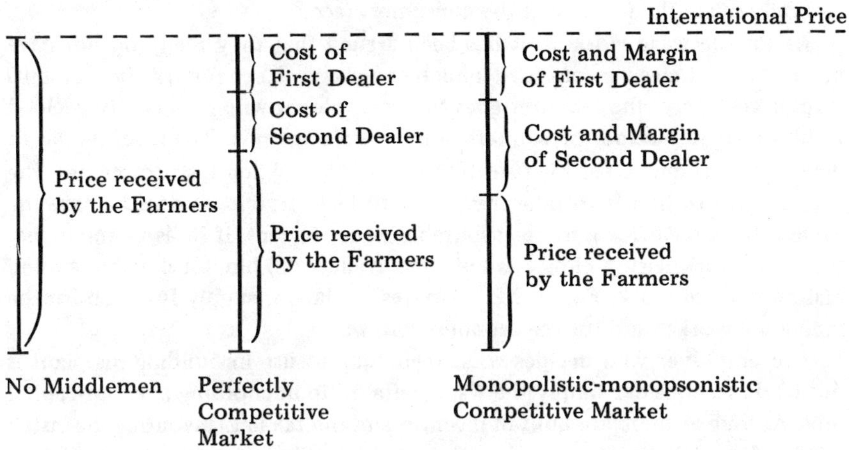

served that the extent of competition at the small- and medium-trade levels is generally keen. However, the margins retained are high, partly necessitated by the small volume of trade handled by each, the cost of credit, and the risk of customer loan default, thus imposing a burden on the farmers. And yet, the income arising from middlemen activities for these small traders is generally modest.

However, our research has shown the extent of concentration of economic power in the hands of the very few, especially the foreign-controlled firms, at the apex of the pyramid. This concentration of economic power affects the prices facing the farmers and hence income distribution in the country in several ways. First, the very small number of large firms within each industry may result in oligopolistic price collusion in the domestic market. This affects the livelihood of the villagers as well as the wage workers. Secondly, since they control the inlets and outlets of particular goods, it is possible for them to influence price increases or reductions, and the volume of business at each level through the granting and withdrawal of agency licences, credit, and discounts. Thirdly, most of the large conglomerates span a wide range of activities, possibly enhancing their ability to bring about the necessary manipulations in order to dictate terms. This is of course a hypothesis needing further research and substantiation.

The Government can influence prices to some extent, but by and large, prices are determined by the marketing structure unless the Government is willing to replace the whole system with a new Government-run system and redistribute any profit back to the villagers. The question is, however, whether such a system can run more efficiently than the present one, such that the overall marketing cost is actually lower than that offered by the present marketing system. It should be recalled that we found the smaller middlemen really making a return equivalent to a pay-off to their labour.

For domestically manufactured goods, the raw materials and parts are frequently imported and then manufactured or assembled locally for distribution. In such cases, there is usually a foreign partner in the few oligopolistic firms, who in addition to being able to dictate the prices of raw materials and parts, and the terms of distribution, can also lobby for tariff protection. This process naturally raises the prices that the consumers face.

As for the wage workers, it has been argued that they really do not have competitive choices as outlined under neo-classical economics. In a labour-surplus economy, the labourer goes to the employer who has already decided to hire a fixed number of workers at a certain wage rate. The labourer has to 'line up' in a queue for his turn to be employed. When his turn comes, the choice open to him is to take the job or to leave it; seldom does he have the chance to bargain for a more favourable wage. In fact, if he is unemployed, the usual work/leisure choice is not even available to him until he has a minimal amount of work. Figure 9.2 illustrates the labour supply function for the individual worker and for the economy as a whole.

The employer who decides what technique to use in building his plant is not likely to consider simply the wage-rental ratio in choosing a labour-capital mix. As long as there are built-in incentives in the tax laws favouring the installation of capital equipment, this will limit the employment creation capacities of new industries. All these limit the bargaining position of the workers. If they were to organize and resort to industrial action to force an increase in wages, employers are likely to resort to more capital-intensive equipment in future investments. In short, the bargaining power of workers is extremely constrained under the present system of decision-making by the very few.

At the international level, this study has attempted initial documenting of the extent of concentration and control of the output of some of the major commodities that Malaysia produces. For example, in the case of tin, one major producer, Charter Consolidated, shares in the control of 42 per cent of Malaysian output. This is in addition to its interest in, or control of, tin mines in Nigeria, Thailand, Bolivia, and elsewhere. In the case of rubber, the large foreign estate owners in Malaysia frequently possess estates in Sri Lanka and Indonesia as well.[7] The point is that when they are also tied up with major British financial and industrial interests, their power in the international market is greatly enhanced. Although this is in itself an insufficient basis to claim that they do exercise significant monopoly-monopsony power, the possibility of significant dictation of trading terms cannot be overlooked, especially in view of the history of price-setting under international cartel arrangements. At the very least, it does show the need for more intensive research into this area in the future.

9.2 REMARKS ON CONCEPTS AND METHODOLOGY

At the conceptual level, this study has tried to introduce two important factors into the study of income distribution. First is the attempt to integrate the study of income distribution with the study of income determination. It is argued that the computation of a Gini coefficient or some other income-distribution reflecting index is not in itself useful. The most important thing is to recognize the factors responsible for poverty and the possible changes

FIGURE 9.2
LABOUR SUPPLY FUNCTION FOR THE INDIVIDUAL AND THE ECONOMY

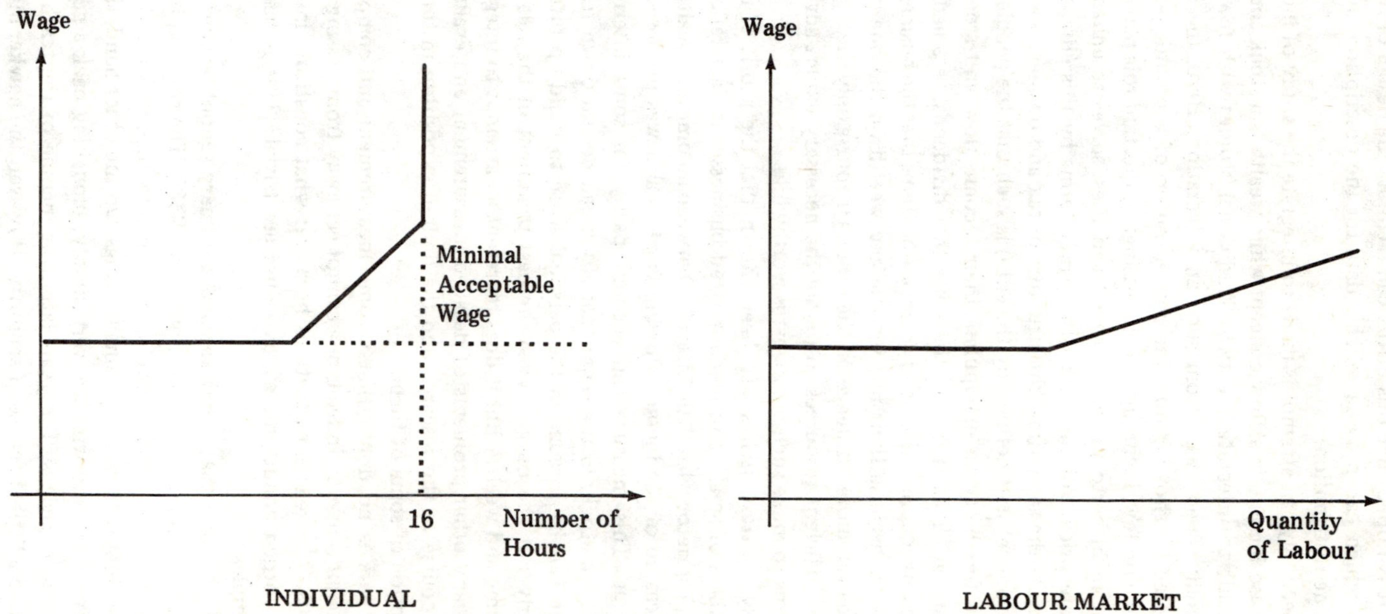

that can be introduced to raise income. As such, much attention is given to the factors influencing income in all the major economic activities in the country. It is hoped that this effort can facilitate the design of future income surveys which can provide reliable data for the description and explanation of income distribution.

Secondly, an attempt is made to integrate the study of income and wealth. Because income is a flow concept while wealth is a stock concept, it has been difficult to integrate the two. Traditional studies with few exceptions have generally shied away from such an integration. Here, the integration is attempted by showing how the concentration of economic power in the hands of an élite few, including the increasingly important role played by the Government in hitherto private business activities, serves to enhance the ability to dictate price, volume, and other trade terms by this élite, foreign and local alike. At the same time, the structure of tax and business laws (which incidentally are set and defined by the élite) is such that the people at the apex have great flexibility to manipulate their income flow and stock assets to their advantage. This is true in the sense that dividends, retained profits, expense accounts, depreciation, and so on, are all items that the businessmen can manipulate to disguise their real income and wealth on the one hand, and to generate even more affluence on the other. Of course only the biggest businessmen have sufficient resources to obtain the necessary expert advice and sufficient returns to make such manoeuvres worthwhile.

By contrast, it has also been shown that the profit of most of the large numbers of small- and medium-sized businesses in fact reflects the labour of the proprietor with little interplay between income and wealth. In this context, a measure of the income flowing from wealth was proposed: gross operating surplus. This measure can account partly for some interrelations between flow and stock, in the sense that stock can be run down for income and income can be forgone in the personal sense to build up future stock. This is clearly not the only or even the best treatment of the relationship between income and wealth. But it does represent an attempt to integrate the two.

Many other problems of detailed measurement and evaluation surfaced in the course of the research and the limited exposition in the text is but a description of some of them.

There is no doubt that income measurement and comparison are full of value judgements. Indeed, one cannot get away from passing such value judgements. The relevant questions here are: what constitute important values to be worried about and which values are trivial? This is best discussed with examples.

1. Assume that a hawker and a primary school teacher both started out with the same income per month, say $300. The social upbringing and background of the teacher impinges upon him to live a certain life-style which leaves him with relatively small savings. On the other hand, the hawker can be 'allowed' to, and will, live very simply, ploughing back a good part of his income into savings. Ten years later, the income of the teacher would have increased a little, because of seniority. However, the hawker may have been able to utilize his savings to obtain higher returns, or buy a house, etc. This may or may not cause his income to be higher than that of the teacher; but in terms

of wealth, his savings with its generated wealth may put the hawker in a more affluent position. Based on investigations at the end of ten years, the hawker may be seen to be better off, but meanwhile the teacher has had a better standard of living. How does one pass a value judgement on the relative welfare of the two?

2. Should the small landed padi farmer and rubber smallholder who each makes about $2,000 per household per year be considered on a par with a small tenant farmer with little possession of non-labour means of production (i.e., land, buffalo, etc.) but also an income of $2,000? What about the urban wage earner who generally does not own any non-labour means of production nor a house? Should not some consideration be given to these differences in the construction of income distribution welfare measures?[8]

9.3 INCOME AND WEALTH DISTRIBUTION IN MALAYSIA

A. Poverty Level

Not unexpectedly, the great majority of Malaysians are poor. Without going into a detailed discussion of what constitutes a poverty level of income, it is possible to make some observations based on common sense and a general familiarity with the local economy.[9]

As an approximate gauge, any household with an annual income below $3,000 (or less than $42 per capita per month) may be considered poor. Others may take issue with this criterion and ask if an annual household income of $2,000 (or $28 per capita per month) may not be more appropriate.[10] In our judgement, an annual household income of $3,000 enables us to take into account pertinent differences in rural-urban living and include the urban poor in our consideration of poverty.

Most of the small rural producers tend to provide themselves with some food—be it padi, vegetable, fruit, poultry, or other animals. This reduces their need to purchase these items from market sources and provides them with the option of either selling some or more of these products or keeping them for home consumption. This has obvious implications on their cost of living and the flexibility is particularly important in times of rising food prices such as in 1973 and 1974. The urban wage earners, however, must purchase all their food needs from their take-home pay. Consequently, an urban wage earner with an annual income of $2,000 to $3,000 is no better off than his rural counterpart earning about $1,500 to $2,000 once the cost of food and rent have been deducted.

From an overall perspective, the difference between households with an annual income of $2,000 and those with an annual income of $3,000 is marginal in terms of economic well-being. The significant gaps in income lie between those who earn less than $3,000 annually and the high-income-bracket earners who receive more than $12,000 per year. Nevertheless, it is necessary to point out that by adopting two different criteria, the number and racial composition of people considered as poor is different. The difference however is not dramatic—on the $2,000 criterion, the proportion of Malays in the poverty group is 75 per cent and on the $3,000 criterion it is probably about

60 to 65 per cent. If one's interests lie in a genuine desire to identify poverty groups rather than giving the issue of poverty a racial undertone, the reasons for accepting the $3,000 are compelling enough.[11]

B. Summary of Distribution

It is now possible to identify the poor households in the late sixties and early seventies. These were the landless agricultural labourers, the small padi cultivators and small rubber smallholders (especially those with only partially replanted land), unmotorized fishermen (especially those on the East Coast), the unskilled urban and estate workers, the employees and some of the owner-operators in the small family enterprises (catering, retailing, hawking, etc.). They seldom received more than $1,500 per year in income, frequently less. A rough approximation is that they formed about 50 per cent of the total households.[12]

At the next level, the Malaysians with $1,500 to $3,000 per household per year were the larger and/or double cropping padi farmers, the larger rubber smallholders with matured, replanted land, the trawler fishermen, the semi-skilled and skilled workers in the urban-based activities (manufacturing, construction, mining, and the Government sector), the more affluent self-employed traders and middlemen, some hawkers, some clerks, and sales workers in retailing and catering. Approximately 25 per cent of the Malaysian population was in this category.[13]

As was indicated in Chapter 4, the middle class, with incomes ranging from $3,000 to $6,000 per household per year, probably constituted 15 per cent of the population. These were the clerks, highly skilled workers, technicians, some supervisors, teachers, sales-related workers, some medium-sized agricultural producers, and Government employees with seniority but not highly qualified or in high positions. Some households entered into this category by having more than one wage earner in the family.

Approximately a little more than 5 per cent of the population were in the upper-middle income bracket with incomes in excess of $6,000 but less than $12,000 per household per year. High-level technicians, university graduates without seniority working in the Government or within the private sector, teachers, medium-sized traders, businessmen, and some of the large smallholders made up the main components in this category.

The less than 5 per cent of the population left were the rich, i.e., those receiving in excess of $12,000 per person per year. It is necessary to divide them into two subgroups: the salary-receiving professionals and executives on the one hand, and the property and wealth holders on the other. Income levels of the first subgroup frequently reached $20,000 to $30,000 a year while many of the self-employed professionals, large traders, and businessmen received more than $50,000 per year. It must be stressed that only a very small minority, probably numbering no more than several thousand households, possess substantial property and wealth. We have documented in Chapters 5–8 the interlocking structure through which a very substantial portion of the locally-owned corporate wealth is concentrated. Obviously only an élite few—the biggest businessmen—are privileged to possess ownership and exercise control at this level.

In short, the income distribution pattern of Malaysia in the late sixties and early seventies was one stacked as follows:

Income Characteristics	*Percentage of Total Households*
Lowest-income group—$1,500 per year	50
Low-income group—$1,500 to $3,000	25
Middle-income group—$3,000 to $6,000	15
Upper-middle income group—$6,000 to $12,000	5
High-income group—$12,000+	3
Very high income group—$50,000+	2

C. Income and Wealth Distribution: Trends and Projections

From the preceding Table, it is obvious that there is very unequal distribution of income amongst Malaysians. Up to 1970, the trend was for these inequalities to widen further as the different income groups experienced disproportionate benefits from economic changes and Government policies. Thus while the top 5 per cent of the population continued to enjoy the largest relative share of total income as well as the largest increase in absolute average income, the income share of the bottom 40 per cent had in fact decreased over the thirteen-year period from 1957 to 1970.

The reasons for this are not hard to find. Up to 1970, the income of the poorest group, i.e., the small Malay farmers living in the rural areas, remained stagnant as the impact of irrigation projects on productivity and income had yet to be felt. The middle- and high-income groups did, however, benefit very rapidly from the manpower requirements arising from the expansion of the civil service, increasing manufacturing activities, and the emphasis on industrialization, as well as the provision of educational opportunity. The strides taken in industrialization also provided substantial profits for the scores of businessmen who took advantage of it. What can we project for the immediate future? We can get a clearer overall picture by tracing developments in each subgroup/sector.

We have already noted the rising inequality up to 1970 largely because of disproportionate increases in income for different income levels. This not surprisingly is reflected in increasing income inequality within each of the three major ethnic groups.

The increase in inequality amongst the Malays has been the sharpest. Up to 1970, we noted that the income of the Malay poor stagnated largely because of the lagging impact of rural development policies. On the other hand, post-Independence education policy and the expansion of the civil service with Malayanization created a more significant share of Malay middle and upper-middle income brackets. While the absolute number of Malays joining the ranks of the middle and upper-middle income groups is still slightly smaller than that of the non-Malays, their rate of increase has been very sharp.

By 1975, the Muda, Kemubu, and Besut irrigation projects were completed and double cropping was under way. Barring unforeseen circumstances, such as the extremely severe drought of 1977–8, the income of the majority of the

FIGURE 9.3
INCOME EFFECT OF THE INTRODUCTION OF DOUBLE CROPPING

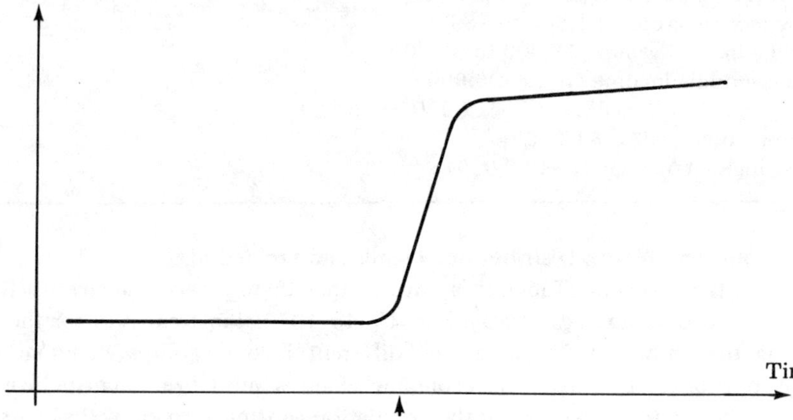

padi farmers, agricultural labourers, and traders in the newly irrigated areas should have improved.[14] One can anticipate an almost stepwise one-time increase in income for the padi farmers (Figure 9.3). The income and livelihood of a sizeable number of padi farm related families (perhaps close to 100,000) would have been pushed up, some from the lowest 40 per cent into the next higher 40 per cent.[15] However, as argued in Chapter 2, the benefits are likely to be uneven, with the poorer, smaller-plot cultivators benefiting the least and perhaps still lingering in the ranks of the bottom 40 per cent. This will be especially true in the pockets where single cropping continues to be practised. Moreover, the livelihood of the padi farmers scattered in the other states would not have improved and hence the income inequality gap within padi farming will increase.

As for the rubber smallholders, by 1975 the replanting programme should have been completed. But income in this case is difficult to anticipate because of the big fluctuations in the price of rubber (see Figure 9.4). However, the price trend of rubber took a favourable upward turn from 1975 to 1978 after the two dips in prices in 1972 and 1974 which caused widespread difficulties to the rubber smallholders.[16] Therefore, the income of the rubber smallholders should have grown by between 50 and 100 per cent in the 1975 to 1978 period after the declines in 1972 and 1974 due to the increased yield and better prices, perhaps due more to the latter than the former. In short, the magnitude of the increase in their income roughly kept pace with that of the double-cropping padi farmers. Projecting ahead, with the so-called 'energy crisis' forcing up the price of synthetic rubber and the increased use of natural rubber with the switch-over to the consumption of radial tyres which requires the use of more natural component, perhaps a new 'minimum' price floor much higher than its historical trend may have emerged, thus ensuring a reas-

FIGURE 9.4
PRICE OF RSS 1 RUBBER OVER TIME

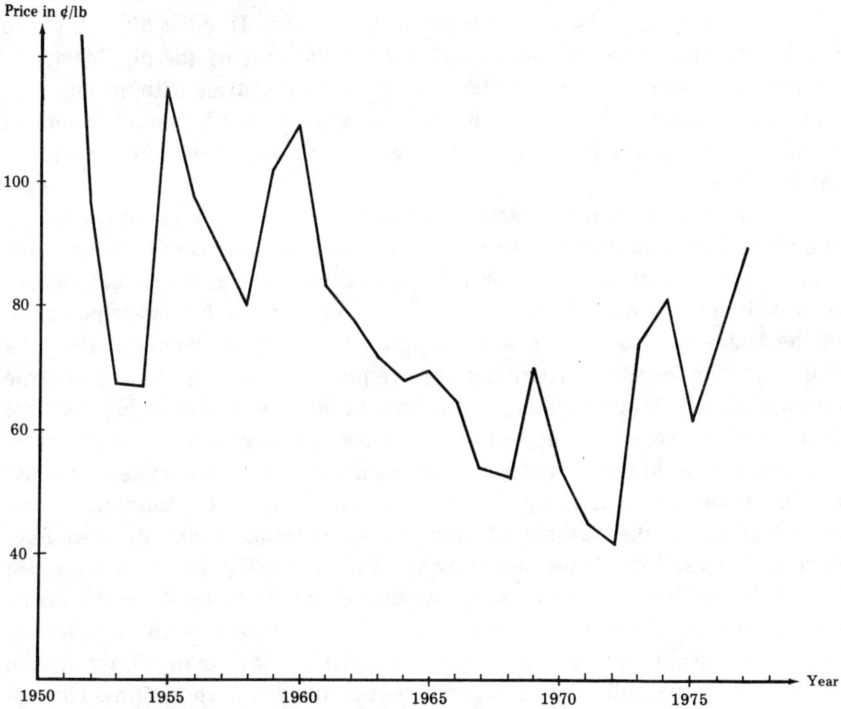

onable level of income for the rubber smallholders with replanted seedlings and fair-sized holdings in the near future.

Furthermore, by 1978, the number of Felda settlers would have reached a significant figure. As pointed out in Chapter 3, although the bulk of the settlers did not come from the landless or the poorest farmers, the income from participating in a Felda scheme with 10 to 12 acres of holding and the planting of high-yielding rubber and oil palm can ensure a better income once the trees come into production. Their income level generally exceeds $3,000 per household per year despite steep loan repayment schedules to the Government. If the prices of rubber and palm oil remain at a high level, the income of these settlers will improve further as the trees come into their most productive periods and the burden of debt eases somewhat. These settlers would have moved into the second lowest 40 per cent in the income ladder, some perhaps even higher.

As for the other rural poor, such as the fishermen, coconut smallholders, pineapple smallholders, and the like, there have been no significant income-raising packages for their benefit. It is most likely that their income level would have lingered around the old level, thus sinking them to the bottom of the income profile along with the small padi farmers with no irrigation facilities, and the rubber smallholders with small plots in remote areas and old seedlings.

For the middle and upper-middle income brackets whose ranks have grown rapidly up to 1970, their pace of expansion should have further quickened under the NEP as evidenced by redoubled efforts to increase Malay enrolment in the tertiary education system, and the push for hiring Malay executives and direct Government participation in private enterprises. It seems likely that the number of Malays in this group will soon equal that of the non-Malays.[17] Their income would also rise rapidly, certainly keeping pace with the improvement witnessed by the farmers in relative terms and substantially more in absolute terms in the light of the three salary revisions in the public sector in the seventies.

Only a small number of Malays participate in the top level of ownership and control of corporate wealth—i.e., within the top 2 per cent of the population in terms of income—but some Malays possess substantial concentrations of wealth in the form of landholdings.[18] Here again, the NEP has helped some of the Malay rich to succeed in building up big business conglomerates. The expressed aim of some interpreters of the policy is precisely to increase the number of Malays participating at this level of business and enjoying this level of income. Hence, we can expect their numbers to increase in the near future.

Nevertheless, in the short-term future of the next five to ten years, the bulk of Government restructuring of wealth is not likely to be translated into a large increase in the number of Malay conglomerates. After all, as we have seen, it has been the Government-owned and controlled corporations which have held the lion's share of the restructured wealth in trust for the Malay general public. The share of corporate wealth of Malay-related interests has been raised from less than 2 per cent in 1970 to more than 10 per cent in 1978,[19] with the bulk of it in Government-controlled corporations. The real significance of these acquisitions, however, goes far beyond that indicated by the percentage of ownership, as the Government has gained dominating control of the financial sector, especially the commercial banks, the tin mining sector, and appears to be making important inroads into the plantation and property development sectors. It is only in manufacturing and trading that Malay initiatives are secondary.

Bearing in mind all the above developments, it does not appear likely that the intra-Malay income distribution could have improved significantly, as a large minority of the Malay populace have stagnated whereas the top 5 per cent has made great strides with those in between making some improvement in their income. At best, overall intra-Malay inequality improves a little—if the number of those in between and the benefits to them increase by an amount such that the narrowed gap between them and the top 5 per cent is adequate to offset the widened gap between themselves and the bottom group, as well as that gap between the top 5 per cent and the bottom group. At worst, the inequality between the privileged and those in the bottom group who have stagnated would have increased greatly in the midst of a swelling middle rank (which is, however, still in the minority) in such a way that the inequality between the top and the middle, and that between the middle and the bottom have both widened. We are inclined towards the latter possibility.[20]

Inequality has also increased amongst the non-Malays. While the Chinese started out as the race with the greatest inequality in 1957, inequality also widened, but by a smaller amount, such that intra-Chinese inequality has become less when compared to the intra-race inequality of the other two major races up to 1970. This can be understood in terms of the significant number of Chinese who were able to find employment as skilled blue- and white-collar workers in the expanding manufacturing industries thus bolstering the number in the upper-lower and lower-middle income brackets. Concurrently, the expanded tertiary education opportunity and the opening up of business opportunities meant that the ranks of the upper-income brackets increased a little with substantial increase in the concentration of corporate wealth. At the other extreme, however, the Chinese poor in the new villages and urban areas have continued to stagnate in poverty and difficulty.

Government policies stressing double cropping and land development have brought minimal direct benefits to the Chinese poor who are largely urban. The introduction of the NEP and the harder push for greater Malay employment at all levels of manufacturing employment in the scenario of a stagnating manufacturing investment in the mid-seventies is bound to have some impact on the number of unemployed Chinese in the absence of a strong and compensating provision of rural employment for the Chinese. Manufacturing activities have been the only ones in which the Chinese poor have been able to participate for improving their welfare and to absorb the labour of a rising population. In view of the relatively more restrictive tertiary education enrolment and the need to employ more Malay executives, the growth in the ranks of the Chinese middle- and upper-income brackets is also likely to slow down somewhat, but not in absolute terms. As for the Chinese rich, while many of them would have preferred to curtail expansion plans in view of difficulties encountered with the ICA, the build-up of wealth from post-Independence expansion up to the early seventies is bound to guarantee a continued flow of high income which can still, and probably does, increase with present high commodity prices and fairly strong domestic demand. In short, it is again unlikely that the intra-Chinese inequality would have improved.

Amongst the Indians, there has also been increasing inequality up to 1970. The reasons are not difficult to surmise. On the one hand, the few Indians who belong to the upper-income levels have, like similar segments within the other ethnic groups, experienced increases in income. And children from better socio-economic backgrounds have been able to join the higher income occupations by obtaining the necessary access to higher education. On the other hand, the welfare of the Indian poor has not improved. The lack of opportunities for an increasing population to be absorbed into existing channels of employment has resulted in the Indians having the highest unemployment rate among the three major races. Moreover, with the switch from rubber to oil palm, one of their traditional major employment channels is contracting instead of increasing! This trend has not been improved by the NEP, for their relative proportion in the tertiary education level has dropped to a very low level thus further blocking the path of upward mobility for the middle section of the population. The very few Indian conglomerates are truly the exceptions.

Figure 9.5 is a set of stylized Lorenz Curves summarizing the above features.

FIGURE 9.5
POSSIBLE STYLIZED LORENZ CURVES FOR
WEST MALAYSIA, 1970 AND 1975

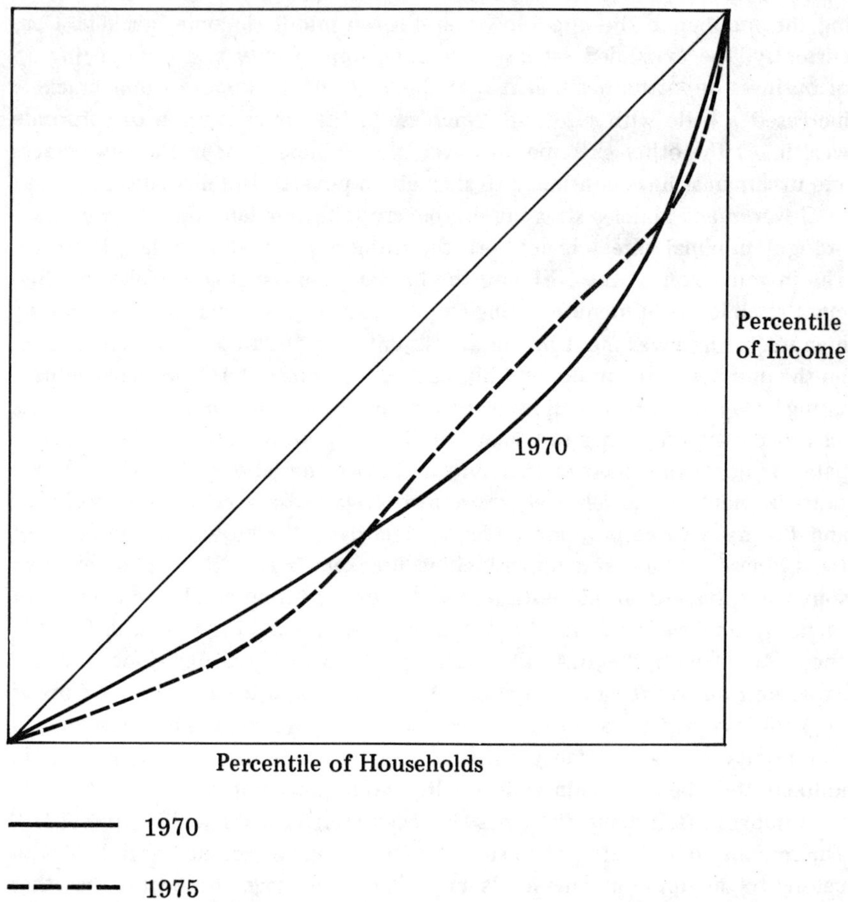

With regard to the role of the foreigners in the corporate sector of the economy, we have seen that they were able to maintain their predominating role after Independence. Few local businessmen succeeded in challenging them and wresting control of any major companies in the plantation and tin sectors from them. Even in fields like the financial and manufacturing sectors, where the post-Independence Government has taken pains to promote local interests, the foreigners have been able to maintain their share, though the British are no longer the sole beneficiaries. However, with the introduction of the NEP and rigorous Government efforts aimed principally at restructuring corporate wealth to allow for Malay participation, the situation has begun to change. In the last few years, the restructuring of major corporations has seen the decline of foreign dominance in the plantation and tin sectors. Projecting into the future, we can expect foreign share-ownership in the traditional sectors to decline further, though not necessarily their control as they would probably attempt to float shares widely to the Malaysian Malays and public while retaining a working minority of controlling interests in general. In so far as Malaysia has a need to expand the manufacturing sector rapidly and lacks the know-how, the foreigners' role will continually be promoted but perhaps with some gentle pressure to allow for local, especially Malay, participation.

9.4 THE POLITICS OF INEQUALITY: PERCEPTIONS AND REALITIES

In a country such as Malaysia, where racial sensitivities run high, it is not surprising that both the issues of poverty and inequality, as well as the related question of who has benefited from development since Independence, have become the central issues around which much conflict and misunderstanding have developed. Nor is it surprising that these are emotionally charged issues. The common tendency, especially since 1969, has been to see economic inequality in racial terms—the Malays are economically worse off in comparison to the non-Malays (especially the Chinese). This contention is often defended by comparing the mean income of the Chinese as a group against the mean income of the Malays, as well as the respective percentages of the ownership of share capital. In either comparison, the poor and the rich tend to be identified in simplistic racial terms.

The preceding chapters have already revealed some of the answers to the question of who has benefited most in the years after Independence. From the documentation of this study, it is clear that the higher income groups, comprising both Malays and non-Malays, were the major beneficiaries.

Without the opportunities created by the post-Independence Government, such as the promotion and protection of manufacturing and a generally more favourable financing climate, non-Malay businessmen would not have been able to expand their economic activities. The big businessmen, in particular, who were poised for growth from trading activities during the colonial era were able to step neatly into the manufacturing drive undertaken by the Government, and into a little banking and finance. They were also able to expand their holdings in large plantation companies, increase their participation in tin dredging and later engage in large-scale property development. While many of them were already affluent before Independence, it was only after 1957 that they were able to consolidate into big conglomerates. Such big businessmen of course number no more than a few score.

The several hundred other non-Malay businessmen, however, were also able to enjoy the fruits of development. Many of their factories and firms were able to prosper into medium-sized organizations with the protection provided for local markets and other investment incentives offered by the Government.

For the big Malay businessmen, life has never been so good. In their case, special opportunities and substantial assistance are provided by the Government. This has enabled a small group of Malay rich who have close links with the centres of political power to consolidate their position. However, because of the lack of penetration by the Malays into the commercial sector prior to

Independence, many other Malay businessmen have not yet been able to blossom into huge conglomerates or to spread extensively throughout the economy. Thus, fewer giant Malay conglomerates exist and there is no extensive network of small and medium-sized firms. At this point, the sum wealth of the non-Malay rich still exceeds that of the Malays. However, an important foundation has been laid for eventual Malay domination in several key aspects of the economy—finance and mining being the two most obvious sectors (see Chapters 5 and 6).

Whereas the upper-income bracket has reaped the most benefits, the numbers in the middle and upper-middle income groups have been the fastest growing in relative terms in the last ten years or so. While the absolute number of Malays joining this rank is still slightly smaller than that of the non-Malays, their rate of increase has been very sharp. In the post-Independence period, the first impetus to this increase came from the rapid expansion of the Government sector in which the bulk of those hired were Malays. The Government education policy provides a supply of Malay graduates to be absorbed by the public as well as the private sector. The details of this up to 1970 have been documented in Chapter 4.

Under the NEP, the Government has been exerting its drive on behalf of the Malays in the private sector. This has given rise to a rapid increase in the number of well-paid Malay executives as the private sector rushes to increase its hiring of Malay executives to meet with prescribed racial proportions in their organizations. But only a small minority which has the training, the financial background, and the connections can seize this opportunity to rise into the highest income bracket.

The number of non-Malays in the ranks of the middle and upper-middle income groups has also been on the increase. They too have been the ones to take advantage of better opportunities in education and employment. In fact, the predominance of non-Malays in this category in the past is due to the fact that the urban communities had always had access to better schools and were the first group to benefit from the setting up of the universities. Thus the enrolment of non-Malays in tertiary institutions up to the late sixties was high. The current admission policy of the universities is consciously formulated to reverse the low Malay participation in universities and ensure a rapid increase of Malay graduates, and from them, a stream of Malay professionals and executives. For example, 75 per cent of the new intake of students into universities and colleges during the 1976 and 1977 academic years were Malays.

It is clear from our discussion that Malays as well as non-Malays in the high, upper-middle, and middle income brackets have benefited in terms of income since Independence. Yet, unhappiness is most vocally expressed by these groups. The formulation and implementation of the NEP was obviously undertaken as a response to Malay unhappiness that the Chinese especially have economically benefited most from development and the rightful role of the Malays was being threatened. While many Malays are already beginning to reap the benefits of the NEP in their income, yet, in public statements, parliamentary debates, and gatherings such as economic conventions, unhappiness continues to be expressed that the total amount of wealth in Malay hands is still small.[21] The quickening pace of change under the new and favourable policies is often relegated to the background as politicians push for even more concessions and privileges and play on chauvinistic sentiments. There is also a concurrent and continued unwillingness to recognize the contributions made by the non-Malays to the development of Malaysia and the existence of a large number of non-Malay poor whose rights to make a decent living must not be denied.

Meanwhile, the non-Malays perceive the New Economic Policy as a threat to their opportunities and economic well-being and their leaders have been equally vocal in expressing their unhappiness. Government policies ensuring more rapid Malay entry into the higher income brackets do have implications on opportunities open to non-Malays. In particular, the very rapid and drastic reversal in their access to education touches on an extremely raw nerve. Non-Malay politicians have been equally opportunistic: while championing the recognition of non-Malay rights, they frequently fail to draw a distinction between the plight of the non-Malay poor and the desire by the non-Malay middle- and upper-income brackets (who have greatly benefited in post-Independence development) for more unrestrained opportunities and a better way of life. More importantly they fail, or are unwilling, to recognize the need to promote the interests of both non-Malay and Malay poor. Instead they merely attack unfair treatment for non-Malays as if all the Malays are culprits in causing all non-Malays to suffer racial oppression, thus fanning further racial sentiments.

While these perceptions dominate the political scene given that these groups are more vocal and articulate, the most important issue that is often missed out is that the poor comprise the vast majority in each ethnic group.

In the economic development of Malaysia since Independence, the Government has promoted rural development through double cropping and price support for padi in the sixties and new land development and settlement in the seventies. In terms of impact, however, the rural populace did not benefit in a significant manner until the middle seventies, part of the benefits coming because of rising commodity prices. Moreover, while the benefits of irrigation and land development accrue to the rural farmers with larger plots and higher income (see Chapters 2 and 3), the impact on the poorest and/or landless has been relatively minor, save in those cases where they can find waged employment on or off farm. Even after the coming on-stream of the rural development projects and the rise in commodity prices to push the income of the majority of rural farmers to a level between $2,000 and $3,000 per year, their livelihood still cannot be considered comfortable, or indeed, off poverty. Not only is it still a far cry from the income of the middle- and upper-income groups, it is clearly not so secure as witnessed by the impact of the recent drought on the Muda farmers and unfavourable tapioca prices for the new villagers in Perak.

Concurrent with the push on rural development, the Government also promoted industrial development and, later on, restructuring in the seventies. The former benefited the non-Malay urban poor through the provision of employment with stable income, though the benefits tend to be more narrowly based as the bulk of the factories are concentrated in the State of Selangor. In addition, through the efforts of organized labour and changing economic conditions, there have been small wage increases in recent years. Nevertheless, the income of the factory workers at $2,000 to $4,000 per year is also far from affluent. With the NEP, non-Malay manufacturing employment is still growing, but at a slower rate, and is beginning to limit the basic job openings for the younger generation of poor non-Malays.

If indeed, as we have observed, the upper-income and the middle-income brackets, whether Malays or non-Malays, have both benefited substantially from post-Independence development pre- and post-NEP, why should there be so much sensitivity and conflict around the question of who benefited and will benefit? By contrast, the poor of all races who have benefited much less, are seemingly more subdued in their demands. One can understand this issue better from the viewpoints of self-interest and expectations.

For the vast majority of the population belonging to the lower-income bracket, they have recognized the limitation imposed by their socio-economic background on their upward mobility in the present structure of society. To the Malay farmers, the opportunity to plant two crops instead of one, or to acquire a couple more acres of land for cultivation to raise their current income, would perhaps be good enough. To some of their children, aspirations can perhaps be temporarily fulfilled if they can migrate to the urban areas and work in 'modern' employment. To the non-Malay poor living in the new villages or squatting in the depths of urban slums, their primary concern would be the ability to secure titled cultivation land or employment opportunity as the case may be. In most cases, the opportunity of primary and secondary education for their children would be treasured as a step in upward mobility for future generations. A place in tertiary education, while still being hoped for perhaps, would have been accepted as beyond the realistic reach of most of them. In neither case is there likely to be much entertainment of the idea of becoming a businessman and ultimately a wealth holder. To those who have entered into hawking out of necessity following a long period of unemployment, the example of the few hawkers who have made good may perhaps inspire the rest to work harder and hope. But then again it is the exception rather than the rule. Therefore, the main concern of the poor is to make a decent living. Issues of tertiary education opportunity, medium of instruction, and which race owns what, are very important no doubt, but secondary to them.

It is only among those who have received very tangible and significant benefits and who are in a position to realize even more tangible gains that expectations run high and aspirations even higher. It is among these people for whom the stakes are high that reactions are sharpest. Thus, access to and opportunity for tertiary education become a heated and possibly explosive issue. After all, for both the Malays and the non-Malays alike, tertiary education has historically been a passport to high income and greater potential.

The non-Malay upper- and middle-income groups which have benefited tremendously in the fifties and sixties from the expansion in tertiary education opportunities not only do not realize that the pace at which their ranks have swelled is highly exceptional, but they unrealistically also expect their children to continue to enjoy the same or even better opportunities. But there is such rapid creation of middle- and upper-income communities only when a nation is in transition from colonialism to Independence with the concurrent rapid economic development. This is bound to slow down when old positions have been replaced with young locals and as rapid economic expansion moderates. Even without the NEP, it would have been unlikely that the rate of expansion of the middle- and upper-income groups could maintain its former pace. The most that the NEP has done is to hasten and aggravate a situation that would have been inevitable.

The Malay middle- and upper-income groups have also experienced an extremely fast and unusually high rate of post-Independence benefits. Their expectations have therefore been similarly inflated. The promises of the NEP with all its new possibilities further heighten their expectations for the well-educated professionals and executives are in the logical position to step into the roles created by the NEP. It is hardly surprising that this group of people is impatient. A life-time is too short. If they perceive the wealth as belonging to them by right, the benefits should be regained and safeguarded as quickly as possible. Therefore, many of them welcome and fervently support Government initiatives such as the ICA and higher percentage admissions to the universities and colleges for these are seen as necessary and desirable to the fulfilment of their aspirations. Any challenge to these policies is viewed not only as a threat but even as a denial of what they perceive to be their right.

Actions invite reactions. The non-Malay middle- and upper-income groups also entertain high hopes themselves and for their families but are willing to tolerate some accommodation in terms of opportunities in education and jobs. However, a constant exclusive emphasis on, and a too rapid promotion of, Malay interests is soon seen as a threat. A non-Malay looking at the statistics on admissions into tertiary education institutions would fear that by some year in the eighties there may not be any possibility of his children entering the universities at all![22] While it is unlikely that such a point would be reached, the perceived threat and the disillusion of the expectant parents are real enough.

However, among the big wealth holders and the leading politicians of all races, accommodation and co-operation have been the norm. Conflict and confrontation are quite unnecessary, as they both have benefited tremendously and continue to benefit under the NEP. After all, their interests go hand in hand. In the past, the medium to big, up-and-coming businessmen were able to share in the fruits of development and there were no gripes. However, they are now faced with the need to restructure, which means retarding the growth of benefits. More importantly, they are not able to find willing and influential Malay partners, unlike the very big businessmen. The ambitions of the Malays who are in the position to offer suitable partnerships have had their sights lifted to be on a par with only the biggest businessmen. Thus, the medium-sized non-Malay businessmen also become dissatisfied under this squeeze of the NEP.

Unfortunately, these conflicts centring around the middle- and upper-income brackets have been blown so out of proportion that the crux of the issues—the welfare of the poor of any race—has been subordinated in attention.

The non-Malay poor have traditionally been dependent on job creation in the urban manufacturing sector to provide employment and income. This opportunity is bound to diminish as the NEP, with its emphasis on Malay employment in the manufacturing sector to reflect the national racial composition, and incentives to disperse new industries to the more rural and predominantly Malay areas, continues to take effect. New alternatives, such as the possibility of dispersing them into rural agricultural employment, have to be pursued if the problem of unemployment is to be resolved and the welfare of the non-Malay poor taken care of. However, this is an extremely sensitive issue given the structure of the political organization and realities.

On the other hand, it is also clear that the Malay poor have not benefited as much from development policies as those in the higher income brackets. While the NEP does provide additional venues of employment for the Malay poor, the fundamental reasons for rural poverty have yet to be tackled. This is bound to leave the predominantly Malay peasantry where they are, living in poverty. This problem has to some extent been perceived and at the Third Bumiputra Economics Convention in 1978, anxiety was clearly expressed that the NEP would merely create a hundred Malay millionaires while failing to resolve the more fundamental problem of poverty. Dispersal of industries to the rural areas is a step in the right direction. The provision of adequate tilling land for the farmers with small plots and the selection of only the most needy to participate in the new Felda schemes are other possibilities.[23] While middleman activities are exploitative to some extent, Government programmes to replace them or force them to be more competitive will work only if the Government agencies can provide better prices and services at a lower cost.

It is true that the bottom 50 per cent of the population which comprises the lowest income group is largely composed of Malays living in the rural areas. It is also true that in the top 2 per cent which comprises the highest income group, there are few Malays. Yet it would be wrong to see economic inequality in terms of race. Some researchers have established that intra-racial inequality and inter-occupational inequality are much more significant dimensions than inter-racial inequality. Anand, for example, estimated that the racial aspect of inequality accounted for only 8.6 per cent of total income inequality whereas the occupational aspect accounted for 23.8 per cent of income inequality.[24]

Looking at it from another viewpoint, the mean non-Malay to Malay income ratio is about 2 : 1; but that between the low-income non-Malays and Malays is only one and one-quarter to one and one-half, and there is little difference between the income of middle- and high-income Malays and non-Malays. It is the smaller number of non-Malay poor and the relatively larger number of non-Malays in middle- and high-income brackets which cause the mean income of the non-Malays to be larger than that of the Malays by about 100 per cent.[25]

There is no denying that the NEP can be considered a brilliant policy formulation. The creation of a Malay business community and the restructuring of economic occupation can indeed help to do away with the identification of economic activity with race, and hopefully thereafter ease off racial tension. However, it is important to recognize that the creation of a Malay business community, the restructuring of wealth such that the Malay community holds 30 per cent of wealth, and the movement of Malays into urban and more modern employment cannot in themselves ease racial tension and achieve national unity. These are necessary but not sufficient conditions. On the other hand, the over-zealous pursuit of the above without adequate consideration for the needs of the non-Malay would heighten their discontent and aggravate racial tension.

National unity can only be achieved when the majority of Malaysians of all races have access to fair opportunities to make a good living, and the structure of economic activities and social environment is such that people of all races can live and work closely together, learning from, and fostering, mutual understanding and respect for one another.

1. R. Wikkramatileke, 'Variable Ethnic Attributes in Malayan Rural Land Development', *Pacific Viewpoint*, 5, 1964.

2. Post-secondary school participation rate by the sons of the rich is 5.5 per cent as opposed to the 0.7 per cent rate by those from the bottom quintile (Meerman, *The Distribution of Public Expenditure in Peninsular Malaysia*, Summary Table).

3. The rates are 48 per cent for the rich and 33 per cent for the poor, ibid.

4. It is necessary to appreciate the differences introduced through the receipt of education and through other policies. A farmer who can participate in double cropping of padi or a Felda scheme can have his household income doubled from $1,000—$1,500 to $3,000—$4,000 on the average. However, the completion of tertiary education can bring about an income level of at least $9,000 per year per person, twice that brought about by the participation in one of the rural development schemes. It is also a level of income which an urban manufacturing employment cannot bring. However, even more importantly, the graduate pay scheme has built-in, more or less automatic, increment and the way of life takes on a distinctly different look. In that sense, even if Felda schemes and urban skilled employment can produce income equal to the graduates, it is still true that the general populace will look at a higher education in a very different manner and with a much higher regard.

5. This is in addition to the other constraints due to the presence of clans and related bias against others and the newcomers. The small traders generally make too small a level of profit (and hence savings for investment) to be able to move up to the bigger operations.

6. Oliver Popenoe, 'A Study of Malay Entrepreneurs', *Quarterly Journal of the Institute Teknoloji MARA*, 1 September 1969, reprinted in David Lim, ed., *Readings on Malaysian Economic Development*, pp. 350—9.

7. This observation came up in the course of the search into *Fraser's Facts and Figures* and Zorn and Leigh-Hunt's *Manual of Rubber and Tin Companies*. Examples include Harrisons and Crosfield and Socfin.

8. To put it another way, if one were to possess a house, however modest, and a piece of land which one could cultivate, one should be more secure than an unskilled worker with no land or house. In the former case, the farmer can always make a marginal living, and has at least one opportunity to mortgage or sell his possessions to tide over difficulties. In the latter case, none of these courses are possible. From a welfare point of view, both are inferior to someone with a higher and more secure income, but between the two, is the choice clear cut?

9. People have tried to define the poverty line according to some biological or sociological minimum. There is no attempt to conduct a similar exercise here since it is both difficult and unfruitful. In that sense, any other cri-

teria used may be considered arbitrary. Here, some controlling factors are proposed to make the arbitrariness reasonable.

10. As Chapter 2 pointed out, the level of income of the padi farmers at the poorer end of the scale is $1,000 to $1,500 per year. The chosen level for comparison here is $1,500 to $2,000 which is a little higher. The difference is not excessive in the sense that the padi income has been imputed using the price of padi, whereas the food the other wage earners have to pay for is in terms of the price of rice, a higher level. Some attention has to be paid to this valuation problem which has not been done here or elsewhere in other researches.

11. When Anand ('The Size Distribution of Income in Malaysia') changed his criterion for poverty from $25 *per capita* per month to $33 *per capita* per month, he found that the proportion of Malays in it had fallen by only a few per cent from 78.1 per cent (see his supplementary Tables). Therefore, one can expect that when the criterion is further raised to $42, the change in percentage should again not exceed several percentage points; here, more than 10 per cent change has been allowed.

12. This is reasonable in view of the discussion in Chapters 2 to 4. The percentage is also roughly consistent with Anand's finding. He reported that the bottom 40 per cent averaged $75 per household per month which works out to about $900 per household per year.

13. Again, refer to the discussion in Chapters 2 to 4 and Anand, op. cit. In the latter's finding, the bottom 80 per cent together averaged only $147 per household per month or $1,765 per household per year. Allowing for this to vary over a range of income, the proposed division here is reasonable.

14. For details, see FAO, *The Muda Survey—A First Report.* Some of the results on income of the farmers have been summarized in Chapter 2. The livelihood of the agricultural labourers has also improved because the concentration of effort necessary has taken many family members off the off-farm jobs market, creating the opportunity for the landless labourers to fill the vacuum. In fact, there are now rather acute shortages of labour during the harvesting seasons and the Muda authority is introducing staggered planting schedules to try to overcome this, and the problem of supply of water.

15. In fact, the criterion of the lower-income group, middle-income group, and so on should be adjusted since we are no longer talking about 1970 but about 1978. At the very least, we should raise the levels by about 40 per cent to allow for the cumulative effect of inflation in the eight-year period. However, when we are talking about movements from the bottom 40 per cent to the next higher 40 per cent and so on, there is no need for any readjustment.

16. From Chart 9.4, it is clear that the price in 1972 hit an all-time low. For 1974, the price for most of the year stayed high but dipped very sharply in November to reach a point lower than in 1972. The resultant difficulties for the rubber smallholders must have been quite substantial as some of them demonstrated to protest against their conditions and the university students staged sympathetic rallies. The Government responded by stockpiling to try to push up the price.

17. The Malay participation rates in secondary school and tertiary education are higher than those of the Chinese (Meerman, op. cit., Summary Table). The rich Chinese have no worry because their participation rate will remain high (the children of the rich have a much higher participation rate than those of the poor); besides, their more privileged socio-economic background may help to ensure high future income through inheritance. The same is not true for the Chinese poor and it may mean that their prospect for upward mobility (via education) has been further reduced.

18. Apart from Mokhzani's study cited in note 77 of Chapter 2, there are

the works of S. Husin Ali, 'Land Concentration and Poverty among Rural Malays', *Nusantara*, 1, 1972, pp. 100—13; and *Malay Peasant Society and Leadership*, Kuala Lumpur, Oxford University Press, 1975.

19. There is as yet no firm figure to support this. If, however, the proportion of limited company shares held by bumiputras and agencies holding in trust for bumiputras has risen from about 2 per cent in 1970 to 8.01 per cent in 1974 (see statement by Dr Mahathir, the Deputy Prime Minister, in Parliament, *New Straits Times*, 20 October 1978), then it is hardly surprising to see at least 3 per cent growth in this percentage from 1974 to 1978.

20. However, if the shares and dividends held in trust by the Government agencies are redistributed to the general Malay public, especially the poor, it is possible that the inequality will narrow.

21. For example, recently a no less distinguished UMNO leader than Ghafar Baba claimed when launching the 10th Bumiputra Trust Fund that the Malays owned less than 2 per cent or $400 million of the $18.9 billion worth of shares traded on the Kuala Lumpur Stock Exchange (*Business Times*, 25/10/1978). It seems likely that the comparison is erroneous. If one is using the worth of shares as the base for comparison, it is necessary to use the worth of shares owned by the Malays as well, rather than the total face value of the shares they own. It appears that it is the latter figure that Ghafar Baba used. Let us illustrate with a few examples: Pernas and other Government agencies owned at least 20 per cent of Sime Darby, which is about $33 million in face value but worth about $100 million on the market; 10 per cent of Highlands & Lowlands which is $7.4 million in face value but about $22.5 million on the market, 30 per cent of Island & Peninsular which is about $9 million in face value but $27 million on the market, and a big chunk of the major tin mining companies through the Malaysia Mining Corporation that is worth at least $200 million on the market; the summation of these items alone adds up to more than $350 million in market value. In addition, we only have to include the $30 million in market value of the $15 million in special issue of K.L.–Kepong to Malay interests recently, and the $33 million in market value of the 30 per cent Malay interest in Guthrie Ropel for the total Malay shareholding on the Kuala Lumpur Stock Exchange to be worth in excess of $400 million! This has yet to take into account major Malay shareholdings in New Straits Times, Kulim, Dunlop, Malaysia Building Society, Malayan Banking, etc.

The problem is that when such a grossly underestimated figure of Malay shareholdings is cited and given wide publicity by the press, it can only aggravate the erroneous impression that the Malays are really far behind in terms of ownership of corporate wealth, despite the New Economic Policy.

22. One only has to project from the changing trend in admissions from 1970 to 1977 onwards to understand the fear that 100 per cent Malay admission point may one day be reached. Of course no one seriously believes that this will indeed happen. Nevertheless, there is no confidence as to where the cut-off point will be: 75 per cent, 80 per cent, or 90 per cent? The problem becomes more real when Ministers keep citing the larger number of non-Malay college students overseas when all along parents are acutely aware that it is becoming prohibitively costly and difficult to send children overseas.

23. Other policies are possible. For instance, in Chapter 3 we discussed the burden of the rubber export duties and cesses on the rubber smallholders. While it may be sensible to introduce a highly progressive export duty on the estates, it makes little sense to tax the basically poor smallholders so heavily. The restructuring of rubber duty and cesses is one way of quickly benefiting the large number of poor rubber smallholders.

24. Anand, op. cit., Table 9, and pp. 75 and 77.

25. This can be seen quite easily with an example: Assume that there are 100 Malays, 80 of whom make $1,200 per year while the other 20 make $10,000 per year; their average income as a group works out to be $2,960 per year. If there are 100 non-Malays, 60 of whom make $1,500 each a year and 40 make an average of $12,000 per year, their average income per year as a group is $5,700. Here, the income of the low-income group and the income of the high-income group of one race are only 20—25 per cent higher than that of another, but the average for one race is twice as much as that of another.

Select Bibliography

I. GOVERNMENT DOCUMENTS

Malaysia, *Second Malaysia Plan 1971–1975*, Kuala Lumpur: Government Printers, 1971.

_____ *Mid-term Review of the Second Malaysia Plan 1971–1975*, Kuala Lumpur: Government Printers, 1973.

_____ *Third Malaysia Plan 1976–1980*, Kuala Lumpur: Government Press, 1976.

_____, Bank Negara Malaysia, *Annual Report*, various years.

_____, _____ *Quarterly Economic Bulletin*, various issues.

_____, Department of Statistics, *Census of Agriculture 1960*, 16 vols. of preliminary reports.

_____, _____ *Census of Distributive Trades 1966.*

_____, _____ *Census of Manufacturing Industries 1968.*

_____, _____ *Census of Mining Industries 1968, 1969 and 1970.*

_____, _____ *Census of the Construction Industries 1968.*

_____, _____ *Census of Professional and Institutional Establishments 1971 and 1972.*

_____, _____ *Financial Survey of Limited Companies 1967.*

_____, _____ *Financial Survey of Limited Companies 1970.*

_____, _____ *Monthly Statistical Bulletin of West Malaysia.*

_____, _____ *National Accounts of Malaya 1955–1960.*

_____, _____ *National Accounts of West Malaysia 1960–1968.*

_____, _____ *National Crop Cutting Survey 1967/68.*

_____, _____ *Oil Palm, Coconut and Tea Statistics, West Malaysia 1970.*

_____, _____ *Socio-Economic Sample Survey of Households 1967/68*, 2 vols.

_____, _____ *Rubber Statistics Handbook*, various years.

_____, _____ *Survey of Construction Industries*, various years.

_____, _____ *Survey of Manufacturing Industries*, various years.

_____, _____ *Survey of Mining Industries*, various years.

_____, _____, Hawley, A. H., Fernandez, O. Z., and Kandiah, V., *The Expectation of Working Life in Peninsular Malaysia 1970.*

_____, Federal Agriculture Marketing Authority, *Proceedings of the National Agricultural Marketing Seminar*, 1968.

_____, Federal Land Development Authority, *Felda Settler Census 1976:*

Survey on Household and Socio-economic Conditions of Felda Settlers October–November 1976, Kuala Lumpur: Institute Pembangunan Tanah dan Jabatan Memproses Data, Felda, 1978.

_____, Malayan Rubber Fund Board, *Annual Report*, various years.

_____, Ministry of Agriculture and Fisheries (or Co-operatives in some years), *A Preliminary Report on the Survey of Coconut Smallholdings in West Malaysia*, Kuala Lumpur, 1968.

_____, _____ *Acreages of Miscellaneous Crops, West Malaysia, 1971*.

_____, _____ *Annual Fisheries Statistics*, various years.

_____, _____ 'Farm Economic Survey of the Muda River Project 1966'.

_____, _____ *Paddy Calendar*, various years.

_____, _____ *Perangkaan Padi* (Rice Statistics), various years.

_____, _____ 'Socio-Economic Survey of 6 Pilot Project Areas in Kedah 1968'.

_____, _____ *Statistical Digest, West Malaysia*, various years.

_____, _____ *Statistical Review 1971*.

_____, _____, Berube, L., 'Outlook of the Fish Marketing Problem in Malaya', Economic Progress Report No. 3, 1966.

_____, _____, Biggs, H. C., 'Report on the Marketing of Agricultural and Other Rural Produce in Malaysia'.

_____, _____, Narkswasdi, Udhis and Selvadurai, S., *Economic Survey of Padi Production in West Malaysia*, 3 reports, 1967.

_____, _____, Selvadurai, S., *A Preliminary Report on the Survey of Coconut Smallholdings in West Johore*, 1968.

_____, _____, _____ *Padi Farming in West Malaysia*, 1972.

_____, _____, _____ *Krian Padi Survey*, December 1972.

_____, _____, _____ *Padi Survey: Sungei Manik and Changkat Jong Irrigation Areas, Perak*, November 1972.

_____, _____, _____ *Socio-Economic Survey of Rubber Smallholdings in West Johore*, 1972.

_____, _____, _____ and Ani bin Arope, *Socio-Economic Study of Padi Farms in Province Wellesley 1968*, March 1969.

_____, _____, _____, _____ and Nik Hassan, *Socio-Economic Study of Padi Farms of the Kemubu Area of Kelantan 1968*, October 1969.

_____, _____, Stead, 'General Report of the Malayan Fishing Industry'.

_____, _____, Tan Cheng Eng, 'Preliminary Report on the Trawling Schemes at Kuantan and Kuala Trengganu', 1968.

_____, _____, Wilson, T. B., *Economics of Padi Production in North Malaya*, 1958.

_____, _____, _____ 'The West Johore Coconut Production Survey', 1958.

Malaysia, Ministry of Education, Education Planning and Research Division, *Educational Statistics of Malaysia*, various years.

_____, Ministry of Finance, Treasury, *Economic Report*, various years.

_____, _____, _____ *The Annual Report of the Director General of Insurance*, various years.

_____, Muda Agricultural Development Authority, *The Economic Implications of Machinery Use in Padi Production: A Study of the Muda Irrigation Scheme*.

_____, Trengganu, Pejabat Daerah Besut, Yap Kim Lian and Dixon, John,

Socio-Economic Study of Padi Farms in the Besut Project Area of Trengganu, April 1972.

Malaya, Bauer, P. T., *Report on a Visit to Rubber Growing Smallholdings of Malaya*, London: HMSO, 1948.

_____, Mudie, R. F., Rarburn, J. R., and Marsch, 'Report of the Mission of Enquiry into the Rubber Industry of Malaya'. Legal Council Paper No. 58, Kuala Lumpur, 1954.

II. BOOKS, JOURNAL ARTICLES AND MONOGRAPHS

Abdul Aziz, Ungku, 'Facts and Fallacies in the Malayan Economy', *Straits Times*, 28/2/1957 to 5/3/1957.

_____'Land Disintegration and Land Policy in Malaya', *Malayan Economic Review* 3 (1958).

_____'The Interdependent Development of Agriculture and Other Industries', *Malayan Economic Review* 4 (April 1959).

_____*Subdivision of Estates in Malaya 1951–1960*, 3 vols., Kuala Lumpur, 1963.

Adelman, Irma and Morris, Cynthia, *Economic Growth and Social Equity in Developing Countries*, Palo Alto, California: Stanford University Press, 1973.

Affifudin bin Haji Omar, 'Some Aspects of the Socio-Economic Value System of the Muda Rice Farmers in Development Perspective', Alor Star, Kedah: Muda Agriculture Development Authority, 1973.

_____'The Social Political and Economic Framework of Muda Rice Farmers: A Historical Perspective', Alor Star, Kedah: Muda Agriculture Development Authority, 1973.

Agarwal, M. C., 'Marketing Margins for Malayan Cabbage', *Journal of Agricultural Economics* XVIII (May 1966).

Aigner, D. J., and Heins, A. J., 'A Social Welfare View of the Measurement of Income Inequality', *Review of Income and Wealth* (March 1967).

_____'On the Determinant of Income Equality', *American Economic Review* (March 1967).

Allen, G. C., and Donnithorne, A. G., *Western Enterprise in Indonesia and Malaya*, London: Allen and Unwin, 1957.

Anand, Sudhir, 'The Size Distribution of Income in Malaysia', Washington, D.C.: World Bank, 1973.

Ani bin Arope and Lai Kok Chew, 'Towards Optimal Size of Rice Farms', *Agriculture Economics Bulletin*, Malaysian Agricultural Research and Development Institute (April 1971).

Atkinson, Anthony B., 'On the Measurement of Inequality', *Journal of Economic Theory* (September 1970).

Barlow, Colin and Chan Kwong Wah, *Towards an Optimum Size of Rubber Holding*, Kuala Lumpur: Rubber Research Institute, 1968.

Bauer, P. T., 'The Working of Rubber Regulation', *Economic Journal* 56 (1946).

_____*The Rubber Industry*, London: Longman, Green and Co., 1948.

_____'Malayan Rubber Policy', *Pacific Studies Quarterly* (March 1957).

Becker, Gary, *Human Capital and the Personal Distribution of Income: An Analytic Approach*, Ann Arbor, Michigan: University of Michigan, W. A. Woytinsky Lecture No. 1, 1967.

Bell and Janet Tai, 'Marketing, Middleman and Technology: Agricultural Supply Response in the Dualistic Economy of South East Asia', *Malayan Economic Review* 14 (April 1969).

Bentzel, R., 'The Social Significance of Income Distribution Statistics', *Review of Income and Wealth*, Income and Wealth Series 16 (1970).

Bevan, J. W. L., *A Report on the Marketing of Smallholders' Rubber with special reference to the First Buyer Level*, Kuala Lumpur: Rubber Research Institute, Research Archives No. 7, 1956.

——— *A Study of Yields, Labour Inputs and Incomes on Rubber Smallholdings in the Coastal Area of Selangor*, Kuala Lumpur: University of Malaya, Department of Agriculture, 1962.

Bhati, U. N., 'Farmers' Technical Knowledge and Income—A Case Study of Padi Farmers of West Malaysia', *Malayan Economic Review* 18 (April 1973).

———'Cost Functions for Selangor Padi Farms', *Kajian Ekonomi Malaysia* 11 (December 1974).

Bjerke, Kjeld, 'Income and Wage Distribution—A Survey of the Literature', *Review of Income and Wealth* 16 (September 1970).

Bonney, R., *Kedah 1771–1821*, Kuala Lumpur: Oxford University Press, 1971.

Bronfenbrenner, Martin, *Income Distribution Theory*, Chicago: Aldine, 1971.

Chan, Francis K. W., 'A Preliminary Study of the Supply Response of Malayan Estates between 1948 and 1959', *Malayan Economic Review* 7 (October 1962).

Chandra Muzaffar, 'Some Political Perspectives on the New Economic Policy', Malaysian Economic Association, Fourth Malaysian Economic Convention, *Agenda for the Nation: Public Policies for restructuring Society*, Kuala Lumpur (May 1977).

Cheam Soon Tee, *A Study of the Marketing of Smallholders' Lower Grade Rubber*, Kuala Lumpur: Rubber Research Institute, Economic Report No. 8 (1971).

Cheng Siok Hwa, 'The Rice Industry of Malaya—A Historical Survey', *Journal of the Malaysian Branch of the Royal Asiatic Society* XLII (December 1969).

———*The Rice Trade of Malaya*, Singapore: University Education Press, 1973.

Chye Kooi Onn and Loh Wee Yat, 'The Cabbage Industry in West Malaysia', *Review of Agriculture Economics Malaysia* 4 (December 1972).

Dasgupta, P., Sen, A. K. and Starrett, D., 'Notes on the Measurement of Inequality', *Journal of Economic Theory* (June 1973).

Djojohadikusumo, Sumitro, *Trade and Aid in South-East Asia*, 2 vols., Kuala Lumpur: University of Malaya Co-operative Bookshop, 1968.

Drabble, J. H., *Rubber in Malaya 1876–1922: The Genesis of the Industry*, Kuala Lumpur: Oxford University Press, 1973.

Edwards, C. T., *Public Finance in Malaysia and Singapore*, Canberra: Australian National University Press, 1970.

Elliston, G. R., 'The Role of Middlemen in the Fishing Industry in West Malaysia', *Review of Agricultural Economics* 1 (December 1967).

Eltetö, O., and Frigyes, E., 'New Income Inequality Measures as Efficient Tools for Causal Analysis and Planning', *Econometrica* 36 (1968).

Esman, Milton, *Administration and Development in Malaysia*, Ithaca, N.Y.: Cornell University Press, 1972.

Firth, R., 'Economics of the Malayan Fishing Industry', *A Record of Anthropological Society* (August 1941).

_____ and Yamey, B. S., eds., *Capital, Saving and Credit in Peasant Society*, London: Allen and Unwin, 1964.

Fisk, E. K., 'Establishment Cost of Small Rice Farms: An Analytical Model of Return to Capital', *Malayan Economic Review* 7 (1962).

_____ 'Productivity and Income from Rubber in an Established Malay Reservation', *Malayan Economic Review* 6 (April 1961).

_____ 'The Mobility of Rural Labour and the Settlement of New Land', *Journal of Farm Economics* (November 1961).

Food and Agriculture Organisation of the U.N. and International Bank for Reconstruction and Development Co-operation Programme, *The Muda Survey—A First Report*, Rome: Food and Agriculture Organisation of the U.N., September 1975.

Fredericks, L. J., 'Market Structure Analysis and Integration in Agriculture', *Kajian Ekonomi Malaysia* 3 (December 1966).

_____ 'Marketing Boards and Prospects for Malaysian Agriculture', *Kajian Ekonomi Malaysia* 3 (June 1966).

_____ and Wells, R. J. G., 'Pattern of Labour Utilisation and Income Distribution in Rice Double Cropping System: Policy Implications', *Developing Economies* XVI, 1 (March 1978).

Freedman, Roger, *Socialism and Private Enterprise in Equatorial Asia: The Case of Malaysia and Indonesia*, Palo Alto, California: Stanford University Press, 1968.

Gamba, Charles, 'Poverty and Some Socio-Economic Aspects of Hoarding, Saving and Borrowing in Malaya', *Malayan Economic Review* 3 (October 1958).

Goh Ban Lee, *Survey of Small Scale Industries in Butterworth Town, April 1976—September 1976*, Penang, Malaysia: Universiti Sains Malaysia, mimeo, 1976.

Goh Keng Swee, 'Entrepreneurship in a Plural Economy', *Malayan Economic Review* 3 (1958).

Goldman, Richard, 'Staple Food Self-Sufficiency and the Distributive Impact of Malaysian Rice Policy', *Food Research Institute Studies* XIV (1975).

Greenwood, J. M. F., 'Rubber Smallholdings in the Federation of Malaya', *Journal of Tropical Geography* 18 (August 1964).

Gullick, J. M., *Indigenous Political Systems of Western Malaya*, London: Athlone Press, 1958.

Hamada, K., 'A Simple Majority Rule on the Distribution of Income', *Journal of Economic Theory* (June 1973).

_____ 'On the Optimal Transfer and Income Distribution in a Growing Economy', *Review of Economic Studies* (July 1967).

Hara, Fujio, 'Hawkers in Penang', 2 parts, アジア 经济 [Ajia Keijai Kenkyujo—Bimonthly Bulletin of Asia Economics] 15 (January and March 1975).

Hill, R. D., 'Agricultural Land Tenure in West Malaysia', *Malayan Economic Review* 12 (April 1967).

Hirschman, Charles, *Ethnic and Social Stratification in Peninsular Malaysia*, American Sociological Society, Arnold and Catherine Rose Monograph, Washington, D.C., 1975.

_____'Net External Migration from Peninsular Malaysia 1957 to 1970', *Malayan Economic Review* XX (October 1975).

_____'Ownership and Control in the Manufacturing Industries in West Malaysia', *UMBC Review* VII (1971).

_____'The Determinants of Ethnic Inequality in Peninsular Malaysia', *UMBC Review* XII (1976).

Ho, Robert, 'Labour Inputs of Rubber Producing Smallholders in Malaya', *Malayan Economic Review* 12 (April 1967).

_____'Land Ownership and Economic Prospects of Malayan Peasants', *Modern Asian Studies* (January 1970).

_____'Mixed Farming and Multiple Cropping in Malaya', *Journal of Tropical Geography* 16 (1962).

_____'Rice Production in Malaya: A Review of Problems and Prospects', *Journal of Tropical Geography* 29 (December 1969).

_____'Rubber Production by Peasants of the Terachi Valley', *Transaction of the Institute of the British Geographer* (June 1967).

Hoerr, O. D., 'Education, Income and Equity in Malaysia', *Economic Development and Cultural Change* (January 1973).

Hoffmann, Lutz and Tan, S. E., 'Employment Creation through Export Growth: A Case Study of West Malaysia's Manufacturing Industries', in H. Giersch, ed., *The International Division of Labour: Problems and Perspectives*, Tübingen: Mohr and Siebeck, 1974.

_____and Tan Tew Nee, 'Pattern of Growth and Structural Change in West Malaysia's Manufacturing Industries, 1959–1968', *Kajian Ekonomi Malaysia* VIII, December 1971, reprinted in David Lim, ed., *Readings on Malaysian Economic Development*, Kuala Lumpur: Oxford University Press, 1975.

Horii, Kenzo, 'The Land Tenure System of Malay Padi Farmers—A Case Study of Kampong Sungei Bujor in the State of Kedah', *The Developing Economies* 10 (March 1972).

黃枝連 [Huang Chih Lien], 馬華社會史導論 *An Introductory Exposition into the Social History of the Malayan Chinese*, Singapore: 萬里文化企業出版社 Wan Li Cultural Enterprise Publisher (1971).

Huang Yu-kon, 'Some Reflections on Padi Double Cropping in West Malaysia', *Malayan Economic Review* 17 (April 1972).

_____'The Behaviour of Indigenous and Non-Indigenous Farmers: A Case Study', *Journal of Development Studies* (January 1974).

Husin Ali, Syed, 'Land Concentration and Poverty among Rural Malays', *Nusantara* 1 (1972).

_____*Malay Peasant Society and Leadership*, Kuala Lumpur: Oxford University Press, 1975.

International Bank for Reconstruction and Development, Report of Mission organized by, *Economic Development of Malaya*, Baltimore: John Hopkins Press, 1955.

International Tin Council, *Report on the World Tin Position with Projections for 1965 and 1970*, by W. Robertson, London, 1965.

Jackson, James, *Planters and Speculators: Chinese and European Agricultural Enterprise in Malaya 1786–1921*, Kuala Lumpur: University of Malaya Press, 1968.

_____'Rice Cultivation in West Malaysia', *Journal of the Malaysian Branch of the Royal Asiatic Society* XLV (1972).

_____'Smallholding Rubber Cultivation in Malaya, 1952–1962', *Oriental Geographer* 9 (1965).

Jackson, R. N., *Immigrant Labour and the Development of Malaya 1786–1920*, Kuala Lumpur: Government Printers, 1961.

Johns, B. L., 'Import Substitution and Export Potential: The Case of Manufacturing Industry in West Malaysia', *Australian Economic Papers* 21, December 1973, reprinted in David Lim, ed., *Readings on Malaysian Economic Development*, Kuala Lumpur: Oxford University Press, 1975.

Khairi bin Haji Mohamed, 'An Outline of the Development of the Land Tenure System in Malaya', *Malayan Agriculture* 2 (1961).

Kongress Bumiputra Malaysia, *Kertas Kerja*, Kuala Lumpur: Government Printers, 1965.

Kongress Ekonomi Bumiputra Malaysia, *Kertas Kerja*, Kuala Lumpur: Government Printers, 1971.

Kratoska, Paul, *The Chettiar and the Yeoman: British Cultural Categories and Rural Indebtedness in Malaya*, Singapore: Institute of Southeast Asian Studies, Occasional Paper No. 32, 1975.

Krueger, Anne, 'Factor Endowments and Per Capita Income Differences among Countries', *Economic Journal* 78 (September 1968).

Kuchiba, M. and Tsubouchi, Y., 'A Padi Farming Community in Kedah, Malaysia', *The Developing Economies* 5 (September 1967).

_____'Cooperation Patterns in a Malay Village', *Asian Survey* 8 (1968).

Kuznets, Simon, 'Economic Growth and Income Inequality', *American Economic Review* 45 (March 1955).

_____'Quantitative Aspects of the Economic Growth of Nations: Part VII Distribution of Income by Size', *Economic Development and Cultural Change* (January 1963).

_____*Economic Growth and Structure: Selected Essays*, N.Y.: Norton, 1965.

_____*Modern Economic Growth, Rate, Structure and Spread*, New Haven: Yale University Press, 1966.

Lee Hock Lock, *Household Saving in West Malaysia and Problem of Financing Development*, Kuala Lumpur: University of Malaya Press, 1971.

Lee Kok Huat, 'The 1960 Agriculture Census', *Kajian Ekonomi Malaysia* (December 1967).

Lee, Y. L., 'Kukup: A Chinese Fishing Village in South West Malaysia', *Journal of Tropical Geography* 16 (September 1962).

Levine, D. and Singer, N., 'The Mathematical Relationship between the Income Density Function and the Measurement of Income Inequality', *Econometrica* (March 1970).

Li Dun Jen, *British Malaya: An Economic Analysis*, New York: American Press, 1955.

Lim Chong Yah, 'Export Taxes on Rubber in Malaya, A Survey of Post-War Development', *Malayan Economic Review* 5 (October 1960).

_____ 'The Malayan Rubber Replanting Taxes', *Malayan Economic Review* 6 (October 1961).

Lim, David, *Economic Growth and Development in West Malaysia, 1947–1970*, Kuala Lumpur: University of Malaya Press, 1973.

_____ ed., *Readings on Malaysian Economic Development*, Kuala Lumpur: Oxford University Press, 1975.

Lim Lin Lean, *Some Aspects of Income Differentials in West Malaysia*, Kuala Lumpur: University of Malaya, Faculty of Economics and Administration, Monograph No. 2, 1971.

Lim Sow Ching, *A Study of the Marketing of Smallholders' Rubber at the First Trade Level in Selangor*, Kuala Lumpur: Rubber Research Institute, Economics and Planning Division Report No. 4, 1968.

_____ *An Agro Economic Study of Intercrops on Rubber Smallholdings*, Kuala Lumpur: Rubber Research Institute, 1969.

_____ 'Analysis of Smallholders Rubber Marketing in West Malaysia', *Journal of Rubber Research Institute Malaya* 21 (1969).

_____ *Land Development Schemes in Peninsular Malaysia. A Study of Benefits and Costs*, Kuala Lumpur: Rubber Research Institute, 1976.

_____ 'Marketing of Rubber by Smallholders in Peninsular Malaysia', *Economic Bulletin for Asia and the Far East* XXVI (September/December 1975).

_____ and Barlow, C., *A Report on the Survey of Malay Group Processing Centres*, Kuala Lumpur: Rubber Research Institute, Economic Report No. 1 (1964).

Lim Teck Ghee, Gibbons, D. S., and Elliston, G. R., *Land Tenure Survey: Farm Locality DII Muda Irrigation Scheme, Final Report on Work Undertaken in 1973*, Penang: Universiti Sains Malaysia, Centre for Policy Research, 1974.

Loh Fook Seng, Philip, *The Malay States 1877–1895*, Kuala Lumpur: Oxford University Press, 1969.

Low Wan Kim, 'Fish Marketing in Malaysia', *Review of Agricultural Economics Malaysia* 1 (June 1967).

_____ 'The Supply and Demand Prospect for Fish in West Malaysia', *Review of Agricultural Economics Malaysia* 2 (December 1968).

Lydall, H. F., *The Structure of Earnings*, Oxford: Clarendon Press, 1966.

Maeda, K., *Alor Janggus: A Chinese Community in Malaya*, Kyoto: Kyoto University, Center for Southeast Asian Studies, Social Science Series No. 1 (1971).

Maeda, N., *Economic Activity among the Orang Hulu*, Kyoto: Kyoto University, Center for Southeast Asian Studies, Research Paper No. 23 (1971).

McLure, Charles, 'The Incidence of Taxation in West Malaysia', *Malayan Economic Review* 17 (October 1972).

Means, Gordon, *Malaysian Politics*, London: University of London Press, 1970.

Meerman, Jacob, *The Distribution of Public Expenditure in Peninsular Malaysia*, Washington, D.C.: International Bank for Reconstruction and Development, 1977.

Milne, R. S., 'The Politics of Malaysia's New Economic Policy', *Pacific Affairs* 49 (Summer 1976).

Mokhzani bin Abdul Rahim and Khoo Siew Mun, eds., *Some Case Studies on Poverty in Malaysia: Essays Presented to Professor Ungku A. Aziz*, Kuala Lumpur: Persatuan Ekonomi Malaysia, 1977.

Moore, Basil J., *Restructuring Wealth Ownership*, Penang: Universiti Sains Malaysia, Centre for Policy Research, Discussion Paper No. 2, 1975.

Munro, G. R. and Chee Kim Loy, *The Economics of Fishing and the Developing World, a Malaysian Case Study*, Penang: Universiti Sains Malaysia Press, 1978. (References in this book are cited from the earlier mimeo version entitled 'Fishermen and Fishing Development in Penang and Kedah', 1972.)

Ness, Gayl D., *Bureaucracy and Rural Development in Malaysia*, Berkeley, California: University of California Press, 1967.

_____'Subdivision of Estates in Malaya 1951–1960: A Methodological Critique', *Malayan Economic Review* 9 (1964).

Ng Choon Sooi, *Some Aspects of Estate Replanting and New Planting Costs*, Kuala Lumpur: Rubber Research Institute.

_____, Barlow, C., and Chan, F., *Factors Affecting the Profitability of Rubber Production in West Malaysian Estates*, Kuala Lumpur: Rubber Research Institute.

Ooi Jin Bee, 'Rural Development in Tropical Areas with special reference to Malaysia', *Journal of Tropical Geography* (March 1959).

Oshima, H. T., 'Income Inequality and Economic Growth', *Malayan Economic Review* 15 (October 1970).

_____'The International Comparison of Size Distribution of Income with special reference to Asia', *Review of Economic Studies* (November 1962).

Purcal, John T., *Rice Economy, Employment and Income in Malaysia*, Honolulu: University of Hawaii Press, 1972.

Puthucheary, James J., *Ownership and Control in the Malayan Economy*, Singapore: Eastern Universities Press, 1960.

_____'Changes in Ownership and Control in Malaysia', paper presented at the Fourth Malaysian Economic Convention, *Agenda for the Nation: Public Policies for Restructuring Society*, Kuala Lumpur: Persatuan Ekonomi Malaysia, May 1977.

Puthucheary, M. C., 'Public Enterprise and the Creation of a Bumiputra Entrepreneurial Community', paper presented at the Fourth Malaysian Economic Convention, *Agenda for the Nation: Public Policies for Restructuring Society*, Kuala Lumpur: Persatuan Ekonomi Malaysia, May 1977.

Rawls, J., *A Theory of Justice*, Cambridge, Massachusetts: Harvard University Press, 1971.

Ray, Elizabeth, 'The International Tin Cartel', in William Y. Elliot, ed., *International Control in the Non-Ferrous Cartel*, New York: Macmillan Co., 1937.

Roff, William, *Kelantan: Religion, Society and Politics in a Malay State*, New York: Oxford University Press, 1974.

Rothschild, M. and Stiglitz, J. E., 'Some Further Results on the Measurement of Inequality', *Journal of Economic Theory* (June 1973).

Rudner, Martin, 'The Malayan Quandary: Rural Development Policy under the First and Second Five Year Plans', *Contributions to Asian Studies*

(1971), reprinted in David Lim, ed., *Readings on Malaysian Economic Development*, Kuala Lumpur: Oxford University Press, 1975.

Sarkar, K., 'Marketing Margin of Certain Agricultural Commodities in Kuala Lumpur', *Review of Agricultural Economics* 5 (June 1974).

Sato, K., 'The Neoclassical Theory and Distribution of Income and Wealth', *Review of Economic Study* (1966).

Seers, Dudley, *The Meaning of Development*, New York: ADC Reprint, September 1970.

Sen, A. K., *On Economic Inequality*, Oxford: Clarendon Press, 1974.

Sheshinski, E., 'Relation between a Social Welfare Function and the Gini Index of Inequality', *Journal of Economic Theory* 4 (1972).

Sieh Mei Ling, 'Size Distribution of Shareholdings in Manufacturing Companies of Malaysia, 1974–75', paper presented at the Fourth Malaysian Economic Convention, *Agenda for the Nation: Public Policies for Restructuring Society*, Kuala Lumpur: Persatuan Ekonomi Malaysia, May 1977.

Silcock, T. H. and Fisk, E. K., *The Political Economy of Independent Malaya*, Canberra: Australian National University Press, 1963.

Smith, Eldon and Geothals, Peter, *Tenancy Among Padi Cultivators in Malaysia*, Ford Foundation and Economic Planning Unit of Malaysia (mimeographed) (1965).

Snodgrass, Donald, *Inequality and Economic Development in Malaysia*, Kuala Lumpur: Oxford University Press, 1980.

Song Ong Siang, *One Hundred Years' History of the Chinese in Singapore*, London: J. Murray, 1923.

Stiglitz, Joseph, 'The Distribution of Income and Wealth among Individuals', *Econometrica* 37 (July 1969).

Swammy, Subramanian, 'Structural Change and the Distribution of Income by Size: The Case of India', *Review of Income and Wealth* (June 1967).

Sweezy, Paul, 'Demand under Conditions of Oligopoly', *Journal of Political Economy*, XLVII, 1939.

Takei, Yoshimitsu, Brock, John C., and Saunders, Bruce, *Education Sponsorship by Ethnicity: A Preliminary Analysis of the West Malaysian Experience*, Athens, Ohio: Ohio University Center for International Studies, Southeast Asia Series No. 28, 1973.

Tan Tat-wai, 'Employment and Labour Utilisation in West Malaysia', unpublished World Bank Paper, Income Distribution Division, Economic Research Centre, 1973.

Tang Loon Boon, *Production Costs of Various Agricultural Commodities*, Kuala Lumpur: Federal Agricultural Marketing Authority, 1971.

Thomas, P. O., *Malaysian Natural Rubber in the Seventies: A Forecast of Production Trend*, Kuala Lumpur: Rubber Research Institute, September 1970.

Thurow, Lester C., *Generating Inequality (Mechanisms of Distribution in the U.S. Economy)*, New York: Basic Books, 1975.

Tinbergen, T., 'A Positive and Normative Theory of Income Distribution', *Review of Income and Wealth* 16 (1970).

Tsubouchi, Y., 'Paddy Farming and Social Structure in a Malay Village: A Social and Anthropological Study of a Community in Kedah', *The Developing Economies* 5 (1967).

Wharton, C. R., 'Marketing, Merchandising and Money Lending: A Note on Middlemen Monopoly in Malaya', *Malayan Economic Review* 7 (October 1962).

_____ 'Malayan Rubber Supply Condition: Some Policy Implications', in T. H. Silcock and E. K. Fisk (eds.), *The Political Economy of Independent Malaya*, Canberra: Australian National University Press, 1963.

Wheelwright, Edward, *Industrialisation in Malaysia*, Melbourne: Melbourne University Press, 1963.

Wikkramatileke, R., 'State Aided Rural Land Colonisation in Malaya: An Appraisal of Federal Land Development Authority Programme', *Annals of the Association of American Geographers* 55 (1965).

_____ 'Trends in Settlement and Economic Development in Eastern Malaya', *Pacific Viewpoint* 3 (1962).

_____ 'Variable Ethnic Attributes in Malayan Rural Land Development', *Pacific Viewpoint* 5 (1964).

Wilson, T. B., 'Some Aspects of Padi and Land Ownership in Krian', *Malayan Agriculture Journal* 37 (1954).

_____ 'Sungei Manik Farm Survey—Composition and Land Tenure', *Malayan Agricultural Journal* 40 (1957).

_____ 'The Inheritance and Fragmentation of Malay Padi Lands in Krian, Perak', *Malayan Agricultural Journal* 38 (1955).

Wong, D., *Tenure and Land Dealings in the Malay States*, Singapore: University of Singapore Press, 1975.

Wong Lin Ken, *The Malayan Tin Industry to 1914*, Tuscon, Arizona: University of Arizona Press for the Association of Asian Studies, 1965.

Yap Chan Ling, 'Cost and Construction of the Pukat Terut Gear and Boat', *Malayan Agricultural Journal* 48 (1972).

_____ 'Fish Marketing Mechanism with special reference to the Development of the Kuala Lumpur Wholesale Market', *Review of Agricultural Economics Malaysia* 4 (June 1972).

_____ 'Over-expansion in the Trawler Industry with Special Reference to the Dindings District of West Malaysia', *Kajian Ekonomi Malaysia* X (December 1973).

Yeoh Chong Hoe, Ghazali Noor, and Tyer, G. C., *A Report on the Survey of Group Processing Centres*, Kuala Lumpur: Rubber Research Institute, 1974.

Yip Yat Hoong, *The Development of the Tin Mining Industry of Malaya*, Kuala Lumpur: University of Malaya Press, 1969.

Yuen Choy Leng, 'Japanese Rubber and Iron Investment in Malaya 1900–1941', *Journal of Southeast Asian Studies* (March 1974).

Zahara Haji Mahmud, 'The Period and Nature of Traditional Settlement in the Malayan Peninsula', *Journal of the Malaysian Branch of the Royal Asiatic Society*, XLII (December 1970).

III. DISSERTATIONS

Barnard, Rosemary, 'Organisation of Production in a Kedah Rice Farming Village', Ph.D. dissertation, Australian National University, 1971.

Chee Peng Lim, 'Small Scale Industries in Peninsular Malaysia', Ph.D. dissertation, University of Malaya, 1976.

Edwards, Christopher B., 'Protection, Profits and Policy—An Analysis of Industrialisation in Malaysia', Ph.D. dissertation, School of Development Studies, University of East Anglia, 1975.

Lee Poh Ping, 'Chinese Society in Nineteenth and Early Twentieth Century Singapore: A Socioeconomic Analysis', Ph.D. dissertation, Cornell University, 1974 (published by Oxford University Press, Kuala Lumpur, 1978).

Leong Keng Yuen, 'The Palm Oil Market: Outlook and the Malaysian Estate Producers', Ph.D. dissertation, Massachusetts Institute of Technology, 1976.

Lim Mah Hui, 'Ownership and Control in a Dependent Economy: The Case of Malaysia's One Hundred Largest Corporations', Ph.D. dissertation, University of Pittsburgh, 1977.

Lim Sow Ching, 'A Study of the Marketing of Smallholders' Rubber at the First Trade Level in Selangor', M.Sc. dissertation, University of Malaya, 1968.

Lim Teck Ghee, 'Peasant Agriculture in Colonial Malaya: Its Development in Perak, Selangor, Negeri Sembilan and Pahang 1874–1941', Ph.D. dissertation, Australian National University, 1971 (published by Oxford University Press, Kuala Lumpur, 1977).

Lindenberg, Marc Merrill, 'Foreign and Domestic Investment in the Pioneer Industry Program, Malaysia 1965–70, Political, Economic and Social Impacts', Ph.D. dissertation, University of Southern California, 1973.

Mamajiwala, R. K., 'Ownership and Control of Public Limited Planting Companies Incorporated in the Federation of Malaya', M.A. thesis, University of Malaya, 1965.

Mokhzani bin Abdul Rahim, 'Credit in a Malay Peasant Economy', Ph.D. dissertation, University of London, 1973.

Ooi Sang Kuang, 'A Study of the Fishing Industry in Penang', B.E. graduation exercise, University of Malaya, 1970.

Pillay, Chandrasekaran, 'Protection of the Malay Community: A Study of UMNO's Position and Opposition Attitudes', M.Sc. thesis, Universiti Sains Malaysia, 1974.

Purvis, Malcolm J., 'Evaluation and Use of Underdeveloped Agricultural Statistics: The Food Economy of Malaysia', Ph.D. dissertation, Cornell University, 1966.

Smith, D., 'Tin Producers' Collusive Cartel under Oligopoly', B.A. honours thesis, Harvard College, 1966.

Tai May Chean, 'Design of a Management Control System for the Manufacturing Subsidiary of a Malaysian Holding Company', M.Sc. dissertation, Massachusetts Institute of Technology, 1975.

Tan Chee Beng, 'Baba and Nyonya: A Study of the Ethnic Identity of the Chinese Peranakan in Malacca', Ph.D. dissertation, Cornell University, 1979.

Tan Tat-wai, 'Income Distribution and Determination in West Malaysia', Ph.D. dissertation, Harvard University, 1977.

Voon Phin Keong, 'Chinese Rubber Smallholding Industry in Selangor', M.A. dissertation, University of Malaya, 1967.

IV. OTHERS

Fraser & Co. (Stock broker), *Facts and Figures*, various issues.

Jane's Major Companies of Europe, 1974.

Kassim and Chan, *SGV Survey of the Commercial Banks 1974.*

_____, *SGV Survey of the Finance Companies 1974.*

Kuala Lumpur Stock Exchange, *Annual Company Handbook, 1977, 1978 and 1979.*

_____, *Biography of Directors.*

_____, *Gazette*, various issues.

Singapore Stock Exchange, *Journal*, various issues.

_____, *Company Handbook*, 1974, 1975, 1976, 1978 and 1979.

Stock Exchange of London, *Stock Exchange Official Yearbook 1975–76.*

Straits Times Press, *Directory of Malaysia*, various years.

_____ *Information on Malaysia and Malaysia Year Book*, 1975/76.

Various companies' Annual Report.

Who's Who in Malaysia and Singapore, various years.

Zorn and Leigh-Hunt, *Manual of Planting and Mining Companies.*

V. NEWSPAPERS

Far Eastern Economic Review, various issues.

Malaysian Business, various issues.

New Straits Times, various issues.

Straits Times, various issues.

南洋商報 *Nanyang Siang Pau.*

南洋年鑑

星洲十年

Index